VENGEANCE IN THE MIDDLE AGES

Vengeance in the Middle Ages
Emotion, Religion and Feud

Edited by

SUSANNA A. THROOP
Ursinus College, USA

and

PAUL R. HYAMS
Cornell University, USA

LONDON AND NEW YORK

First published 2010 by Ashgate publishing

Published 2016 by Routledge
2 Park Square, Milton Park, Abingdon, Oxon OX14 4RN
605 Third Avenue, New York, NY 10017

First issued in paperback 2020

Routledge is an imprint of the Taylor & Francis Group, an informa business

Copyright © The Editors and Contributors 2010

Susanna A. Throop and Paul R. Hyams have asserted their right under the Copyright, Designs and Patents Act, 1988, to be identified as the editors of this work.

All rights reserved. No part of this book may be reprinted or reproduced or utilised in any form or by any electronic, mechanical, or other means, now known or hereafter invented, including photocopying and recording, or in any information storage or retrieval system, without permission in writing from the publishers.

Notice:
Product or corporate names may be trademarks or registered trademarks, and are used only for identification and explanation without intent to infringe.

British Library Cataloguing in Publication Data

Vengeance in the Middle Ages: Emotion, Religion and Feud.
 1. Revenge – Europe – History – To 1500.
 2. Revenge – Europe – History – To 1500 – Historiography.
 3. Revenge – Religious aspects – History – To 1500.
 4. Civilization, Medieval.
 I. Throop, Susanna A. II. Hyams, Paul R.
 909'.07–dc22

Library of Congress Cataloging-in-Publication Data

Throop, Susanna A.
 Vengeance in the Middle Ages: Emotion, Religion, and Feud / Susanna A. Throop and Paul R. Hyams.
   p. cm.
 ISBN 978-0-7546-6421-5 (hardcover : alk. paper) 1. Revenge.
2. Revenge – Religious aspects. 3. Europe – History. I. Hyams, Paul R. II. Title.
 BF637.R48T47 2009
 940.1–dc22

2009018788

ISBN 13: 978-0-367-74012-2 (pbk)
ISBN 13: 978-0-7546-6421-5 (hbk)

Contents

Notes on Contributors		*vii*
Acknowledgements		*ix*
Introduction: The Study of Vengeance in the Middle Ages Susanna A. Throop		1
1	"Vengeance is Mine": Saintly Retribution in Medieval Ireland Máire Johnson	5
2	The "Fyre of Ire Kyndild" in the Fifteenth-Century Scottish Marches Jackson W. Armstrong	51
3	Living in Fear of Revenge: Religious Minorities and the Right to Bear Arms in Fifteenth-Century Portugal François Soyer	85
4	Feudal War in Tenth-Century France Dominique Barthélemy	105
5	The Way Vengeance Comes: Rancorous Deeds and Words in the World of Orderic Vitalis Thomas Roche	115
6	Verbal and Physical Violence in the *Historie of Aurelio and Isabell* Marina S. Brownlee	137
7	Was There Really Such a Thing as Feud in the High Middle Ages? Paul R. Hyams	151
8	Zeal, Anger and Vengeance: The Emotional Rhetoric of Crusading Susanna A. Throop	177
Afterword: Neither Unnatural nor Wholly Negative: The Future of Medieval Vengeance Paul R. Hyams		203
Index		*221*

Notes on Contributors

Jackson W. Armstrong is Lecturer in History at the University of Aberdeen. His work is broadly concerned with the British Isles in the period 1300–1600, with a particular focus on the fifteenth century and the borderlands between Scotland and England. He is primarily interested in themes of frontiers, conflict, law, social organization and political society.

Dominique Barthélemy was born in Paris, in 1953. He is now Professor in the University of Paris IV Sorbonne, and *directeur d'études* in the Ecole Pratique des Hautes Etudes. After having studied under Georges Duby, he began to reconsider the social history of feudal France; he found help and encouragement in Great Britain from historians like Janet Nelson, Susan Reynolds, Sir Rees Davies, David Bates, John Hudson and others. His recent works include *Chevaliers et miracles* (Paris, 2004) and *La chevalerie, de la Germanie antique à la France du XIIè siècle* (Paris, 2006). In 2009, an updated version of *The Serf, The Knight, and The Historian* was published in English. He is now preparing other studies about *Démons et saints dans la France romane* and *L'ordre féodal en France, Xè-XIIè siècle*.

Marina S. Brownlee writes on a variety of issues pertaining to medieval and early modern literature and theory. Her interests include periodization (and its discontents), cultural and linguistic translation, the literary representation of gender and of the senses, and the relationship of early tabloid literature to the seventeenth-century short story. She works primarily in Spanish, French and Italian contexts. Her books include *The Cultural Labyrinth of María de Zayas*, *The Severed Word: Ovid's "Heroides" and the "Novela Sentimental"*, *The Status of the Reading Subject in the "Libro de Buen Amor"* and *The Poetics of Literary Theory in Lope and Cervantes*. She has co-edited a number of volumes on medieval and early modern topics, and most recently has edited a special issue of Duke University's *Journal of Medieval and Early Modern Studies* entitled *Intricate Alliances: Early Modern Spain and England*. She is currently working on Hispanic articulations of poesis and modernity in the sixteenth century.

Paul R. Hyams, Professor of History at Cornell University, and Director of Medieval Studies there for several years, was a fellow of Pembroke College, Oxford from 1969–89. An escaped lawyer, he has always sought to place medieval law back in the outside world in a human context, and uses the results to illuminate the whole culture. Though he works best at article length, he has published two books *King, Lords and Peasants in Medieval England* on the law of villeinage and

Rancor and Reconciliation in Medieval England on the changing notion of Wrong and the ways in which people dealt with it. He is currently at work on a study of manumission charters in the "long" thirteenth century, *The Joy of Liberty and the Price of Respectability.*

Máire Johnson presently teaches world civilization for Clarion University of Pennsylvania. A soon-to-be graduate of the Centre for Medieval Studies, University of Toronto, she has recently defended her dissertation, "Holy Body, Wholly Other: Sanctity and Society in the *Lives* of Irish Saints." She has written and presented several other papers on the subject of Ireland's saints. Among these may be counted her peer-reviewed article, "Preserving the Body Christian: The Motif of 'Recapitation' in Ireland's Medieval Hagiography," *The Heroic Age: A Journal of Early Medieval Northwestern Europe*, 10 (2007), at http:www/heroicage.org. Current projects include a paper on the use of the apocrypha in the *Lives* of Ireland's saints for the Harvard Celtic Colloquium in October 2009 and the preparation for publication of the appendix to her dissertation, "Towards the dating of *Vita I S Brigitae.*"

Thomas Roche is a former teaching assistant at the Sorbonne (Université Paris-4) and is now Head of Archives in the *département* of Nièvre. His current research interests focus on legal history and charters in the Anglo-Norman world and also in Burgundy, during the High Middle Ages.

François Soyer Ph.D. (2006) in History, University of Cambridge, held a Leverhulme Trust postdoctoral research award between 2006 and 2008. During this period he was also a visiting Research Fellow at the University of Evora (Portugal) and the Universidad Complutense of Madrid (Spain). He has published on religious minorities and the Inquisition in Medieval and Early Modern Spain and Portugal. He is presently a Lecturer in Early Modern History at the University of Southampton (United Kingdom).

Susanna A. Throop received her Ph.D. in History in 2006 from the University of Cambridge, where she was a Gates Cambridge Scholar from 2001–2005. Now an Assistant Professor of History at Ursinus College, she is interested in interdisciplinary perspectives on religion, violence, ideology and emotion in the High Middle Ages, particularly in the context of the medieval crusading movement. Her recent publications include two peer-reviewed articles, as well as a short essay and source translation in *Medieval Christianity in Practice*, edited by Miri Rubin (Princeton Readings in Religion 2009). She is currently completing her first monograph for Ashgate, *Crusading as an Act of Vengeance, 1095–1216.*

Acknowledgements

This collection began as a session at the International Medieval Congress in July 2005 titled "Vengeance in the Middle Ages." Organized by Susanna and moderated by Paul, the session's original speakers included Dominique Barthélemy and Guy Halsall. Our thanks are owed to the International Medieval Congress and our original contributors for getting the ball rolling, and also to our audience that day, whose interest in the subject inspired us to continue with the project.

We are grateful to many institutions in the U.S. and the U.K. for their help and support while working on this project: Ursinus College, Cornell University, the University of New Hampshire at Manchester, the Gates Cambridge Trust and the University of Cambridge, as well as all the schools involved with the Boston Library Consortium (especially Boston College). Without their generous assistance and access to their collections, the project would not have been possible. Susanna would particularly like to thank Cindy Tremblay and Annie Donahue at UNH-Manchester, who worked patiently and creatively to help her obtain materials.

There are a number of people we want to thank. For Susanna, first among them are her co-editor, Paul, whose belief in the project was instrumental, and Jonathan Riley-Smith, her Ph.D. supervisor, whose generous encouragement and tireless professional support are deeply appreciated. Paul prefers not to appear too complimentary of his co-editor, the true progenitor of this book. He just wishes his colleagues the good fortune to have such a rewarding and challenging student once in a while. Thanks are owed likewise to Tom Gray, Miri Rubin, Tom Brown, Tamsin Palmer, Carol Lambert and Deborah Brown for their kind support.

To our spouses, Elaine and Matt, we owe a debt too large to ever be repaid. They cheered us on when our spirits flagged, inspired us when we lost sight of our goal and always believed in us.

Susanna Throop and Paul Hyams

Introduction
The Study of Vengeance in the Middle Ages

Susanna A. Throop

Vengeance certainly draws a crowd. Back at the International Medieval Congress in Leeds in July 2005, the audience for our session on medieval vengeance spilled out into the hallway. And it's not just academics who are interested, either. Search online for movies or novels with "vengeance" in the title, and it's easy to see that people everywhere are prepared to lay down cold hard cash for a little revenge.

But what is vengeance, anyway?

Well over a century ago Friedrich Nietzsche noted that "the word 'revenge' is said so quickly it almost seems as if it could contain no more than one conceptual and perceptional root," and in many ways this observation holds true today.[1] In popular culture "vengeance" is an explanatory word used with little hesitation to explain why people do things. It is generally assumed that we all know what it means and that the term itself does not require its own explanation.

But as anthropologists and social scientists continue to demonstrate, the different words used for vengeance, and the variety of different ways in which a desire for vengeance may be expressed or sanctioned within different cultures, is truly boggling.[2] For historians, the puzzle is more difficult still. It can be tricky to follow the convoluted twists and turns of event and explanation in our own media-saturated times; it is downright exasperating to try to construct valid interpretations when the historical evidence is scanty and highly subjective at best. And as hard as it is to pin down the meaning of our modern words and idioms for vengeance, how can we hope to understand a whole gamut of terms and metaphors in historical languages?

Given these inherent difficulties, it may seem odd that the study of vengeance continues to draw scholars with such a siren's song. But then, vengeance is that most intriguing of human creations, an explanatory idea—a concept used to explain events. With vengeance, these events relate to human conflict. Often, perhaps always, they involve violence of one form or another. And vengeance has not only been used to *explain* violence, it has frequently been used by some to *justify* violence. So vengeance has a moral weight—of some kind.

---

[1] Friedrich Nietzsche, *Human, All Too Human*, in K. Ansell-Pearson (ed.) and C. Diethe (trans.), *On the Genealogy of Morality* (Cambridge, 1994), p. 131.

[2] A place to start is Raymond Verdier (ed.), *La vengeance: etudes d'ethnologie, d'histoire et de philosophie* (4 vols, Paris, 1980–84).

Therein lies the difficulty. We are not agreed on that moral weight—not in our popular cultures, not in our scholarly research. Vengeance seems universal, in that some sort of relative concept appears throughout history and across cultures. Yet vengeance also seems specific, since the rules that govern vengeance differ widely among, and even within, societies. Similarly, vengeance seems personal and deeply tied to the individual's sense of injured honor. But then we remember the stereotypical "vengeful mob" or the phenomenon of vengeance for kith and kin, and vengeance seems to have a communal function, as well. Vengeance seems a purely negative phenomenon that creates anarchy and chaos and points a society towards a time when "man is wolf to man"—yet it emerges from study that vengeance can be used constructively within a society to bolster the social fabric and enhance social stability. And so on and so forth.

It quickly appears that vengeance is not singular, but plural—that over time we are examining a variety of vengeances, all related but few (if any) identical. And as to whether the sum of these vengeances, when all their qualities and characteristics are catalogued, is a social "good" or "bad"—the jury is most certainly still out.

Strictly speaking, therefore, this collection should be titled *Vengeances in the Middle Ages*. For the essays all quite rightly attempt to clarify the natures of vengeance within specific and different medieval contexts—a particular region, a particular text, a particular social movement. By asking what relationship a distinct factor like authorship or religion has with the concept of vengeance, each author points us ever closer to the meanings of medieval vengeance, to the heart of the deeper and broader questions that spur our interest.

Several of our contributors examine the relationship between a specific geographical region and the concepts and practices of vengeance. In Chapter 1, Máire Johnson wonders if Irish saints had a notorious medieval reputation for vengefulness simply because they were Irish (and thus by ethnic stereotype vengeful). By carefully matching stories of saintly vengeance in medieval Ireland with scriptural parallels, she is able to show that, in fact, vengefulness and holiness walked hand in hand in early Irish Christianity—not because ethnic norms had overwhelmed Christian values, but because the Irish model of sanctity was based on both biblical interpretation and distinct characteristics of Irish culture. Moving forward several centuries, in Chapter 2 Jackson Armstrong visits a cross-border dispute crossing the Scottish marches, where political allegiances (public and private) shifted and divided, and emotions waxed and waned. Armstrong's detailed analysis offers a fresh take on the question of public "justice" versus private "vengeance," and provides insight on the specific role of vengeance within frontier communities. Meanwhile, François Soyer looks at a community of religious frontiers and explores the tension between top-down law and order and private desires for vengeance in late medieval Portugal. His work in Chapter 3 provides much-needed perspective on vengeance and feuding on the Iberian peninsula, and suggests that, for some at least, conflict inside a religious group often took precedence over conflict between different religious communities.

The focus narrows as Dominique Barthélemy and Thomas Roche ask how the identity of a source's author influences the presentation of vengeance within that source. Both Barthélemy and Roche invite us to read our primary sources closely, persuasively demonstrating the effect of the individual author on a text's presentation of vengeance, and suggesting ways for scholars to approach such thorny and multi-layered evidence.

In Chapter 4, Barthélemy dissects the nature of war in tenth-century France and introduces his own concept of "feudal war"—in which adult noblemen revenge themselves upon each other's peasants, rather than each other's persons. At the same time, his comparative treatment of two different medieval authors (Flodoard and Richer of Rheims) demonstrates the importance of careful, canny reading. Roche in Chapter 5 visits a familiar medieval voice, that of Orderic Vitalis. He shows us that the discourse of vengeance functioned on three different levels within Orderic's *Ecclesiastical History*—first, in the way Orderic narrates specific events, second, in the actions and speeches of individuals within Orderic's narrations, and third, in the overarching themes Orderic creates in the work as a whole.

Finally, three chapters ask if it matters what words are used to talk about vengeance, in the Middle Ages and our own times—and if so, what words *should* be used? In Chapter 6, Marina Brownlee takes us inside an extraordinary medieval tale of gender war, incest, love and vengeance. She reveals the relationships between verbal and physical violence in a text we lightly refer to as "literature," thereby illustrating the dangerous potential of words to become deeds, and warning that we trivialize verbal violence at our own risk. Paul Hyams decisively revisits the question of the words scholars use to talk about vengeance, in particular that contentious term familiar to historians and anthropologists alike, "feud," in Chapter 7, while in Chapter 8 I look at the interplay between crusading ideology and religious emotion, using frequently repeated vocabulary as a starting point.

These contributions all have in common an acceptance of Robert Solomon's assertion that vengeance involves intensely personal emotional experiences.[3] In chapter after chapter we are brought face to face with the emotions enduringly labeled as "taboo" by Sigmund Freud—fear, grief, anger, shame.[4] Moreover, we do so within a world where emotion and violence are not separate from religion; a world where religion, emotion, violence and various ideologies coexist and co-inform each other. The medieval discourse that results from such a heady mixture is often striking, sometimes shocking; these essays purposefully direct your attention towards a subject many today may find embarrassing or even repellent.

---

[3] Robert C. Solomon, *A Passion for Justice: Emotions and the Origin of the Social Contract* (London, 1995), p. 41.

[4] Thomas Scheff, "The Taboo on Coarse Emotions," *Review of Personality and Social Psychology*, 5(1984), p. 153.

When all is said and done, we see our work here as one further step in an ongoing investigation—a genuine *enquête à poursuivre*. For those prepared to be challenged, this collection will surely spark a desire to learn and discover more about the varieties of medieval vengeance.

Chapter 1
"Vengeance is Mine":
Saintly Retribution in Medieval Ireland[1]

Máire Johnson

Gerald of Wales, in one of the earliest extant observations concerning the character of Ireland's saints, wrote in the late twelfth century that Irish holy men and women had a greater penchant for vindictive behavior than their foreign colleagues, a viewpoint that has survived even to the present day.[2] Lester Little, for example, has stated that Ireland's saints are often depicted as "matchless champions of the spontaneous, hostile, and efficacious curse" delivered through the vehicle of divinely sanctioned rage.[3] The hagiographical dossiers of such icons of Irish Christianity as Patrick, Brigit and Columba certainly portray their holy subjects bringing all manner of punishments down upon those who challenge their authority, sometimes with deadly results. But is the dire quality of their reputation as straightforward as has been assumed? Do the punitive episodes merely represent holy temper tantrums, or is there something more significant at work?

Numerous approaches have been employed in the study of Ireland's hagiography, a corpus of surviving texts that span the seventh through fourteenth centuries and are written both in Latin (*vitae*) and in Irish (*bethada*). Academic opinion originally saw the genre as the descendant of pagan vernacular lore and saints the inheritors of traits once ascribed to deities or druids, attributing unusual

---

[1] The quotation in the title is from Deut. 32:35, which begins *Mea est ultio et ego retribuam* [Vengeance is mine, and I shall exact retribution]. The version of the *Biblia Sacra* I have used is that available through the University of Chicago's ARTFL Project Online, at http://www.lib.uchicago.edu/efts/ARTFL/public/bibles. Latin translations in this chapter are my own; translations from the vernacular rely in part on those of other scholars. My thanks are owed to the editors of this project, as well as to Ann Dooley, Michael Herren, Andy Orchard, David Klausner, Nicole Lopez-Jantzen and Mark Kowitt for their helpful comments. Any remaining errors are my own.

[2] *Topographia Hiberniae* 2.83, ed. John J. O'Meara, "Giraldus Cambrensis in *Topographia Hibernie*: Text of the First Recension," *Proceedings of the Royal Irish Academy* (hereafter *PRIA*), 52C (1949), p. 156. For dating, see *The History and Topography of Ireland*, trans. John O'Meara (Portlaoise, 1952), pp. 14–15.

[3] "Anger in Monastic Curses," in Barbara H. Rosenwein (ed.), *Anger's Past: The Social Uses of an Emotion in the Middle Ages* (Ithaca, 1998), pp. 28–9.

or apparently non-ecclesiastical acts to that same lineage.[4] Since that time, it has been recognized that a strict definition of Ireland's literary tradition as "secular" or "ecclesiastical" is misleading at best; the two branches grew side by side in the same monastic medium, and influence between them must be understood as reciprocal rather than unidirectional. Saints are not, then, merely the offspring of saga literature and heirs of whitewashed pagan traditions, but the siblings of those same heroic protagonists with whom they share characteristics.[5]

Many studies of Ireland's hagiography focus on the abundant wonder-workings of its subjects, and it is among these tales that representations of vengeance are found. The strong roots of Irish miracle stories in both continental and native sources have been demonstrated by several scholars.[6] Irish hagiographers' influence has also been shown to have extended outward from Ireland, as their portrayals of cursing Irish saints seemingly altered religious expression in areas settled by Irish missionaries.[7] Examinations of links between malediction and anger suggest that

---

[4] Scholars using this approach include Charles Plummer (ed.), *Vitae Sanctorum Hiberniae*, 1 (Oxford, 1910), pp. cxxix–clxxxviii, especially xcccii–cxlix, clxiv–vi; Felim Ó Briain, "Saga Themes in Irish Hagiography," in Séamus Pender (ed.), *Essays and Studies Presented to Professor Tadhg Ua Donnchadha (Torna)* (Cork, 1947), pp. 33–42; William W. Heist, "Myth and Folklore in the Lives of Irish Saints," *The Centennial Review*, 12 (Spring 1968): 181–93; also Heist, "Irish Saints' Lives, Romance, and Cultural History," *Medievalia et Humanistica*, n.s., 6 (1975): 25–40.

[5] See, for example, Ludwig Bieler, "Hagiography and Romance in Medieval Ireland," *Medievalia et Humanistica*, n.s., 6 (1975): 13–24; Joseph Falaky Nagy, "Close Encounters of the Traditional Kind in Medieval Irish Literature," in Patrick K. Ford (ed.), *Celtic Folklore and Christianity* (Santa Barbara, 1983), pp. 129–49; Joseph Nagy, *Conversing with Angels and Ancients: Literary Myths of Medieval Ireland* (Ithaca, 1997); Kim McCone, *Pagan Past and Christian Present in Early Irish Literature* (Maynooth, 1990). McCone particularly emphasizes the scriptural roots of vernacular Irish saga.

[6] Jean-Michel Picard, "The Marvelous in Irish and Continental Saints' Lives of the Merovingian Period," in H.B. Clarke and Mary Brennan (eds), *Columbanus and Merovingian Monasticism* (Oxford, 1981), pp. 91–103; Tomás Ó Cathasaigh, "Curse and Satire," *Éigse*, 21 (1986): 10–15; Dorothy Ann Bray, "Heroic Tradition in the Lives of the Early Irish Saints: A Study in Hagio-Biographical Patterning," in George MacLennon (ed.), *Proceedings of the First North American Congress of Celtic Studies* (Ottawa, 1988), pp. 261–71; Clare Stancliffe, "The Miracle Stories in Seventh-Century Irish Saints' Lives," in Jacques Fontaine and J.N. Hillgarth (eds), *Le Septième Siècle: Changements et Continuités* (London, 1992), pp. 87–115; Dorothy Ann Bray, *A List of Motifs in the Lives of the Early Irish Saints* (Helsinki, 1992); Lisa M. Bitel, "Saints and Angry Neighbors: The Politics of Cursing in Irish Hagiography," in Sharon Farmer and Barbara H. Rosenwein (eds), *Monks & Nuns, Saints & Outcasts: Religion in Medieval Society* (Ithaca, 2000), pp. 123–50; Dorothy Ann Bray, "Miracles and Wonders in the Composition of the Lives of the Early Irish Saints," in Jane Cartwright (ed.), *Celtic Hagiography and Saints' Cults* (Cardiff, 2003), pp. 136–47.

[7] Lester K. Little, *Benedictine Maledictions: Liturgical Cursing in Romanesque France* (Ithaca, 1993); see also Little, "Anger in Monastic Curses," and Bitel, "Saints and Angry Neighbors."

act and emotion are disconnected in most instances, a separation that defies the assertions of Gerald of Wales that Irish saints were impatient and hasty to pursue retribution.[8] Furthermore, most curses are theorized to be responses to insult or dishonor, which constitute challenges both to the saint's authority and to the authority of God himself. Thus curses not only coerce malefactors to turn from sin toward redemption, but also reinforce ecclesiastical rights and define the political relationship between church and secular powers.[9]

The body of scholarship on *miracula* and maledictions in the saintly biographies of medieval Ireland provides considerable material for scholastic discussion. Despite the attention devoted to cursing, however, light has not been shed on the wider field of hagiographical retribution, of which curses comprise but one element. Moreover, the question of the relationship between holiness and saints' reprisals has yet to be addressed. In particular, what do depictions of vengeful saints reveal about the perceptions of sanctity among hagiographers of the Irish Middle Ages? In this chapter, I will map the general topography of saintly vengeance in the landscape of Ireland's medieval hagiography. I will argue, based on this map, that the retaliatory episodes of Ireland's early saints comprise powerful statements concerning the Irish understanding of the nature of sanctity and sainthood, a sanctity that includes not just aspects of the scriptural, moral and spiritual, but also of the legal world of the Irish.[10]

The problem of chronology

Any investigation of Ireland's hagiography must confront the vexing issue of chronology, a matter complicated both by the length of the tradition and by its survival in two languages. Though some works have been reliably placed, most of the time there are few clues that might permit dating. Among vernacular texts, evidence such as intertextual relationships or historical references in the narratives can be augmented by the use of linguistic analysis, fitting the grammar and orthography of *bethada* into an evolutionary outline of Irish. Because written

---

[8] *Topographia Hiberniae* 2.83, O'Meara, "Giraldus Cambrensis in *Topographia Hibernie*," p. 156. Note, however, that Little ("Anger in Monastic Curses") disagrees with the separation of emotion from cursing only in Ireland's hagiography.

[9] See Wendy Davies, "Anger and the Celtic Saint," in Rosenwein (ed.), *Anger's Past*, pp. 191–202; Bitel, "Saints and Angry Neighbors"; and Dorothy Ann Bray, "Malediction and Benediction in the Lives of the Early Irish Saints," *Studia Celtica*, 36 (2002): 47–58.

[10] To avoid confusion between historical and hagiographical events in this study, the vengeful acts of saints are to be understood as the deeds of hagiographical holy men and women of early Ireland, and not the actual undertakings of historical individuals unless specifically stated as such. In other words, representations of retribution used by the biographers of Irish saints are to be taken as textual devices, not as reports of true occurrences.

Latin changed very little over time, however, *vitae* must generally be dated from other clues, and a significant number have not yet been shown to possess sufficient data for chronological labeling.

In fact, whether in Latin or Irish, most *Lives* show signs of repeated redaction. In such texts, early elements mingle with accretions and alterations from throughout the medieval period, mirroring, in a sense, the hagiographical genre's development.[11] There are, however, five important *vitae* of the seventh and early eighth century that provide a solid foundation to Ireland's hagiography. *Vita S Brigitae* of Cogitosus dates to between 650 and 675.[12] Two texts regarding Saint Patrick are extant, the mid-seventh-century *Collectanea Patriciana* of Tírechán and the slightly later, much more narrative *Vita S Patricii* of Muirchú.[13] *Vita S Columbae* of Adomnán places between 689 and 704.[14] Finally, there is the anonymous *Vita I S Brigitae*, the exact dating of which is disputed but is known to originate in either the seventh or the first half of the eighth century.[15] These

---

[11] See, for example, the introduction to the edition of the Book of Lismore *bethada*. Though the manuscript itself is from the 1400s, the texts are linguistically mixed, possessing elements from Old, Middle and Early Modern Irish. *Lives of the Saints from the Book of Lismore*, ed. and trans. Whitley Stokes (Oxford, 1890), pp. v, xlv. Also see the comments of Ailbhe S. Mac Shamhráin on the *Vita Coemgeni* in *Church and Polity in Pre-Norman Ireland: The Case of Glendalough* (Maynooth, 1996), especially p. 149; the work of Máire Herbert demonstrating early elements in the *Vita Cainnechi*, in "The *Vita Columbae* and Irish Hagiography: A Study of *Vita Cainnechi*," in *Studies in Irish Hagiography: Saints and Scholars*, ed. John Carey, Máire Herbert and Pádraig Ó Riain (Dublin, 2001), pp. 31–40; and the analysis of the *Bethu Phátraic*, a text which possesses a core of around 900 but also shows evidence of repeated redaction up through at least the late 1000s, in Kenneth H. Jackson's "The Date of the Tripartite Life of St. Patrick," *Zeitschrift für celtische Philologie* (hereafter *ZCP*), 41 (1986): 5–45.

[12] *Acta Sanctorum*, Februarius I, cols 0135B–0141E. There is also available a translation, based upon the translators' unpublished edition: Seán Connolly and Jean-Michel Picard, "Cogitosus' Life of St. Brigit: Content and Value," *Journal of the Royal Society of Antiquaries of Ireland* (hereafter *JRSAI*), 117 (1987), p. 5. See Seán Connolly, "*Vita Prima Sanctae Brigitae*: Background and Historical Value," *JRSAI*, 119 (1989), p. 6 for dating.

[13] Both texts are edited and translated by Ludwig Bieler, *The Patrician Texts in the Book of Armagh* (Dublin, 1979). Tírechán's collection of anecdotes relating to Patrick is labeled the *Collectanea* by its editor, not its author; see pp. 35–42 for the text. Muirchú's work is found at pp. 60–123.

[14] Alan Orr Anderson and Marjorie Ogilvie Anderson (eds and trans), *Adomnán's Life of Columba* (Edinburgh, 1961). For the dating of the text see Jean-Michel Picard, "The Purpose of Adomnán's *Vita Columbae*," *Peritia*, 1 (1982): 160–77.

[15] *Acta Sanctorum*, Februarius I, cols 0119E–0135B. Also available in a translation based upon the translator's unpublished edition; see Connolly, "*Vita Prima Sanctae Brigitae*," pp. 5–49. The *Vita I* is so named due to its placement in the *Acta Sanctorum*, not to its chronological or textual primacy. Arguments concerning the *vita*'s date center on whether it precedes or follows the work of Cogitosus. Those who place it among Cogitosus' sources include Mario Esposito, "On the Early Latin Lives of St. Brigid of

vitae underlie not only later *Lives* of Brigit, Patrick and Columba, but nearly all Irish saints' *Lives*, their elements and episodes refracted repeatedly throughout the hagiographical genre.

Additionally, the dates of five significant collections of medieval *Lives* may act as terminal reference points for the texts they contain where other chronology is lacking. In Irish, there are the many-layered *bethada* of the late fifteenth-century Book of Lismore.[16] In Latin, there are three large compilations of *vitae*, conveniently designated by Richard Sharpe as the Salamanca, the Dublin and the Oxford, among which there are both shared and unique texts.[17] The most recent studies of these collections place the Salamanca to the later 1200s, the Dublin to around the middle of the 1300s, and the Oxford to the later fourteenth century.[18]

The representation of saintly vengeance

For the present chapter, any miraculous punitive reprisal may be considered a vengeance episode. While there are often linguistic clues, including the use of terms such as the Latin *vindicta* or *ultio* (vengeance, revenge) or, in Irish, of *maldacht* (a curse), such clues are not universal. The marvelous remains the primary component of saintly revenge, differentiating it from more mundane corrections. Moreover, expressions of hagiographical vengeance generally appear to conform to four broad categories, which I define primarily according to the action undertaken by the saint. These categories are prayer, outright malediction, negative or maledictory prophecy, and passive retaliatory judgment.

Kildare," *Hermathena*, 24 (1935): 120–65; Richard Sharpe, "*Vita S. Brigitae*: The Oldest Texts," *Peritia*, 1 (1982): 91–106; and David Howlett, "*Vita I Sanctae Brigitae*," *Peritia*, 12 (1998): 1–23. On the opposing side may be found Donncha Ó hAodha (ed.), *Bethu Brigte* (Dublin, 1978), pp. ix–xxv; Kim McCone, "Brigit in the Seventh Century: A Saint with Three Lives?" *Peritia*, 1 (1982): 107–45; and Connolly, "*Vita Prima Sanctae Brigitae*."

[16] See footnote 11 above.

[17] Richard Sharpe, *Medieval Irish Saints' Lives: An Introduction to* Vitae Sanctorum Hiberniae (Oxford, 1991), pp. 228–39, 246–52 and 347–63. The Salamanca vitae are edited by William W. Heist, *Vitae Sanctorum Hiberniae ex Codice olim Salmanticensi nunc Bruxellensi* (Brussels, 1965). The Dublin texts and those vitae unique to the Oxford compilation have been edited by Charles Plummer, *Vitae Sanctorum Hiberniae* (2 vols, Oxford, 1910).

[18] Pádraig Ó Riain, *Beatha Bharra: St Finbarr of Cork, The Complete Life* (London, 1994), pp. 94–8 and 109–12; also Ó Riain, "*Codex Salmanticensis*: A Provenance *Inter Anglos* or *Inter Hibernos*?" in Toby C. Barnard, Daíbhí Ó Cróinín and Katharine Simms (eds), *"A Miracle of Learning": Studies in Manuscripts and Irish Learning* (Aldershot, 1998), pp. 91–100; and Caoimhín Breatnach, "The Significance of the Orthography of Irish Proper Names in the *Codex Salmanticensis*," *Ériu*, 55 (2005): 85–101.

The earliest *vitae*

In order to understand the branches and leaves of vengeance in Ireland's hagiography, it is useful to begin with its roots. We therefore examine first the earliest *vitae* of Brigit, Patrick and Columba.

Prayer vengeance

In some episodes, saints invoke a divine verdict through prayer alone. Quite often the supplications offered are very detailed, resulting in equally exact consequences. Prayer vengeance makes clear the saint's role as conscious mediator of God's punitive intervention; the saint acts rather like a prosecutor bringing a case before the divine judge, and it is God's final sentence that demonstrates the saint's identity as a sanctified agent of God's will.

Prayer is particularly well represented in the seventh-century hagiography of Ireland's premier saint, Patrick. When, for example, the druid Lochru mocks Patrick and his faith, the saint asks that Lochru be lifted up and removed both from their company and from life. Lochru is immediately borne aloft outside and dashed headfirst on the stones.[19] As pagan armies then gather to avenge the druid's death, Patrick prays that God rout his enemies; the result is an earthquake and darkness that cause mass confusion in the midst of which the opposing host slays many of its own members.[20] Significantly, Patrick's prayer is the beginning of Psalm 67, hinting at the importance of the Psalter and the rise of the *sailm escaine*, the "cursing psalms," in early Ireland.[21]

---

[19] Muirchú, ch. 1.17, pp. 88, 90; see also Tírechán, ch. 85, pp. 130–32, where Lochru is called Lochletheneus.

[20] Muirchú, ch. 1.18, p. 90. The story was retained in subsequent Patrician *Lives*, including the *Vita II* and *Vita IV* of the early ninth century and the great tripartite *Bethu Phátraic*, begun in the ninth century and modified repeatedly through at least the twelfth century. *Vita II*, ch. 36 and *Vita IV*, ch. 42, in Ludwig Bieler (ed.), *Four Latin Lives of St. Patrick: Colgan's Vita Secunda, Quarta, Tertia and Quinta* (Dublin, 1971), p. 91. See F.J. Byrne and Pádraig Francis (trans), "Two Lives of St. Patrick: *Vita Secunda* and *Vita Quarta*," *JRSAI*, 124 (1994), p. 8 for dating on linguistic and internal references. For the vernacular *Life*, see the edition of Kathleen Mulchrone, *Bethu Phátraic: The Tripartite Life of Patrick Vol. I: Text and Sources* (Dublin, 1939), ll. 476–502, pp. 29–30, also the edition and translation of Whitley Stokes, *The Tripartite Life of Patrick with Other Documents Relating to that Saint, Part One* (Nendeln, 1965), pp. 44–9. For the dating of the *Bethu*, see the comprehensive study of Kenneth Jackson, "The Date of the Tripartite Life of St. Patrick," *ZCP*, 41 (1986): 5–45.

[21] "*Exsurgat Deus et dissipentur inimici eius et fugiant qui oderunt eum*" (May God rise up, and may his enemies be scattered and those who hate him put to flight). Both Muirchú (*maledictum*) and the later *Bethu Phátraic* (*mallachtain*) label the prayer a curse despite its delivery as prayer. Muirchú, ch. 1.18, p. 90; *Bethu Phátraic*, ll. 487–502, Mulchrone, pp. 29–30 and Stokes, pp. 44–7. For more on the important place of the Psalter,

In another episode a defiant king, Corictic, mocks Patrick's repeated letters demanding that the king cease his attacks on Christians. Corictic's derision prompts Patrick to pray that the ruler be expelled both "from this world and the next" (*de praesenti saeculoque futuro*). Upon learning of this petition, Corictic's bard and nobles chant a verse calling for the king to forfeit his sovereignty. Before their eyes, the recalcitrant fellow is transformed ignominiously (*miserabiliter*, literally "wretchedly") into a fox. The animal flees and is never seen again.[22]

Ireland was a highly stratified culture in which individual status was hedged around by the determination of honor-price, or *enech*, the value of which compensation for injury depended upon gender and position. Mocking someone constituted a form of insult by verbal assault, entailing a penalty of full honor-price for its victim; in this instance it is paid with Lochru's life.[23] Moreover, if a king like Corictic allowed any challenge to his honor to go unanswered, including the challenge of satires like the chant of his nobles, he could lose his honor-price, and with it his sovereignty.[24] For Corictic, metamorphosis into a base little fox, a beast known for a sly cleverness reminiscent of the manipulative serpent of Genesis, not only strips him of his status, utterly shaming him, it also removes him from his earthly sovereignty. Proper recompense is paid to Patrick, the permanent emendation of Corictic's wicked ways is accomplished, and the king himself is exiled not only from his participation in the community of Christ but also from humanity and any hope of heaven.[25]

---

see, for example, canon 2.3 of the *Canones Hibernenses*, a text from around the middle 600s and therefore roughly contemporary with Muirchú, in Ludwig Bieler (ed. and trans.), *The Irish Penitentials* (Dublin, 1975), p. 164. Also see the eighth-century Rules of Ailbe and of Comgall, *The Rule of Ailbe*, §§16–20, ed. and trans. Joseph Ó Néill, "The Rule of Ailbe of Emly," *Ériu*, 3 (1907), pp. 98–101; also trans. Uinseann Ó Maidín, *The Celtic Monk: Rules and Writings of Early Irish Monks* (Kalamazoo, 1996), pp. 21–2. The *Rule of Comgall*, §§3–4, 13, ed. and trans. John Strachan, "An Old-Irish Metrical Rule," *Ériu*, 1 (1904), pp. 193, 196–7; also trans. Ó Maidín, *The Celtic Monk*, pp. 31–3. On the *sailm escaine*, see Dan M. Wiley, "The Maledictory Psalms," *Peritia*, 15 (2001): 261–79.

[22] Muirchú, ch. 1.29, p. 100.
[23] Fergus Kelly, *A Guide to Early Irish Law* (Dublin, 1988), p. 137.
[24] *Críth Gablach*, §21, ed. D.A. Binchy (Dublin, 1941), pp. 12–13; also see "*áer*, 'satirizing'," p. 69 and "*enech*, 'honour, dignity'," pp. 84–5 for Binchy's further explanation of the impact of a just satire and of dishonor in general. This eighth-century vernacular law tract has been translated by Eoin MacNeill, "Ancient Irish Law: The Law of Status and Franchise," *PRIA*, 36C (1923): 265–316; see §§100–101, pp. 295–6 for the translation of the present passage. Also see Kelly, *Guide to Early Irish Law*, pp. 137–9.
[25] It would seem the early Irish felt that foxes were not possessed of souls. In addition, if one cannot properly perform penance or engage in the rituals of the faith, one cannot gain entry into the community of believers on earth or in heaven.

Prayer and fasting with vigil

A particularly interesting manifestation of prayer vengeance in these early *vitae* is the combination of prayer with fasting and vigil to summon retribution. In the only such episode of this era, St. Brigit fasts against a layman who refuses to depart an island claimed by the saint's anchorite. Though an eagle swoops up the layman's infant son and carries him to the mainland shore, the layman is not moved to comply with Brigit's requests until he is himself blown off the island by a great gust of wind. Finally the frazzled fellow does penance to Brigit and cedes to her his land.[26]

It is notable that this female saint's punitive urgings are not as instantly devastating as the prayer-summoned vengeance of her male counterpart, Patrick. Instead, they are increasingly insistent encouragements to emend. No one in the episode is harmed. The clearly divine power manifest demonstrates the divine source of Brigit's authority, humbles the layman and demands compliance. We shall soon see, however, that Brigit and the other lady saints of Ireland are not always so demure.

Fasting itself has a complex lineage in Ireland, beginning with a long legal history as a means of compelling someone of equal or superior status to comply with demands of due restitution. Contemporary vernacular legal texts explain that seizure of property, or distraint, a final stage in the process of gaining due recompense, was often to be preceded by notice of the plaintiff's case. If no response was forthcoming and the defendant was of sufficiently exalted status, fasting could follow.[27] A defendant who failed to give the appropriate pledges or to counter-fast against the plaintiff before the conclusion of the plaintiff's vigil could legally lose property, status or both.[28]

---

[26] *Vita I S Brigitae*, §12.72, col. 0129C. Also §72, Connolly, pp. 35–6.

[27] Neither notice nor fasting was necessary when a defendant's status was inferior to that of a plaintiff, as the superior grades could simply appropriate the defendant's property. Defendants of fasting had to be kings, nobles, clerics or poets, the higher grades of Irish society. §§8–9, ed. and trans. D.A. Binchy, "A Text on the Forms of Distraint," *Celtica*, 10 (1973): 72–86. The largest tract on fasting (*troscud*) is a subsection of the *Cetharslicht Athgabála* (*The Four Classes of Distraint*) 365.5–367.7, ed. D.A. Binchy, *Corpus Iuris Hibernici* (Dublin, 1978). English translation (not always accurate) in *Ancient Laws of Ireland*, §§112.14–118–7, ed. and trans. W.N. Hancock et al. (Dublin, 1865). German translation plus discussion of the practice of fasting against a defendant by Rudolf Thurneysen, "Das Fasten beim Pfändungsverfahren," *ZCP*, 15 (1925): 260–75. Also worth consulting are D.A. Binchy, "Distraint in Irish Law," *Celtica*, 10 (1973): 22–71, especially 34–5, and Kelly, *Guide to Early Irish Law*, pp. 9, 182–3.

[28] See Kelly, *Guide to Early Irish Law*, pp. 182–3. Binchy observes that in *Cetharslicht Athgabála* fasting replaced the tendering of notice by the plaintiff, while other legal tracts still required the announcement of the suit prior to engaging in the fast ("Distraint in Irish Law," pp. 34, 66).

This type of legal fasting did influence Ireland's later hagiography. In *Lives* outside the earliest texts, Saints Patrick, Maedóc and Énda all fast against God to obtain boons for them and their followers.[29] Patrick's boons are even called a *les*, a legal term for redress gained through court proceedings, underlining the assumption that the fast itself is seen as a lawsuit brought against God as the defendant.[30]

Fasting also belongs to an illustrious scriptural heritage, although the context in the Bible is somewhat different. Usually an expression of despair or mourning, a part of ritual atonement or an element of purification, fasting in the Old and New Testaments is often associated not only with spiritual cleanliness but with proving commitment and contrition to gain mercy, forgiveness, inspiration or aid from God.[31]

Elements of this scriptural fasting also appear in Ireland's hagiography. In the seventh century, Tírechán's Patrick not only fasts for God's aid but also undertakes a forty-day and forty-night fast according to the example of Moses, Elijah and Christ.[32] When this same epic vigil appears in the later *Bethu Phátraic*, it has become a legal fast; Patrick's protracted deprivation moves a wearied angel to accede to the saint's demands.[33]

Brigit, for her part, observes all the legal niceties. She gives notice of her suit and asks the layman to leave. When he refuses, she fasts against him for the legal minimum of one night.[34] Having gained little response by the end of the fast, Brigit pursues "distraint," and the layman is pointedly removed from the island. Property, produce, independence, physical and spiritual health, even life itself are often targets for saintly seizure, but in Brigit's case it is only land, claimed by the plaintiff through persuasive force once other methods have failed.

Brigit's episode of fasting and vigil also represents the first sign we have yet seen of penance in the early *vitae*. Whether the association of penance with Brigit is due

---

[29] *Bethu Phátraic*, ll. 1289–1374, Mulchrone, pp. 71–5; Stokes, pp. 112–19. *Vita S Aidui sive Maedoc* (Vespasian MS), ch. 33, Plummer, vol. 2, p. 304; also *Vita S Aedani seu Maedoc Episcopi Fernensis* (Salamanca), ch. 28, Heist, p. 241, and *Vita S Maedoc Episcopi de Ferna* (Dublin), ch. 33, Plummer, vol. 2, pp. 153–4. *Vita S Endei Abbatis de Arann* (Oxford), ch. 31, Plummer, vol. 2, pp. 73–4.

[30] 'Les', *Dictionary of the Irish Language Based Mainly on Old and Middle Irish Materials: Compact Edition* (hereafter *DIL*) (Dublin, 1998).

[31] For just a few examples, see Exod. 24:18; 1 Kgs. 7:6; 2 Kgs. 1:12, 12:16–23; 3 Kgs. 21:27; Neh. 1:4; Esther 4:16; Ps. 34:12–14; Matt. 6:16–18; Mark 2:18–20; Luke 2:37, 18:12; or Acts 13:2, 14:23.

[32] Chs 3.19.4, 3.38, pp. 138, 152.

[33] Lines 1289–1374, Mulchrone, pp. 71–5; Stokes, pp. 112–19.

[34] Binchy, "Distraint in Irish Law," pp. 34–5. Biblical precedent for one-night fasts can be found in 2 Kgs. 12:16–17 or Dan. 6:18, for example. Other than vigils of one night, the most common duration in hagiography is three days and nights; one instance of scriptural fasting for this period of time is Esther 4:16.

to the category of prayer vengeance itself or is a result of Brigit's femininity is not clear. It is useful to observe, however, that the prosecution of a legal fast inherently provides a defendant multiple opportunities to reform, offering considerable room for a saint's mercy. Prayer alone, by contrast, has no waiting period. In these early *vitae*, prayer invokes an immediate judgment with no recourse for appeal.

Outright malediction

Some saints deliver the stunning and often lethal pronouncements of outright malediction. Using both language and, in some cases, gestures to indicate the maledictory act, curses have an instantaneous fulfillment that cannot fail to impress the *Life*'s audience. Importantly, God's involvement in outright malediction is not always explicitly acknowledged. Instead it is understood that it is the saint's identity as a vessel of God's grace that permits the successful infliction of the curse.

In the earliest *vitae*, Patrick stands forth as the master of outright malediction. He curses rivers to immediate and permanent sterility because the riverbank inhabitants refuse to share their fish with him, or because two boys in his retinue drown in the affected waters.[35] In a similar vein, Adomnán depicts Columba of Iona pronouncing the instant death and damnation of a man who brazenly slays a girl cowering at his feet.[36]

An important part of the rights due to a person of exalted social status in medieval Ireland was the receipt of hospitality. The noble classes had the reasonable and legal expectation that they would be welcomed, housed and fed by landholders they approached when traveling. According to the early vernacular legal writings, refusal of hospitality due a person of quality—whether lay or ecclesiastical—entitled that person to the payment of his full honor-price.[37] Two forms of rejection are specified.

---

[35] Tírechán, chs 3.46.4–5, pp. 158, 160. The episodes are retained in later Patrician hagiography, but altered to negative prophecy, the boys not drowned but whipped. *Vita IV*, ch. 51, Bieler, pp. 98–9; Byrne and Francis, p. 52. *Bethu Phátraic*, ll. 1692–3, 1718–29, Mulchrone, pp. 89–91; Stokes, pp. 146–9.

[36] *Vita S Columbae*, ch. 2.25, pp. 382, 384. The episode is retained in the later twelfth-century *Betha Coluim Chille*, §25, ed. and trans. Máire Herbert, "The Irish Life of Colum Cille," *Iona, Kells, and Derry: The History and Hagiography of the Monastic Familia of Columba* (Oxford, 1998), pp. 245, 267. For dating, see Herbert, pp. 184–93.

[37] *Críth Gablach*, §§6, 11, 12, Binchy, pp. 1–2, 5–6; §§66, 83, 84, MacNeill, pp. 283, 288–9. See also Binchy, *Críth Gablach*, p. 81 (*cóe*, "coshering"), and pp. 87–8 (*esáin*, "driving away"), as well as the seventh-century *Canones Hibernenses*, Book 5, ed. and trans. Ludwig Bieler, *The Irish Penitentials* (Dublin, 1975), pp. 172, 174, for the penalties and penances incurred by rejecting ecclesiastical figures. Ecclesiastical ranks were paralleled with their secular counterparts, for example a king and a bishop commanded the same honor-price. See *Uraicecht Becc*, §§8–9, trans. MacNeill, "Ancient Irish Law," pp. 273–4; *Bretha Nemed Toísech*, §20, ed. and trans. Liam Breatnach, "The First Third of *Bretha Nemed Toísech*," *Ériu*, 40 (1989), pp. 16–17. Both are legal texts of the eighth century. Also Kelly, *Guide to Early Irish Law*, p. 139.

The first is *étach*, or "refusal," and the second, more severe type is *esáin*, "driving away."[38] Further, any missed meals the denied party should suffer are considered forced fasts, qualifying the hungry elite for an additional recompense.[39] While a rejected king might demand a payment of cattle or other goods to restore his honor, a saint's exaction is more severe. Patrick, by damning a river to fishlessness, imposes upon its region a permanent hunger akin to that inflicted upon him by its inhabitants and accomplishes thereby both the restitution of his own injury and the turning onto his injurers of the *étach* he suffered.

A person of elevated rank also held the right to extend his protection, his *snádud* or *turtugud*, to those of equal or lesser status. The elite individual was thereby able to guarantee safe conduct and, if necessary, immunity from prosecution for a period of time determined by his own social grade. Violation of this protection, or *díguin*, by the wounding or death of someone under its aegis constituted a serious injury to the protector's honor, incurring the protector's full honor-price as penalty.[40] Patrick's malediction upon the rivers that drown his young followers essentially deprives their waters of their life; Columba's curse likewise removes its target from existence. In these texts, the price for violating a saint's protection is death.

Other motives for malediction include a deceiving attempt to test Patrick, which results in the malefactor's death; when his companions convert, however, he is returned to life in an uncharacteristic display of mercy.[41] Attempts on Patrick's life prompt him to raise his left hand and condemn the ringleader of the plot, who is instantly immolated by lightning "as a sign of vengeance" (*in signum vindictae*).[42] Nor are the men the only saints to curse. Brigit, displeased (*displicuit*) that a laywoman refuses to share apples she brought for the saint with a leper seeking alms, pronounces the perpetual fruitlessness of the laywoman's trees.[43]

---

[38] Kelly, *Guide to Early Irish Law*, pp. 139–40.

[39] Binchy, *Críth Gablach*, pp. 106–7 (*snádud*); also Kelly, *Guide to Early Irish Law*, p. 140.

[40] *Críth Gablach*, §§6, 11, 12, Binchy, pp. 1–2, 5–6; §§66, 83, 84, MacNeill, "Ancient Irish Law," pp. 283, 288–9. Also see *Críth Gablach*, "*díguin*," pp. 82–3.

[41] Muirchú, ch. 1.23, pp. 102, 104. The tale is retained in *Bethu Phátraic*, ll. 2612–46, Mulchrone, pp. 131–4; Stokes, pp. 220–23.

[42] Tírechán, ch. 3.42.2–6, p. 156. The same story is found in both the *Vita IV* and the later *Bethu Phátraic*, where the malefactor is dropped on his head *quasi* Lochru. In both cases, the crime is refusal to convert, not a murder plot against Patrick, and the mode of vengeance is passive retaliatory judgment rather than malediction. *Vita IV*, ch. 66, Bieler, pp. 103–4; Byrne and Francis, p. 56. *Bethu Phátraic*, ll. 1488–1511, Mulchrone, pp. 81–2; Stokes, pp. 130–31.

[43] *Vita I S Brigitae*, ch. 4.28, col. 0122D; §32, Connolly, p. 21. In the later version of the Book of Lismore, the curse is extended to the permanent emptiness of the laywoman's overflowing storage barns as well. *Bethu Brigte* (ninth century), §32, Ó hAodha, pp. 12, 29, and *Betha Bhrigdi* (Lismore), ll. 1424–30, Stokes, pp. 42–3, 190. For the dating of the Old Irish text, see Ó hAodha, *Bethu Brigte*, pp. ix–xxv.

Negative or maledictory prophecy

Closely related to outright malediction is the saintly use of what I label "negative or maledictory prophecy." In delivery, intent, language and often in judgment duration, negative prophecy is identical to outright cursing. Episodes of negative prophecy, however, also include language such as *prophetavit* (he or she prophesied), *praedicere* (to foretell) or *fáistinid* (he prophesies). The difference, a distinction not made by the Irish themselves, lies in the time of onset. Straightforward malediction always produces instantaneous result. Negative prophecy, however, has a delayed onset, its full manifestation not appearing for anywhere from one day to many years later.

The motivation to distinguish between outright malediction and maledictory prophecy is found in Book 61 of the early eighth-century Irish canon law compendium, the *Collectio Canonum Hibernensis*, which specifically addresses cursing.[44] On the one hand, Book 61 relies upon scriptural and scholastic precedent to encourage avoidance of cursing and the practice instead of humility and forgiveness (Matt. 5:44/Luke 6:27–8, Rom. 12:14, Jas. 3:8–12). On the other, the book concludes with a string of prohibitive maledictions that closely parallel those pronounced upon any who disobey God or Moses (Deut. 27:15–26). This apparently muddled message is clarified in the first two chapters, which consider that curses are to be a last resort utilized only against a malefactor who "does not fear God's face" (*non timet faciem Dei*), are to correct rather than to permanently condemn, and are to be pronounced "not with the spirit of one desiring, but of one prophesying [them]" (*non optantis animo, sed prophetantis*). In other words, malediction should, by virtue of prophetic pronouncement, both avoid even the appearance of an act of rage and provide time during which the wrongdoers might make satisfaction and alleviate or obviate their sentence.[45] At the same time, the list of potent curses at the end of the book make plain that certain infractions do demand instant, irredeemable judgment.[46]

This canon law draws considerable inspiration from a scriptural precedent that both exemplifies and condemns curses. Most cases of malediction occur in the Old Testament. While there are a few curses delivered in the New Testament (Matt. 21:18–21/Mark 11:12–14, Acts 5, Acts 13:11–12), the overall emphasis is on rejection of cursing. The tenets of Book 61 in the *Collectio* thus balance between

---

[44] "*De Maledictionibus*," ed. Hermann Wasserschleben, *Die irische Kanonensammlung* (Leipzig, 1885), pp. 227–8. Other scholars to observe the canon law prescriptions urging that malediction be pronounced as prophecy include Little, *Benedictine Maledictions*, pp. 88–91; Wiley, "The Maledictory Psalms," pp. 271–3; Bitel, "Saints and Angry Neighbors," p. 129 and Bray, "Malediction and Benediction," p. 52. Both Bitel and Bray have used the term "negative prophecy." Neither, however, have utilized the alternate term, "maledictory prophecy."

[45] "*De Maledictionibus*," p. 227.

[46] Ibid., ch. 6, p. 228.

both the Old and the New Testament, between the outright malediction so frequent in the former and the general tendency to prohibit it in the latter. That fulcrum is the pronouncement of what I term "negative prophecy."

The single most common maledictory foretelling is that which dooms a lineage to servitude, removing it from a sovereignty that is often then bestowed upon a competing kindred. Patrick is a virtuoso of the skill, condemning the descendants of Coirpre mac Néill and of Derclaid for attempting to kill him, and removing the line of an unnamed son of Fíachu mac Néill from kingship for the murder of some of the saint's followers.[47] Rule is taken from the Uí Eircc for the theft of Patrick's horses, and Loegaire's descendants are deposed due to their progenitor's defiantly reluctant conversion.[48]

Negative prophecy is also given other expression. In an apparent hagiographical enforcement of the tenets found in the apocryphal "Letter of Jesus on Sunday Observance," Patrick warns pagans building an embankment around a fort on Sunday that their work will come to naught. The ditch is destroyed that night by the sea.[49] The "Letter," thought to have been known in Ireland from around 700, contains an extensive list of the activities forbidden from Saturday sunset until Monday morning—including domestic chores in and outside of the house—and the penalties for engaging in them.[50]

Adomnán's Columba of Iona also foretells doom upon certain deserving souls. An unrepentant sinner is told he will suffer debasement and decapitation, while poverty and murderous betrayal are the portion for one who denies hospitality

---

[47] Tírechán, chs 3.8.9, 3.16.4, 3.36, pp. 132, 136, 150. Coirpre mac Néill's condemnation is found in both the *Vita IV*, ch. 51, Bieler, pp. 98–9; Byrne and Francis, p. 52, and in the *Bethu Phátraic*, ll. 736–41, Mulchrone, p. 45; Stokes, pp. 68–71. Derclaid's downfall is only retained in *Bethu Phátraic*, ll. 1257–63 (where Derclaid is Derglám), Mulchrone, pp. 69–70; Stokes, pp. 110–11.

[48] Tírechán, ch. 3.31.2–3, p. 148. Also Muirchú, ch. 1.21.2, p. 98. The debasement of the Uí Eircc is in *Bethu Phátraic*, ll. 1231–3, 1664–8, Mulchrone, pp. 68, 88; Stokes, pp. 108–9, 144–5. Loegaire's unwilling conversion is also in the *Bethu*, ll. 622–32, Mulchrone, pp. 36–7; Stokes, pp. 60–61.

[49] Muirchú, ch. 1.26, p. 106. The tale is retained by *Bethu Phátraic*, ll. 2647–54, Mulchrone, p. 134; Stokes, pp. 222–5.

[50] §10, ed. and trans. Máire Herbert and Martin McNamara, *Irish Biblical Apocrypha: Selected Texts in Translation* (Edinburgh, 1989), p. 52. For dating, see McNamara, *Apocrypha in the Irish Church* (Dublin, 1975), pp. 60–63. The apparent use of the "Letter" by Muirchú suggests a slightly earlier availability in the seventh century than has been supposed. It must be acknowledged, however, that the proscriptions of Mosaic Law on the Sabbath rest may also apply (Lev. 23:3). Notably, some early Irish, even in the seventh century, viewed the Sabbath as Saturday, and Sunday as *Dies Dominica*, the Lord's day; Adomnán makes this distinction in the *Vita S Columbae*, and does not condemn travel or domestic chores on Sunday as does the "Letter." See Anderson and Anderson, *Adomnán's Life of Columba*, pp. 25–9.

to Columba; in another instance, sudden death is predicted for a supposed ally who kills a man under Columba's protection.[51] Columba also prophesies death by shipwreck and drowning upon a brigand who repeatedly raids Columba's ally, Saint Colmán Élo.[52] Known in Latin as *fures, latrones* or *latrunculi* and in Irish as *díbergaig*, brigands were particular targets of ecclesiastical censure, and frequent subjects of saintly vengeance, due in no small part to their irritating habit of raiding church properties and involving noncombatants in acts of violence.[53]

A number of Columban episodes may relate to the interests of the author of *Vita S Columbae*, Adomnán. As abbot of Iona himself, Adomnán wrote and promulgated the *Cáin Adomnáin*, also called the Law of Innocents (*Lex Innocentium*), in 697.[54] This law set forth heavy fines for those who involved women, children, clerics or slaves in warfare or raiding.[55] In one such case, Columba foretells the mortal illness of a Pictish druid, Broichan, because he refuses to release an Irish slave girl. Broichan is only saved from his demise when he relents and sets the girl free, whereupon Columba arranges his healing.[56]

Adomnán's Columba often prophesies some form of pollution as part of a malefactor's downfall. In one instance Columba tells a penitent he will consume horsemeat in the company of outlaws because, in an act of pride, he refuses a food indulgence the saint has offered to the entire community.[57] In Ireland's early penitentials, the eating of horseflesh called for a minimum of three and a half years of penance on bread and water, in keeping with the prohibitions of Mosaic Law (Lev. 1:1–8).[58] Furthermore, to dine with outlaws, whatever the dish may be, implies apostasy, the ultimate pollution for a supposed penitent.

---

[51] *Vita S Columbae*, chs 1.41, 2.20, 2.23, pp. 290–92, 368, 376–8.

[52] Ibid., ch. 2.22, pp. 372–6.

[53] For discussion of this topic, see Richard Sharpe, "Hiberno-Latin *laicus*, Irish *láech* and the Devil's Men," *Ériu*, 30 (1979): 75–92; Kim McCone, "Werewolves, Cyclopes, *Díberga*, and *Fíanna*: Juvenile Delinquency in Early Ireland," *Cambridge Medieval Celtic Studies*, 12 (Winter 1986): 1–22; Máire Johnson, "Preserving the Body Christian: The Motif of 'Recapitation' in Ireland's Medieval Hagiography," *The Heroic Age: A Journal of Early Medieval Northwest Europe*, 10 (May 2007): n.p. Available online at http://www.heroicage.org.

[54] *Annals of Ulster*, ed. and trans. Seán Mac Airt and Gearóid Mac Niocaill, *The Annals of Ulster (to A. D. 1131)* (Cork, 2000), pp. 157, 158. Available online through the Corpus of Electronic Texts, http://www.ucc.ie/celt.

[55] Kuno Meyer (ed. and trans.), *Cáin Adomnáin: An Old-Irish Treatise on the Law of Adomnán* (Oxford, 1905).

[56] *Vita S Columbae*, ch. 2.33, pp. 398–404.

[57] Ibid., ch. 1.26, 1.41, pp. 250, 252, 290, 292.

[58] *Canones Hibernenses*, canon 1.13, Bieler, *The Irish Penitentials*, p. 160. The *Canones* are from the first half of the seventh century. See Bieler, *The Irish Penitentials*, p. 9. Also §1.2, ed. and trans. E.J. Gwynn, "An Irish Penitential," *Ériu*, 7 (1914), pp. 146–7. The penitential is from the late eighth century; see p. 130.

Apostasy is also a critical part of Columba's prophecy of doom upon a wrongly ordained regicide, Áed Dubh, whom Columba predicts will forsake his vows, return to his bloody ways, and then be slain. As for the bishop who ordained Áed, Columba's foretelling removes the source of his pollution and its threat to his soul, in accordance with the scriptural injunction to remove those parts that offend (Matt. 5:29–30). The bishop's right hand, used to bless the regicide's head, slowly and agonizingly rots from his arm.[59]

Brigit also pronounces maledictory prophecy. Irked (*displicuit*) by the arrogance of a leper seeking alms, she tells him to take her cow, but warns that the animal will do him no good. While his humble companion makes it home safely with his own cow, the haughty leper and his prize are swept away during a river crossing.[60] The episode is inspired at least in part by an extended sermon of the seventh century, the *De Duodecim Abusivis Saeculi* (*Concerning the Twelve Abuses of the Age*). Brigit's vengeance echoes the lesson of the eighth abuse, *pauper superbus*, emphasizing the proper humble acceptance of poverty as the key to attaining heaven.[61]

As with prayer vengeance and outright malediction, penance is again curiously lacking in the episodes of negative prophecy. The only display of mercy is that shown by Columba in the healing of Broichan, but since the druid does not convert, he cannot perform penance, and merely releases the slave girl to gain his cure.

Passive retaliatory judgment

Passive retaliatory judgment is the term I use to describe instances of apparent vengeance in which the saints commit no act, either of speech or of gesture, to invoke the punitive miracles that occur. These portrayals most clearly display the saint's identity as a recipient of God's favor; he or she is a conduit not for his or her own power or authority but for a "divine strength," a *divina virtus* that moves independently of the saint when necessary.

---

[59] *Vita S Columbae*, ch. 1.37, pp. 280–82.

[60] *Vita I S Brigitae*, §12.78, cols 0130A–0130B; §78–9, Connolly, p. 37.

[61] This use by the *Vita I* of *De Duodecim Abusiuis* may have implications for the dating of the *vita*, an issue I will be exploring in a future essay. Siegmund Hellmann (ed.), "Pseudo-Cyprianus *De XII Abusivis Saeculi*," *Texte und Untersuchungen zur Geschichte der altchristlichen Literatur*, 34 (1909), pp. 49–51. For the date, 630x650, see Aidan Breen's studies of the *De XII Abusivis*: "Pseudo-Cyprian *De Duodecim Abusivis Saeculi* and the Bible," in *Irland und die Christenheit: Bibelstudien und Mission / Ireland and Christendom: the Bible and the missions*, ed. Próinséas Ní Chatháin und Michael Richter (Stuttgart, 1987), pp. 230–31; "The Evidence of Antique Irish Exegesis in Pseudo-Cyprian, *De Duodecim Abusivis Saeculi*," *PRIA*, 87C (1987), p. 76; and "*De XII Abusiuis*: Text and Transmission," in *Ireland and Europe in the Early Middle Ages: Texts and Transmission/ Irland und Europa im früheren Mittelalter: Texte und Überlieferung*, ed. Próinséas Ní Chatháin und Michael Richter (Dublin, 2002), p. 84. These sentiments take as biblical support Matt. 5:3–5 and 1 Tim. 6:17–19.

In the earliest *vitae* of Ireland, this form of retribution falls almost exclusively to Saint Brigit. In *Vita Brigitae* of Cogitosus, raiders who make off with Brigit's cattle are confronted by a river which, rising "like a wall" (*instar muri*) against them, engulfs them and washes them away. The cows, released, return home.[62] In *Vita I*, the expanded story softens the punishment with a healthy mix of public shame. In order to cross the flooded river, the thieves strip and bind their clothing onto the horns of their stolen herd, but the cows turn back midstream. The sodden, naked men are forced to chase the animals all the way back to Brigit's settlement, where they are recognized by everyone and perform immediate penance to Brigit.[63]

In another example, passive retaliatory judgment paralyzes the hands of disputing lepers, compelling the two men to stand immobile, their arms raised and their fists bunched, until they do penance. Notably, Brigit heals only their hands, not their leprosy, perhaps as an ongoing penitential lesson.[64] This episode also relates to *De Duodecim Abusivis*, but here it is the seventh abuse, *Christianus contentiosus*, with which *Vita I* is concerned. This sermon asserts that a Christian should observe the habits of Christ in order to attain heaven, and since Jesus did not fight over earthly things, neither should those who profess to follow him.[65]

Brigit is also associated with several other cases of passive retaliation. A nun who defies Brigit is punished with a one-hour bout of putrid leprosy.[66] The arrogance of a haughty, newly-healed leper incurs a full relapse of his disease while his humble friend is completely cured—another reflection of the eighth abuse of *De Duodecim Abusivis*.[67] In an interesting portrayal of political activism by the female saint, a king who rejects Brigit's chosen candidate for an appointment falls from his chariot and dashes out his brains.[68]

One episode may relate to the *Cáin Adomnáin*. Here, Brigit seeks the release of a slave girl who takes sanctuary with her. The girl's mistress rudely rebuffs Brigit and hauls the girl from the saint's side, displeasing (*displicuit*) Brigit. Immediately the hand with which the woman grasps her slave's arm withers, and it remains shriveled until she does proper penance and releases the slave to Brigit.[69]

---

[62] §19, col. 0137D; also ch. 16, Connolly and Picard, "Cogitosus' Life of St. Brigit," p. 18.

[63] *Vita I S Brigitae*, §6.43, cols 0124B–0124C; §45, Connolly, p. 25.

[64] §4.30, col. 0122F; §34, Connolly, p. 22. The episode continues in *Bethu Brigte* and the Lismore *Betha Bhrigdi*, in both of which not only the lepers' paralysis but their leprosy is cured. *Bethu Brigte*, §34, Ó hAodha, pp. 12, 29; *Betha Bhrigdi*, ll. 1431–4, Stokes, pp. 43, 190.

[65] Hellmann, "Pseudo-Cyprianus *De XII Abusivis Saeculi*," pp. 46–9.

[66] §8.54, col. 0126A; §56, Connolly, p. 29.

[67] §12.76, col. 0129F; §76, Connolly, p. 37. For the eighth abuse, refer to Hellmann, "Pseudo-Cyprianus *De XII Abusivis Saeculi*," pp. 49–51.

[68] §17.107, col. 0134B; §118, Connolly, p. 47.

[69] §12.74, cols 0129D–0129E; §74, Connolly, p. 36. If *Vita I* does mirror *Cáin Adomnáin*, it (*Vita I*) would not predate the early eighth century.

In Patrick's solitary early example of passive retaliatory judgment, the horses of a wealthy man, Dáire, drop dead after being pastured on land promised to Patrick. Dáire sends men to kill Patrick in retaliation, but dies himself; the deceased are all raised at the earnest behests of Dáire's wife and kin.[70] Pasturing one's horses on another's land without permission was one way to claim property ownership, a claim denied if the horses were expelled.[71] Dáire's act of trespass is thus a hubris-filled statement that his own claim supersedes that of a saint, and both earthly and heavenly penalty—for arrogance as much as for trespass—naturally follow.

Scriptural parallels and models of sanctity in the early vitae

Despite the small number of texts at the foundation of Ireland's hagiography, a particular view of sanctity is apparent in the scriptural parallels of and antecedents to the vengeful episodes of the early *vitae*. The most significant of these is the explicit comparison drawn by Muirchú between Patrick's conflict with Lochru and the apocryphal confrontation of Peter with Simon Magus in *The Acts of Peter and Paul*, a comparison discussed by Aideen O'Leary.[72] The apocryphon depicts Simon Magus committing an act of thaumaturgical barnstorming to undermine the identity of Jesus as the Christ, from which flight he is fatally brought down by Peter's prayers.[73] By placing Patrick on the same footing as Peter, Muirchú declares Patrick a recipient of the same apostolic dispensation as that bestowed by Jesus upon Peter. Just as Peter is the Rock of the universal Church, so Patrick is the first apostle to and bedrock of the Irish church, his primacy and authority given by the Son of God.[74]

Overall, the majority of scriptural inspiration for the men seems to have been either apostolic, as in the immediate decease that befalls the lying Ananias and Sephira at Peter's curse (Acts 5), or based upon texts of the prophets, such as

---

[70] Muirchú, ch. 1.24, pp. 108, 110.

[71] Kelly, *Guide to Early Irish Law*, pp. 109–10 ("usucaption") and 186–7 (legal claim process). Also Fergus Kelly, *Early Irish Farming* (Dublin, 1997), pp. 432–3.

[72] *Vita S Patricii*, ch. 1.18, p. 90. Aideen O'Leary, "An Irish Apocryphal Apostle: Muirchú's Portrayal of St Patrick," *Harvard Theological Review*, 89 (July 1996): 287–301. Patrick's contest with Lochletheneus/Lochru in Tírechán clearly relies on the same comparison, if tacitly. That both authors use the episode suggests that their shared source takes the apocryphal roots of Irish sanctity farther back than the middle of the 600s. See *Collectanea Patriciana*, ch. 85, pp. 130–32.

[73] See §14, Herbert and McNamara, *Irish Biblical Apocrypha*, pp.103–4, 181 for a translation of the Irish version of the text.

[74] See Matt. 16:15–19, where Peter—also named Simon Peter—is called by Jesus the foundation upon which Jesus will build his church, and is given by Jesus the power to bind and to free from bonds both in heaven and on earth because the apostle recognizes Jesus as the Messiah. Jesus also bestows upon all the apostles the ability to heal and cast out devils (Luke 9:1–2).

the vengeful divine fire that incinerates 250 Levites for rebelling against Aaron's authority (Num. 16:35). One might also note the long Old Testament tradition of negative prophecies that depose one lineage in favor of another, beginning with the refusal of Cain's offering and patent favoring of his brother, Abel, by God (Gen. 4:4–5, 11–12) (see Table 1.2 in the Appendix). In these *vitae* of Patrick and Columba, very little direct modeling upon Jesus is accomplished through the canonical Gospels. Instead, aside from the echo of a hungry Jesus' curse of fruitlessness upon the barren fig tree (Matt. 21:19–20/Mark 11:12–21) seen in the condemnation to sterility of lands and waters that fail to provide for a saint's empty stomach, most parallels to the Savior appear to draw from apocryphal works like the *Infancy Gospel of Thomas*, in which those interfering with the child Jesus are cursed to instant death (see Table 1.2).[75]

In fact, Patrick is compared explicitly and implicitly to Moses, Elijah and Christ. Patrick brings to Ireland the written Law of God (Moses), witnesses to the divinity of Jesus (Moses and Elijah), teaches the revelations of the Gospel message (Christ) and performs many miracles (Elijah, Christ).[76] He is also considered, among other things, to have the right to judge the Irish at the end of days just as the apostles are to judge the tribes of Israel.[77] Adomnán, for his part, ranks Columba of Iona alongside Elijah, Elisha, Peter, Paul, John and Jesus, because the saint both raises the dead and has the gift of prophecy.[78]

For both these male saints, their lineage, legitimacy and power descend from the initial apocryphal parallel drawn between Patrick and Peter. Just as Peter was the first to receive the apostolic dispensation that placed him in the illustrious lineage and tradition of the Old Testament prophets, followed by the rest of the apostles, so also Patrick was first in Ireland, and all other Irish saints stand in the shadow of his primacy.

In contrast, nearly all of the Brigitine scriptural inspirations for vengeance, particularly in *Vita I*, are drawn from the reports of Jesus' words and deeds in the four Gospels. Brigit seems to influence the natural forces of wind and water (Matt. 8:23–8/ Mark 4:37–40/Luke 8:22–5), and curses in a manner uncannily close to

---

[75] Verses 1, 8–12, 15–16, Herbert and McNamara, *Irish Biblical Apocrypha*, pp. 44–5. Also §§8–12, ed. Martin McNamara et al., *Apocrypha Hiberniae I: Evangelia Infantiae* (Turnhout, 2001), Corpus Christianorum Series Apocryphorum 13, pp. 460–63.

[76] Tírechán, *Collectanea* 2.3.1, 3.38, 3.43.1, 13.1, 33.1, 45.2, pp. 122, 132, 150, 152, 158, 160, 164. The implicit equation is made clearer in the preface of the early ninth-century *Vita IV*, Byrne and Frances, p. 17; it later reappears in *Bethu Phátraic*, ll. 1289–374, Mulchrone, pp. 71–3. For more on Moses in the literature of early Ireland, see John Hennig, "The Literary Tradition of Moses in Ireland," *Traditio*, 7 (1949–51), pp. 246–54, wherein Hennig discusses the explicit and implicit correspondences between Patrick and Moses and between St. Brendan and Moses. Elijah is depicted alongside Moses witnessing Christ's transfiguration in Matt. 17:1–5, Mark 9:2–7, Luke 9:25–39, Rom. 3:21.

[77] Muirchú, chs 1.2.1, 1.13.1 1.15.2, 1.16.1, 2.5, pp. 68, 82, 84, 86, 116.

[78] *Vita S Columbae*, 2.32, p. 398.

Jesus' malediction of the fig tree. When Brigit is compelled to handle pairs of paupers, one of whom is humble and the other arrogant, not only does the narrative rely upon the sermons of *De Duodecim Abusivis* but it also resonates with Jesus' message that the lowly will be exalted and the haughty cast down (Luke 14:11, 18:14). This latter reference further provides inspiration—in the form of a literal interpretation of the text—for the punishment of death by the dashing of the hubris-driven ruler's head on the stony ground.

There are incidents, such as the wall of water rising against brigands in Cogitosus' *Vita Brigitae* that relate to Old Testament stories, in this case the crossing of the Red Sea (Exod. 14:27–9). These parallels suggest that Brigit was viewed as ranking among the elite prophets, including Moses. Because there are no biblical women who did what Brigit does in her *Lives*, she is modeled upon modified versions of the examples of the men. There are also several cases where Brigidine vengeance may be drawn from apocryphal or extra-canonical texts such as the *Acts of Thomas* or the *Book of Wisdom* (see Table 1.2), augmenting the perception that Brigit is possessed of a power and authority as legitimate as that of her male colleagues. Nevertheless, early Brigitine inspiration arises overwhelmingly from the canonical New Testament stories of Jesus.

This dichotomy between male and female sanctity is reflected in the sorts of retribution associated with Patrick, Columba and Brigit. Nearly all of Brigit's vengeful episodes in these earliest *vitae* occur as passive retaliatory judgment, and visibly involve mercy and penance. The men, however, are fully engaged in the punishments they invoke. Passive retaliatory judgment is rare in the *Lives* of Patrick and absent entirely from Columba's *vita*, while maledictory prophecy dominates for both men. Moreover, almost no cases of penance, implied or otherwise, appear in the texts concerning Patrick and Columba (see Table 1.1 in the Appendix).

Part of the explanation for this penitential difference may be found in the identity of the saints' *provocateurs*. Patrick and Columba are served a main dish of defiant, reviling pagans of varying social status and few redeeming qualities, along with a small side order of clerical and lay antagonism. Brigit, on the other hand, must contend much more often with issues of disobedience, arrogance and contention among the lay and religious around her. There is little room for mercy when one's foes are more than merely obstreperous.

It must be noted that though Brigit's vengeance often does not involve her active participation, she does still pronounce both curse and negative prophecy. She is also the only one of the trio to engage in a fasting and vigil that summons retribution. Nevertheless, Brigit's results are not usually as lethal as those of the men, and her retribution often presents multiple opportunities for malefactors to emend their ways. In fact, while penance is only represented in 8 percent of the vengeance episodes of Patrick and Columba combined, it is found in almost half of Brigit's reprisals (see Table 1.1).

With respect to these early *vitae*, the outline of sanctity is evident. Brigit's retribution reflects the saint as a model of humility, generosity, charity and mercy, drawn primarily from the canonical New Testament with a light flavoring of the Old. Patrick and Columba, on the other hand, possess a power, an authority and an apostolic grace rooted in the apocrypha and clarified with both canonical and apocryphal Old Testament parallels, the combination of which further legitimizes the place of the saints in a lineage that extends all the way back to Moses and beyond.

Vengeance after the early *vitae*

Once we depart from the early Latin *Lives*, Irish hagiography slowly expands, encompassing two languages and a steadily increasing number of texts. A considerable proportion of the motives and manifestations of saintly vengeance remain the same between the texts of the earliest *vitae* and the remainder of Ireland's hagiography. Aside from a few examples of this sort of continuity, the greater emphasis in this section will be on the new expressions of retribution.

Prayer vengeance

Outside of the earliest *vitae* and the episodes from them that are retained in later *Lives* of Patrick, Brigit and Columba of Iona, vengeance invoked by prayer alone occurs less than a dozen unique times. Throughout, penance is barely apparent (see Table 1.1). The petitions of Monenna, for example, afflict permanent wasteland upon the English king for plundering church lands.[79] The prayer and sign of the cross delivered by Saint Faenche paralyzes men attempting to drag the newly tonsured Énda from her church, rendering them immobile until they perform penance for this violation of her *snádud* and the sanctuary of her church.[80]

Fasting and vigil

Fasting and vigil episodes are more common in *vitae* than in *bethada*, and outside the early texts only involve men. Penance occurs in more than half of the Latin accounts, but appears in none of the Irish (see Table 1.1). Familiar motives and manifestations are seen when, for instance, Saint Eógan fasts for one night against a settlement denying him hospitality, resulting in the permanent fruitlessness of its surrounding fields.[81]

---

[79] Conchubranus, *Vita S Monennae*, ch. 1.14, ed. Mario Esposito, "*Conchubrani Vita S Monennae*," *PRIA*, 28C (1910), pp. 215–16. For dating, see Esposito, "The Sources of Conchubranus' *Life of St Monenna*," *English Historical Review*, 35 (1920): 71–8, where the text is dated on internal evidence to the first half of the eleventh century.

[80] *Vita S Endei Abbatis de Arann* (Oxford), ch. 4, Plummer, vol. 2, pp. 61–2.

[81] *Vita S Eogani Episcopi Ardsratensis* (Salamanca), ch. 16, Heist, pp. 403–4.

Outright malediction

Outright malediction is the third most common form of vengeance in *vitae* of male saints, but is rare in *vitae* of women. By comparison, cursing episodes are the second most numerous type of retribution in *bethada* of men, but the most common in *bethada* of female saints. Penance is more frequent among male saints in the Latin than in the Irish; in *Lives* of women, all Latin malediction episodes involve penance, but only a fraction of those in *bethada* do so (see Table 1.1). Denial of hospitality with the lie that the host is mourning a dead son causes Moling to pronounce the healthy boy's immediate decease.[82] Disobedience prompts Brigit to curse a miller and his mill to total destruction; the vernacular text uses the legal phrase *dib línaib*, "both parties," defining the punishment as justified legal exaction.[83] Lasair, overcome by "great fury" (*mór feirge*), curses with bad luck, poverty, family contention and war all those who did not tender the tribute due her.[84]

Negative prophecy

Among the male saints outside the earliest *vitae*, negative prophecy constitutes the second most common form of vengeance in the Latin, about one quarter of which include penance; in their Irish *Lives*, however, negative prophecy is the most numerous type of reprisal and never involves penance. In contrast, female saints rarely offer maledictory prophecy in these texts. When they do it is in the *vitae*, and always includes penance (see Table 1.1). Prophecies that deny sovereignty or ecclesiastical eminence to entire lineages remain common. Adomnán deposes a significant number of lineages in his tenth-century *Betha*, mirroring the political nature of the text.[85] In an example that may reflect the tenets of the *Cáin Adomnáin*, Adomnán forecasts the downfall of a dynast's descendants for condemning a murderess to execution.[86]

---

[82] *Genemain Moling ocus a Bethu*, §§62–4, ed. and trans. Whitley Stokes, *The Birth and Life of St. Moling* (London, 1907), pp. 48–9.

[83] *Bethu Brigte* (ninth century), Anecdote 7, Ó hAodha, pp. 18–19, 35. The anecdote itself is a later addition in Middle Irish; it may date to the eleventh century. For the legal terminology see "*Lín*," *DIL*.

[84] *Beatha Lasrach*, ll. 3–17, ed. and trans. Lucius Gwynn, "The Life of St. Lasair," *Ériu*, 5 (1911), pp. 100–101.

[85] For discussion of the political foundation of the text, see Máire Herbert and Pádraig Ó Riain (eds and trans), *Betha Adamnáin* (London, 1988), pp. 1–44, and Herbert, *Iona, Kells, and Derry*, pp. 151–68, 203.

[86] Herbert and Ó Riain, *Betha Adamnáin*, §3, pp. 48–51.

Passive retaliatory judgment

Passive retaliatory judgment is the most commonly depicted mode of retribution outside the earliest texts, and many saints associated with no other forms of vengeance appear here. In total, there are some 150 cases of passive retaliatory judgment in *Lives* of male saints. More than half include penance, the vast majority of which occurs in their *vitae*. Among the women, however, passive retaliatory judgment is more common in *bethada*, and penance is dominant (see Table 1.1). Recognizable elements abound, such as punishments for brigandage and denial of hospitality.[87]

Sensory deprivation as saintly vengeance

Aside from the many cases of familiar motive or manifestation, there are quite a few novel forms. Many occur repeatedly across the different categories of vengeance, making it profitable to consider them thematically. Among the most numerous of these new types of vengeance are inflictions of sensory deprivation, each case of which acts as a penitential exaction, preventing thereby the need for more drastic or deadly consequence. The impairments suffered by wrongdoers both demonstrate the identity of the saint as sanctified and mark the afflicted as separated—literally, figuratively or both—from the community of the faithful. Further, once recognition of the saint's holy authority and of their own wrongdoing is shown through acts of contrition, the remission of physical penalty not only stands as visible proof of the erasure of sin following penance but also makes clear the re-inclusion of the now-forgiven sinners into the body Christian.

Blindness The removal of sight, whether permanent or temporary, total or partial, is the most common form of punitive sensory deprivation. This frequency suggests that Ireland's hagiographers held a perception that far too many professed Christians remained in some manner unable or unwilling to see the true nature of their place in the body of the faithful. Such loss of sight thus both physically manifests an extant spiritual blindness and, where it is a temporary correction rather than a permanent affliction, also acts to open the spiritual eyes of those previously unable to see. Saint Maedóc's prayers, for instance, render Saxon brigands blind for one year, a common period of penance for a number of sins, including brigandage.[88]

---

[87] *Vita Prior S Lugidi seu Moluae Abbatis de Cluain Ferta Molua* (Salamanca), ch. 44, Heist, pp. 140–41. *Vita S MacNissei Episcopi Connerensis* (Salamanca), ch. 10, Heist, p. 406.

[88] *Vita S Aidui sive Maedoc Episcopi ex Codice Cottoniano* (Vespasian MS), ch. 18, Plummer, vol. 2, pp. 299–300. According to the evidence of this vengeance episode, its redactor seems to have viewed the Saxons as errant Christians requiring a period of correction, and not as pagans deemed irretrievably 'blind' to the message of the faith. The Vespasian text is believed to date to the late eleventh century based on its relationship to other *Lives* of Maedóc. See Sharpe, *Medieval Irish Saints' Lives*, pp. 25–6, 223–7, 394. Also "An Irish Penitential," §§1.11, 15; 2.17; 3.2, 22; 5.9, Gwynn, pp. 143, 150–51, 154–5, 158–61, 168–9.

In another episode, Saint Mochoemóg, enraged (*irati*) by the illegal pasturing of King Failbe's horses on his land, engages in a full-scale yelling match with the ruler. Failbe mocks both Mochoemóg's stature and probably his tonsure in an act of verbal assault, calling him a "bald little man" (*calve parve*). In response to this unjustified satire, Mochoemóg declares, "If I am bald, then you are one-eyed" (*Si ego sum calvus, tu eris luscus*). Instantly Failbe suffers sharp agonies in one eye, losing its sight.[89] The pain, partial blindness and chronic ridicule of being one-eyed act as penalty for the injury to Mochoemóg's honor, while simultaneously declaring that though Failbe may be Christian and therefore not totally blind to the revelation of the faith, he is certainly half-blind, unable thereby to perceive the holiness of the man whom he insults. Moreover, Failbe's mocking satire only calls attention to what already exists, while Mochoemóg's malediction creates what it pronounces.

In an episode from Brigit's Old Irish *Bethu* that mirrors in part the legal status of women, Brigit's brother, Bacéne, attempts to force her to marry in order to gain her bride-price. In response, Brigit damns him and his entire lineage. As a mark of her condemnation and of Bacéne's refusal to recognize his sister's sanctified identity, Bacéne's eyes immediately burst.[90] The core concept of this episode is the conflict between Bacéne's legal right to determine his sister's future and the divine right bestowed upon God's saint to follow her calling. In Ireland, a woman had little independent legal status, her value contingent upon and worth only a fraction of the honor-price of her male guardian, that is, her father, her husband or her brother.[91] Bacéne believes it is he who acts as Brigit's guardian. In fact, it is God, and every one of Brigit's acts, even when she appears to behave independently, is undertaken with God's approval. Brigit defies only her brother's claims over her, not those of her actual legal—and spiritual—protector.

---

[89] *Vita S Mochoemog* (Dublin), ch. 19, Plummer, vol. 2, p. 174. Whether they mock a natural baldness or—in an even more wicked attack—satirize the status, faith and election inherent in the saint's tonsure, Failbe's words call attention to a feature of Mochoemóg's appearance, an act that constitutes only one of a number of forms of verbal assault in vernacular Irish law. See Kelly, *Guide to Early Irish Law*, p. 137.

[90] *Bethu Brigte*, §15, Ó hAodha, pp. 5, 23. This same conflict between Brigit's brother and Brigit's calling is found in both the preceding Latin and following vernacular *Lives* of this saint. In the *Vita I*, Brigit prays to God to disfigure her, whereupon one of her own eyes bursts (§2.15, col. 0125B; §19, Connolly, p. 18). In both the ninth-century *Bethu* and the Lismore text, Brigit plucks out her own eye (*Betha Bhrigdi*, ll. 1332–40, Stokes, pp. 40, 188). In all three variants, it is with Bacéne's capitulation, granting permission for her to become a nun, that Brigit's own sight is restored. Only in the Old Irish text does Brigit curse her kin.

[91] *Críth Gablach*, §24, Binchy, p. 14; also see *cétmuinter*, p. 80 for comments. Also §109, MacNeill, "Ancient Irish Law," p. 297. For further discussion, see Kelly, *Guide to Early Irish Law*, pp. 68–78, especially 75–6.

Blindness in combination with other forms of deprivation Occasionally, loss of sight is not sufficient punishment, and additional types of sensory and physical deprivation are added to the vengeance. In one case, individuals who pretend blindness and deafness in order to deceive Maedóc are cursed to retain these conditions the rest of their days.[92] In another instance, a king who refuses to release the captive kindred of Saint Camna, despite the requests of her elder saint, Colmán Élo, is struck blind, deaf and mute through passive retaliatory judgment.[93]

Muteness Muteness is usually inflicted upon those who contradict the saint, who revile the faith, or who lie, and acts to immediately prevent the sin as much as to correct the sinner and demonstrate the saint's access to God's power. Refusal to convert and cease blaspheming the faith, for instance, brings maledictory muteness upon an unrepentant *magus*, through Saint Berach.[94] Brigit signs a woman's face with the cross before asking her to name her father's baby. When the woman lies, her head and tongue swell up, rendering her speechless until she does penance.[95] A king who speaks against Saint Ciarán of Saigir is literally silenced when his voice vanishes for seven days through passive retaliatory judgment; it is restored after that period when he performs penance.[96]

Punishment as a consequence of pollution

The vengeance of lethal sickness has an interesting new motivation in forms of pollution where the violation of the sacred by the profane causes diseases of the soul that manifest as bodily ailment. In one case, a man known for blaspheming Saint Baithéne requests, receives and drinks leftover milk from the saint's community, and is instantly cast into the throes of a grave illness. He realizes just before he dies that he has poisoned himself by "touching something holy with a polluted mouth" (*sanctum polluto ore tangens*).[97] In another episode, an English seneschal with the temerity to hitch his horses to the stone upon which Saint Féchín prays sickens and dies that night for his act of presumption and profanation.[98]

---

[92] *Vita S Aidui sive Maedoc* (Vespasian), chs 17, 23, Plummer, vol. 2, pp. 299–301; *Vita S Aedani seu Maedoc* (Salamanca), chs 14, 19, Heist, pp. 236, 238; *Vita S Maedoc* (Dublin), chs 18, 23, Plummer, vol. 2, pp. 147, 149.

[93] *Vita S Colmani* (Salamanca), ch. 44, Heist, pp. 222–3; (Dublin), ch. 30, Plummer, vol. 1, pp. 270–71.

[94] *Vita S Berachi* (Oxford), ch. 21, Plummer, vol. 1, p. 84.

[95] *Bethu Brigte*, §40, Ó hAodha, pp. 14–15, 31.

[96] *Vita S Ciarani Episcopi Saigirensis* (Salamanca), ch. 9, Heist, p. 349; *Vita S Ciarani Episcopi de Saigir* (Dublin), ch. 28, Plummer, vol. 1, pp. 228–9.

[97] *Vita S Baithini Abbatis Hiensis* (Salamanca), ch. 7, Heist, p. 380.

[98] *Vita S Fechini Abbatis de Favoria* (Oxford), ch. 19, Plummer, vol. 2, p. 83. Political commentary in the *Lives* produced after the 1170 English incursions are not uncommon, but they are particularly frequent in the texts relating to Féchín of Fore and to Senán of Scattery.

The vengeance of chthonic consumption

One of the more startling manifestations of saintly vengeance is the awakening of a hungry earth under the feet of sinners whose crimes against saints demand immediate conveyance to hell. Saint Berach's petitions, for instance, cause a sorceress and all her wicked female co-conspirators to be devoured by the earth for plotting grievous bodily harm to her step-son.[99] Colmán mac Lúacháin's malediction pronounces the submergence of his foe's island residence and the swallowing into the soil of that foe's horses and chariots.[100] A troop of performers who threaten Patrick with satire if he does not feed them are consumed by the earth as soon as they receive their food, both saving Patrick's honor and exacting his honor-price through passive retaliatory judgment.[101]

Debasement and pollution as vengeance

Forms of debasement and pollution are not uncommon manifestations of saintly retribution. In most cases, they act as elements of a saint's just exaction of his or her honor-price. Although not an entirely new expression of vengeance in the *Lives*, the wry humor of these later texts makes their inclusion worthwhile. In an episode of fasting and vigil, for example, Saint Mocholmóg's fast against King Áed Róin for the illegal distraint of Mocholmóg's plough-team brings about the scattering of the king's body among Ireland's saints. When Áed Róin is slain in battle, wolves dismember him, then seize his *membrum virile* and carry it to all the saints of Ireland.[102] Áed Róin's death and subsequent canine-facilitated dismemberment graphically destroy the king's nobility, while the sign of his secular and sexual prowess is removed and displayed to Ireland's saints in the ultimate humiliating distraint of his masculine sovereignty.

In another instance of fasting and vigil, Saint Finnian fasts against King Tuathal to compel him to allow the building of a church in his kingdom. During Finnian's one-night vigil, the king's beloved son suddenly dies. The next morning Tuathal, still obdurate, goes to a neighboring field to attend *ad necessitatem nature* (to the need of nature), and abruptly finds himself paralyzed. He remains thus immobilized until he does penance and yields the land to God and his saints, whereupon Finnian releases him and resurrects his son.[103] The death of Tuathal's

---

[99] *Vita S Berachi Abbatis de Cluain Coirpthe* (Oxford), ch. 10, Plummer, vol. 1, pp. 78–9.

[100] *Betha Colmáin maic Lúacháin*, §68, ed. and trans. Kuno Meyer (Dublin, 1911), pp. 70–71.

[101] *Bethu Phátraic*, ll. 2379–406, Mulchrone, pp. 122–3; Stokes, pp. 202–5.

[102] *Betha Colmáin maic Lúacháin*, §§90–91, Meyer, pp. 92–5. This text is datable by internal evidence to the early 1100s; see p. vi. It is Meyer who delicately refers to the offending organ in the episode as a *membrum virile*.

[103] *Vita S Finniani Abbatis de Cluain Iraird* (Salamanca), ch. 30, Heist, p. 105.

son represents an initial stage in the process of a distraint where the eventual value of the "property" to be taken is too considerable to be seized all at once.[104] Tuathal himself is physically distrained, frozen in a humiliating stance until penance is satisfied. In both of these episodes, the utter obliteration of honor and social status through literal and figurative emasculation is a natural consequence of defaulting upon a saint's fast.

Other modes of vengeance also exact punitive debasement and pollution. A princeling responsible for the injury of twenty-seven of Columba of Iona's monks is cursed with madness when he hears the saint ring his sacred bell, and is lucid thereafter only when defecating.[105] A king who insults Saint Fintan is prophesied to be betrayed and decapitated, his blood mixing with buttermilk in a vivid adulteration of its nobility.[106] A raider who not only refuses to release Saint Comgall's illegally distrained beasts but also verbally assaults the saint dies that night while in bed with his wife. The ellipsis in the text may be hinting at a sort of emasculation, the raider taken by "the worst death" (*morte pessima*) during the conjugal act.[107]

Punitive transformations

A saint's malediction occasionally results in the transformation of the sinner into something else, particularly stones, a departure from the Patrician metamorphosis of Corictic into a fox. Fifty pursuers intent on Patrick's death, for example, are turned into stones by the saint's curse.[108] Saint Finnchúa, angered (*feargaigther*) by the repeated release of horses on the lush meadow he guards from grazing, inflicts a similar consequence on the animals. In one curious divergence from the stone motif and return to the Patrician pattern, the curse of Columba of Iona causes a woman to metamorphose into a crane for the unjustified satire of calling the saint "crane-like" (*corrclerech*), possibly taunting a hunched back.[109]

Saintly retribution and sticking to one's crime

Adhering to items, both animate and otherwise, is a common punitive theme in episodes of passive retaliatory judgment outside the early *vitae*. Such episodes make

---

[104] Binchy, "Distraint in Irish Law," p. 50.

[105] *Betha Coluim Chille*, Appendix §4, Herbert, pp. 244–5, 266.

[106] *Vita Prior S Fintani seu Munnu* (Salamanca), ch. 29, Heist, p. 207; *Vita Altera S Fintani seu Munnu* (Salamanca), ch. 25, Heist, p. 254; *Vita S Munnu sive Fintani* (Dublin), ch. 26, Plummer, vol. 2, pp. 236–7.

[107] *Vita S Comgalli Abbatis de Bennchor* (Dublin), ch. 53, Plummer, vol. 2, p. 19.

[108] *Vita IV*, ch. 74, Bieler, p. 105; Byrne and Francis, p. 57. The tale is also in the *Bethu Phátraic*, where it appears the men may only be drowned, ll. 2146–53, Mulchrone, pp. 111–12; Stokes, pp. 182–5.

[109] *Betha Coluim Chille*, Appendix §6, Herbert, pp. 245, 267.

plain to all eyes the cause and content of a sinner's wrongdoing, simultaneously compelling the admission and preventing the denial of the sin, while also creating a public state of penitential correction through a thorough demonstration of the saint's holy otherness. In *Vita IV* of Patrick, for instance, a pagan merchant who receives an enormous cauldron in exchange for selling the saint into servitude is not only glued to the thing himself, but finds that his wife and all others who attempt to free him also become stuck. The merchant hauls everyone with him back to Patrick to seek pardon, where the saint's forgiveness liberates everyone.[110] In another case, rustlers who make off with Saint Mochta's horses in the night ride until dawn, but they not only make no distance from the scene of their crime, they are also stuck on the backs of the poor exhausted animals until they do penance before Mochta.[111]

Punitive hair loss

In some episodes, vanity reaps a harvest of hairlessness. Saint Coemgen, for example, blesses water and sends it—with instructions to use it as a rinse—to a soldier whose absorption with his lush locks displeases (*displicuit*) the saint. Upon pouring the water on his head, the soldier instantly becomes bald. His vanity turned to shame, the abruptly hairless man does penance; Coemgen's blessing returns the soldier's mane, but it does not quite attain its previous glory, preventing any chance of the soldier suffering a relapse into his former self-absorbed habits.[112]

The tenets of the "Letter of Jesus on Sunday Observance" are reflected when girls who insist on washing their hair on Saturday evening despite the warnings of Saint Áed mac Bricc find their pates utterly smooth on Sunday morning.[113] They perform penance, but in what seems both a sign of their ongoing penance and a refusal by the saint to work miracles during the Sunday rest, Áed compels them to remain thus disgraced until Monday morning. On Monday, a wash with blessed water restores their tresses in full, ending their penitential embarrassment and returning them to the community of the faithful with both their heads and their souls newly cleansed.[114]

---

[110] Ch. 22, Bieler, pp. 69–70; Byrne and Francis, pp. 32–3. The tale survives in the *Bethu Phátraic*, Mulchrone, p. 15 (lower notes, taken from a Latin translation of the now lost pages); Stokes, p. 23.

[111] *Vita S Mochtei Episcopi Lugmadensis* (Salamanca), ch. 15, Heist, p. 399.

[112] *Vita S Coemgeni* (Dublin), ch. 41, Plummer, vol. 1, p. 254.

[113] See p. 17 and note 50 above.

[114] *Vita S Aidi Episcopi Killariensis* (Salamanca), ch. 41, Heist, pp. 178–9; *Vita S Aedi Episcopi Filii Bricc* (Dublin), ch. 30, Plummer, vol. 1, p. 43.

Punishment of the aithech fortha or "substitute churl"

During these various episodes of saintly vengeance, it is not unusual to see someone other than the actual eminent target of a saint's complaint receive punishment. When, for example, Saint Fínán Cam tries to obtain remission of his community's tax from King Failbe, it is not Failbe but his tax collector who refuses the demand. Fínán warns that if the tax is not forgiven, the tax collector's house will be consumed by fire. In a split second lightning strikes and immolates the building, and simultaneously the tax collector himself is made mute. Penance, however, is not performed by the tax collector, but by the king, satisfaction of which restores the former to his usual talkative self.[115]

The tax collector is apparently acting as an *aithech fortha*, or "substitute churl," a commoner who could legally stand in for the king as defendant and who would be held liable for any penalties incurred by the king.[116] Fínán's response is twofold: he exacts a price from the tax collector as the king's stand-in, and then makes it impossible for him to continue to act on the king's behalf by rendering him unable to speak. With the *aithech fortha* out of commission, the king himself is compelled to satisfy Fínán's claim directly, or lose honor, status and possibly even his life and soul.

Beating the bad guys with a bachall

In a number of stories, the saintly subject marks his or her foes for death by striking them with a staff of office, or *bachall*. This punishment most often occurs when Irish saints feel that not only their own and their churches' rights but also the very survival of the Irish body Christian are threatened at the hands of foreigners who deny the holiness of Ireland's saints. Féchín of Fore whacks a contemptuous English vicar for blaspheming the saint's church and sanctity, causing the vicar's swift expiration that night.[117] Senán, whose *post-mortem* miracles nearly all involve cases of *bachall* batting practice, appears in one case to Richard de Clare to avenge Richard's plundering of Senán's church and lands. Richard, too, dies rapidly.[118]

---

[115] *Vita S Finani Abbatis de Cenn Etigh* (Salamanca), ch. 26, Heist, p. 158; (Dublin), ch. 19, Plummer, vol. 2, p. 92. Note that in the Dublin version, the prophecy only warns that the tax collector will suffer God's vengeance (*vindicta*).

[116] D.A. Binchy, "A Text on the Forms of Distraint," *Celtica*, 10 (1973), §9, pp. 80–81, and especially discussion of the section on pp. 84–5. The translation of *aithech fortha* as "substitute churl" is that of Binchy. The legal aspects of Ireland's hagiography see more in-depth treatment in my Ph.D. dissertation, *Holy body, Wholly Other: Sanctity and Society in the Lives of Irish Saints* (University of Toronto, 2010).

[117] *Vita S Fechini* (Oxford), ch. 18, Plummer, vol. 2, pp. 82–3.

[118] *Míorbuile Senáin*, §§7–8, ed. and trans. Charles Plummer, "The Miracles of Senán," *ZCP*, 10 (1915), pp. 12–15. The text is datable by internal reference to identifiable figures of the early 1300s. See pp. 1–2.

Scriptural parallels in the later Lives

As in the earlier *vitae*, an emphasis on Old Testament texts is common, whether they are canonical or apocryphal in origin. A reliance on some New Testament scriptures is also apparent, but as before many of the probable inspirations are apocryphal. Nearly all of the parallels visible in the founding *Lives* continue to be woven into the tapestry of the saint in these later works, leaving only a few new threads to add.

Both the Old and the New Testament, canonical or otherwise, play roles in the affliction of sensory and bodily deprivation. Whether the vengeance involves blindness alone or summons some other disability, such as limb withering or tumorous growths, parallels to the Old Testament are largely canonical, while New Testament models are almost entirely apocryphal (*Infancy Gospel of Thomas* verses 1, 8–21, 15–16, 21, *Transitus Mariae* pars. 36–9, *Acts of Thomas* 6:51–2, *Acts of Andrew and Matthias* 22).[119] The same is true of lethal sickness and the consumption of the unruly, dishonest or murderous by the hungry earth (see Table 1.2 in the Appendix).[120]

Other punitive consequences, however, bear almost exclusively on Old Testament precedent, drawing from standard, non-standard and apocryphal texts. The predictions of death and dismemberment in which a pertinent body part is brought back to the prophet by an animal, for instance, are drawn from the *Acts of Thomas* 1:6–8, in which tale Thomas tells a cupbearer who strikes him that the offending hand will be dragged by dogs. The cupbearer is later torn apart by a lion, his presumptuous appendage carried from the carnage to Thomas by a little dog (see Table 1.2).[121]

The use of such *exempla* makes extraordinarily clear the perception of the saint's status as sharing in the authority and power of prominent biblical figures. Saints whose reprisals invoke punitive consequences similar to those of Moses, Elijah or the apostles are favored by the legitimacy of their predecessors. Moreover, the particular inspiration taken makes important statements about both saint and malefactor, depending upon the nature of the tale.

A saint whose vengeance, for instance, turns the earth into a devouring maw is aligned with Moses (Num. 16) as the chosen voice of God, the dispenser of God's will and the vessel through which God's power may be manifest. His foe, inhaled into hell, is made to stand alongside Dathan and Abiram—an equation some *Lives* make explicit—as a foolhardy rebel against God's elected agent and therefore against God himself. Alternatively, the saint may be ranked with the apostle Andrew (*Acts of Andrew and Matthias* 31), heir to the apostolic dispensation

---

[119] McNamara, *Apocrypha Hiberniae I*, pp. 456–67; Herbert and McNamara, *Irish Biblical Apocrypha*, pp. 44–5, 128. J.K. Elliott (ed.), *The Apocryphal New Testament* (Oxford, 1993), pp. 293, 468–9.

[120] Elliott, *The Apocryphal New Testament*, p. 298.

[121] Elliott, pp. 449–51.

bestowed by Jesus upon his disciples, while his opponent is equated with both a father who willingly surrenders his children to be slaughtered in order to save his own hide and the executioner willing to take their innocent lives.[122]

The common thread in any scriptural parallel is election. It is the saint's identity as the chosen vessel of God's grace that grants him or her authority to speak with God's voice. When Saint Ruadán contests with King Diarmait mac Cerbhaill, for instance, it is Ruadán's saintly authority that makes his negative prophecies so much more potent than those of the king, even though Diarmait is a just and righteous Christian ruler. While Diarmait can only prophecy maiming and blemishes, Ruadán foretells death, dismemberment and devastation not just on the present but on future generations. Diarmait concedes the victory to Ruadán because, as the hagiographer puts it, God loves the saint more.[123] Whichever scriptural source provides inspiration, the message is the same. The saint acts on behalf of God, through a divine dispensation that invests every deed and pronouncement with heavenly authority.

Penance and the issue of audience in the depiction of vengeance

It is evident, from both the portrayals of penance and the different categories of vengeance present in Latin and Irish *Lives*, that there are two sets of sanctity models, one for the men and women of *vitae* and one for the male and female saints of *bethada*. The explanation for the separation can be found in the intended audience of each language.

Vitae clearly had an audience capable of understanding the Latin language, implying that they were written for ecclesiastical and lay elites. By virtue of the language alone, these texts could and did extend beyond Ireland. Many, if not most Latin *Lives* were known on the Continent, including the *Vita II* and *Vita IV* of Patrick, Adomnán's *Vita S Columbae*, and *Vita I S Brigitae*.[124] Ireland's hagiographers knew their Latin works could travel. In their *vitae*, saints had to conform to more universal notions of sanctity or risk being labeled irrelevant or heterodox by non-Irish audiences unable to resonate with them. Thus women are involved with vengeance less and penance more than the men, while the reprisals of male saints are more often those of a passive retaliatory vengeance dominated by penitential episodes than the maledictory actions on which all other scholars have focused (see Table 1.1 in the Appendix).

Bethada, by contrast, only needed to appeal to the Irish. The hagiographers of *bethada* seem to have been vastly more comfortable portraying saints wreaking

---

[122] Ibid., p. 298.

[123] *Vita S Ruadani* (Salamanca), ch. 12, pp. 163–5, (Dublin), chs 15–17, vol. 2, pp. 245–8.

[124] Byrne and Francis, "Two Lives of Saint Patrick," pp. 8–10. Also Picard, "The Purpose of Adomnán's *Vita Columbae*," *Peritia*, 1 (1982): 160–77, and Connolly, "*Vita Prima Sanctae Brigitae*," pp. 5–6.

holy havoc when needed. In *vitae* of Patrick, for instance, there are only twenty-four retribution episodes, but in *Bethu Phátraic* there are at least fifty cases of vengeance, most of which are unique to the text and not drawn from the *Bethu*'s predecessors. Irish *Lives* are dominated by malediction and negative prophecy, and portray penance less often than do the *vitae*.

It would seem that in the vernacular hagiography, aimed exclusively at Irish Christians of any rank or station, saints were expected to be more active, and proactive, than those depicted for an international audience. The women, too, are more overtly connected with vengeance in *bethada* than in *vitae*, suggesting that the Irish responded to women who could and did stand up for themselves and for God. Indeed, where Brigit in the early *vitae* is nearly entirely modeled on the deeds of Jesus in the Gospels, the Brigit of her later *bethada* invokes maledictory response as lethal as that of any man in stories of clear Old Testament and apocryphal apostolic parallel. Brigit and her female peers are as potent as their male colleagues, even if their saintly power is not summoned for vengeance quite as often (see Table 1.1).

The identity of the Irish saint

One of the medieval period's most influential thinkers, Pope Gregory the Great (d. 604), expressed in his writings the belief that "the essence of sanctity" is embodied by *imitatio Christi*, the imitation of Christ, and thus "ultimately involves the exercise of all the virtues" Christ displayed. Gregory particularly embedded this view in his well-known work on saints' miracles, *The Dialogues*, a text with significant and lasting influence on Ireland's hagiography.[125] As a consequence of this influence, it might be expected that the model of *imitatio Christi* would predominate. The evidence of scriptural parallels, however, would seem to say otherwise. Over and over again, the emphasis of vengeance in Ireland's hagiography is on other models, making subtle and not-so-subtle comparisons between Irish saints and key Old Testament figures—particularly Moses, Elijah and Elijah's successor, Elisha, on prayers and invocations from the Psalter, and on the powerful apostolic figures of the apocryphal New Testament.[126]

There is a body of evidence that suggests the medieval Irish *literati* not only viewed Mosaic Law, the religious code of the Old Testament, as a living Law even after the revelation brought by Christ, but also considered the Irish people to have a close relationship with Moses himself. Both the secular and canon law codes of the Irish Middle Ages are founded upon the principles of the Law of Moses as laid

---

[125] William D. McCready, *Signs of Sanctity: Miracles in the Thought of Gregory the Great* (Toronto, 1989), pp. 70–71. For more concerning the influence of *The Dialogues* on seventh-century Irish hagiographers, see especially Stancliffe, "Miracle stories," p. 88.

[126] Elisha is said to inherit Elijah's grace in 4 Kgs. 2:8–12, and Elisha's subsequent miracles mirror those of his elder.

out in the Pentateuch.[127] This may in part be because observance of Mosaic Law agrees with the New Testament injunction that the revelation of Christ does not abolish the laws of the Pentateuch, it perfects them, and the former is not to be set aside for the latter (Matt. 5:17–20/Luke 16:16–17).

Furthermore, a mytho-historical poem of the ninth century reveals a tradition that the eponymous ancestor of the Irish knew Moses in Egypt. This same ancestor later led his tribespeople, the Gaels, through trial, tribulation, settlement and expulsion to their promised land—Ireland.[128] The twelfth-century *Lebor Gabála Érenn* elaborates on the tradition, drawing so closely upon the Old Testament that the story of the Israelites is only barely prevented from becoming that of the Gaels.[129]

Within the embrace of this lengthy tradition we find nestled the literary genre of Ireland's hagiography. From its inception, its male saints were explicitly and implicitly equated with Old Testament prophets and with the apostles of the apocryphal New Testament, with Patrick at the head of the phalanx as heir to the same apostolic grace and status as Peter. While initially Brigit's vengeance tales show stronger reliance on *imitatio Christi*, including the reliance of *Vita I* on the sermons of *De Duodecim Abusivis* and their patent messages to imitate Christ in order to gain heaven, these overt parallels all but disappear after *Vita I*. The vengeance episodes of the lady saints in later texts draw in their own way on the models of authority and election provided by figures such as Moses or Elijah, or upon the apocryphal representations of the apostles.

Emotion is represented in both Irish and Latin texts, although infrequently, and involves both male and female saints. Whenever a saint is displeased or angered, as occurs with Brigit, Mochoemóg and Coemgen in Latin and with Patrick, Lasair and Finnchúa in Irish, negative consequences for the *provocateurs* are assured.[130] In this manner, too, Ireland's saints are linked to the Old Testament prophets. One has only to think of Moses' rage at the creation of the golden calf for a well-known

---

[127] For a full discussion of Irish law and its reliance on the Pentateuch, see Donnchadh Ó Corráin, Liam Breatnach and Aidan Breen, "The Laws of the Irish," *Peritia*, 3 (1984): 382–438.

[128] The ninth-century poem *Can a mBunadus na nGáedel?* (Whence the origin of the Gael?), is edited by R.I. Best and M.A. O'Brien, *The Book of Leinster, formerly Lebar na Núachongbála*, III (Dublin, 1957), pp. 516–23; a summary of its contents can be found in Kim McCone, *Pagan Past*, pp. 24, 68. McCone also discusses the relationship between Irish law and the scriptures, pp. 85–104.

[129] Ed. and trans. R.A.S. Macalister, *Lebor Gabála Érenn: The Book of the Taking of Ireland*, 118–20, II (Dublin, 1939, repr. 1986), pp. 32–5. Macalister provides a table of the two narratives, i.e. the Pentateuch exodus and the Irish origin story, in his introduction, presenting the plots in parallel and demonstrating unequivocally the extremely close correspondence. See volume I (London, 1938; repr. 1993), pp. xxvii–viii. Further analysis also by McCone, *Pagan Past*, pp. 29–30, 68–77.

[130] See pp. 15, 19, 20, 25, 27, 30 and 31 above. Note that Lasair is female.

example of justifiable wrath (Exod. 32:19). The disconnection between emotion and act theorized by prior scholars seems not to be quite so straightforward as necessarily thought.[131]

The involvement of canon and secular Irish law in the representations of vengeance adds another layer to the image of the saint. The saints conform particularly to native Irish law, even in the prosecution of vengeance, where Irish legal codes are used to bolster the saint's right to pursue just recompense. As has been asserted by scholars with respect to the portrayal and function of cursing in the hagiography, saintly retribution from all categories—not just malediction, which is now revealed to be a relatively minor constituent of saintly reprisal—reinforces social, cultural, legal and spiritual lessons.[132] If the identity of any saint is as one emulating the models of the Old and New Testaments, what sets apart the Irish saint is, in part, this adherence to Irish law.

But there is more to the story still. The same Irish saints who curse also cure. They pronounce negative prophecy and potent blessing, invoke lethal retribution and raise the dead. Ireland's saints are thus depicted not only enacting retribution in a legitimate tradition rising from the great Old Testament prophets and inherited by the apostles of the New Testament, but also performing the merciful, healing miracles of both these models and Jesus.[133] Even without explicit acknowledgement of divine involvement, the foundation of sanctity in heaven is clear.

From Moses to Elijah and Elisha, and then to Christ and his disciples, Ireland's hagiographers seemingly trace the Christian religion from the birth of Mosaic Law, through the forerunners of the Messiah, to the Law's completion in Christ's revelation, placing the entire narrative of the Bible into the persons of their saints. The vengeful holy person, far from the flawed and vindictive individual assumed for so long, thus becomes a completed saintly being, an heir to an indisputably ancient authority and a vessel of God's grace—the same grace bestowed upon Old Testament prophet, New Testament apostle and the Messiah himself. As the embodiment of the full scriptural dispensation, from Genesis to Acts and beyond, the Irish saint is the personification of the living Christian faith.

---

[131] See p. 7, footnotes 8 and 9 above.

[132] See pp. 11, 12–13, 14–15, 18, 20–21, 25, 26, 27, 29, 30 and 32 above.

[133] Elijah raises the dead (3 Kgs. 17:19–24); Elisha purifies and heals water (4 Kgs. 2:19–22), raises the dead (4 Kgs. 4:31–7), multiplies food (4 Kgs. 4:41–4) and heals leprosy (4 Kgs. 5:1–15). The miracles of Christ and the apostles are sufficiently well-known not to require any listing of them here.

APPENDIX

Table 1.1   Relative Distribution of Vengeance Categories

	Early *vitae* of Brigit (2)	Later *vitae* of women (4)	Later *bethada* of women (3)	Early *vitae* of men (3)	Later *vitae* of men (58)	Later *bethada* of men (13)
Prayer	0	1	0	6	6	3
Prayer + Penance	0	1	0	0	0	0
Fasting and Vigil	0	0	0	0	2	2
Fasting and Vigil + Penance	1	0	0	0	5	0
Malediction	1	0	6	4	20	31
Malediction + Penance	0	1	1	1	7	2
Negative prophecy	1	0	0	11	42	42
Negative prophecy + Penance	0	2	0	1	11	0
PRJ*	5	1	2	1	56	18
PRJ + Penance	4	1	3	0	72	4
Total vengeance episodes	12	7	12	24	221	102
Total penance episodes	5	5	4	2	95	6
% without penance	58%	29%	67%	92%	57%	94%
% with penance	42%	71%	33%	8%	43%	6%

*Passive retaliatory judgment

Table 1.2   Representative Table of Scriptural Parallels

Type of vengeance (and associated saints)*	Scriptural parallels	Summary of scriptural story
Abduction of target's infant by eagle (**Brigit**)	Lev. 26:22	Prophecy of wild beasts sent to tear children from parents for defying Mosaic Law/God
Bad luck, poverty, discord, strife, sickness (**Lasair**)	Lev. 26:14–41	Prophecy of terror, disease, famine, crop failure, war against those defying Mosaic Law/God
	Deut. 28:15–62	Malediction of starvation, thirst, sickness, crop failure, nakedness, war, oppression against those defying Mosaic Law/God
	4 Esdr. 15:12–16.17	Prophecy of strife, violence, anarchy, pestilence part of God's vengeance at apocalypse
Blindness (of any sort) (Abbán, Áed mac Bricc, Ailbe, **Brigit**, Cainnech, Ciarán of Clonmacnoise, Ciarán of Saigir, Coemgen, Colmán Élo, Comgall, Finnian, Flannán, Maedóc, Mochoemóg, Mochutu, Molaisse of Devenish, **Monenna**, Patrick, Ruadán, Tigernach)	Gen. 19:11	Angels of the Lord blind men trying to break into Lot's house
	Exod. 10:22–3	Moses invokes three days of total darkness
	Lev. 26:16	Prophecy of plagues of blindness against those defying Mosaic Law/God
	Deut. 28:28–9, 65	Malediction of blindness against those defying Mosaic Law/God
	4 Kgs. 6:18	Elisha asks God to strike Aramaean host with blindness
	Ps. 68:24	Prayer for God to afflict enemies with blindness
	Matt. 5:29–30	Jesus enjoins followers to pluck out eye if it offends rather than be carried to hell by its pollution
	Zach. 14:12–13	Prophecy of rotting disease that putrefies eyes upon God's foes
	Acts 13:11–12	Paul/Saul curses sorcerer Elymas with temporary blindness for interfering with preaching of Lord's word
	Infancy Gospel of Thomas, verse 21	Child Jesus portrayed punishing those threatening/accusing him with blindness
	Transitus Mariae, par. 36	Men attempting to slay apostles at Mary's bier struck blind

*   Normal type = Latin texts, *Italics* = Irish, Underline = both Latin and Irish, **Bold** = female saint

Type of vengeance (and associated saints)	Scriptural parallels	Summary of scriptural story
Blindness and deafness (Colmán Élo, Maedóc)	*Infancy Gospel of Thomas*, verse 21	Child Jesus portrayed punishing those threatening him with deafness and blindness
Confusion and wandering, with/without darkness/blindness; misdirection in travels (*Brigit*, Buite, Cainnech, Coemgen, Colmán Élo, *Colmán mac Lúacháin*, **Lasair**, Mochta, **Monenna**, *Senán*)	Deut. 28:28–9	Maledictions of blindness, confusion, wandering upon those defying Mosaic Law/God
	Isa. 19:2–3	Egyptian armies thrown into confusion
	Ps. 6:9–10	Prayer asking God to cast enemies into confusion
	4 Esdr. 2:5–6	Malediction of confusion part of punishment upon those breaking covenant with God
	3 Macc. 5:28	Ptolemy struck with incomprehension, forgetfulness to prevent destruction of Jews
Damnation/ excommunication (numerous; these are just a few key scriptures) (*Adomnán, Colmán mac Lúacháin*, Columba of Iona, Mochutu, *Patrick*, *Senán*)	1 Cor. 16:22	Malediction expelling those who do not love the Lord from Christian society
	Gal. 1:8–9	Malediction of expulsion/outcast status on anyone preaching heterodoxy
	Apoc. 22:18–19	Expulsion and excommunication part of the malediction upon anyone changing report of plagues prophesied in Revelations
Death of target (battle), dismemberment, seizure of body part by animal, display of body part to saint(s) (*Finnian, Mocholmóg*)	*Acts of Thomas*, ch. 1:6–8	Thomas tells cupbearer who struck him that hand will be dragged by dogs. Cupbearer killed and dismembered by lion at fountain, but lion does not eat him; hand that struck Thomas brought to Thomas at banquet
Death of target (dashed headfirst) (*Patrick*)	Ps. 9:4 (?)	Enemies said to fall headlong before God
	Ps. 136:9	He who smashes Babylon against rock of God will be blessed
	Wis. 4:19	Unrighteous prophesied to be dashed against the ground
	Acts of Peter, ch. 32:3	Peter's prayer to Jesus causes levitating Simon Magus to crash to ground and break leg in three places
	Acts of Peter and Paul, §14	Peter's prayer causes Simon Magus to crash to ground and break into four pieces

Type of vengeance (and associated saints)	Scriptural parallels	Summary of scriptural story
Death of target (drowning) (**Brigit**, Ciarán of Saigir, *Colmán mac Lúacháin*, Columba of Iona, Comgall, <u>Patrick</u>, *Senán*)	Gen. 7:10–12, 17–23	All humanity save Noah and Noah's family drowned in great flood
	Exod. 14:27–9	Pharaoh and Pharaoh's armies drowned in Red Sea
	Wis. 5:21–3	Seas and rivers prophesied to rise against and overwhelm the unrighteous
Death of target (flaming sword of fiery charioteer) (Cainnech)	4 Kgs. 2:11–12	Elijah taken to heaven by flaming chariot driven by fiery charioteer, drawn by fiery horses
	2 Macc. 3:25–6	Angelic warriors fighting on behalf of Jews described as cavalry with flashing golden armor, swords, thunderbolts, who throw enemies into chaos and cut them to pieces
	2 Macc. 5:2–3	
	2 Macc. 10:29–30	
	4 Macc. 10	
Death of target (immolation by lightning) (Cainnech, Declán, MacNisse, Mochutu, <u>Patrick</u>)	Num. 16	Korah's 250 Levite followers immolated for rebelling against Aaron
	see also 'immolation of target' below	
Death of target (instant/sudden) (**Brigit**, Cainnech, *Ciarán of Clonmacnoise*, Coemgen, Columba of Iona, Columba of Terryglass, Comgall, Declán, *Féchín*, <u>Finnian</u>, Lugaid, Maedóc, Mochoemóg, <u>Moling</u>, **Monenna**, <u>Patrick</u>, *Senán*)	2 Kgs. 6:6–8	Uzziah struck instantly dead for touching Ark of Covenant
	4 Kgs. 7:18–20	Elisha prophesies sudden death upon doubters of the Lord
	Ps. 16:14	Prayer asking God to remove enemies from life
	Ps. 54:16	Malediction/prayer that death strike down enemies
	Wis. 1:16	Ungodly said to summon death by words and deeds
	Acts 5	Ananias, Saphira drop dead from malediction of Peter for their deceit
	Infancy Gospel of Thomas, verses 1, 8–12, 15–16	Child Jesus portrayed cursing to sudden death children who interfere with his will/annoy him
Death of target (poison turned serpent) (Ailbe)	*Acts of John/ Episodes from the Life of John the Beloved Disciple*, ch. 7	John drinks poison that kills others and lives, to prove truth of God to Aristodemus

Type of vengeance (and associated saints)	Scriptural parallels	Summary of scriptural story
Death of target (sickness) (Áed mac Bricc, Baithéne, Féchín, Maedóc, Mochutu, **Samthann**, *Senán*)	Lev. 26:16	Prophecy of wasting disease, recurrent fever upon those defying Mosaic Law/God
	Lev. 26:25	Prophecy of pestilence upon those defying Mosaic Law/God
	Deut. 28:20	Malediction of lethal dysentery upon those defying Mosaic Law/God
	Zach. 14:12–13	Prophecy of rotting sickness upon enemies of God
	Acts 12:23	Herod struck with lethal vermiform illness by Angel of God for usurping honor due to God
Death of target (slain by animals) (*Ciarán of Clonmacnoise*, Ciarán of Saigir)	4 Kgs. 2:23–25	Elisha curses forty-two boys who mock him, call him bald; two bears tear up children
Death of target (swallowed by earth) (Berach, Buite, Colmán of Dromore, *Colmán mac Lúacháin*, Declán, *Finnchúa*, Laisrén of Leighlin, Patrick)	Num. 16	Dathan, Abiram, Korah swallowed by earth for rebelling against Moses
	Ps. 30:18	Prayer that the wicked be led to hell
	Ps. 54:16	Malediction/prayer that enemies descend living into hell
	Acts of Andrew and Matthias, ch. 31	Old man who surrenders children to be slaughtered in his place when lots fall to him during famine swallowed by earth, along with all executioners of children
Death of target's child, children of target's allies (instant/sudden) (Áed mac Bricc, Ailbe, Finnian, Maedóc, Mochoemóg, *Moling*, Ruadán)	Exod. 12:28–9	Death of all first-born in Egypt except Israelites
Death of target's horses/cattle (any means) (Áed mac Bricc, *Colmán mac Lúacháin*, Féchín, Fínán Cam, Flannán, Mochoemóg, Molaisse of Devenish, Patrick, *Senán*)	Exod. 12:28–9	Passover plague kills firstborn animals along with firstborn children
	Lev. 26:22	Prophecy that wild beasts will kill cattle of those defying Mosaic Law/God

Type of vengeance (and associated saints)	Scriptural parallels	Summary of scriptural story
Debasement of target's dead body (*Adomnán*, Fintán/Munnu, MacCarthinn, Ruadán)	Deut. 28:26	Malediction of body being food for birds, beasts for defying Mosaic Law/God
	Ps. 62:11	Bodies of the unjust prophesied to be food for foxes
Destruction of target's fortress/house/mill/crops (lightning, burning hail, other means except sea) (**Brigit**, Comgall, *Féchín*, Fínán Cam)	Josh. 6:21, 24, 26	Fall of Jericho at hands of Joshua
	Ps. 10:7	Prophecy of burning coals upon unjust
	Ps. 17:13	God's anger and arrival said to be accompanied with burning hail
	Matt. 11:20–24	Jesus' prophecy of downfall of Chorazin, Bethsaida, Capernaum for arrogance, lack of repentance, refusal of Jesus' message
	Luke 10:13–15	
	Matt. 23:37–9	Jesus' prophecy of Jerusalem's downfall for rejecting Jesus' message
	Luke 19:42–4	
Destruction of target's labors/fortress (swamped by sea) (*Senán*, Patrick)	Wis. 5:21–3	Seas prophesied to rage against, and rivers to overwhelm unrighteous
Displacement of target by wind (**Brigit**)	Ps. 1:4	Impious men said to be like dust the wind drives from the earth
	Wis. 5:23	Mighty wind prophesied to rise against unrighteous
	Matt. 8:23–8	Jesus calms wind and sea
	Mark 4:37–40	
	Luke 8:22–5	
Earthquake, darkness, confusion, with/without mutual slaying among enemies (Laisrén of Leighlin, Patrick)	Isa. 19:2–3	Egyptian armies thrown into confusion, forced to fight each other
	Isa. 29:5–8	Prophecy of earthquake, thunder, destruction against God's enemies
	Ps. 17:8	God's anger and arrival said to be attended with earthquake
	Ps. 67 (directly quoted in Patrician *Lives*)	Prayer invoking God to rise up, scatter enemies; fulfillment includes earthquake, confusion, mutual slaying among enemies
	Wis. 4:19	Prophecy of unrighteous being shaken from their foundations, cast to the ground

Type of vengeance (and associated saints)	Scriptural parallels	Summary of scriptural story
Earthquake, darkness *cont.*	4 Esdr. 15:12–16.17	Prophecy of strife, confusion, violence, slaughter, earthquakes, destruction among other vengeances at apocalypse
	Apoc. 15:10–11	Prophecy of darkness part of apocalypse
	Apoc. 15:20–1	Prophecy of earthquakes as part of apocalypse
	Apoc. 22:18–19	Prophecy of plagues of darkness, earthquakes among the plagues at apocalypse
Enervation, loss of bodily strength (Ciarán of Clonmacnoise)	*Infancy Gospel of Thomas*, ch. 14.2	Child Jesus curses teacher for striking him; teacher faints and falls to ground
Expulsion, loss of kingdom, and ignominious death (Mochoemóg, Mochutu, *Patrick*)	Lev. 26:16–20, 31–3	Prophecy of crops, country stolen by enemies, destruction of kingdom for disobeying Mosaic Law/God
	Deut. 8:19–20	Prophecy of destruction against those disobeying Mosaic Law/God
	Deut. 28:20, 22, 25–6	Malediction of starvation, destruction, loss of promised land, routing, rejection by other nations, death, lying unburied to be eaten by animals/birds, against those disobeying Mosaic Law/God
	Ps. 24:3–4	Shame to fall on those breaking faith with God
	Ps. 30:18	The wicked to be put to shame, damned
Forced fasting (Lugaid)	Ps. 106:18	Punishment of God said to include food becoming loathsome, near death from hunger for sinners
Foreign domination/ oppression (Mochutu, *Patrick*)	Lev. 26:25	Prophecy of giving Jews over to enemy for defying Mosaic Law/God
	Deut. 28:33–4, 36	Prophecy of foreign nation eating harvests, ruling lands of those defying Mosaic Law/God
	Deut. 28:49–53	Malediction/prophecy of foreign nation invading and oppressing those defying Mosaic Law/God

Type of vengeance (and associated saints)	Scriptural parallels	Summary of scriptural story
Gangrenous tumors (Colmán Élo)	Deut. 28:27	Malediction of Egyptian boils and tumors for defying Mosaic Law/God
	Deut. 28:35–6	Malediction of malignant boils for defying Mosaic Law/God
Grain eaten by mice (Comgall)	Deut. 28:38–9, 42	Prophecy of loss of crops to animals/insects for defying Mosaic Law/God
Hair loss (Áed mac Bricc, Coemgen)	Ps. 67:22	God prophesied to smite the heads of proud sinners with flowing hair
Hand loss (sudden) (Columba of Iona, Colmán Élo, Maedóc, Mochoemóg)	2 Kgs. 4:12	David has hands, feet cut off Rechab, Baaneh for killing innocent man
	Ps. 35:12	Prayer that the hand of the sinner not affect one praying
	Matt. 5:29–30	Jesus enjoins followers to cut off hand rather than be carried to hell by its pollution
	Acts of Thomas, ch. 1.6–8	Hand of cupbearer who strikes Thomas brought to Thomas by dog after cupbearer killed by lion
	Transitus Mariae, par. 39	Hands of man attempting to knock Mary's body from bier adhere to bier, then separate from arms; restored after conversion
Immolation of target, target's house/fortress, or target's crops by lightning/burning hail (Comgall, *Féchín*, Fínán Cam, Fintán of Dún Blésci, Moling)	Gen. 19:24	Fire and burning hail part of the destruction of Sodom and Gomorrah
	Exod. 9:22–6	Moses invokes hail and lightning storm that destroys crops
	Lev. 10:1–3	Sons of Aaron immolated by divine fire for disrespect to God, making inappropriate offering
	Num. 16:35	Two hundred and fifty Levites rebelling against Aaron's authority immolated by divine fire
	Josh. 7:15	God pronounces burning for those breaking covenant of the Lord by harboring items forbidden in Mosaic Law
	4 Kgs. 1:9–14	Elijah calls down fire upon messengers, soldiers of king of Samaria
	Ps. 10:7	Lord's vengeance said to include red-hot coals falling from sky

Type of vengeance (and associated saints)	Scriptural parallels	Summary of scriptural story
Immolation of target *cont.*	Ps. 20:9–10	Prophecy that fire will strike down and consume enemies of the faithful
	Ps. 96:3–5	Divine fire said to burn up God's enemies
	Wis. 5:21–3	Lightning part of prophesied vengeance upon unrighteous
	Apoc. 15:20–21	Prophecy of lightning, thunder, hail part of final plague at apocalypse
	Apocalypse of Abraham, ch. 8.5–7	God immolates Abraham's father, his father's house, household for continuing to make, sell, and worship pagan idols
Insanity (*Columba of Iona*)	Deut. 28:28–9, 65	Malediction of madness upon those defying Mosaic Law/God
Lake protecting target's island fortress removed (Mochoemóg)	Ps. 17:16	Beds of the seas, foundations of earth said to be laid bare at God's coming
	Ps. 73:15	God said to have disrupted flowing waters, dried up rivers
	Ps. 106:3	God said to have dried up rivers and springs because inhabitants of region wicked
	Wis. 4:19	Unrighteous prophesied to be left utterly dry and barren by God's vengeance
Lameness (Cainnech)	2 Kgs. 4:12 (?)	David has hands, feet cut off Rechab, Baaneh for killing innocent man
	Ps. 35:12	Prayer that the foot of the arrogant not approach one praying
Land/orchard rendered sterile/uninhabitable/ waste (**Brigit**, Eógan, Fintán/ Munnu, **Monenna**, Patrick, Ruadán, *Senán*)	Lev. 26:20	Prophecy of sterility of crops, orchards against any who defy Mosaic Law/God
	Lev. 26:33–4	Prophecy of land made desolate, cities in rubble for defying Mosaic Law/God
	Deut. 28:18	Malediction on fruits of land and tree in punishment for defying Mosaic Law/God
	Ps. 106:34	God said to have turned fruitful lands into salt barrens because inhabitants wicked
	Josh. 6:21, 24, 26	Fall of Jericho through Joshua, Joshua's malediction upon any who attempt to rebuild

Type of vengeance (and associated saints)	Scriptural parallels	Summary of scriptural story
Land/orchard rendered sterile *cont.*	Wis. 5:21–3	Prophecy that sea will rage against, rivers will swamp unrighteous
	Isa. 19:5–10	Prophecy that Egypt will be barren of crops, plants
	Matt. 21:19–20	Christ curses unfruiting fig tree to permanent barrenness
	Mark 11:12–21	
Leprosy (**Brigit**, *Columba of Iona*, Lugaid, Molaisse of Devenish)	Num. 12	Miriam afflicted with leprosy for speaking against Moses
	4 Kgs. 5:20–27	Elisha's servant, Gehazi, struck with leprosy for asking payment from man Elisha healed of the disease
	2 Par. 26:16–23	King Uzziah struck with leprosy for attempting to burn incense on Lord's altar, being rude to priests
Lifespan abbreviated, violent/ignominious death, lineage removed from sovereignty, grave forgotten (*Adomnán*, Columba of Iona, *Finnian*, Maedóc, Mochutu, *Patrick*)	Deut. 28:20, 22, 25–6, 41	Malediction of destruction, debasement, death upon those defying Mosaic Law/God
	Ps. 30:18	The wicked to be put to shame, damned
	Ps. 108:8–15	Prayers that enemies have short life, poverty, loss of family/lineage, damnation
	Jer. 28:16	Jeremiah prophesies death within year of false prophet Hananiah
Limb/head loss by gangrene/rotting off (Buite, *Ciarán of Clonmacnoise*, Colmán Élo)	Zach. 14:12–13	Prophecy that God will strike down enemies with plague that rots off flesh
Limb withering, with/without paralysis (Abbán, **Brigit**, Cainnech, Lugaid, MacCarthinn, Maedóc, Mochutu)	Lev. 26:16	Prophecy of wasting disease against those disobeying Mosaic Law/God
	3 Kgs. 13:4–7	King Jeroboam afflicted with withered hand, paralysis for pointing at and condemning to death a man of God
	Acts of Thomas, ch. 6.51–2	Hands of murderer trying to take communion shrivel so he cannot put them to his mouth; are restored after confession to Thomas
	Infancy Gospel of Thomas, ch. 3.2–3	Child Jesus curses son of Annas the scribe; son of Annas withers like old man

Type of vengeance (and associated saints)	Scriptural parallels	Summary of scriptural story
Lineage/patrimony lost (Flannán, Mochutu, Patrick)	Josh. 6:21, 24, 26	Lineage of Jericho cursed with debasement after destruction through Joshua
	Ps. 36:38	Unjust and impious will scatter and perish
	Ps. 108:13	Malediction/prayer that all progeny of accuser of psalmist be wiped out and name of family lost
	Wis. 3:10–13	Ungodly said to have accursed offspring
	4 Esdr. 1:33–4	Expulsion and lack of progeny prophesied for evildoers
	4 Esdr. 2:5–6	Malediction of lack of progeny and forced diaspora upon those breaking covenant with God
Lineage removed from sovereignty (*Adomnán*, Áed mac Bricc, Fínán Cam, Fintán/Munnu, Mochoemóg, Mochutu, Molaisse of Devenish, Patrick, Ruadán, *Senán*)	Gen. 4:4–5, 11–12	Cain's offering rejected by God after Abel's offering accepted; Cain cursed and banished for Abel's death
	Gen. 25:23	One of Rebecca's sons prophesied to be ascendant over other
	Gen. 27:29	Isaac prophesies Jacob's ascendancy over brothers, thinking he is Esau
	Gen. 27:39–40	Isaac prophesies Esau's servitude to Jacob
	3 Kgs. 14:9–11	Ahijah prophesies devastation of house and lineage of King Jeroboam for disobedience to Mosaic Law/God
	3 Kgs. 16:1–5	Jehu prophesies devastation of house, lineage of Baasha for disobedience to Mosaic Law/God
	3 Kgs. 21:23–6	Elijah prophesies downfall, destruction of house of Ahab for worshipping Baal
	Ps. 108:14–15	Prayers asking God to end, damn entire lineage of enemies
	Jer. 29:31–2	Jeremiah prophesies end of lineage of false prophet Shemaiah for preaching rebellion against God
Misdirection	See *'Confusion and wandering'* above	

Type of vengeance (and associated saints)	Scriptural parallels	Summary of scriptural story
Muteness (Berach, **Brigit**, Ciarán of Saigir, Colmán Élo, Fínán Cam)	Ps. 30:19	Prayer that those speaking with contempt against righteous be struck dumb
	Ps. 62:12	Mouths of those speaking unjust/dangerous things prophesied to be stopped
	Wis. 4:19	Unrighteous prophesied to be struck speechless
	Zach. 14:12–14	Prophecy against God's enemies of rotting disease that putrefies tongue
	3 Macc. 2:22	Ptolemy struck speechless by God's judgment for plotting destruction of Jews
	Infancy Narrative, §41.1	Zacharias struck mute for not believing Gabriel's announcement that wife, Elizabeth, would give birth to John the Baptist
Paralysis (frozen in place/stuck to earth) with/without adhering to stolen/ill-gotten goods (Abbán, Áed mac Bricc, Berach, **Brigit**, Cainnech, Ciarán of Clonmacnoise, Colmán Élo, **Faenche**, Finnian, Fintán/Munnu, Flannán, MacCarthinn, Maedóc, Mochoemóg, Mochta, Patrick, Ruadán, *Senán*)	3 Kgs. 13:4–7	King Jeroboam paralyzed when points at, condemns to death man of God
	3 Macc. 2:22	Ptolemy struck with paralysis by God's judgment for plotting destruction of Jews
	Acts of Andrew and Matthias, ch. 22	Andrew's prayers to Jesus turn hands of executioners into stone
	Transitus Mariae, par. 38	Men attempting to slay apostles at Mary's bier paralyzed in hands and feet
	Transitus Mariae, par. 39	Hands of man attempting to knock Mary's body from bier adhere to bier and separate from arms
Poverty, debasement (*Adomnán*, **Brigit**, Ciarán of Saigir, *Colmán mac Lúacháin*, Columba of Iona, Énda, Fínán Cam, Mochutu, *Patrick*)	Ps. 108:10	Malediction/prayer of poverty, begging, expulsion upon wicked men accusing psalmist
River rendered sterile (Énda, Patrick)	Exod. 7:19–21	Egypt's rivers turned to blood by Moses and Aaron
	Apoc. 15:3–4	Prophecy of rivers turning to blood, seas rendered lifeless as second, third plagues of apocalypse

Type of vengeance (and associated saints)	Scriptural parallels	Summary of scriptural story
Servitude, confusion, blindness, and discord (*Adomnán, Colmán mac Lúacháin*, Columba of Iona, Mochutu, *Patrick*)	Deut. 28:20, 28–9, 30–5, 41, 48–9, 65	Malediction of destruction, blindness, confusion, oppression, loss of lineage into captivity upon those defying Mosaic Law/God
Sickness, non-lethal (Columba of Iona, Mochutu)	Lev. 26:16, 25	Prophecy of wasting disease, recurrent fever, plague, pestilence for defying Mosaic Law/God
	Deut. 28:27–8	Malediction of Egyptian boils, tumors, scabs, itches with no cure for defying Mosaic Law/God
Transformation of target (animal/bird) (*Columba of Iona, Patrick*)	Exod. 7:10–12 (?)	Transformation of rod into serpent and back by God through Aaron, Moses
	Infancy Gospel of Thomas 40 (Syriac or Arabic texts)	Child Christ turns group of boys into goats and back into children
Transformation of target / target's horses (stone) (*Finnchúa*, Flannán, Patrick)	Gen. 19:26	Lot's wife turned to salt for disobeying Angel of God
Uselessness of labour (*Patrick*)	Lev. 26:16–20	Prophecy of seeds sown to no purpose, strength of labour in vain for defying Mosaic Law/God
	Deut. 28:30–31, 38–41	Malediction of not enjoying any of fruits of labors for defying Mosaic Law/God
	Wis: 3.10–13	Ungodly said to have unprofitable labours

Chapter 2
The "Fyre of Ire Kyndild" in the Fifteenth-Century Scottish Marches[1]

Jackson W. Armstrong

Recent studies concerned with the theme of vengeance in late medieval Europe have focused attention on the management of conflict through "feud," and its processes of violence and peacemaking, in the context of the building of early modern "states."[2]

Even if feud is now well understood to be as much a legal phenomenon as an extra-legal one, the expectations of the transition from a medieval to a modern society bring into focus a perennial assumption about feud in different contexts: that the justice of feud is essentially a "private" apparatus flourishing when and where the mechanisms of justice provided by a "public" governing authority are

---

[1] I am grateful to Christine Carpenter, Andrea Ruddick, the editors and anonymous readers, and to audiences at Cambridge (2004), Swansea (2005) and Edinburgh (2006), all for comments on earlier versions of this paper, in some of which the English *Causa de Heron* was also examined (see my essay "Violence and Peacemaking in the English Marches Towards Scotland, *ca.* 1425–1440," in Linda Clark (ed.), *The Fifteenth Century VI: Identity and Insurgency in the Late Middle Ages* (Woodbridge, 2006), pp. 53–71). I wish to acknowledge the generous assistance towards the research undertaken for this paper provided by the Social Sciences and Humanities Research Council of Canada, the Overseas Research Students Awards Scheme and various bodies at the University of Cambridge.

[2] Claude Gauvard, *"De grace espécial:" Crime, état et société en France à la fin du moyen âge* (2 vols, Paris, 1991); Hillay Zmora, *State and Nobility in Early Modern Germany: The Knightly Feud in Franconia, 1440–1567* (Cambridge, 1997); Daniel L. Smail, "Hatred as a Social Institution in Medieval Society," *Speculum*, 76 (2001): 90–126; Howard Kaminsky, "The Noble Feud in the Later Middle Ages," *Past & Present*, 177 (2002): 55–83; Jeppe B. Netterstrøm, "Feud, Protection and Serfdom in Late Medieval and Early Modern Denmark (c. 1400–1600)," in Paul Freedman and Monique Bourin (eds), *Forms of Servitude in Northern and Central Europe: Decline, Resistance and Expansion* (Turnhout, 2005), pp. 369–84; Stuart Carroll, *Blood and Violence in Early Modern France* (Oxford, 2006); Peter Crooks, "Factions, Feuds and Noble Power in Late Medieval Ireland, c. 1356–1496," *Irish Historical Studies*, 35 (2007): 425–54. The study of feud in late medieval Europe begins with Otto Brunner, *Land und Herrschaft: Grundfragen der Territorialen Verfassungsgeschichte Österreichs im Mittelalter* (5th edn, Vienna, 1965), trans. as *Land and Lordship: Structures of Governance in Medieval Austria*, trans. Howard Kaminsky and J.V.H. Melton (Philadelphia, 1992).

weak or non-existent.[3] Consequently, central to much of this recent late medieval work is the question of how local societies and their noble leaders regulated disputes by making use of expanding governmental structures, and of developing conceptions of governance by public authorities with exclusive claims to the use of legitimate violence and the right to punish "crime" through coercive judicial systems which were far more intrusive than their early medieval antecedents. This chapter addresses such questions by examining vengeance and its quenching in a dispute which, in part, stretched across the international boundary between two late medieval "states" on the periphery of Europe.[4] Outstanding here are the marginal role of the judicial system, the ways in which Scotland's frontier with England was important, the effect of Scottish national political upheavals and the significance of ties of lordship in local processes of violent disputing and the making of peace.

Some historians have argued that in late medieval and early modern Scotland, private mechanisms of justice—including the processes which can be described as feud—had a stabilizing function.[5] On the other hand, others highlighted competitive and disruptive violence as a natural and important part of late medieval Scottish politics,[6] a point of view which suggests parallels with other parts of Europe, notably Germany.[7] The Scottish realm's government and judicial system, especially when compared with England at this time, was relatively localized,

---

[3] A topic reviewed in Paul R. Hyams, *Rancor and Reconciliation* (Ithaca, 2003), pp. 6–8. See also W.C. Brown, *Unjust Seizure: Conflict, Interest, and Authority in an Early Medieval Society* (Ithaca and London, 2001), pp. 5–6; W.C. Brown and Piotr Górecki (eds), *Conflict in Medieval Europe: Changing Perspectives on Society and Culture* (Aldershot, 2003), pp. 23–5, 279–82; Guy Halsall (ed.), *Violence and Society in the Early Medieval West* (Woodbridge, 1998), pp. 7–16.

[4] Historians of late medieval Scotland tend to avoid the term "state," whereas historians of England in the same period tend to embrace it. For the wider historiographical issues, see John Watts, *The Making of Polities: Europe, 1300–1500* (Cambridge, 2009), pp. 23–34. For England and Scotland, see, for example, G.L. Harriss, "Political Society and the Growth of Government in Late Medieval England," *Past & Present*, 138 (1993): 28–57; J.M. Wormald, *Court, Kirk and Community: Scotland 1470–1625* (London, 1981); Julian Goodare, *State and Society in Early Modern Scotland* (Oxford, 1999).

[5] J.M. Wormald, "Bloodfeud, Kindred and Government in Early Modern Scotland," *Past & Present*, 87 (1980): 54–97; J.M. Wormald, *Lords and Men in Scotland: Bonds of Manrent 1442–1603* (Edinburgh, 1985). On the problem of "feud" and its definition, see K.M. Brown, *Bloodfeud in Scotland 1573–1625* (Glasgow, 1986), p. 4; Hyams, *Rancor*, pp. xvi, 8–9, 33 and Chapter 7 below.

[6] S.I. Boardman, *Politics and the Feud in Late Medieval Scotland* (St. Andrews University Ph.D. thesis, 1989), especially pp. vi and 434; Brown, *Bloodfeud*, pp. 72–3; M.H. Brown, "Scotland Tamed? Kings and Magnates in Late Medieval Scotland: A Review of Recent Work," *Innes Review*, 45 (1994): 120–46.

[7] Zmora, *State and Nobility*; Gadi Algazi, "The Social Use of Private War: Some Late Medieval Views Reviewed," *Tel Aviver Jahrbuch für Deutsche Geschichte*, 22 (1993): 253–73.

privatized and informal. In this way, the norms of conflict management provided by the king's common law accommodated accustomed disputing practices related to feud, notably the payment of compensation to kinsmen in redress of injury, a process which was built into Scottish law.[8] Disputants in the Scottish marches used a vocabulary which further indicates the currency of feud and related concepts, especially private wars and enmities. For example, a pair of landowners spoke in 1453 of "fedis" that might emerge between their followers, in the 1460s "*guerras*" and "*inimicicias capitales*" arose and, in a dispute from 1498, the word "feyd" was used interchangeably with "ennemyte."[9] Thus, the management of conflict in the Scottish marches towards England was, as elsewhere in the Scottish realm, an endeavor which relied upon a normative balance achieved between expectations of royal justice and of customary practices.

Drawing on scholarship which emphasizes the importance of social relationships in the generation, pursuit and resolution of conflict, what follows is a close analysis of a dispute that escalated dramatically in the 1440s.[10] The case to be examined involved members of the Hume, Hepburn and Dunbar families, and concerned especially the Benedictine priory of Coldingham in south-eastern Scotland. At issue were the relationships among lay and ecclesiastical individuals and groups in the region, and the power structure into which these parties fitted at the local, regional, national and international levels. This example illustrates how events escalated to violence, and how acts of violence, and especially violent revenge-taking, were provoked. It offers a glimpse, rare in the evidence surviving from late medieval Scotland, of the role of emotion and honor in such violent disputing. The case is also extraordinarily well-documented, thanks in part to the

---

[8] Alexander Grant, *Independence and Nationhood: Scotland 1306–1469* (London, 1984), pp. 156–69; A.M. Godfrey, "Arbitration and Dispute Resolution in Sixteenth Century Scotland," *The Legal History Review*, 70 (2002): 109–35. On England, see Edward Powell, *Kingship, Law and Society: Criminal Justice in the Reign of Henry V* (Oxford, 1989); M.C. Carpenter, *Locality and Polity: A Study in Warwickshire Landed Society, 1401–1499* (Cambridge, 1992).

[9] Historical Manuscripts Commission (hereafter HMC), *Fourteenth Report, Appendix, Part 3* (London, 1894), p. 9; University of Durham Library, Archives and Special Collections, Durham Cathedral Muniments (hereafter DCM), Reg. IV, fols 162v–163v; *The Correspondence, Inventories, Account Rolls and Law Proceedings of the Priory of Coldingham*, ed. James Raine (Surtees Society, vol. 12, London, 1841) (hereafter *Coldingham*), pp. 196–201; *The Acts of the Lords of Council in Civil Causes, 1496–1501*, ed. George Neilson and Henry Paton (Edinburgh, 1918), p. 280. On mortal enmities, see Robert J. Bartlett, *"Mortal Enmities:" The Legal Aspect of Hostility in the Middle Ages* (T. Jones Pierce Lecture, Aberystwyth, 1998); Smail, "Hatred as a Social Institution."

[10] Patrick J. Geary, "Vivre en conflit dans une France sans état: typologie des mechanisms de règlement des conflits, 1050–1200," *Annales E.S.C.*, 41 (1986): 1107–33, trans. as "Living with Conflicts in Stateless France: A Typology of Conflict Management Mechanisms, 1050–1200," in Patrick J. Geary, *Living with the Dead in the Middle Ages* (Ithaca, 1994), pp. 125–60, at pp. 136–41.

survival of evidence for multiple attempts at resolution. It is in these peacemaking processes that we can see when and how compromise was effective, and why it failed when it did. In this way, the dispute is representative of patterns of local conflict in the Scottish marches, and it speaks to the central importance of the desire for vengeance (and the elimination of that desire) in the prosecution of lethal disputes.[11]

What follows is placed into three sections. The first is a simplified account of the conflict and its background. Next is an examination of the violent processes of this dispute and, third, is an assessment of the processes of peacemaking.

The conflict over Coldingham

Scotland in the fifteenth century was an independent realm which had overcome the threat to its autonomy once posed by England's imperial ambitions from the late thirteenth century. Since the end of the "Wars of Independence" in the early fourteenth century, Scottish border lords like the Douglas earls of Douglas (the Black Douglases) and the Dunbar earls of March had re-conquered land previously lost to English control. In this process the border line had, with a few exceptions like the English stronghold of Roxburgh, returned to the position on which it had settled in 1237 under the treaty of York.[12]

Nevertheless, the fifteenth-century Anglo-Scottish marches were still a sporadic war zone that from time to time witnessed major military campaigns on a national scale. England and Scotland were officially at war throughout this period, although international truces were almost always in effect. Frequent local border raids in both directions, which violated the truce agreements, were the substance of diplomatic negotiations between special commissioners from both countries. The frontier zones in both realms were divided administratively into regional "marches," each with a powerful crown officer known as a warden of the march. The wardens were regional magnates who were responsible for frontier defense and the administration of "march law," the evolving body of international law recognized between England and Scotland.[13]

---

[11] A topic explored in my doctoral thesis, which I plan to develop in print in due course—Jackson Armstrong, *Local Conflict in the Anglo-Scottish Borderlands, c. 1399–1488* (Cambridge University Ph.D. thesis, 2007).

[12] *Anglo-Scottish Relations 1174–1328: Some Selected Documents*, ed. E.L.G. Stones (London, 1965), pp. 38–53. On the thirteenth-century marches, see K.J. Stringer, "Identities in Thirteenth-Century England: Frontier Society in the Far North," in Claus Bjørn, Alexander Grant and K.J. Stringer (eds), *Social and Political Identities in Western History* (Copenhagen, 1994), pp. 28–66. On the fourteenth century, see A.J. Macdonald, *Border Bloodshed: Scotland, England and France at war 1369–1403* (East Linton, 2000).

[13] Anthony Goodman, "The Anglo-Scottish Marches in the Fifteenth Century: A Frontier Society?" in R.A. Mason (ed.), *Scotland and England, 1286–1815* (Edinburgh,

Coldingham was a daughter cell of the powerful English Cathedral Priory of Durham, and by the early fifteenth century it was the only remaining English religious house in Scotland.[14] It was situated in the Scottish east march, on the Lothian coast, a dozen miles north of the border town of Berwick-upon-Tweed.[15] The continued presence of this English priory in Scotland despite over a century of warfare was testament to the spiritual weight of Durham's patron, St. Cuthbert, from the Forth to the Tees. It was also sustained by the military reality of the English occupation of nearby Berwick.[16] The bishop of St. Andrews in Scotland exercised some influence over Coldingham, as the institution of the prior there was vested in him; however, it was the prior of Durham to whom the presentation of the candidate for prior belonged. Another office which lay solely in the gift of the prior of Durham—the bailiary of Coldingham—was the manifest object of conflict in the early stages of the dispute considered here. A bailie was an estate manager who collected rents, escheats and fines, and held courts on behalf of a landowner.[17] The bailiary of Coldingham came with a negotiable fee and a lease of some of the priory's Scottish lands, but more valuable than these perquisites were the regional influence and status accorded to the bailie, not just on the Scottish side of the border but also in England. A direct personal and institutional tie to the prior of Durham, himself an enormously influential prelate and landlord, could prove useful to a Scottish border laird whose own tenants, kin and friends were no doubt the frequent victims and perpetrators of cross-border raiding.

1987), pp. 18–33; C.J. Neville, *Violence, Custom and Law: The Anglo-Scottish Border Lands in the Later Middle Ages* (Edinburgh, 1998).

[14] R.B. Dobson, "The Last English Monks on Scottish Soil," *Scottish Historical Review*, 46 (1967): 1–25, at pp. 1–6.

[15] We are indebted to various historians for piecing together the story of Coldingham and its interested parties in the fourteenth and fifteenth centuries: A.I. Dunlop, *The Life and Times of James Kennedy Bishop of St Andrews* (Edinburgh, 1950) (hereafter Dunlop); A.L. Brown, "The Priory of Coldingham in the Late Fourteenth Century," *Innes Review*, 23 (1972): 91–101; R.B. Dobson, *Durham Priory 1400–1450* (London, 1973); N.A.T. Macdougall, "Crown *versus* Nobility: The Struggle for the Priory of Coldingham, 1472–88," in K.J. Stringer (ed.), *Essays on the Nobility of Medieval Scotland* (Edinburgh, 1985), pp. 254–69; C.A. McGladdery, *James II* (Edinburgh, 1990) (hereafter McGladdery); M.H. Brown, *The Black Douglases* (East Linton, 1998).

[16] For the significance of the occupation of Berwick, see the comments made in 1478 by the prior of Durham: DCM, Reg. Parv. III, fols 185v–186r. For Durham's historical influence, see Richard Lomas, "St Cuthbert and the Border, c.1080–c.1300," in C.D. Liddy and R.H. Britnell (eds), *North-East England in the Later Middle Ages* (Woodbridge, 2005), pp. 13–28; Anthony Goodman, "Religion and Warfare in the Anglo-Scottish Marches," in Robert Bartlett and Angus MacKay (eds), *Medieval Frontier Societies* (Oxford, 1989), pp. 245–66, esp. 246.

[17] Dunlop, p. 48. For an example of a Scottish bailie, see *Registrum Magni Sigilli Regum Scotorum*, ed. J.M. Thomson et al. (11 vols, Edinburgh, 1882–1914) (hereafter RMS), vol 2, pp. 168–9, no. 786.

The Coldingham conflict took place in the wider context of Scottish politics, and a quick survey of these figures and events will assist in the following analysis (the most important relationships are illustrated in Figure 2.1 in the Appendix). In the late 1420s and early 1430s competitive tensions grew among three substantial houses in the south-east. The oldest of these families were the Dunbar earls of March who, for centuries, had been seated at Dunbar Castle on the Lothian coast, north of Coldingham. However, for the last generation their regional authority had been surpassed by the Black Douglases, earls of Douglas, who were the greatest magnates in the south of Scotland. A cadet branch of the Douglas family, the Red Douglas earls of Angus, had also relatively recently gained lands and interests in the south-east. During the personal rule of James I from 1424, the king actively began to promote the power of the Red Douglases against the interests of the Black Douglases and the earls of March.[18]

In 1434, in response to the growing disaffection of George, tenth earl of March, with James I, the king had William, second earl of Angus, and others arrest the earl and seize his castle of Dunbar. By January 1435 March was disinherited and his lands forfeited to the crown.[19] Another of the royal agents and local beneficiaries of March's removal was Sir Adam Hepburn of Hailes. Although his castle of Hailes was nearly thirty miles from the border, close to Dunbar, the Hepburns were prominent in border affairs and tensions between the Dunbars and Hepburns dated back to the turn of the century. In the event, Adam Hepburn became royal keeper of Dunbar Castle from June 1434 and, afterwards, he was to become the crown steward of the earldom of March. This new arrangement of power was favorable, above all, to the earl of Angus.[20] In response to his father's forfeiture, Patrick ("Paton") Dunbar, eldest son of the former earl of March, jointly led an English raid across the border at the end of

---

[18] Brown, *James I* (Edinburgh, 1994), pp. 52–4, 149–56 and 160–63.

[19] Walter Bower, *Scotichronicon*, book 11, c. 23–4 and book 16, c. 24, trans. and ed. D.E.R. Watt (9 vols, Aberdeen, 1987–98), vol. 6, pp. 67–73 and vol. 8, pp. 290–92; *The Acts of the Parliaments of Scotland*, ed. Thomas Thomson and Cosmo Innes (12 vols, Record Commission, London, 1814–75) (hereafter APS), vol. 2, pp. 22–3; Brown, *James I*, pp. 154–6; Brown, *Black Douglases*, p. 243; McGladdery, p. 38.

[20] Bower, *Scotichronicon*, book 15, c. 10, lines 47–53, vol. 8, p. 33; book 15, c. 13, lines 1–37, vol. 8, pp. 43–4; book 16, c. 25, lines 16–20, vol. 8, p. 293; *The Exchequer Rolls of Scotland*, ed. J. Stuart et al. (23 vols, Edinburgh, 1878–1908) (hereafter ER), 4:620, 5:75, 100, 112, 124, and 144; S.I. Boardman, *Early Stewart Kings* (East Linton, 1996), pp. 228–9, 237, 246; Brown, *James I*, pp. 152–5; McGladdery, p. 38; Brown, *Black Douglases*, p. 266; Dunlop, pp. 51–2, and 75, n. 2; R.G. Nicholson, *Scotland: The Later Middle Ages* (Edinburgh, 1974), p. 344, n. 125. For the Hepburn lands in 1451, see RMS, vol. 2, pp. 115–16, no. 513. In January 1437 Hepburn of Hailes was described as the king's "lieutenant of the marches." See *Calendar of Scottish Supplications to Rome*, ed. E.R. Lindsay et al. (3 vols, Scottish History Society, Edinburgh, 1934–70) (hereafter CSSR), vol. 4 (1433–1447), ed. A.I. Dunlop and David MacLauchlan (Glasgow, 1983), p. 84, no. 343.

the summer. The raiders were repulsed at Piperdean on 10 September 1435 by a force led by Angus and Hepburn of Hailes.[21]

Other Scottish political malcontents arranged the assassination of the king in February 1437. In response to this new upheaval, the next month the Scottish parliament appointed Archibald, fifth earl of Douglas, as lieutenant-general of the realm during the royal minority of the new king, James II. In October of that year the earl of Angus died and was succeeded by his 11-year-old son, James, third earl of Angus. With the Dunbars eliminated, and both the new king and earl of Angus not yet of age, the fifth earl of Douglas was now the ascendant power—not just in the borders, but in the realm as a whole.[22] Earl Archibald's new dominance was brief, for he died in June 1439. He was succeeded by his underage son, but the equally short career of the young earl was dominated by his great uncle, James, nicknamed "the Gross."[23] Tensions at the royal court culminated in November 1440 when James the Gross conspired with others to have the Douglas heir killed in Edinburgh. As a result, James the Gross himself succeeded as the seventh earl and head of the Black Douglas family.[24] In summary, by late 1440 the Scottish political community was divided into two factions. On the one hand was James

---

[21] Bower, *Scotichronicon*, book 16, c. 25, lines 16–24, vol. 8, pp. 293–5; *Proceedings and Ordinances of the Privy Council of England*, ed. Sir Harris Nicolas (7 vols, London, 1834–37), vol. 4, p. 310. For English safe conducts to Patrick Dunbar in July and December 1435, see *Calendar of Documents Relating to Scotland*, ed. J. Bain (5 vols, Edinburgh, 1881–8), vol. 4, p. 222 and vol. 5, p. 293. For comment, see Brown, *James I*, p. 161, who notes the conspicuous absence of Alexander and David Hume in Bower's account of Piperdean, and suggests that they may have been sympathetic to Dunbar. Nonetheless, Angus made grants to both Humes in 1436: HMC, *Twelfth Report, Appendix, Part 8* (London, 1891), pp. 174–5, no. 293; HMC, *Milne-Home Report* (London, 1902), p. 20, nos 5–6.

[22] Brown, *James I*, pp. 154–5; McGladdery, pp. 12, 14, and 16–17; Nicholson, *Scotland*, p. 326; Brown, *Black Douglases*, pp. 246, 248–50; R.J. Tanner, *The Late Medieval Scottish Parliament: Politics and the Three Estates, 1424–1488* (East Linton, 2001), pp. 76–9. Apart from Douglas, the only other adult earl resident in Scotland at this time was David Lindsay, third earl of Crawford: Alexander Grant, "Earls and Earldoms in Late Medieval Scotland 1310–1460," in John Bossy and Peter Jupp (eds), *Essays Presented to Michael Roberts* (Belfast, 1976), pp. 24–40; Alexander Grant, "The Development of the Scottish Peerage," *Scottish Historical Review*, 57 (1978): 1–27.

[23] James "the Gross" Douglas, brother of the fourth earl of Douglas, was lord of Balvenie and Abercorn, and had recently been created earl of Avondale: McGladdery, pp. 14, and 16–17; Brown, *Black Douglases*, pp. 234, 238 and 255.

[24] William, sixth earl of Douglas, was killed with his brother David and their associate Sir Malcolm Fleming of Biggar and Cumbernauld at what was to become known as the "Black Dinner." See Dunlop, p. 39; Brown, *Black Douglases*, pp. 258–60, 274 and 282, n. 37; McGladdery, pp. 23 and 35; *The Douglas Book*, ed. Sir William Fraser (4 vols, Edinburgh, 1885), vol. 2, p. 42; Nicholson, *Scotland*, pp. 330–31.

the Gross with his allies.[25] On the other hand was the queen mother, allied with the teenage earl of Angus and James Kennedy, the new bishop of St. Andrews.

Tensions persisted between James the Gross and the minority council till his death in March 1443. His son William succeeded as eighth earl of Douglas.[26] By October 1444, Earl William and his allies, the Livingstons, had secured control of the 14-year-old king and, in a general council held at Stirling, they dubiously declared James II of age to rule and announced a general revocation of land grants. Civil war erupted in November, pitting the Douglases and Livingstons against Chancellor Crichton, Kennedy, Angus and the queen mother.[27] Douglas had triumphed by the end of the summer and his opponents, including Angus, were forced to come to terms with him. Until the young king's marriage in 1449 Douglas was to dominate Scottish politics.[28]

With these overarching events in mind, we can now return to the conflict with which we are primarily concerned. This dispute began over the right to the bailiary of Coldingham Priory. In the first quarter of the century, the immensely powerful Archibald, fourth earl of Douglas, was bailie of Coldingham. He deputed the office to his knight Sir Alexander Hume of that Ilk, lord of Dunglass (north of Coldingham).[29] (It should be pointed out that the particularly Scottish territorial designation, "of that Ilk," usually means "(lord) of that same (place)," where the place-name is the same as the holder's surname. Thus Alexander Hume was lord of the lands of Hume, and also of Dunglass and other lesser holdings.) George Dunbar, tenth earl of March, whose ancient family were patrons of Coldingham, opposed this arrangement, which nevertheless endured until 1424 when Douglas and Hume met their deaths in battle in France, and the Black Douglases lost their hold on the Coldingham office.[30] The following year, both Alexander's brother, David Hume of Wedderburn, and Alexander's son and heir, another Alexander Hume of that Ilk, had an interest in claiming the bailiary, but they agreed to halve

---

[25] For the moment James the Gross's allies included Sir William Crichton, the chancellor.

[26] Brown, *Black Douglases*, pp. 265–6, 269; McGladdery, pp. 23–8.

[27] HMC, *Twelfth Report, Appendix, Part 8*, pp. 114–15, no. 85; McGladdery, pp. 32–3; Brown, *Black Douglases*, pp. 273–4.

[28] APS, vol. 2, p. 59; Nicholson, *Scotland*, p. 342; N.A.T. Macdougall, *James III: A Political Study* (Edinburgh, 1982), p. 13, nn. 40 and 41; McGladdery, pp. 32–46; Brown, *Black Douglases*, pp. 274 and 282, n. 37.

[29] The surname is also spelled Home. Hume of that Ilk (or Hume of Hume) in this case is the senior line, whereas Hume of Wedderburn is a cadet branch of the family. Alexander Grant, "Acts of Lordship: The Records of Archibald, Fourth Earl of Douglas," in Terry Brotherstone and David Ditchburn (eds), *Freedom and Authority: Scotland c.1050–1650* (East Linton, 2000), p. 256, no. 10; Fraser, *Douglas Book*, vol. 3, p. 367, no. 298; Dobson, *Durham Priory*, p. 321; Brown, *Black Douglases*, p. 177. See also DCM, Reg. III, fol. 41r; *Coldingham*, pp. 86–8, nos 98–9.

[30] DCM, Locellus XXV, no. 137; Brown, *Black Douglases*, p. 266.

the profits of the office, whichever of the two should acquire it from Durham.[31] The prior of Durham at this time was the capable John Wessington, then in the prime of his almost thirty-year tenure as head of the Durham convent. Wessington appointed David Hume of Wedderburn as bailie in 1428, the same year in which he made William Douglas, second earl of Angus, "special protector and defender" of Coldingham, with the assent of the Scottish king James I.[32]

However, by early 1433, Angus was out of favor with Durham, while Prior Wessington drew David Hume closer, granting him and his wife letters of confraternity with Durham and all its dependent cells.[33] In the mounting political competition of the later 1430s, following the assassination of the king, the alignments of the Humes are unclear. Both uncle and nephew were knighted about this time, probably at the coronation of James II on 25 March 1437.[34] Two days after the coronation, David's commission as bailie of Coldingham was renewed for five years.[35] The only other evidence forthcoming is that Alexander Hume lost lands in Berwickshire to the young earl of Angus through an arbitration between

---

[31] *The Scots Peerage*, ed. Sir James Balfour Paul (9 vols, Edinburgh, 1904–14) (hereafter *Scots Peerage*), vol. 4, p. 446; HMC, *Milne-Home Report*, p. 19, no. 3. David was commissioned to act in his brother's stead during his absence in France: DCM, Reg. III, fols 105v–106r, printed in *Coldingham*, p. 97, no. 109. For the Hume family, see *Scots Peerage*, vol. 4, pp. 446–8, and the important correction at vol. 9, pp. 106–7. For Hume relations, see RMS, vol. 2, pp. 115–16, 119, 131, 193, 225 and 289, nos 512, 514, 525, 596, 924, 1092 and 1408; and for David Hume's relations in particular, see RMS, vol. 2, pp. 80–81, no. 349. On 8 March 1425 Alexander Hume and David Hume witnessed a grant by the earl of March to his son Archibald Dunbar, of Wester Spott in the regality of Dunbar. Other witnesses included David Dunbar the earl's brother, Sir Patrick Dunbar the earl's uncle, George Dunbar the earl's son and Patrick Dunbar of Biel: *The Book of Carlaverock*, ed. Sir William Fraser (2 vols, Edinburgh, 1873), vol. 2, p. 428, no. 34.

[32] James Raine, *The History and Antiquities of North Durham* (London, 1852), appendix, p. 98, no. 559; DCM, Reg. III, fols 129r–130r; *Coldingham*, pp. 101–2, nos 113 and 114; Dunlop, p. 77. On this same date Angus and his wife Christiana were given letters of confraternity with Durham: DCM, Reg. III, fol. 126v. See also the leases made to Angus in early 1428 of Coldingham lands: DCM, Misc. Ch. 1092 and 1093. For Wessington's career as prior, from 1416–46, see Dobson, *Durham Priory*.

[33] David Hume's lands were confirmed by the king in 1431 and he was renewed as bailie in 1432: RMS, vol. 2, p. 43, no. 189; Grant, "Acts of Lordship," p. 268, no. 87; HMC, *Milne-Home Report*, pp. 17–18, no. 1; DCM, Reg. III, fols 148v–149r, 149r–v; *Coldingham*, pp. 105–7, nos 117 and 118; Dobson, *Durham Priory*, p. 321; Brown, *James I*, pp. 52–4, 149–56 and 160–63. Prior William Drax of Coldingham and David Hume may have cooperated in robbery at this time: Mary Kennaway, *Fast Castle: The Early Years* (Edinburgh, 1992), pp. 31–8.

[34] The earliest reference to David Hume as a knight is on 30 December 1438 (HMC, *Twelfth Report, Appendix, Part 8*, p. 108, no. 53) and to Alexander Hume as a knight is on 4 September 1439 (RMS, vol. 2, p. 49, no. 204). For the coronation, see APS, vol. 2, p. 31.

[35] *Coldingham*, pp. 108–10, no. 121.

them in 1440. Still, there is no suggestion that Alexander or David had links to Angus's opponents.[36]

The political competition of the early years of the minority of James II coincided roughly, it appears, with the coming of age of an ambitious young Alexander.[37] It was in these changing circumstances that tensions erupted between nephew and uncle. In February of 1439 or 1440, David, now residing at the former Dunbar tower of Cockburnspath north of Coldingham, had written to Prior Wessington asking to have his annual pension "sumthyng amendit," rising from five marks English to 100s, and also for a grant of the bailiary for life. This is the first clear sign of competition between the Humes, the main conflict of this analysis. Wessington consented to the rise, but declined the life grant, and indicated that David's nephew, Alexander, had also approached him for a grant of the bailiary. From the end of 1440 till the autumn of 1441, Alexander continued to apply pressure for the bailiary and its associated lands.[38]

At the same time, David anxiously corresponded with Wessington concerning a number of topics, including the advancement of David's own candidate to succeed the aging prior of Coldingham, William Drax. On this matter, Wessington reminded David that the Scotsman was a brother of Durham, and that the convent trusted David to be more favorable "in savying of their right." In the summer David again asked Wessington for a life grant, for his fee to be increased and to exchange certain Coldingham lands. Once again, the prior gave him his requested rise, but denied him a grant for life.[39] On 16 September 1441, David went in person to Durham and secured a grant of the bailiary for forty years, with a promise to exchange certain lands, apparently in violation of a more recent bond with his nephew which has not survived.[40] Early the next month, an affronted Alexander

---

[36] The arbitration was done at Jedburgh on 27 February and the arbiters were the Roxburghshire men Sir Archibald Douglas of Cavers (a supporter of the earls of Angus) and Nicholas Rutherford of Grubbit, and the lands at issue were Preston and Lintlaws within the barony of Bunkle: Fraser, *Douglas Book*, vol. 3, p. 69, no. 76. On Angus and Douglas of Cavers, see Brown, *Black Douglases*, p. 243. See also a royal grant to Alexander Hume in 1439: RMS, vol. 2, p. 49, no. 204.

[37] Alexander Hume's age at the time of his father's death in 1424 is unknown, but he lived until 1491. In all probability he was still a minor at the time of the agreement with his uncle.

[38] DCM, Reg. Parv. II, fols 101v–102r, and 122v; *Coldingham*, pp. 108–10, and 114, nos 121–3 and 128. In November 1440 Alexander secured a grant of lands from the elderly Prior Drax of Coldingham: HMC, *Twelfth Report, Appendix, Part 8*, p. 108, no. 54. As early as July 1440 the future vacancy of Coldingham after Drax's death was being contemplated: Dunlop, p. 49 and 51.

[39] Dunlop, p. 51, nn. 2 and 3; DCM, Reg. Parv. II, fols 141v–142r, 142r–v, 142v–143v, and 144r–v; *Coldingham*, pp. 116 and 119, nos 132 and 134; quote from pp. 117–18, no. 133.

[40] HMC, *Milne-Home Report*, pp. 20–21, no. 7; DCM, Misc. Ch. 656; DCM, Reg. III, fols 273*r–v; *Coldingham*, pp. 120–21, no. 135; Dunlop, p. 51; Dobson, *Durham Priory*,

wrote to Wessington claiming that it was his own strength, kin and men that allowed David the authority to discharge his office, and that David "taryis in the full fillyng of his band to me, thynkyng till optene my gudewill of your lands."[41]

Shortly afterwards, on 12 October 1441, with Wessington's endorsement, the Humes brought their dispute to the arbitration of Adam Hepburn of Hailes and others, who decreed that the jurisdiction of the bailiary was to be divided evenly between uncle and nephew.[42] Further correspondence on this arrangement traveled to and from Wessington as the year drew to a close. This was the point at which the Scottish national politics discussed above entered into the dispute between the Humes, for, by the end of the year, the earl of Angus was backing Alexander's side. However, the first real test of the Hepburn arbitration came in December, when Prior Drax died. Wessington soon presented the Durham monk John Oll as Drax's successor, telling Oll that he had persuaded both Humes to support his admission as prior of Coldingham.[43]

The Humes cooperated in securing the support of Bishop James Kennedy of St. Andrews for John Oll and, on 22 January 1442, at Coldingham, they both witnessed Oll's induction to the priorate. However, in March, Wessington reproached David for his abrupt behavior the previous autumn.[44] The tenuous cooperation between uncle and nephew had collapsed by April 1442 when the Scottish chancellor approached Wessington about the "mater" between the Humes, advising him that "a sudane deliverance" by an English judge "will causs inqwyet to the Priour & the pure men of the Baronry of Coldynghame." The Scottish council, including Bishop Kennedy, was pleased neither with Durham's choice of Oll for Coldingham, nor with the prior's influence over the Humes' dispute.[45] Taking the hint, Wessington again wrote to Hepburn about dividing the bailiary between the Humes and asked him to intervene once more.[46] However, Alexander seized an

---

p. 322. For the clearest evidence of a bond, perhaps made in early 1441, see *Coldingham*, p. 127, no. 143, and pp. 132–3, no. 148.

[41] *Coldingham*, pp. 135–6, no. 151.

[42] DCM, Misc. Ch. 1089; DCM, Reg. Parv. II, fols 146r–v; *Coldingham*, pp. 122, no. 136; David Hume of Godscroft, *De Familia Humia Wedderburnensi Liber*, ed. John Miller (Abbotsford Club, vol. 15, Edinburgh, 1839) (hereafter Godscroft), p. 8; Dunlop, p. 52, n. 1.

[43] DCM, Reg. III, fol. 270v; *Coldingham*, pp. 121–5, nos 136–41; Dunlop, p. 49; Dobson, *Durham Priory*, p. 323.

[44] It was Alexander who spoke at length before Kennedy on Oll's behalf: Dobson, *Durham Priory*, pp. 322–4; DCM, Misc. Ch. 1098 and 7193; DCM, Reg. III, fols 273*v–275r; DCM, Reg. Parv. II, fols 149–50, and 153r–v; *Coldingham*, pp. 127–33, nos 143–8, and pp. 246–58. See also Dunlop, pp. 49–50.

[45] *Coldingham*, pp. 138–9, no. 153. Sir William Crichton of that Ilk (adopting the style Lord Crichton from the mid-1440s, in the form of title assumed by those newly emerging as lords of parliament), the chancellor, would soon offer his support to Alexander: Dunlop, p. 52.

[46] DCM, Reg. Parv. II, fols 154r–v, printed in *Coldingham*, pp. 136–8, no. 152. See also Dunlop, pp. 51–2.

opportunity to balance the objectives of Durham and the Scottish council in his favor. Striking a deal with Priors Oll and Wessington, who granted him the bailiary for life in May, Alexander secured the council's acknowledgement of himself as bailie and their consent to the underage James II admitting Oll to the temporalities of Coldingham. Oll was duly admitted in June and the king took the priory under royal protection. The international accommodation brokered by Alexander Hume, now bailie for life, was complete.[47]

David Hume had been outmaneuvered by his nephew. Though he had a copy of the recent arbitration made, it was a futile effort. He was left to accuse Alexander of having extracted the support of the king's council by force and to turn for assistance to the Black Douglas earl, James the Gross.[48] Relations between the council and James the Gross had deteriorated since the previous year. The earl welcomed David Hume's appeal for support and readily backed the knight in his claim to Coldingham. By the end of 1442, David had seized the priory by force. However, he was not able to hold it for long and, by 4 January 1443, the English monks had returned to Coldingham and the bailiary was again in Alexander's hands, this time with a new grant of the office for sixty years.[49]

David later accused his nephew of using the priory as a base to raid livestock from him and Adam Hepburn.[50] He lost the support of James the Gross when the earl died on 25 March 1443 and, shortly afterwards, David seems to have resigned himself to his nephew's ascendancy. Cooperation had replaced animosity by 20 June, when a large group of Humes and Hepburns gathered to witness a grant made by Alexander's wife.[51] This apparent cooling of tensions among the combatants may well have been the result of pressure by James, earl of Angus, who had previously lent support to Alexander. Indeed, it was Angus and his comital council to whom the Humes formally submitted their dispute for arbitration in January 1444, and Angus's award finally achieved accommodation between uncle and nephew.[52]

---

[47] The other members of the underage king's council included Crichton, the earls of Angus, Mar and Crawford, and Adam Hepburn: DCM, Reg. III, fols 275v, and 276v–277r; Raine, *North Durham*, appendix, p. 99, no. 567, and p. 105, no. 600; Dunlop, pp. 50 and 52, n. 4; Dobson, *Durham Priory*, pp. 322–4; McGladdery, p. 38; Brown, *Black Douglases*, p. 266.

[48] The transumpt was done at Cockburnspath on 12 May 1442: Godscroft, p. 8; *Coldingham*, pp. 147–8, no. 160. See also DCM, Loc. XXV, no. 6; *Coldingham*, pp. 140–42, no. 155; Dobson, *Durham Priory*, p. 324.

[49] DCM, Misc. Ch. 654, 1087 and 1282; DCM, Reg. III, fol. 287v; *Coldingham*, pp. 139, 141, 147–50 and 164–5, nos 149, 155, 160 and 178; Dunlop, pp. 46–7, 52–3; Dobson, *Durham Priory*, pp. 324–5; McGladdery, p. 39; Brown, *Black Douglases*, pp. 265–6.

[50] DCM, Misc. Ch. 1087; *Coldingham*, pp. 147–50, no. 160.

[51] HMC, Fourteenth Report, Appendix, Part 3, p. 18, no. 31.

[52] HMC, *Milne-Home Report*, p. 21, no. 8; Godscroft, p. 9; McGladdery, p. 39; Dunlop, pp. 53–4. Alexander received a forty-year lease of the lands of Aldcambus from the prior of Durham on 7 May 1444: *Coldingham*, pp. 150–51, no. 161.

By the summer of 1444 national tensions in Scotland were escalating and, reacting defensively to his rival Angus's achievement of the Hume reconciliation, the energetic Black Douglas heir, William, eighth earl of Douglas, sought to forge new links with both the Humes and the Hepburns. On 29 June he made grants to Patrick Hepburn, the son and heir of Adam Hepburn of Hailes, witnessed by David Hume, and to Alexander Hume on 24 August.[53] In October 1444, William, earl of Douglas made a further gesture of good will to Alexander. The following month events led the political community into civil war.[54]

During the course of hostilities in July 1445 Douglas besieged Dunbar Castle, then held by its keeper, Adam Hepburn, and the queen mother. The queen died during the siege and Hepburn surrendered the castle to the triumphant Douglas "throu trety." Relative stability returned for the rest of the year, but not all were happy with the Douglas victory. Further violence erupted in the spring of 1446. In April, Adam Hepburn's son and heir, Patrick, recaptured Dunbar Castle, and assaulted and kidnapped Prior Oll of Coldingham and others, holding them for ransom at Dunbar. His violent actions drew the condemnation of the minority council and, though the details are unclear, Hepburn was soon driven from the castle in a siege ordered and paid for by the crown. Later that year, the Hepburns themselves were the victims of violence when Archibald Dunbar, another son of the former earl of March, captured the Hepburns' castle of Hailes, holding it for a short time before turning it over to the control of the Black Douglases.[55] After these bursts of violence in 1446, the next two years were relatively uneventful. Then, in February 1449, a double marriage contract was signed between the Hepburns and Humes, which appears to have secured a lasting resolution between these families.[56]

---

[53] Fraser, *Douglas Book*, vol. 3, pp. 76–7, no. 81 (29 June 1444); RMS, vol. 2, p. 124, no. 557 (24 August 1444); National Archives of Scotland (hereafter NAS), RH 6/310; Fraser, *Douglas Book*, vol. 3, p. 426, no. 412. Alexander also received a grant from Robert Hog of Hogiston, done at Kelso on 7 July 1444: RMS, vol. 2, p. 62, no. 271. See also Brown, *Black Douglases*, pp. 273–5. In 1444 Adam Hepburn was described as steward of the earldom of March: Dunlop, p. 75, n. 2.

[54] Alexander Hume received a letter from the king (under Douglas's control) assuring him that the general revocation issued at Stirling would not affect his own rights. HMC *Twelfth Report, Appendix, Part 8*, pp. 114–15, no. 85; McGladdery, pp. 32–3; Brown, *Black Douglases*, pp. 273–4.

[55] "Auchinleck Chronicle," fol. 111r, printed in McGladdery, p. 162, see also pp. 24 and 39–40; ER, vol. 4, p. 620; Dunlop, pp. 76–7; Brown, *Black Douglases*, p. 275.

[56] *The Scotts of Buccleuch*, ed. Sir William Fraser (2 vols, Edinburgh, 1878), vol. 2, pp. 39–41, no. 44; McGladdery, p. 40; Dunlop, pp. 77 and 121. In 1448 Alexander Hume was appointed sheriff-depute of Berwickshire under John Lord Haliburton, of Direlton, who also leased lands to Hume: RMS, vol. 2, pp. 70–71, no. 305. From at least Whitsunday in 1450 Patrick Hepburn of Hailes served as royal steward of March: ER, vol. 5, p. 486.

Violent disputing

With the foregoing narrative of this conflict in mind, we can now look at this case more closely. As we have seen, the dormant competitive tensions between uncle and nephew erupted to the surface in 1440, in the context of a major renegotiation of regional and national power structures following the death of the fifth earl of Douglas during a royal minority. In this process, both Humes turned to lay lords for support. When the prior of Durham warned David Hume in 1440 that he had been approached by "notabill persons" asking "to prefer certayn persons to the said office," he was doubtless referring to Alexander Hume, with the probable support of James, earl of Angus.[57] The following year, when David corresponded with Wessington about having his own candidate succeed as prior of Coldingham, he was backed by the local knight Adam Hepburn of Hailes. Once he had lost the bailiary to Alexander in 1442, David brought his complaint to James the Gross, earl of Douglas, who had reason to oppose the interests of Alexander, and who was already antagonistic towards Angus.[58] In 1446, faced with attacks from the Hepburns and Dunbars, the reconciled Humes relied on William, eighth earl of Douglas, for backing.[59] When local events escalated, such appeals to lordship allowed the contending parties to link their local dispute into larger regional, national and, indeed, international tensions, thus expanding their conflict and drawing greater interests and resources into the pursuit of their objectives.

The role of Prior John Wessington of Durham illustrates how bonds of lordship in this dispute stretched across the border. As the English prior of Durham, Wessington appointed the bailie of Coldingham and so had control over an important local office in the Scottish marches. As bailie in the 1430s, David Hume had cultivated strong relationships with both Wessington and Prior William Drax of Coldingham. The strength of these earthly bonds was enhanced by Wessington's grant of confraternity to David and his wife in 1433, a grant which the prior chose to remind David of nine years later when their relationship became strained.[60] His reminder to David indicates that Wessington expected the spiritual bond with his Scottish bailie to involve mutual assistance. Yet, the cross-border link between David and Wessington was unstable. Alexander Hume's

---

[57] DCM, Reg. Parv. II, fols 101v–102r, and 122v; *Coldingham*, pp. 109–10, and 114, nos 123 and 128. Both Hepburn and Angus offered written support for Alexander to Prior Wessington in 1441 (ibid., pp. 123–4, nos 138 and 140); Dobson, *Durham Priory*, pp. 321–2; Dunlop, p. 51.

[58] Dunlop, pp. 46–7, 52–3 and 51, nn. 2–3; DCM, Reg. Parv. II, fols 141v–142r, 142r–v and 144r–v; *Coldingham*, pp. 116–19, nos 132 and 134; McGladdery, p. 39; Brown, *Black Douglases*, pp. 265–6.

[59] HMC, *Fourteenth Report, Appendix, Part 3*, pp. 24–5, no. 49; Fraser, *Douglas Book*, vol. 3, p. 427, no. 415.

[60] DCM, Reg. III, fols 148v–149r; DCM, Reg. Parv. II, fols 142v–143v; *Coldingham*, pp. 106 and 117–18, nos 118 and 133; Dobson, *Durham Priory*, p. 321.

application of pressure on these two men, by which he aimed to secure the office for himself, generated significant tension between David and the English prior. In 1441–2, when Wessington needed help to secure Scottish support for John Oll as the new prior of Coldingham, David, under pressure and attempting to forward his own candidate, misguidedly chose to ignore the prior. With his uncle in a corner, Alexander was able to attain Wessington's support by recognizing and fulfilling the English prior's goal. In return, Wessington gave Alexander the office of bailie in place of David.[61]

At certain junctures, tensions escalated beyond mere political maneuvering and the parties in this dispute turned to violence in the pursuit of their objectives. However, they did not do so at random. Violence here arose from specific changes in the political situation, furthered certain objectives, followed norms and relied on particular relationships. When David Hume wrote to ask Prior Wessington for a life grant of the bailiary in 1440, he told the prior "3e knaw qwhat debatis & striffis is lyk to ryss in our land [,] the qwilk is abill to wast 3our place [of Coldingham]." Allusion became implicit threat the following year, when he referred to rumors that he was planning to "overlay" the house of Coldingham with his "repayr" (following). In the spring of 1442, Wessington made a statement indicating that the presence of a hostile frontier further complicated the issue of potential violence. The prior reported in a stern letter to David that the talk in the border town of Berwick and the county of Northumberland was that David was planning to build a castle or tower on the priory's lands "which were likely to be to England great harme."[62]

David ultimately fulfilled his threats of violence when, in his own words, he took "the stepil of Coldingham" in 1442. Once his nephew had deprived him of the office of bailie, and David had secured the support of James the Gross, earl of Douglas, he later said that, perceiving opposition from Alexander and John Oll, prior of Coldingham, "in defens of the kyrk rycht and me [,] I put my familiars in the strentht of the kyrk." He claimed to do this with the consent of Prior Oll but, in fact, the prior and monks fled the monastery for Berwick. Prior Wessington was later to describe David's actions as sacrilegious and warlike.[63]

Part of the explanation for why violence erupted in 1442 and not before can be found in David's appeal to James the Gross. In his capacity as royal justiciar in southern Scotland, "avysit be a worthy consale," the Black Douglas earl

---

[61] DCM, Misc. Ch. 1098 and 7193; DCM, Reg. III, fols 273*v–275r, 275v and 276v–277r; DCM, Reg. Parv. II, fols 149–50; *Coldingham*, pp. 127–32, nos 143–7 and pp. 246–58; Raine, *North Durham*, appendix, p. 99, no. 567 and p. 105, no. 600; Dunlop, pp. 49–50 and 52, n. 4; Dobson, *Durham Priory*, pp. 322–4; McGladdery, p. 38; Brown, *Black Douglases*, p. 266.

[62] DCM, Reg. Parv. II, fols 142r–v, 142v–143v and 153r–v; *Coldingham*, pp. 113, 117–18 and 132–3, nos 127, 133 and 148.

[63] DCM, Misc. Ch. 1087; Reg. III, fol. 276r; *Coldingham*, pp. 139–40 and 147–50, nos 154 and 160. See also Brown, *Black Douglases*, p. 266; McGladdery, p. 39.

overturned the decision in favor of Alexander by the king's "partiale consale," finding David to be the rightful bailie, and had as much proclaimed "in heryng of all the peple."[64] This caused the previously peaceful dispute between the Humes to link into an already violent, and wider, web of conflict. Relations between Douglas and other Scottish magnates, including Bishop Kennedy and the earl of Angus, had grown tense since the previous year. Moreover, in 1442, Kennedy had promoted Alexander's "ner kynnesman," Patrick Hume, to replace Douglas's own adherent as archdeacon of Teviotdale. In the summer, Douglas made a show of force against his opponents.[65] It seems that this escalation of the wider conflict now gave David pretext to take similar action. Indeed the opportunity to do so may well have been what drew him to Douglas in the first place. Still, unable to hold on to the priory by force, David soon lost control and backed down.

Alexander Hume also made use of violence to advance his cause. In a letter written to Prior Wessington in March 1443, David described the violence of his nephew Alexander. He accused Prior Oll of delivering Coldingham to Alexander who then held it "as a hous of weer" in which he kept "a garyson of refars" (reivers) with whom he raided more than two thousand head of livestock from David and his son, and from David's supporter Adam Hepburn. We are reminded again of the presence of the English border by David's allegation that Alexander sold these stolen goods to "Inglish men" in violation of the Anglo-Scottish truce.[66]

Obviously David was concerned here to portray his opponent's actions as negatively as possible; nevertheless, from this narrative we can detect possible motives for Alexander's resort to violence. It was in some part retaliatory, a proportionate response to his uncle's own actions. More importantly though, his use of violence at this juncture was probably intended to stamp his authority on the new arrangement of power with a public show of force against his opponents, plundering their lands and animals. In David's words, Alexander had earlier "sent thither his power to be seen" when James the Gross had publicly proclaimed his

---

[64] DCM, Misc. Ch. 1087; *Coldingham*, pp. 147–50, no. 160; Dunlop, pp. 52–3.

[65] The chancellor, Sir William Crichton, had become another Douglas adversary at this stage: Brown, *Black Douglases*, pp. 265–6. On the archdeaconry of Teviotdale, and William Croyser, Douglas's agent in church affairs, see DCM, Reg. Parv. III, fol. 108v; *Coldingham*, p. 187, no. 203 (quotation); HMC, *Twelfth Report, Appendix, Part 8*, p. 176, no. 297; Dunlop, pp. 46–7 and 52–3; McGladdery, p. 39. Patrick Hume may have been a son of David Hume of Wedderburn's brother, Patrick Hume of Rathburn. See *Scots Peerage*, vol. 4, p. 444. It is improbable that he was one and the same with Patrick Hume of Fastcastle, another son of Sir Alexander: William Douglas, "Fast Castle and its Owners: Some Notes on their History," *Proceedings of the Society of Antiquaries of Scotland*, 55 (1920–21): 56–83, at p. 65; Kennaway, *Fast Castle*, pp. 44–5.

[66] DCM, Misc. Ch. 1087; *Coldingham*, pp. 147–50, no. 160; Alexander allegedly raided David's lands of Upsettlington, Flemington and Wedderburn, driving off his flocks and usurping the teinds [tithes] of Thurston: Godscroft, p. 8; Fraser, *Douglas Book*, vol. 2, p. 41. See also Brown, *Black Douglases*, p. 266; McGladdery, p. 39; Dunlop, pp. 52–3; Dobson, *Durham Priory*, p. 324.

support for his uncle. No doubt Alexander's subsequent violent actions were also meant as both a practical and a symbolic posture of dominance.[67] Certainly in 1443 archdeacon Patrick Hume reported to the Pope that he only visited Teviotdale with a band of armed men, almost certainly furnished by Alexander, for fear of attacks from his rivals, by whom he meant James the Gross and David.[68]

For David, the use of violence was tied up with issues of honor and status. He complained to Wessington that Alexander had interfered with his possession of the bailiary, and declared "that unamendit I sall never remit qwhill I am lyfand." David was acutely aware that his reputation had been sullied and told the prior that he was held in derision, with "dyverss contre men saying 'Se nw his rewarde for lang gude service.'" However, he turned the issue around and sought to justify his actions and condemn those of his rival in the same terms of honor. He protested that in his nephew he had "fand na deids folwand his words, but grete unkyndeness don to my men." He took matters even further when it came to violence, claiming that Alexander's raids on him and Hepburn did "harm til us, bot mykill [much] mar schame & harme til hym [Alexander]." David also spoke of the "greif" he suffered himself and implied that Alexander had no eye "to trewthe, ne dreds na schame."[69]

Shame is an emotion which is often equated with dishonor.[70] In his narrative David cited his nephew's unfaithfulness (his failure to act upon his word or to

---

[67] DCM, Misc. Ch. 1087; *Coldingham*, pp. 147–50, no. 160. On the related topic of symbolic violence, see J.B. Thompson's introduction to Pierre Bourdieu, *Language and Symbolic Power*, trans. Gino Raymond and Matthew Adamson, ed. J.B. Thompson (Cambridge, 1991), pp. 23–5.

[68] William Croyser was James the Gross's favored archdeacon of Teviotdale. The papal reply to Patrick Hume's entreaty recounted: "*quique potenciam inimicorum tuorum merito perhorrescens ad visitandum proptera ecclesias et alia loca ecclesiastica dicti archidiaconatus absque multitudine armatorum tibi assistentium accedere non audes.*" *Calendar of Entries in the Papal Registers Relating to Great Britain and Ireland*, ed. W.H. Bliss et al. (20 vols, London, 1893–2005), vol. 9, p. 565; CSSR, vol. 4, pp. 219 and 318, nos 882 and 1289. Note that no. 882 is a dispensation for the marriage of Alexander Hume's daughter Joneta to Robert Lauder of the Bass, made on 21 July 1442. See also Dunlop, p. 47, n. 6.

[69] DCM, Misc. Ch. 1087; *Coldingham*, pp. 147–50, no. 160.

[70] F.H. Stewart, *Honor* (Chicago, 1994), pp. 128–9. On honor and the emotion of joy, see S.D. White, "The Politics of Anger," in Barbara H. Rosenwein (ed.), *Anger's Past: The Social Uses of an Emotion in the Middle Ages* (Ithaca, 1998), pp. 127–52, at pp. 142–3. Further on honor and status, see Julian Pitt-Rivers, "Honour and Social Status," in J.G. Peristiany (ed.), *Honour and Shame: The Values of Mediterranean Society* (London, 1965), pp. 21–77; Pierre Bourdieu, "The Sentiment of Honour in Kabyle Society," in Peristiany (ed.), *Honour and Shame*, pp. 193–241; M.E. James, "English Politics and the Concept of Honour, 1485–1642," *Past & Present*, Supplement 3 (1978): 1–30; P.C. Maddern, "Honour Among the Pastons: Gender and Integrity in Fifteenth-Century English Provincial Society," *Journal of Medieval History*, 14 (1988): 357–71, at pp. 358–9; P.C. Maddern, *Violence and Social Order: East Anglia 1422–1442* (Oxford, 1992), pp. 227–32; Jacob Black-Michaud,

regard truth) and unkindness (his failure to act as a kinsman should), and used the concept of shame to portray Alexander's violent actions as dishonorable, thus turning back on to his opponent the dishonor which David, as victim, should have suffered himself. Admitting to his own harm and grief, but finding himself in no position to respond with anger and violent revenge against Alexander following the death of his powerful supporter, James the Gross, the aggrieved David used this careful narrative of honor to save face.[71]

Violence particular to this conflict did not erupt again until 1446. We have seen that this followed a civil war fought in the interim, during the course of which Adam Hepburn of Hailes had surrendered Dunbar Castle to William, the new earl of Douglas. In the spring of 1446, almost a year after the end of hostilities, Adam's son Patrick Hepburn recaptured the lost castle. We possess some additional details of this incident. With "malicious hands and heart" Patrick's followers "drawing and brandishing their swords" ambushed and kidnapped Prior Oll and six of his men on the king's highway between Edinburgh and Coldingham, holding them for ransom at Dunbar.[72] Hepburn's attack was condemned on 28 April 1446 by the king as "þe maisest tressonable takyn off our castell of dunbar Byrning heirschipp' [plundering] slawchtyr prisonying opprissyon' of our peple & distructyon' off our land." The king also ordered Hepburn to release his prisoners and Oll not to pay his ransom. As we have seen, he was eventually driven from the castle by a government-sponsored siege.[73]

Hepburn's obvious motive was the recovery of the castle. However, this does not explain his attack on Prior Oll. It is probable that the assault was done in reprisal for Alexander Hume's plundering raids on Hepburn's lands in 1442–3, in which Hume had used the priory as a base. By kidnapping Oll, the young Hepburn challenged Hume's ability to protect the priory. He also seems to have targeted Hume's allies with deadly violence. As will be shown below, Hepburn was later

---

Cohesive Force: Feud in the Mediterranean and the Middle East (Oxford, 1975), pp. 42–3 and 178–84; William I. Miller, *Bloodtaking and Peacemaking: Feud, Law and Society in Saga Iceland* (Chicago, 1990), esp. pp. 29–34, 193, 200, 207, 271–83 and 301–3.

[71] Cf. White, "Politics of Anger," pp. 138–46. On emotion and "the moral sentiments behind the violence," see Smail, "Hatred as a Social Institution," p. 92; Hyams, *Rancor*, ch. 2.

[72] DCM, Reg. Parv. III, fols 10r–v, printed in Coldingham, pp. 156–7, no. 168. Oll later described Patrick Hepburn's assault: "*Idem enim Patricius per iniquitatis suae fautores, quorum ipse auctor et caput existit, jacentes in insidiis, ac solum versantes in manibus et corde maligno dolos et obices contra insontes, in me et meos in via regia insultum gravem fecerunt, ac, gladiis extractis et vibratis, minas et terrores graves intentarunt, manus in nos violentas injecerunt, bona nostra direpcioni et praedacioni dederunt, et ad castrum de Dunbar, ubi dictus Patricius, ut violentus intrusor dominatur, adduxerunt.*"

[73] Raine, *North Durham*, appendix, p. 22, no. 96; *Coldingham*, pp. 156–7, no. 168. Patrick Cockburn, the royal keeper of Dalkeith castle, was later reimbursed for his part in the siege: ER, vol. 5, p. 305; Dunlop, pp. 76–7; McGladdery, pp. 24 and 39–40; Brown, *Black Douglases*, p. 275.

to make an endowment for the souls of "Robyne of Nesbet" and "Williame of Chyrnside," implying that he bore responsibility for killing these men. In all probability these were the slaughters to which the king referred in his letter. Moreover, one of the hostages taken by Hepburn was James Nisbet, perhaps a relation.[74] Violence was no longer confined to plundering raids, but was now directed with lethality against supporters. Oll's description of the assault, which highlighted his opponents' malice of heart and ambush on the king's highway, elements of Scottish and English homicide law at the time, further illustrates this point.[75] Thus, Hepburn's attack was both deadly and directed against Alexander Hume's interests.

Such grave violence seems to have led to a chain of vengeance in 1446. It will be recalled that in the 1430s Adam Hepburn of Hailes had been pivotal in the fall of George Dunbar, earl of March, and in repelling the border raid of Patrick Dunbar at Piperdean. When, in April 1446, Patrick Hepburn violently reclaimed the Dunbars' ancestral castle as his own, this public action (later said by Oll to be common gossip "under all the skies of Britain") was intolerable to the disinherited Dunbars, and seems to have stirred their long-standing animosities with the Hepburns.[76] Archibald Dunbar, another son of the former earl of March, turned to violence on St. Andrew's day, 30 November, when he captured the Hepburns'

---

[74] "Robyne" may be identified with the Robert Nisbet who was Alexander Hume's messenger to Durham in 1442, and the same man mentioned by Alexander in the foundation charter for his collegiate church of Dunglass in 1444: DCM, Reg. Parv. II, fol. 154r–v, printed in *Coldingham*, pp. 136–8, no. 152; Raine, *North Durham*, appendix, p. 22, no. 96; Fraser, *Buccleuch*, vol. 2, pp. 39–41, no. 44; HMC, *Twelfth Report, Appendix, Part 8*, pp. 124–6, no. 123. Chirnside was a place in Berwickshire and William may have been Alexander's tenant there. Patrick Nisbet of that Ilk acted as a witness at Coldingham in 1433 (NAS, GD 12/31). Thomas Nisbet became the new prior of Coldingham in 1446 (*Coldingham*, pp. 157–8, no. 169). See also Dunlop, pp. 76–7. A David Chirnside and a William Nisbet sat on an assize at Lauder in 1440: HMC, *Twelfth Report, Appendix, Part 8*, p. 161, no. 256.

[75] See above, n. 71. F.W. Maitland, "The Early History of Malice Aforethought," in *The Collected Papers of Frederic William Maitland*, ed. H.A.L. Fisher (3 vols, Cambridge, 1911), vol. 1, pp. 304–28; W.D.H. Sellar, "Forethocht Felony, Malice Aforethought and the Classification of Homicide," in W.M. Gordon and T.D. Fergus (eds), *Legal History in the Making* (London, 1991), pp. 43–59; W.D.H. Sellar, "Was it murder? John Comyn of Badenoch and William, earl of Douglas," in C.J. Kay and M.A. MacKay (eds), *Perspectives on the Older Scottish Tongue: A Celebration of DOST* (Edinburgh, 2005), pp. 132–8.

[76] DCM, Reg. Parv. III, fols 10r–v; Coldingham, pp. 156–7, no. 168: "*cum per omnia climata tocius Britanniae in ore omnium tam magnatum quam popularium fabula sit et publice praedicatum.*" Translated quotation from Dunlop, pp. 76–8. Boardman, *Early Stewart Kings*, pp. 228–9, 237, 246; Brown, *James I*, p. 154; Brown, *Black Douglases*, p. 275; McGladdery, pp. 39–40; Dobson, *Durham Priory*, p. 325.

castle of Hailes.[77] It is worth speculating that the timing of Dunbar's attack on this feast day may have been meant to draw the attention of James Kennedy, bishop of St. Andrews, his father's feudal superior. It is probable that Dunbar's attack was also lethal, for, after this time, Adam Hepburn disappears from record.[78]

A chain of reciprocal events in 1446 thus began when, taking revenge against both the earl of Douglas and Alexander Hume, Patrick Hepburn captured Dunbar Castle and Prior Oll. In response, Archibald Dunbar retaliated against the Hepburns by capturing Hailes Castle. Finally, the Douglases responded in force and Archibald Dunbar soon lost Hailes when he "cowardlie gaf it ower to the master of douglas sodanlie." The Humes seem to have stood back from this cycle of violence, choosing not to seek revenge for the deaths of Nisbet and Chirnside. Both Alexander and David waited patiently in Stirling with the earl of Douglas, witnessing a charter there on 10 May 1446.[79] It may have been the hand of Douglas that restrained the Humes and stopped this cycle of retaliatory violence from expanding further. If so, the Humes had much to gain from holding back. With the Dunbars excluded and the Hepburns marginalized, and both the castles of Dunbar and Hailes under Douglas dominance, the Humes were the local winners of 1446.

A final point to be made regarding this violent disputing concerns those who were involved. Ties of kinship were obviously important in determining who acted in vengeance. Patrick Hepburn retaliated on his father's behalf for the loss of the family's stronghold. Likewise, Archibald Dunbar retaliated on behalf of his brother Patrick, and his family's wider interest. William, earl of Douglas was able to count on his brother (the "master of Douglas," probably Archibald, earl

---

[77] "Auchinleck Chronicle," fol. 111r, printed in McGladdery, p. 162. The death of the earl of Angus, whose interests were opposed to those of the Dunbars, sometime before September 1446 (Fraser, *Douglas Book*, vol. 2, p. 42) may have presented an opportunity for the settling of scores. After his forfeiture, the former earl of March was known as Sir George Dunbar of Kilconquhar, an estate in Fife held of the bishop: ER, vol. 5, pp. 383, 435 and 497; *Scots Peerage*, vol. 3, p. 277; Brown, *James I*, pp. 154–6; Dunlop, p. 78, n. 1.

[78] A verse quarrel ("flyting") written about 1505, between the poets William Dunbar and Walter Kennedy, alludes to this incident, claiming that "Archbald Dunbar betrasd the house of Hailis/Because the 3ung Lord had Dumbar to keip." See *The Flyting of Dunbar and Kennedy* in William Dunbar, *The Poems of William Dunbar*, ed. John Small et al. (5 vols, Scottish Text Society, Edinburgh, 1893), vol. 2, p. 21, lines 299–300. In the 1570s Pitscottie wrote about the incident: "attour Archebald Dunbar seigit the castell of Haillis in Lowtheane and at the first assault he wan the samin and slew them all that he fand thairin. He schortlie thairefter was beseigit be James Douglas in quhois will he put himself and the castell but ony farder debaitt." Robert Lindsay of Pitscottie, *The Historie and Cronicles of Scotland*, ed. A.J.G. Mackay (3 vols, Scottish Text Society, Edinburgh, 1899–1911), vol. 1, p. 56. I am grateful to Christine McGladdery for this last reference.

[79] "Auchinleck Chronicle," fol. 111r, printed in McGladdery, p. 162; HMC, *Fourteenth Report, Appendix, Part 3*, pp. 24–5, no. 49; Fraser, *Douglas Book*, vol. 3, p. 427, no. 415.

of Moray) to besiege Hailes Castle.[80] However, as the dispute within the Hume family illustrates, Scottish kin groups were hardly monolithic blocs of allies. If a shared surname was the "test of kinship" in late medieval Scotland, it is perhaps not surprising that, when uncle fought against nephew, both parties were denied the full network of relatives to whom they might otherwise turn for support and upon whom they later came to rely.[81] As we shall see shortly, more distant ties of kinship existed between the Humes and the Hepburns, and these too were overcome by conflict.

While kin were clearly important in violent processes as both allies and enemies, the surviving evidence offers little information on the identities of the disputants' other supporters when force was deployed. In a letter dated 1440 to Prior Wessington, David Hume spoke of "my kyn and my frends" who would support him in the defense of Coldingham if he asked them.[82] Even this reference takes us no great distance for, in Scotland, as in some other parts of medieval Europe, the term friend could carry connotations of kinship, and so David may well have been speaking of his close and more distant kin.[83] However, in the violence of 1442, he referred to his own armed following more generally as his "repayr" and, later, as his "familiars." Prior Wessington similarly described David's followers as his "*familia et complicibus.*" These vague terms probably encompassed David's kin and friends, but it is not clear if they were meant to include his tenants as well. When speaking of his opponent, David called Alexander's men "refars [reivers] of the kings liegs," sanctimoniously condemning them as illicit raiders. Still, he did not say what exactly their relationship was to Alexander. He did accuse his nephew of selling stolen livestock to Englishmen who were, by implication, receivers and

---

[80] James and Archibald Douglas were twins and only in 1447 was James recognized as the first-born (RMS, vol. 2, pp. 68–9, no. 301). James, the future ninth earl, was bishop of Aberdeen from 1441 (Brown, *Black Douglases*, p. 269). Of course, Pitscottie's later account, given above in n. 78, claims that it was James.

[81] Wormald, "Bloodfeud," pp. 68–71, quote from p. 68. On intra-kin disputes, see Brown, *Bloodfeud*, pp. 76–9; K.M. Brown, "A House Divided: Family and Feud in Carrick under John Kennedy, fifth Earl of Cassillis," *Scottish Historical Review*, 75 (1996): 168–96, at pp. 94–6; Miller, *Bloodtaking*, p. 160; Black-Michaud, *Cohesive Force*, pp. 28–30, 51 and 228–35.

[82] *Coldingham*, p. 113, no. 127.

[83] Wormald, *Lords and Men*, pp. 79–90, esp. p. 83; Marc Bloch, *La société féodale* (Paris, 1939–40), pp. 183–6; Jacques Le Goff, "The Symbolic Ritual of Vassalage," in *Time, Work and Culture in the Middle Ages*, trans. Arthur Goldhammer (Chicago, 1980), pp. 260–61; Paul R. Hyams, "Homage and Feudalism: A Judicious Separation," in Natalie Fryde (ed.), *Die Gegenwart des Feudalismus* (Veröffentlichungen des Max-Planck-Instituts für Geschichte, vol. 173, Göttingen, 2003), pp. 13–49, at p. 39; Hyams, *Rancor*, pp. 9, 23; Geary, "Conflicts," pp. 136–9; S.D. White, "Clothild's Revenge: Politics, Kinship and Ideology in the Merovingian Bloodfeud," in S.K. Cohn and S.A. Epstein (eds), *Portraits of Medieval and Renaissance Living: Essays in Memory of David Herlihy* (Michigan, 1996), pp. 120 and 125.

may have been contacts in Alexander's wider support group.[84] More specifically, Robert Nisbet and William Chirnside, apparently killed by Hepburn in 1446, as noted above, can be counted among the local supporters of Alexander Hume.

The making of peace

Having examined the violent processes of this case, it now remains to consider the processes of pacification and compromise. Evidence survives for various attempted resolutions in the course of events, in 1425, 1441, 1444 and 1449. These resolutions had different results, and that of 1441, at least, proved completely ineffective. They show that successful peacemaking was not just about the restoration of order (although of course tensions had to de-escalate for negotiations to occur), such as might be achieved through the execution of an offender by a court of law, a forced exile or blunt coercion by a greater authority demanding an end to hostilities. While such outcomes could impose a neutral peace, and even further a party's interests, they did nothing to change the underlying tensions and hostile relationships between combatants which stoked the fires of grievance. By contrast, an effective compromise made peace by building new, positive relationships, transforming the structures which generated conflict.[85] This is an important point which has not been given adequate consideration in existing studies of Scottish dispute and feud.[86] With particular regard to vengeance in this case, we shall see how effective compromise placed disputants into a new arrangement of relations in which the desire to take revenge became irrelevant.

Magnates had a crucial role in peacemaking. This point has been made by Jenny Wormald who, in her pioneering work on feud in Scotland, observed that pacification regularly depended upon strong individual lordship.[87] The same has been found on both sides of the Anglo-Scottish borderlands in the fifteenth century, at least when disputes involved serious violence between opposing groups of supporters.[88] Patrick Geary's work on an earlier period in France helpfully points us towards an explanation for the importance of such strong lordship.[89] A powerful

---

[84] DCM, Misc. Ch. 1087; Reg. Parv. II, fols 142r–v and 142v–143v; DCM, Reg. III, fol. 276r; *Coldingham*, pp. 117–18, 139–40 and 147–50, nos 133, 154 and 160.

[85] Cf. Geary, "Conflicts," pp. 148 and 154–9; Powell, *Kingship*, pp. 102 and 107; Hyams, *Rancor*, pp. 12 and 16.

[86] Wormald, "Bloodfeud," pp. 74–6; Wormald, *Lords and Men*, chs 6 and 7. On lordship in Scottish disputes, see also Brown, *Bloodfeud*, pp. 48–9 and 72–3.

[87] Wormald, "Bloodfeud," pp. 74–6; Wormald, *Lords and Men*, p. 121. On lordship in Scottish disputes, see also Brown, *Bloodfeud*, pp. 48–9 and 72–3.

[88] Armstrong, *Local Conflict*, ch. 8.

[89] Geary, "Conflicts," pp. 150, 155, 159. See also R.V. Gould, "Revenge as Sanction and Solidarity Display: An Analysis of Vendettas in Nineteenth-Century Corsica," *American Sociological Review*, 56 (2000): 682–704, at pp. 699–702; Hyams, *Rancor*, p. 9.

magnate's influence was necessary to overcome the inertia of a group's desire to preserve the relationships of conflict which lent it cohesion. The personal authority of a great lord could facilitate the negotiation of new relationships, oversee the transformation of old enmity into new amity, and enforce the bonds of the new arrangement until, like glue, they stuck on their own.

A letter from Prior Wessington to Adam Hepburn of Hailes some time in 1442, in which he asked Hepburn to intervene again for "good concorde" between the Humes stated simply the role of a peacemaking lord. He asked Hepburn that, lest "the fyre of ire kyndild betwixt thaym grow to fer [too bold], as yhe hafe begun yhe will labor to staunch."[90] This is the only evidence from this dispute for the use of a word for "anger" in our modern sense, and it illustrates the objective of quenching the enmity that might escalate into acts of serious violence. It foreshadows the cycle of vengeance that was to occur in 1446.[91] Nevertheless, it appears that Hepburn was not powerful enough to make peace between the Humes. Despite sitting on the royal minority council, he was still only a laird and did not have the influence of a great magnate. His attempt at arbitration in 1441 failed, and he became a target himself, suffering Alexander Hume's raiding in 1442.[92] By contrast, James, earl of Angus, was powerful enough to broker a peace between the Humes in January 1444. At this stage in the conflict, the failed arbitrator Adam Hepburn took part merely as a supporter of David Hume's cause before the earl's council.[93]

In the early attempts at peacemaking in this dispute we can again see how relationships of lordship stretched across the border. Prior Wessington's register contains correspondence between himself and both Humes, Hepburn, the earl of Angus and others involved in the dispute, and reveals the prelate's efforts to engineer a resolution.[94] However, Wessington's role in the peacemaking process, like Hepburn's, was limited. He relied primarily upon Hepburn to call the disputants to compromise and it is revealing that after Hepburn's attempt at arbitration failed, Wessington soon lost influence over the dispute as well.

---

[90] DCM, Reg. Parv. II, 154r–v, printed in *Coldingham*, pp. 136–8, no. 152. Internal evidence suggests this undated letter was probably written after Palm Sunday, 25 March 1442.

[91] Elsewhere David Hume uses the verb "to aungyr," but in the obsolete sense of to bother or trouble (his kin and friends to support him) (*Coldingham*, p. 113, no. 127). Wessington seems to have drawn on imagery from Deuteronomy 32:22: '*ignis succensus est in furore meo et ardebit usque ad inferni novissima*' (a fire is kindled in my anger/wrath, and shall burn even to the last/lowest hell).

[92] DCM, Reg. Parv. II, fols 146r–v; *Coldingham*, p. 122, no. 136; Godscroft, p. 8; Dunlop, p. 52, n. 1; Brown, *Black Douglases*, pp. 257–8.

[93] According to Godscroft, David was supported in the arbitration by Adam Hepburn and Alexander was supported by his brother, George Hume of Spott: Godscroft, p. 9; HMC *Milne-Home Report*, p. 21, no. 8; McGladdery, p. 39; Dunlop, pp. 53–4.

[94] *Coldingham*, pp. 109–65.

Wessington's ties of ecclesiastical and cross-border lordship did not rival the immediate regional lordship of a lay Scottish magnate like James the Gross, seventh earl of Douglas, who was able to break apart the Hume compromise in 1442, or like Angus, who was able to resolve it in 1444. Wessington resigned as prior of Durham in June 1446, and he had no role in the episodes of conflict erupting that year or after. Instead, it was clearly the regional and national pre-eminence in the late 1440s of William, eighth earl of Douglas that created the climate for reconciliation between the Humes and Hepburns. Douglas, dominant before the young king emerged as an independent adult sovereign in 1449, led the realm in war against England in 1448–9.[95] Thus, military concerns may have made the repair of relationships between border lairds paramount, and the Hume–Hepburn agreement of February 1449 was a sign of the Hepburns' return to favor with the Black Douglas regime.[96] It is clear that effective peacemaking was best achieved under the influence of great lay lords.

The risk of failure in achieving compromise was high. If tensions between parties were addressed ineffectively, or if circumstances changed, they were liable to resurface. For example, consider the agreement made in 1425 between Alexander Hume of that Ilk and David Hume of Wedderburn, to share the profits of the bailiary of Coldingham no matter who should acquire it.[97] In this instance, a cooperative financial arrangement was reached between uncle and nephew, and it is impressive that this compromise endured successfully for fifteen years through significant regional and national upheavals. Nevertheless, competitive tensions between uncle and nephew remained dormant. The simple terms of this agreement could not restrain their re-emergence in 1440 as Alexander reached adulthood and as major political renegotiations occurred on a national scale.

---

[95] Fraser, *Buccleuch*, vol. 2, pp. 39–41, no. 44. Warfare was mostly focused in the west march in 1448–9. In December 1448, Douglas held a conference to codify new wartime statutes for the marches: APS, vol. 1, pp. 714–16; George Neilson, "The March Laws," ed. T.I. Rae (Stair Society, Miscellany 1, Edinburgh, 1971); George Neilson, "The Battle of the Sark," *Transactions of the Dumfriesshire and Galloway Natural History and Antiquarian Society*, 13 (1898 for 1896–7): 122–31; "Auchinleck Chronicle," fols 113r and 123r, printed in McGladdery, pp. 164, 173, and see also p. 40; Brown, *Black Douglases*, pp. 276–7; Dunlop, p. 77.

[96] From at least Whitsunday 1450 Patrick Hepburn of Hailes served as royal steward of March: ER, vol. 5, p. 486. Unlike Alexander Hume, Hepburn does not seem to have accompanied the earl of Douglas on his pilgrimage to the papal jubilee between October 1450 and April 1451. Yet, in March 1451, the Hepburns married into another family of long-time Douglas adherents in Lothian, the Haliburtons: RMS, vol. 2, p. 98, no. 437. However, Brown views Patrick Hepburn as an enemy of Earl William right up to Douglas's death in 1452: Brown, *Black Douglases*, pp. 287, 289 and 292.

[97] HMC, *Milne-Home Report*, p. 19, no.3. Prior Wessington later recalled the two men coming to him in agreement at this time: DCM, Reg. Parv. II, fols 154r–v, printed in *Coldingham*, pp. 136–8, no. 152.

The consequences of a clumsy or partial resolution can also readily be seen in 1444–6. Even though the Hepburns had already been drawn into the conflict between Alexander and David Hume, the peace agreed in 1444 encompassed the Humes alone. As a result, in 1446, an unsatisfied Patrick Hepburn sought revenge against Alexander by means of his ransom-taking and attack on Dunbar Castle. Similarly, peace had not been made between the Hepburns and the Dunbar family after the fall of the earl of March in 1434–5; the Dunbars had simply been removed from power. This abrupt rearrangement, far from a mutually acceptable compromise, left the Dunbars with almost nothing to lose. Even after their elimination from the local network of landed society, the Dunbars' relationship of enmity with the Hepburns endured, to be acted upon at a later date.[98] Although hardly inevitable, the cycle of vengeance which played out in 1446 can be understood as a result of these ineffective or un-attempted compromises.

A powerful tool for successfully constructing new amicable relationships between former enemies was the giving and receiving of gifts.[99] One type of gift-giving was the donation of reparation, and, in Scotland, the term "assythment" denoted compensation payments of this sort offered in dispute resolutions. The principle of gift exchange in assythment is made clear in a letter from David Hume to Prior Wessington. Hume stated that, for the outstanding money owed to him by his nephew, he was ready "to mak asythe, & to hafe the same" (1443).[100] While Wormald has argued that such reparations served to restore the status quo,[101] it would appear that, in this dispute at least, the giving of assythment as a gift was not about returning relationships to their previous terms (which had generated conflict), but part of the process of making new bonds of friendship between old enemies, thus redrawing the very relationships between offender and offended, and in this way eliminating the desire of the aggrieved party for vengeance.

Some exchanges served not only to recognize the new arrangement of Alexander's ascendancy in the locality, but also to augment the strained ties of kinship between the disputants. The award between the Humes brokered in January 1444 by the earl of Angus provided for David to concede the office of bailie to his nephew and for him, in turn, to receive all the livestock taken from him by Alexander, silver in compensation for any not returned and half of the profits of

---

[98] The former earl of March lived out his days as Sir George Dunbar of Kilconquhar, in Fife: ER, vol. 5, pp. 383, 435 and 497; *Scots Peerage*, vol. 3, p. 277; Brown, *James I*, pp. 154–6; Dunlop, p. 78, n. 1. And see above, n. 77.

[99] S.D. White, "'*Pactum ... Legum Vincit et Amor Judicium*': The Settlement of Disputes by Compromise in Eleventh-century Western France," *American Journal of Legal History*, 22 (1978): 281–308, at p. 302; Geary, "Conflicts," p. 156, and see Geary's comments at p. 156, n. 88.

[100] *Coldingham*, p. 149, no. 160.

[101] Wormald, "Bloodfeud," pp. 74–6; Wormald, *Lords and Men*, p. 121.

the bailiary for the preceding term.[102] A further gesture of good will came in March, in the chapter house at St. Andrews Cathedral, when Alexander mentioned David as one of the spiritual beneficiaries of the foundation of his collegiate church of Dunglass.[103] Here friendly acts renovated the bonds between kinsmen, restoring not the undesirable status quo, but the expectations of kindly behavior.

An illustrative contrast is the unsuccessful arbitration of 1441, which may have collapsed not only because of Hepburn's limited authority, but also because it did not include an equivalent friendly exchange of gifts. However, the Hume–Hepburn reconciliation of 1449 did involve analogous gift giving. The contract itself required Hepburn to endow a perpetual priest in Hume's college of Dunglass "for the plesance of God and the frendis of" the deceased Robert Nisbet and William Chirnside. Then, in August 1450, both Alexander Hume and Patrick Hepburn made grants to Dunglass church. Hepburn's grant, stating specifically that it was for the salvation of the souls of the dead King James I, the bishop of St. Andrews, Hepburn himself, Hume, Nisbet and Chirnside was, therefore, a publicly visible gift made in part to Hume and the dead men. Two days earlier, Hume had made a similar donation to his own church, for the salvation of the dead king, the living bishop and his dead father. His gift was of various lands in Chirnside, which may suggest some significance for the dead William Chirnside.[104] The charters were dated only two days apart, and were confirmed together by the king within three weeks. Although Hume's gift was not made to Hepburn, and Hepburn's gift appears larger than Hume's—details which may indicate acknowledgement of Hume's superiority in the arrangement—the implication is that they were complementary acts, symbolizing the shared objectives of the new friendship.[105]

---

[102] According to Godscroft, Angus awarded that Alexander restore to David 800 sheep and 35 oxen, and any teinds (tithes) taken by dubious right: HMC, *Milne-Home Report*, p. 21, no. 8; Godscroft, p. 9; McGladdery, p. 39; Dunlop, pp. 53–4.

[103] Dunlop, p. 54; HMC, *Twelfth Report, Appendix, Part 8*, pp. 124–6, no. 123. Alexander's father had been a patron of the chapel of St. Mary of Dunglass: ibid., pp. 123–4, no. 122. That the charter was done in St. Andrews led Dunlop to suggest, reasonably, that Bishop Kennedy had played a role in the Hume reconciliation. Nevertheless, both Humes acted as procurators that year and the next for Coldingham against Kennedy in litigation over the patronage of Berwickshire churches: DCM, Reg. IV, fol. 25. See also Dunlop, pp. 53–4 and 80.

[104] In 1380, George Dunbar, then earl of March, had exchanged with Coldingham Priory the lands of Chirnside for the lands of Aldcambus: Brown, "Priory of Coldingham," p. 93.

[105] Fraser, *Buccleuch*, vol. 2, pp. 39–41, no. 44; RMS, vol. 2, p. 89, nos 387 and 389; HMC, *Twelfth Report, Appendix, Part 8*, pp. 126–7, nos 124–5. Dunlop suggests that the mention of Bishop Kennedy implies he again had a role in peacemaking: Dunlop, pp. 77 and 117. Hepburn's grant was witnessed by his brothers William and George, and by his relative Alexander Hepburn, esquire, among others. Hume's grant was witnessed by his eldest son Alexander, his brothers Thomas Hume of Tyninghame (on whose property the contract was made) and George Hume of Spott, and by his relatives James and Finlay Hume (perhaps sons of Thomas), among others.

As they were in violent processes, disputants' supporters were integral to efforts at conciliation. In 1442 the Prior Wessington expressed his hope that both David and Alexander Hume, "and thar frendshipp" (in the sense of their groups of friends) should be content with a compromise plan. In the same place he listed four witnesses in Alexander's "party," and it is reasonable to count these men among his "frendshipp." They were George Hume (probably his brother, of Spott), Edmund Hay (probably another Scot) and two others, John Ogle and one "Collyngwood," whose names suggest that they were lesser Northumberland gentlemen. In this instance we can see friendly supporters in peacemaking stretching across the frontier, links evidently facilitated by Durham Priory.[106]

The concept of friendship appears a number of times in the Hume–Hepburn contract of 1449. The mention of Nisbet and Chirnside's friends has been noted, but the agreement also included provisions that "supprisis [attacks] and scathis [injuries]" done by each party "salbe amendit" to the "plesance and worschipe [honor]" of the other, by the sight of their "speciale frendis," not named.[107] Contingency plans were laid that any future "strevis" (strifes) happening between them "and thair frendis or men" should be resolved through the "ordenance and consale of four or sex of thair nerrest frendis." The success of the previous resolution between Alexander and David is apparent here in that they are mentioned as being one party, with the same special friends, seeking amends from Hepburn.[108] Friends were fundamental to the pacification of the present dispute and, more importantly, they were to be called upon again should this agreement fail.

Kinship was an important bond of support for contending parties and for a lesser peacemaker. To some extent, it was a flexible category that overlapped with friendship. Although the exact relationship between the families is unclear, in 1441 Wessington asked Adam Hepburn of Hailes to treat between the Humes as he was the "most worthy of thayre kyn."[109] When he did arbitrate that year, he involved as co-arbitrators his eldest son, Patrick, his relative Patrick Hepburn

---

[106] DCM, Reg. Parv. II, fols 154r–v; *Coldingham*, p. 137, no 152. The Ogles were prominent in Northumberland (although a family of the same name resided at Papple near Haddington), and the lesser Collingwoods had branches in northern Northumberland.

[107] On the concept of "worship," a term for reputation and honor, see Carpenter, *Locality and Polity*, pp. 198–9, 245 and 347–50; Maddern, "Honour Among the Pastons," pp. 357–8.

[108] Fraser, *Buccleuch*, vol. 2, pp. 39–41, no. 44 (20 February 1449).

[109] DCM, Reg. Parv. II, fols 146r–v; *Coldingham*, p. 122, no. 136. In his will of 1424, Alexander Hume's father appointed his brothers Patrick and David Hume, and Patrick Hepburn of Waughton, as his executors, perhaps suggesting that Hepburn was Hume's brother-in-law: HMC, *Twelfth Report, Appendix, Part 8*, pp. 87–8, no. 1. A possible link through the Lauders and Landells is hinted at in CSSR, vol. 1, pp. 96–7. See the papal dispensation sought by Alexander Hume and Agnes Hepburn, on 2 January 1451, being within the third and third degrees of affinity. Their request, supported by the king, also noted that Agnes's father, Adam Hepburn, had been godfather to Alexander at his baptism: *Calendar of Entries in the Papal Registers*, vol. 10, pp. 217–18.

of Waughton "and other common friends."[110] In June 1443, when cooperation seems to have prevailed as the various disputants witnessed a Hume deed at Dunglass, a number of kin were involved at the proceedings. David Hume was present with his son David junior, Alexander Hume brought his brothers George and Thomas, and Adam Hepburn of Hailes appeared with his kinsmen Patrick Hepburn of Waughton and William Hepburn.[111] In 1444, when the dispute came before Angus's comital council, Alexander Hume was supported by his brother George.[112] It seems that the unsuccessful arbitrator Adam Hepburn recognized his relatively weak authority and thus sought to reinforce his position with a network of kin. By contrast, the more confident earl of Angus does not seem to have done the same.

Finally, we return to the point that vengeance was eliminated through the building of new relationships. The ideal of new amity was well expressed in the most effective resolution, the Hume–Hepburn agreement of 1449. The principal parties, called "honorabile men [,] ... accordit that fathful frendschipe, kyndnes, and lawte salbe kepit betuix thaim, lelely and threuly, withoutyn fraude or gile for all the dayis of thair lifis."[113] Thus, honorable virtues like faithfulness, loyalty and truthfulness buttressed the relationships of friendship and kinship ("kyndnes"),[114] terms which were the polar opposite of those expressed by the aggrieved David Hume in his letter of 1443, discussed above. The Hume–Hepburn agreement backed up its high expectations with clear action. It was built around a double marriage contract between the two (already distantly related) families. Wormald has demonstrated that marriage contracts were often associated with late medieval and early modern Scottish dispute pacifications. She has argued that they could be used to compensate for a killing, in which case the daughter or sister of a deceased victim might wed a close relative of the man who had killed her "natural protector," thereby making suitable reparation.[115] However, like assythment, such

---

[110] *"aliosque communes amicos."* Hepburn of Waughton was called *"comarcho"* (borderer?) by Hume of Godscroft, writing more than a century later: Godscroft, p. 8. See also Dunlop, p. 52, n. 1.

[111] HMC, *Fourteenth Report, Appendix, Part 3*, p. 18, no. 31: Alexander Hume's wife Mariot Lauder made a grant to Andrew Kerr of Altonburn, and the other witnesses included William Seton, the son of deceased Alexander Seton Lord Gordon, and Robert Lauder of Edrington.

[112] George Hume of Spott: Godscroft, p. 9.

[113] Fraser, *Buccleuch*, vol. 2, pp. 39–41, no. 44.

[114] *Dictionary of the Scots Language*, ed. S.C. Rennie et al. (Department of English, University of Dundee, 2001–). Consulted at http://www.dsl.ac.uk/ (last accessed 1 July 2007). S.v. "kind."

[115] Wormald, "Bloodfeud," p. 74. For other examples, see Brown, *Bloodfeud*, p. 130; H.L. MacQueen, "Survival and Success: The Kennedys of Dunure," in S.I. Boardman and Alasdair Ross (eds), *The Exercise of Power in Medieval Scotland* (Dublin, 2003), pp. 67–94, at p. 87; M.H. Brown, "Earldom and Kindred: The Lennox and its Earls, 1200–1458,"

peace-weaving marriages were not meant to return relationships to their previous structure of conflict, but rather to forge a new structure entirely. The Hepburns were no strangers to such marriages for, in 1431, one Archibald Hepburn and his bride had sought dispensation to marry within the third degree of kinship, in order "to settle discords among their kinsfolk."[116]

In 1449 a contract of kinship between the Humes and Hepburns was not just coincidental to peacemaking, but it actually functioned as *the* tool of compromise itself, incorporating the other terms of conciliation.[117] By this means, existing and strained kinship ties between the Humes and Hepburns were renovated with new betrothals. Ellen Hume, the daughter of Alexander, was to marry Adam, the underage son of Patrick Hepburn, and Alexander Hume junior, the son of Alexander, was to marry Agnes, the sister of Patrick Hepburn. Provision was made to ensure that marriages would be secured between the families even if the engaged couples died.[118] The principle of linking the kindreds in marriage was a powerful symbol for the resolution of conflict, especially if marriage is understood as a highly ritualized ceremony of gift-exchange. Both parties transformed their enmities into new bonds of amity through the public giving and receiving of daughters, sisters, sons and spouses into a new web of kinship. In this way, the relationships of the old dispute, the only context in which vengeance would remain relevant, were superseded. Both these marriages proved successful and produced children and heirs.[119]

---

in Boardman and Ross (eds), *Exercise of Power*, pp. 201–24, at p. 214. Richard Hoyle has also argued that marriages were used to heal rifts among the nobility in mid-sixteenth-century northern England: Richard W. Hoyle, "Faction, Feud and Reconciliation Amongst the Northern English Nobility, 1525–1569," *History*, 84 (1999): 590–613, at pp. 612–13. For pacifying marriages in earlier periods and on the continent, see Hyams, "Homage and Feudalism," p. 29; Le Goff, "Symbolic Ritual of Vassalage," pp. 237–87; Emile Chénon, "Recherches historiques sur quelques rites nuptiaux," *Nouvelle revue historique de droit français et étranger*, 36 (1912): 573–660.

[116] The bride was Christian Herring: CSSR, vol. 3, pp. 197–8. Cooperation between the families is found in June 1443, when a deed by John Herring "lord of Edmerisdene" was witnessed by Sir Adam Hepburn of Hailes, Patrick his son and heir, and Sir Patrick Hepburn of Waughton: RMS, vol. 2, p. 112, no. 497. B.A. McAndrew, *Scotland's Historic Heraldry* (Woodbridge, 2006), p. 303, shows that the Herrings (also spelled Heron) bore arms of feudal dependence on the Hepburns.

[117] On contracts of lordship and friendship in peacemaking, see Wormald, *Lords and Men*, pp. 21–3, 85, 122, 126, 129–30; Armstrong, *Local Conflict*, ch. 8.

[118] Fraser, *Buccleuch*, vol. 2, pp. 39–41, no. 44.

[119] *Scots Peerage*, vol. 2, p. 158 and vol. 9, p. 107. On marriage as gift-exchange, see Geary, "Conflicts," p. 156.

Conclusions

This foregoing discussion illustrates an exceptionally well-documented late medieval Scottish dispute. This case conveys the importance of accustomed practices of conflict management, including the use of violence and the negotiation of compromise. Although illustrative of the way in which such accustomed practices worked, it inevitably under-represents the degree to which these practices, especially those related to compromise, could be facilitated by the king's law and the judicial system. For medieval Scotland there is very limited evidence to show the use of the law (relevant legal records, other than stray items, which might have pointed us in this direction simply do not survive until the later fifteenth century); and there is equally limited evidence for the law of the march used in its domestic or international guises. Still, in this particular dispute, remarkably little of the judicial system is visible: all that can be seen is James the Gross as justiciar promoting David Hume in 1442. Even the arbitrations which took place do not seem to have arisen from or run parallel to judicial activity.

Nevertheless, there is much to be learned from this example. Violent processes in this dispute were not confined to threats or restrained symbolic acts, or even to disruptive raiding, for violence escalated up to lethal assaults against people and fortresses. Even this last step, the most serious type of violence, was not atypical of Scottish disputing, but it was a sign of extreme tensions shooting beyond the more commonplace, and usually non-lethal, plundering of lands and tenants which was a regular part of political competition in Scotland. All these degrees of violence tended to provoke a retributive response and, in such a way, this case from the Scottish marches is representative of patterns detected by others elsewhere in the realm. Even so, an important consideration in future work on this theme will be to investigate regional differences across the kingdom.[120]

With regard to the making of peace, this analysis brings to the existing literature on conflict resolution in Scotland a highly significant point derived from studies of conflict in other contexts. Restoration of the status quo was only a first step in pacification, not the final objective. If opposing parties sought to make a sincere conciliation with each other, what was typically described as "good concorde," the necessary requirement was the building of new amicable relationships in place of old hostile ones. The result was to extinguish the context in which any lingering desires for revenge could be acted upon. Of course this was not the only way for pacification to be achieved. A greater authority could simply impose a ceasefire on combatants, or one side could be driven off; the latter is what happened to the

---

[120] On the non-lethal objectives of violence between magnates see Brown, *Black Douglases*, p. 90. On political competition, see Brown, "Scotland Tamed?"; Boardman, "Politics and the Feud," pp. vi and 434, and ch. 6 (on the Montgomery–Cunningham and Murray–Drummond disputes). On the degree to which violence could be kept within, or exceed, limits acceptable to both sides, see Brown, *Bloodfeud*, pp. 4–8, 27, 30–33, 72–3, 76–9, 97, 113.

Dunbars in the 1430s. Nevertheless, especially when a dispute had escalated to severe, lethal violence, relationship building was the surest road to success.[121]

The shape of the Hume–Hepburn–Dunbar conflict was defined by the relationships of friendship, kinship and lordship among the disputing parties, and these relationships were integral to how conflict was managed. All these bonds were of course soluble, and fights could arise between kin, friends, lords and men. Disputants relied upon kin and friends as allies when violence was necessary and, when parties came to compromise, they were involved as supporters and witnesses, and sometimes as arbitrators. The ties between lesser and greater men were important in all aspects of this dispute, from local competition, to violent action, and to the making of peace. Indeed the direct involvement of great lay magnates, like the earls of Douglas and Angus, seems to have moved the processes of conflict forward, causing violence to erupt (as in 1442) and peace to be made (as in 1444 and 1449). In the latter two examples of peacemaking, where new relationships were constructed, the powerful influence of magnates was a crucial coagulant.

The evidence for this dispute is all the more valuable for demonstrating that participants understood conflict in normative terms of status, honor and emotion. Violence was an assertion of authority, but it was also an honorable means to respond to grief and anger, by inflicting dishonor and shame on an enemy, in turn provoking further retribution. Yet once kindled the emotion of ire could grow "too" bold, crossing an invisible threshold beyond which lords, kin and friends compelled the enemies among them to make peace. When peace was made, honor and status remained at the forefront, and faithfulness, loyalty and truthfulness were to define new relationships of friendship and kinship. These relationships were far more than tools used in arid political gambits.[122] On the contrary, these were real ties between people with emotions and ambitions, and were no doubt shaped by the forces of personality and personal preference. Nevertheless, they existed within a wider social and political structure which gave them shape and purpose.

From a wider perspective on vengeance and feud in the Middle Ages, this example illustrates the significance of a firmly established border between two late medieval "states." Although not described by contemporaries as a feud, this conflict, which was certainly feud-like, not least in the exercise of vengeance, had a cross-border dimension in terms of its participants and in certain episodes of its prosecution. However, the international frontier presented such a barrier that tensions could not be resolved in a cross-border context. When an ecclesiastical lord like Prior Wessington attempted to direct pacification, he met with failure. This was a consequence of the Scottish realm's increased integrity during the fifteenth century, and the decline of English influence north of the border. Gone were the days of a peaceful thirteenth-century cross-border society and the English military

---

[121] Armstrong, *Local Conflict*, ch. 8.

[122] See the concerns expressed by A.J. Macdonald, "Kings of the Wild Frontier? The Earls of Dunbar or March, c.1070–1435," in Boardman and Ross (eds), *Exercise of Power*, pp 139–58, at p. 158, n. 100. Cf. White, "Politics of Anger," pp. 151–2.

domination of southern Scotland during much of the fourteenth century. Although Durham's cross-border links were the strongest among religious houses on both sides of the frontier at this time,[123] the English priory's influence in Scotland was waning quickly.[124] Thus, as a test-case for the significance of the frontier to conflict overlapping two late medieval "states," we can safely conclude that, despite its English dimension, this became a Scottish dispute, to be decided by participants on the northern side of the border.

The integrity of the Scottish realm in the fifteenth century, and the growing strength of the Stewart dynasty notwithstanding,[125] this example shows that the Scottish "state" had only a limited claim to the exclusive use of legitimate violence and an even more limited power to enforce public authority through coercive royal justice. Scottish governmental involvement in feud-like conflict management was best expressed in the arrangement of compensation for injuries through the king's law. But a strong king was needed for the royal judicial system to function effectively. In the borderlands at least, although the active rule of an adult king might exacerbate local conflict (and direct it to the royal courts), royal minorities could prove particularly destabilizing.[126] This dispute erupted during the minority of James II, which followed upon the assassination of James I, and escalated in a period of severe political strife during the mid-1440s. In pursuit of their objectives, disputants relied almost entirely on customary practices in the management of conflict. Acts of violent retribution were part of the normal course of Scottish political competition. But, at a time when governmental authority was at a low ebb, disputants relied almost entirely on customary practices in the management of conflict. An uncertain political settlement following the turbulent civil war of 1444–5 prompted a swift cycle of lethal vengeance to play out in 1446 and throughout the episodes of this conflict combatants relied upon great lay magnates to provide support and to direct the making of an honorable peace.

---

[123] See, for example, *Liber Sancte Marie de Melros*, ed. Cosmo Innes (2 vols, Bannatyne Club, vol. 56, Edinburgh, 1837), pp. 551–2 and 596–9, nos 550 and 577; Fraser, *Douglas Book*, vol. 3, p. 82, no. 86.

[124] Dobson, "Last English Monks."

[125] Brown, *James I*; McGladdery.

[126] Armstrong, *Local Conflict*, ch. 3. Cf. Boardman, "Politics and the Feud," p. 434.

APPENDIX

Figure 2.1 Pedigrees and Lists of Significant Parties (Abridged)

Humes of that Ilk

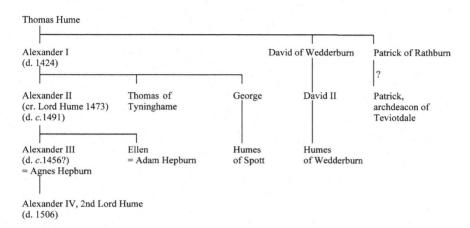

Hepburns of Hailes

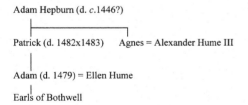

Dunbar earls of March

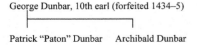

Black Douglases: Earls of Douglas

Archibald Douglas, 5th earl (d. 1439)
William Douglas, 6th earl (k. 1440)
James "the Gross" Douglas, 7th earl (d. 1443)
William Douglas, 8th earl (k. 1452)

Priors of Durham

John Wessington (1416–46)
William Ebchester (1446–56)

Bishop of St. Andrews

James Kennedy (1440–65)

Red Douglases: Earls of Angus

William Douglas, 2nd earl (d. 1437)
James Douglas, 3rd earl (d. 1446)
George Douglas, 4th earl (d. 1463)

Priors of Coldingham

William Drax (1419–41)
John Oll (1442–6)
Thomas Nisbet (1446–56)

Chapter 3
Living in Fear of Revenge: Religious Minorities and the Right to Bear Arms in Fifteenth-Century Portugal

François Soyer

The enforcement of law and order presented an inextricable dilemma for the Crown in the fifteenth-century kingdom of Portugal. The rulers of Portugal were faced by the conflicting necessities of ensuring their subjects were sufficiently well-equipped to serve in their armies in the event of war whilst at the same time tackling the very real threat to public order posed by the proliferation of armed men throughout their kingdom. Significantly, the response of the Crown was never to seek to restrict the *ownership* of weapons but rather to regulate the right of individuals to *carry* them in public. Various laws instituted by João I (1385–1433) attempted to limit the right to bear arms—beyond royal officials—to knights and the citizens of Lisbon. During the minority of Afonso V (1438–81), however, the regent Prince Pedro (d. 1449) liberalized the right to carry weapons publicly to include all free men on condition that no weapons were to be carried in public at night or used inappropriately. The only individuals who continued to be banned outright from bearing arms in public were clerics in holy orders, Jews and Muslims.[1]

This chapter will present the two very different contexts in which Jews and Muslims, notwithstanding the restrictive legislation imposed on them, were allowed to bear arms in medieval Portugal. The first part of this work will briefly examine the official use of Jews and Muslims in royal armies during the period under study. There is incontrovertible evidence that the Portuguese Crown did require the religious minorities to serve in its armies. The second section will focus on the special licenses to bear arms that were granted to Jews and Muslims in the fifteenth century. As was the case with most interdictions imposed upon Jews and Muslims, a few individuals were granted special licenses authorizing them to carry weapons exclusively for their self-defense. A number of these unusual documents have fortunately survived in the registers of the royal chanceries (*livros das chancelarias*) of Afonso V and his son João II (1481–95) which are

---

[1] L. Miguel Duarte, *Justiça e criminalidade no Portugal medievo* (Lisbon, 1999), pp. 285–369; J. Gouveia Monteiro, "Estado moderno e guerra: monopólio da violência e organisação militar," in M.H. da Cruz Coelho and A.L. de Carvalho Homem (eds), *A génese do estado moderno no Portugal tardo-medievo* (Lisbon, 1999), pp. 79–93.

preserved in the Portuguese national archives. After analyzing these documents and highlighting certain differences between those granted to Jews and those conferred on Muslims, this section seeks to prove the value of these licenses as historical evidence for a fierce blood feud that divided the Muslim community of the town of Évora in the middle of the fifteenth century. Additionally, three of the most interesting documents referred to in this article have been edited and translated and are included as an appendix.

Until King Manuel I (1495–1521) put an end to religious pluralism in 1496, Jewish and Muslim minorities resided in the kingdom of Portugal just as they did in the other Christian kingdoms of the Iberian Peninsula.[2] Organized into autonomous communities (*comunas*), they lived in segregated and gated areas of towns (*judiarias* and *mourarias*) and were not allowed to venture out of them after vespers. Furthermore, they were compelled to wear distinctive symbols on their clothing—a six-pointed red star for Jews as well as a yellow crescent for all "free Muslims" (*mouros forros*) and Muslim slaves—and were barred from taking part in municipal government as citizens (*vecinos*).[3] Amongst the long list of restrictions imposed on Jews and Muslims, the fact that they were prohibited from carrying weapons is often overlooked. In a society that valued martial prowess, the legal inability of Jews and Muslims to carry arms was a particularly clear marker of their social inferiority.[4]

The cohabitation of Christians, Jews and Muslims in the Christian kingdoms of the medieval Iberian Peninsula has been frequently upheld as a model of harmonious religious pluralism or, to use the contentious term coined by the historian Américo Castro (1885–1972), "*convivencia*."[5] Recently, however, historians working with the extant documentary evidence have formulated a far less harmonious picture of

---

[2] The forced mass conversion of the Jews and expulsion of the Muslims from Portugal in 1496–7 is the subject of my *The Persecution of the Jews and Muslims of Portugal (1496–7): King Manuel I and the End of Religious Tolerance* (E.J. Brill, Medieval Mediterranean Series, n° 69, 2007).

[3] For the status of Jews and Muslims (free and unfree) in Medieval Portugal, see *Ordenações Afonsinas*, bk II, title 86 (Jews); *Arquivo Nacional da Torre do Tombo* (A.N.T.T.), *Núcleo Antigo*, doc. 118, fols 172v–173 (Muslims) and A.N.T.T., *Chancelaria de D. Afonso V*, bk 16, fol. 39 and bk 17, fol. 84 as well as chapter 1 of Soyer, *Persecution of the Jews and Muslims of Portugal*.

[4] On medieval Portuguese Jewry, see Maria José Pimenta Ferro Tavares, *Os Judeus em Portugal no século XIV* (Lisbon, 1979) and *Os judeus em Portugal no século XV* (2 vols, Lisbon, 1982). On the Muslims, see M.F. Lopes de Barros "As comunas Muçulmanas em Portugal (Subsidios para seu estudo)," *Revista da Faculdade de Letras. História*, Porto, 2ª Serie, 7 (1990): 85–100 and *A comuna muçulmana de Lisboa* (Lisbon, 1998). For Muslim slaves, see F. Soyer, "Muslim Slaves and Freedmen in Medieval Portugal," *al-Qantara: Revista de Estudios Árabes*, 28, fasc. 2 (December 2007): 487–514.

[5] For Américo Castro's elaboration of the concept of *convivencia*, see his influential work, *España en su historia: cristianos, moros y judíos* (Buenos Aires, 1948). Also José Luis Gómez-Martínez, *Américo Castro y el origen de los españoles: historia de una polémica* (Madrid, 1975).

Christian–Muslim–Jewish relations and interaction. David Nirenberg, in particular, has argued that "violence was a central and systemic aspect of the coexistence of majority and minorities in Medieval Spain."[6] Such an observation certainly applies itself to Portugal, where both minorities were conscious of their precarious social position and of their vulnerability to popular violence. Actual violence against Portuguese Jews was relatively rare but their repeated appeals to the Crown for protection demonstrate their unease. Such fears of popular unrest were validated by the fact that the largest of the three Jewish quarters of Lisbon—the *Judiaria Grande*—was sacked by a Christian crowd in December 1449.[7]

The Muslim minority, though numerically less important than the Jewish one, was not exempt from fear of attacks by Christians. A pardon granted on 26 August 1446 to the Muslim Qāsim Láparo, a master carpet maker residing in Lisbon, reveals that he was acutely aware of his community's vulnerability. The document states that in 1444 an unspecified number of Muslim slaves were arrested for the murder of a Christian boy named Afonso in the *mouraria* of Lisbon. The slaves were tortured prior to their execution and some of them implicated Qāsim Láparo. The slaves declared that Láparo had offered them assistance in their attempt to escape. A slave named 'Alī Chanque Cego revealed that Qāsim Láparo had given them 400 *reais brancos* so that they might leave the realm and go to the "lands of the Muslims." To aid their escape Qāsim Láparo had even given them a letter of introduction for the other Muslim communities of Portugal so that they might receive shelter and assistance on their way out of the realm. In his defence Qāsim Láparo claimed that if the Christians had discovered that a Christian child had been murdered by Muslims in the Muslim quarter then "all the Muslims of the *mouraria* would have been put to the sword" and that he had acted in order to prevent "a great riot by the populace of the town." It is, of course, entirely possible that Qāsim Láparo could have invented the fears he expressed to cover up the fact that he had helped the Muslim slaves out of a sense of religious solidarity. The truth will never be known, but the Crown nonetheless accepted Qāsim Láparo's explanation and he received a pardon in return for the payment of a heavy fine.[8]

---

[6] David Nirenberg, *Communities of Violence: Persecution of Minorities in the Middle Ages* (Princeton, 1996), p. 9.

[7] On anti-Jewish feeling in medieval Portugal, see the articles by H.B. Moreno, "As pregações de mestre Paulo contra os judeus bracarenses nos fins do século XV," *Bracara Augusta*, 30 (1976): 53–62; "Novos elementos relativos a Mestre Paulo, pregador do século XV contra os judeus bracarenses," *Bracara Augusta*, 32 (1978): 117–24; "Movimentos Sociais Antijudios em Portugal no século XV," *Marginalidade e Conflictos Sociais em Portugal nos séculos XIV e XV* (Lisbon, 1985), pp. 79–88; and "O Assalto à Judiaria Grande de Lisboa," *Marginalidade e Conflictos Sociais em Portugal nos séculos XIV e XV* (Lisbon, 1985), pp. 89–132. Also of interest is Maria José Pimenta Ferro Tavares, "Revoltas contra os judeus no Portugal Medieval," *Revista de História das Ideias*, 6 (1984): 161–73.

[8] A.N.T.T., *Chancelaria de D. Afonso V*, bk 5, fols 90–90v. Qāsim Láparo, who was himself on the run, was pardoned in return for the payment of a fine of 100 gold crowns.

Bearing arms for the Crown: religious minorities and military service

The laws of João I and Prince Pedro forbade Jews and Muslims to carry weapons in public. Nonetheless, an exception was made when arms were carried in the service of the Crown. The first explicit reference to military service by Jews in Portugal dates from 1366. That year the Jews of Lisbon and Santarém, "who on behalf [of the Crown] were ordered to have horses and weapons at the ready," protested to the Crown that the Christian authorities were compelling Jews to serve "on the borders of the realm and guard prisoners, monies and places to which they were never accustomed to go" and that, in addition, those Jews were ill-treated by the Christians accompanying them. In response Pedro I (1357–67) ordered the municipal judges not to force Jews to serve on the borders, to mistreat them or permit them to be mistreated. Nevertheless, the monarch did not exempt them from military service. The same year identical privileges were also granted to the Jews of Setúbal, Beja, Coimbra and Santiago de Cacém. The privilege granted to the Jews of Setúbal specified that they were only obliged to guard the King's tents and his treasure chest.[9] Only one further complaint about military service was made in 1370, this time by the Jews of Tavira, who protested that the municipal authorities were forcing them to perform guard duty in that town.[10]

In the fifteenth century, it can be inferred that the Jews continued to be liable for military service to the Crown since a law of 1422 exempted Jewish converts to Christianity from having to appear for muster.[11] Although the Jewish population of medieval Portugal included many blacksmiths and a fair number of experts in the manufacture of armor and weapons—including artillery and firearms—evidence of Jews actually taking part in battle is scarce.[12] The registers of the royal chancery record the names of only a handful of Jews who served in Portuguese armies in Morocco and Castile:

- Master José, goldsmith of Prince Henry, participated with his own horse, weapons and two infantrymen in the conquest of Ceuta in 1415 and the unsuccessful attempt to capture Tangier in 1437.[13]

---

[9] A.N.T.T., *Chancelaria de D. Pedro I*, bk 1, fols 121–121v (Lisbon); bk 1, fol. 121v; bk 1, fol. 125v (Beja); bk 1, fol. 129 (Coimbra); bk 1, fol. 129v (Santiago de Cacém).

[10] A.N.T.T., *Chancelaria de D. João II*, bk 8, fol. 149v (confirmation of an earlier privilege granted by King Fernando (1367–83)). A. Iria, *Documentos Portugueses Vol. 2: O Algarve e os Descobrimientos* (Lisbon, 1956), vol. I, pp. 307–8.

[11] *Ordenações do Senhor Rey D. Afonso V* (Lisbon, 1984; facsimile edn of 1792 edn), bk II, title 83, items 1–2.

[12] For instances of Jewish armourers and weapon smiths, see Maria José Pimenta Ferro Tavares, *Os judeus em Portugal no século XV* (Lisbon, 1982), vol. 2, pp. 576–96, 599–600 and 622.

[13] A.N.T.T., *Chancelaria de D. Afonso V*, bk 20, fols 139v–140.

- Master Abraham, a royal physician, was killed fighting alongside Afonso V during the assault upon Arzila in 1471. With him at Arzila was another Jew, Moses Cohen.[14]
- Abraham Abret, tailor to João II, fought at the capture of Tangier and Arzila in Morocco and at the battle of Toro in Castile (1476).[15]

These men were all members of the Jewish elite in Portugal and it appears likely that they were acting on their own account and fighting in the retinues of their Christian patrons rather than because of any military obligations owed to the Crown. One of the leading reasons put forward in 1412 to justify the Crown's decision to exclude Portuguese Jews from having access to the status of municipal citizens, and its attendant privileges, was that they did not serve in the army in time of war.[16] Royal pardons do reveal, however, that Jewish and Muslim criminals were frequently sentenced to periods of exile in Portuguese Moroccan strongholds, presumably to participate in their defense.[17]

The situation concerning the Muslim minority is somewhat clearer. In other Iberian realms the use of Muslim subjects as soldiers by Christian kings—usually against Christian enemies—is well evidenced.[18] In Portugal, however, none of the charters granted to Muslim communities in the twelfth and thirteenth centuries list military service as a duty owed to the Crown. In spite of this, the Muslims were definitely subject to military service during the fourteenth and fifteenth centuries. The first reference to military service by Muslims occurs in a similar context to that of Jewish military service. In 1366 the Muslim communities of Lisbon, Santarém and Alenquer protested to the Crown that the municipal authorities of those towns were forcing them to serve with the armies on the borders of Portugal and perform other services to which they were not accustomed. The three communities claimed that their only obligation was to guard the royal tents and treasury. Convinced by

---

[14] A.N.T.T., *Chancelaria de D. Afonso V*, bk 29, fol. 221v and bk 33, fol. 134.

[15] A.N.T.T., *Chancelaria de D. João II*, bk 1, fol. 62v.

[16] "*nenhũus judeus da nossa terra nom deujam dauer priujllegios de estaaos nem seerem auudos por vizinhoos porque nom serujam em guerra.*" H.B. Moreno, "A sentença do Rei D. João I, contra os judeus de 1412," *LVCERNA. Centro de Estudios Humanísticos. Homenagem a D. Domingos de Pinho Brandão* (Porto, 1984), p. 414.

[17] A.N.T.T., *Chancelaria de D. Afonso V*, bk 22, fol. 121v–122 (served in Arzila); bk 35, fol. 79v (three years of exile in Ceuta); *Chancelaria de D. João II*, bk 9, fol. 37 (one year of exile in Arzila).

[18] For Muslim military service in the Crown of Aragón, see R.I. Burns, *Medieval Colonialism: Postcrusade Exploitation of Islamic Valencia* (Princeton, 1975), pp. 138–48. In Castile the thirteenth-century *Crónica de la poblacíon de Avila* mentions that the Muslims of the town contributed 70 horsemen and 500 infantry to a municipal force in 1255. The bishops of Cuenca and Sigüenza were attacked by Muslim archers in the service of the knights of Santiago in 1241. See François Soyer, 'The Social Status of Muslims in the Realms of León, Castile and Portugal (1100–1300),' unpublished M.Phil dissertation, History Faculty, Seely Library, University of Cambridge (Cambridge, 2003), p. 73.

the arguments of his Muslim subjects, the King ordered the municipal authorities to stop harassing them. According to these documents, the military duties of Muslims from these three communities were thus limited to accompanying the person of the King on his campaigns and guarding the baggage train.[19]

The privileges of 1366 are enlightening but it is not known whether they extended to all Muslim communities in Portugal. Evidence certainly exists that Muslims did serve the King as de facto baggage guards during the fifteenth century. A group of Muslims involved in a dispute with the Cistercian monastery of Alcobaça over the non-fulfillment of the terms of a lease in 1403 claimed in their defense that they had been constrained to serve the King and guard his tents both within and without this realm.[20] Furthermore, a number of royal privileges granted to individual Muslims state that the beneficiary either was, or was not, exempted from having "to serve with weapons and horses." One Muslim of Beja received privileges in 1482 in exchange for his readiness to serve in the Royal Army with a musket (*espingarda*).[21]

In the town of Elvas, situated directly on the border with Castile, the Muslim population also fought alongside the municipal forces during the war that pitted Portugal against its larger neighbor between 1383 and 1411. At the parliament of

---

[19] "*Sabede que o comun dos mouros forros dessa cidade me enujarom dizer que ... elles no tempo del rrey meu padre e em no meu e no tempo dos outros reis que ante mjm forom nunca forom em hoste por fronteyros nem a outros lugares E forom sempre desas cousas escusados saluo se guardauam e armauam as mjmhas tendas e tesouros e dormiam a rredor deles.*" A.N.T.T., *Chancelaria de D. Pedro I*, bk 1, fols 121 (Santarém) and 121v (Lisbon and Alenquer).

[20] A.N.T.T., *Mosteiro de Alcobaça, maço* 64, doc. 19.

[21] A.N.T.T., *Chancelaria de D. Afonso V*, bk 33, fols 22v (28/01/1473) and 156 (12/05/1472); *Chancelaria de D. João II*, bk 5, fols 70–70v (20/05/1492) and bk 12, fols 136–136v (10/07/1482). Exemptions from military service were also granted to Muslim judges (*alcaldes*), religious dignitaries (*capelãos dos mouros*) and those aged over 70—see *Chancelaria de D. Afonso V*, bk 4, fol. 29v (17/06/1452); bk 5, fol. 16v (26/03/1446); bk 10, fol. 133v (19/01/1455); bk 13, fols 130v (02/06/1456), 136 (18/03/1456) and 179v (15/03/1456); bk 14, fols 66v (28/02/1466), 79 (07/03/1466) and 95 (22/02/1466); bk 15, fols 20v (25/03/1455), 46 (08/04/1455), 64 (?/?/1455) and 70v (27/04/1455); bk 16, fols 8 (10/01/1471) and 32v (16/02/1471); bk 18, fol. 11 (13/07/1439); bk 21, fols 72 (27/03/1471); bk 22, fol. 101v (18/10/1471); bk 24, fols 32 (20/04/1444) and 48 (22/03/1444); bk 25, fols 8 (12/01/1445) and 27 (02/07/1445); bk 26, fol. 181v (22/11/1475); bk 27, fols 44v–45 (31/08/1442) and 63 (31/08/1442); bk 31, fols 73v (01/10/1469) and 125v (24/11/1467); bk 33, fol. 201v (11/09/1473); bk 34, fol. 129v (10/07/1450) and 207 (07/02/1450); bk 35, fols 8v (10/03/1466), 10 (02/04/1466) and 90v (20/10/1451); bk 36, fol. 35 (20/02/1459); bk 38, fols 60 (18/06/1466) and 68v (12/09/1471). A.N.T.T., *Chancelaria de D. João II*, bk 3, fol. 41 (04/09/1482); bk 5, fol. 23v (29/01/1492); bk 21, fol. 143v (10/01/1487); bk 24, fol. 4v (26/04/1489). In 1482 Qāsim Mundam of Beja received privileges from the Crown "*por quanto he nosso espingardeiro E ha d'estar prestes pera nos serujr com ssua espingarda quando quer que o mandarmos.*" A.N.T.T., *Chancelaria de D. João II*, bk 3, fol. 41 (04/09/1482).

1441, the town council urged the Crown to exempt the Muslim community from certain taxes in consideration of their "great service" during the war:

> Your Majesty should know of the great service that the Muslims of this *comuna* have rendered during the past wars; keeping watch in its defense and waging war against Castile together with the other inhabitants of this town. Many of them have been killed and captured or have been forced to eat *bagasse* (vegetable pulp) and linseed bread during the defense of this town.[22]

The request was repeated in similar terms in 1455.[23] Later in the fifteenth century the Elvan Muslims sought further exemptions. In 1469 the Crown granted the Muslims of Elvas the privilege of not being conscripted for a period of three years and subsequently renewed it in 1473 and 1475.[24] Even the Muslims of Lisbon, notwithstanding their claims in 1366, thought it necessary to secure royal exemptions from military service for the periods of 1459–64, 1473–6 and for an unspecified period of time after 1481.[25]

Licences to bear arms in public: privilege and self-defense

It is perhaps paradoxical that, even though it was content to conscript Jews and Muslims into its armies, the Crown promulgated laws that prohibited them from bearing weapons within Portugal itself. It is significant to note, however, that these laws never prohibited Jews and Muslims from *owning* weapons and keeping them in their houses.[26] Nonetheless, only individuals who received special licenses from the Crown were exempt from the prohibition on *bearing* arms in public.

---

[22] "*vossa mercee pode bem saber o muyto e muy stremado serviço que os mouros da comuna desta teuem fecto nas guerras pasadas a esta villa, por defensom della vellando e rroldando e indo fazer guerra a Castella em companha dos moradores desta villa, sendo delles mortos e presos e comendo muyto pam de bagaçco e de linhaça por defensom desta villa.*" A.N.T.T. *Chancelaria de D. Afonso V*, bk 2, fol. 7; P. de Azevedo, *Capitulos do Concelho de Elvas apresentados em Côrtes*, (Elvas, 1914), p. 21.

[23] "*Item. Dizees que antigamente, pellos mouros dessa villa nos tempos das guerras servirem com cavallos e armas e com lanças e dardos e beestas, os vertuosos Rex nossos antecessores mandarom de nom pagasem portajem.*" A.N.T.T., *Chancelaria de D. Afonso V*, bk 15, fol. 80v–81; A.N.T.T., Leitura Nova, Odiana, bk 3, fol. 171.

[24] A.N.T.T., *Chancelaria de D. Afonso V*, bk 31, fol. 129; bk 33, fol. 51v (16/02/1473) and bk 30, fol. 175v (06/03/1475).

[25] A.N.T.T., *Chancelaria de D. Afonso V*, bk 8, fol. 174; bk 33, fol. 6v (17/01/1473) and bk 26, fol. 28 (08/02/1481).

[26] On the 1402 law, see A.N.T.T., *Chancelaria de D. João I*, bk 5, fol. 90v. For the 1442 law, see "Fragmentos de legislação escritos no livro chamado antigo das posses da Casa da Supplicação," *Collecção de livros inéditos de historia Portugueza* (Lisbon, 1793), vol. 3, p. 561, doc. 16.

That individual Jews and Muslims did bother to apply for such licenses is evidence that these laws were enforced by Crown officials to a certain degree. As can be seen from the documents collated in the appendix, licenses to bear arms were highly formulaic in nature. These licenses merely instructed Crown officials not to arrest the Muslims or Jews concerned nor to confiscate or requisition their weapons. The petitioner received a license to bear arms in public with the proviso that he should not carry them on him at night outside of the permitted hours—that is, after vespers—or use them for any illegal purpose. These conditions were not specific to religious minorities but had also featured in licenses granted to Christians prior to the liberalization of Prince Pedro and later to foreign Christians.[27] In spite of their formulaic nature, these documents are nonetheless of considerable historical interest.

In the reigns of Afonso V and João II, 88 such licenses were granted to Jews.[28] During the same period, licenses to carry weapons were issued to only 19 Muslims.[29] In the case of the Jews, it appears that the right to carry weapons was usually granted to individuals as just one of a number of other privileges, such as exemption from numerous taxes, not having to wear distinctive symbols on their clothing or even the right to ride horses. The recipients included members of the richest and most influential Jewish merchant families in medieval Portugal—such as the Abravanel, Negro and Navarro families—who were mostly resident in Lisbon. For most Jews it thus appears that the right to bear arms was perceived as a privilege that would increase their prestige in their own community. In comparison, the permits granted to Muslims are of quite a different nature to those granted to Jews. It is certainly the case that some Muslim recipients of licenses to bear weapons received them in addition to a number of other privileges. On 17 December 1473, for instance, two Muslim brothers living in the southern town of Silves, 'Alī Bucar and Aḥmad Bucar, received the right to bear arms anywhere in Portugal alongside exemption from a number of taxes. 'Alī Bucar had his privilege confirmed by João II on 2 February 1486.[30] Another example is Aḥmad Alquiveny,

---

[27] J. Silva de Sousa, "Das autorizações de porte de armas e de deslocação em besta de muar em meados do século XV. Algumas notas para o seu estudo," *Estudos de História de Portugal, Vol. 1 (sécs X–XV). Homenagem a A.H. De Oliveira Marques* (Lisbon, 1982), pp. 293–308.

[28] These are listed in Maria José Pimenta Ferro Tavares, *Os judeus em Portugal no século XV* (Lisbon, 1982), vol. 2, pp. 781–828.

[29] These are the following: A.N.T.T, *Chancelaria de D. Afonso V*, bk 1, fol. 25 (28/05/1462); bk 29, fols 214v (16/11/1472) and 239 (01/12/1472); bk 32, fol. 158v (05/05/1480); bk 37, fols 82v (12/12/1466) and 83v (28/02/1466); A.N.T.T., *Chancelaria de D. João II*, bk 22, fol. 106v (22/05/1484). See also H.B. Moreno, *Os Mudejares no Portugal Medievo* (Porto, 1994), pp. 29–32, docs 4 and 5.

[30] A.N.T.T., *Chancelaria de D. Afonso V*, bk 33, fol. 211 and *Chancelaria de D. João II*, bk 8, fol. 165v.

who received the right to bear arms in May 1480 after the King's own sister, Princess Beatrice, interceded in his favor.[31]

In the majority of cases, however, the Muslim beneficiaries of these licenses were individuals or groups of men who felt themselves to be in very real physical danger. The licenses granted by the Crown specify that the right to bear arms was bestowed because the petitioner(s) had been threatened. One illustration is particularly pertinent in this respect. On 7 February 1459, a Muslim of Évora named Ghālib who had been involved in the death of the Christian Martim Gonçalves received the right to carry weapons in self-defense because he feared reprisals from the relatives of the dead man.[32] In most cases, however, the petitioners were threatened not by Christians but by fellow Muslims or, as we shall see below, in one case by the Muslim family of a convert to Christianity. Another significant difference between Jews and Muslims was that the majority of Muslim recipients of licenses were not from Lisbon, where the largest Muslim community existed, but from the town of Évora. As we shall see in the next section, the reason for this was a specific series of events affecting the Muslim community of that town during the middle decades of the fifteenth century.

Using licenses to bear arms as historical evidence: reconstructing a Muslim blood feud in Évora (1440–66)

At first sight, such highly formulaic documents as the licenses to bear arms would appear to be of only limited historical interest. Nonetheless these permits can provide evidence for the tensions that existed within Muslim communities as is highlighted by a careful examination of the licenses granted to thirteen Muslim residents of the town of Évora between 1440 and 1466.[33] Évora was an important town in the flat south-central Alentejo region of Portugal and boasted Jewish and Muslim communities. Its size in the middle of the fifteenth century is not known but a census carried out at the start of the sixteenth century reveals that it was the third largest town in the kingdom after Lisbon and Porto.[34]

Our case study opens not with these licenses but rather with two extant pardons granted to a Christian of that town named João Fernandes, a potter by trade. At some unknown date, João Fernandes had received a pardon from the Crown for having murdered Aḥmad Caeiro, a Muslim of Évora "about 11 years before" (in 1440). Fernandes was pardoned because he had served in the royal army during the short civil war in 1449 that pitted the King against the regent Prince Pedro. The pardon João Fernandes received was not an unconditional one, however, as he was exiled to the penal colony of Marvão, an inhospitable town on the border

---

[31] A.N.T.T., *Chancelaria de D. Afonso V*, bk 32, fol. 158v.
[32] A.N.T.T., *Chancelaria de D. Afonso V*, bk 36, fol. 28.
[33] For a timeline of events, see Table 3.1 in the Appendix.
[34] See J.J. Alves Dias, "A população," *Nova história de Portugal* (Lisbon, 1998), vol. 5.

with the neighboring kingdom of Castile, for a period of six years. All of these details only survive because Fernandes later petitioned the Crown, protesting that he would not be able to exercise his profession, and thus sustain himself, in Marvão and begged the Crown to change the location of his exile. João Fernandes was successful in his petition and, on 3 May 1451, he was allowed to serve out his period of exile in the more hospitable town of Arronches instead.[35] Later still, on 20 June 1455, João Fernandes was pardoned for the remaining two years of exile which he still had to serve in return for the payment of a fine of 1,000 *reais* to the Crown's charitable fund.[36]

A number of licenses to bear arms in self-defense issued both before and after João Fernandes's petitions start to expose a bitter feud that lasted over twenty years. In effect, three arms-permits granted by the Crown between 1443, 1444 and 1459 reveal that João Fernandes had not committed the murder of Aḥmad Caeiro alone. According to these documents, three Muslims of Évora also received licenses to bear arms in self-defense in fear of reprisals by the relatives of Aḥmad Caeiro:

- On 17 August 1443, the beneficiary was Aḥmad, the son of Muḥammad Dedo.[37]
- On 25 April 1444, the beneficiary was 'Umār Caeiro.[38]
- On 9 June 1459, the beneficiary was another Muslim, known only as Ḥusayn.[39]

The last of these licenses is particularly interesting (see Document 3.1 in the Appendix). According to this license, Ḥusayn had not been directly involved in the murder of Aḥmad Caeiro but his brother Sulaymān had been arrested, charged and then freed. Nevertheless, his kinship with Sulaymān had been enough for the aggrieved relatives of Aḥmad Caeiro—and particularly a brother of his named 'Alī Caeiro—to threaten Ḥusayn's life and cause him to seek to arm himself in self-defense. The document also states that Sulaymān had himself received a license although there is no extant copy of it. The scenario that presents itself thus conforms to the very definition of a protracted family feud in which the relatives of the murder victim sought to avenge their murdered relative by perpetrating retaliatory homicidal assaults on the murderer or his family.

Even though João Fernandes had received a pardon from the Crown for his crime, the relatives of Aḥmad Caeiro neither forgot nor forgave him and he did not live out the rest of his days in peace. His brutal demise is revealed when a group of five Muslims of Évora received the right to bear arms for their own protection on

---

[35] A.N.T.T., *Chancelaria de D. Afonso V*, bk 11, fol. 23v.
[36] A.N.T.T., *Chancelaria de D. Afonso V*, bk 15, fol. 68.
[37] A.N.T.T., *Chancelaria de D. Afonso V*, bk 27, fol. 118.
[38] A.N.T.T., *Chancelaria de D. Afonso V*, bk 24, fol. 60.
[39] A.N.T.T., *Chancelaria de D. Afonso V*, bk 36, fol. 122v.

13 March 1462 (see Document 3.2 in the Appendix). Bakr Caeiro, Ibrāhīm Velho, 'Abd Allāh Caeiro, 'Alī Caeiro and Aḥmad Franco all applied for and received licenses to bear weapons because they had been accused of the death of a man named João Fernandes. Although they had been cleared of the murder, they feared the family and friends of the murdered João Fernandes who had threatened "to kill or injure or stab them." Bakr Caeiro and his associates were thus the family and friends of Aḥmad Caeiro, who had so terrified the presumed accomplices of João Fernandes in the previous decade. The fact that three of the men bear the name Caeiro makes it clear that they were linked to the murdered Muslim by ties of kinship and that 'Alī Caeiro, as we have seen above, was his brother.

The licenses granted in 1462 were not the last to be issued in connection with the death of João Fernandes. On 12 December 1466 Aḥmad de Ceuta, whose nickname was "the boy" (*o moço*), and 'Abd Allāh of Ceuta each received permits to bear arms in self-defense because they feared reprisals from the family of João Fernandes. The description of João Fernandes as an inhabitant of Arronches leaves little room for doubt that this was the same man who had murdered Aḥmad Caeiro a quarter of a century previously. Perhaps the most surprising information contained in these last two permits, however, is that the deceased João Fernandes had in fact formerly been a Muslim.[40] It may have been the case that João Fernandes converted to Christianity following his murder of Aḥmad Caeiro to escape capital punishment. Such conversions by Muslims or even Jews were not unknown in fifteenth-century Portugal and in Évora itself two other such conversions are known to have taken place during the 1450s. The Crown granted a pardon in March 1453 to a Muslim potter, imprisoned for having committed adultery with his sister-in-law, who had converted in prison and taken the name João Vasquez. Another document in November 1459 refers to a certain 'Alī Guedelha who had assaulted an official of the Muslim community but had become a Christian to escape punishment.[41]

At this point it is perhaps worth noting that João Fernandes may not have been the last casualty of this feud. On 28 May 1462, a previously unknown Muslim named Sulaymān with his sons Ibrāhīm and Aḥmad all received the right to bear arms because of the threats they had received from a certain Ḥusayn. The latter had killed Sulaymān's brother 'Umār and was on the run.[42] Was this the same Ḥusayn who had himself received a license in 1459? Unfortunately, there is no information in the license that might help identify the deceased 'Umār or his killer. However, the appearance of another individual named Ḥusayn without any surname does tentatively suggest that these were one and the same man. A decade later Ḥusayn's

---

[40] "*da morte d'huum Joham ferrnandez oleiro que fora mouro.*" A.N.T.T., *Chancelaria de D. Afonso V*, bk 37, fol. 82v. This document is in a very poor state of conservation and I am grateful to Dr. Maria Filomena Lopes de Barros for generously providing me with one of her own transcriptions.

[41] A.N.T.T., *Chancelaria de D. Afonso V*, bk 3, fols 41v–42 and bk 36, fol. 28.

[42] See Document 3.3 in the Appendix.

elderly mother petitioned the Crown to receive some of the property confiscated after he had fled to the emirate of Granada.[43]

Why and how did this protracted feud start? Neither the pardons granted to João Fernandes nor the arms permits granted to the various Muslims of Évora provide any information that might reveal the causes of a feud that left at least two men dead. Consequently, we are left with only two hypotheses. The first is that the feud originated in a dispute between two families. It is indeed striking that on one side were ranged the family of the murdered Aḥmad Caeiro: three of the men share the name Caeiro, strongly suggesting that they formed part of the same kin group. The relationship between the murderers of Aḥmad Caeiro, however, is not at all obvious as no clear kinship links between them can be drawn. The involvement of 'Umār Caeiro in the murder of Aḥmad Caeiro is puzzling. It is possible that Aḥmad Caeiro may have been his uncle. A royal pardon granted to an 'Umār Caeiro of Évora in June 1464 for handling stolen goods specifies that he was the son of an 'Alī Caeiro "the Elder" (*o velho*).[44]

The documentary evidence is simply too fragmentary to permit a clear reconstruction of the kinship networks that existed amongst the Muslim inhabitants of Évora in the fifteenth century. Recent research in the nomenclature of Portuguese Muslims conducted by Maria Filomena Lopes de Barros has demonstrated that Portuguese Muslims only rarely used the patronymic name form common elsewhere in the Islamic world but instead—so far as we can see from the extant documents produced by Christian scribes—they adopted a binomial name form. The second components of names borne by Portuguese Muslims were not simply patronymic but also derived from trades, geographical locations or sometimes simply nicknames such as "*o velho*" ("the old one/the elder").[45] The relationship between the Caeiro, Franco and Ceuta families is therefore unclear. Another problem that surfaces is the fact that the documents of this period present a number of individuals who shared the same name. A contract drawn up for a sale of property on 14 November 1449, for instance, contains a reference to Aḥmad Caeiro, a resident in Évora, who is obviously not the murder victim of 1440. Likewise, another contract, this time dating from the time of the expulsion in 1497, refers to a third individual with this name.[46]

The second and more promising hypothesis is that the feud which pitted two bands of Muslims against one another in Évora for over two decades revolved around a struggle for power within their community. Muslim communities in medieval Portugal were placed under the leadership of a judge or *alcalde* (a title

---

[43] A.N.T.T., *Chancelaria de D. Afonso V*, bk 29, fols 212v.

[44] A.N.T.T., *Chancelaria de D. Afonso V*, bk 8, fols 119v–120.

[45] M.F.L. de Barros, "The Identification of Portuguese Muslims: Problems and Methodology," *Medieval Prosopography*, 23 (2002): 203–28.

[46] *Biblioteca de Évora, Casa Forte, Pergaminhos Soltos, vários* 22, doc. 19 and *Cabido da Sé de Évora*, CEC 3–VI, fols 79–80v. I wish to thank Dr. Barros for providing me with transcriptions of these documents.

clearly derived from the Arabic for judge: *al-qāḍī* القاضي) supposedly elected by the Muslims themselves. With his wide judicial and fiscal powers, the *alcalde* wielded considerable power within his community especially as he was responsible for determining the part of the Crown's taxes that each Muslim family would have to shoulder. Tension often revolved around the partition of the fiscal burden and indeed in February 1450, the *alcalde* of Évora complained to the Crown of two Muslims who refused to contribute to communal expenses due to tax exemptions granted to them by the Crown.[47] By controlling and abusing the powers of the *alcalde*, individuals and factions could favor friends and persecute enemies. Similar conflicts arose in the Jewish communities in this period over the distribution of the fiscal burden and control of the office of "lesser rabbi" (*rabi-menor*, the Jewish equivalent to the *alcalde*).[48]

Evidence exists to suggest that during this period the Muslim community of Évora was gripped by just such a power struggle to control the office of *alcalde*. In late 1454, or early 1455, the Crown received alarming news from the Muslim community, whose members complained that "they are completely ungoverned and are close to lawlessness as they do not have a leader."[49] As a consequence, on 8 February 1455, the Crown appointed 'Alī Caeiro, the brother of Aḥmad Caeiro, as the *alcalde* of the community. The document specifies that 'Alī Caeiro had already served three years as *alcalde* and that the Crown appointed him to that office for a further three years. Although the Crown claimed that the appointment of 'Alī was due to his good service as *alcalde*, it is manifest from the document itself that some Muslims of his community had opposed this continued incumbency. 'Alī Caeiro appears in fact to have consolidated his position and enjoyed something of a dominant position in Évora during the 1450s and early 1460s. Indeed, a later document dated 15 January 1459 testifies to the fact that the Crown renewed his term of office for yet another three years.[50] It thus appears that the violence plaguing the Muslim community of Évora took place at exactly the same time as there was a breakdown of the communal government within that same Muslim community. Although the documentary evidence does not draw a conclusive link between these two developments, the striking coincidence between these two facts is such as to suggest the high probability of a causal link existing between them.

Was the conflict that tore the Muslim community of Évora apart during the middle decades of the fifteenth century simply a straightforward struggle for power, or can it be characterized as a feud between two family groups? In reality, it appears to have been both of these. If the conflict was over control of the office

---

[47] A.N.T.T., *Chancelaria de D. Afonso V*, bk 34, fol. 12.

[48] M.J. Pimenta Ferro Tavares, *Os judeus em Portugal no século XV* (Lisbon, 1982), vol. 1, pp. 125–36.

[49] "*a comuna dos mouros desta cidade d'euora nos fezerom recontamento como ssom desregidos e em ponto de sse perder por nom teerem alcaide.*" A.N.T.T., *Chancelaria de D. Afonso V*, bk 15, fol. 104v.

[50] A.N.T.T., *Chancelaria de D. Afonso V*, bk 36, fol. 45v.

of *alcalde*, as appears likely, the evidence is nonetheless extremely suggestive and indicates that the dispute can be characterized as a feud. The significant lapse of time that separates the two murders—Ahmad Caeiro having been killed in 1440 and João Fernandes losing his life at some point between 1455 and 1462—points to the intensity and persistence of the resentment and hatreds. Moreover, the fact that those asking for licenses to bear arms explicitly justified their applications by citing their fears of reprisals by family members and friends of one or the other of the murdered men only serves to reinforce this impression. The laconic nature of the documents at our disposal, unfortunately, does not allow us to have an exact sense of the extent to which the concepts of "honor" or "kinship" may have played a part in the murders.

Conclusions

Revenge killings and blood feuds in the Middle Ages are popularly associated with the turbulent aristocratic and knightly clans of violent frontier areas such as, for instance, the Anglo-Scottish march or the autonomous city states of Italy. To a certain extent this impression is due to an absence of sources concerning the feuds that must have existed lower down the social hierarchy.[51] This study of extant licenses to bear arms in fifteenth-century Portugal has attempted to reconstruct an example of the feuds and revenge killings that existed in the very different context of a religious minority community. Considering the relative scarcity of sources concerning religious minorities in medieval Europe, these licenses offer historians an unusual and very precious insight into the turbulent inner life of one such community. In the case of Évora, a close examination of these documents actually allows us to reconstruct the outlines of a blood feud and its evolution over time. They do not, however, permit any holistic examination of vengeance and peacemaking in medieval Portugal. The problem of using documentary sources as evidence for feuds has already been remarked upon by Paul Hyams in relation to conflict resolution in medieval England.[52] This is particularly the case insofar as these documents reveal little information concerning the essential sentiments and enmities that underpinned the killings in Évora.

These licenses—though they leave important questions unanswered—nevertheless yield some surprising information. To start with, although religious minorities were conscious of the possibility of violence from the Christian population, it is significant that the Muslims of Évora sought to protect themselves not so much from Christians but rather from fellow Muslims. Another salient feature of these licenses is the manner in which they reveal not only the apparent inability of the Crown and its officials to put an end to the feuding but also the

---

[51] On which, see Paul R. Hyams, *Rancor and Reconciliation in Medieval England* (Ithaca, 2003), pp. 246–51.
[52] Ibid.

fact that individuals from both sides were given the right to arm themselves. It is even quite intriguing that, in one case, the Crown contradictorily describes the beneficiary of a license as having received an acquittal (*sentença de luyramento*) after his arrest on suspicion of murder, but continues to describe him as a "killer" (*matador*).[53]

The study of violence and feuds in the medieval and early modern Iberian Peninsula still lags far behind that in other regions of Europe. Modern research on violence and feuding in medieval and early modern societies has concentrated in northern Europe, particularly Anglo-Saxon England, Scotland, Germany and Iceland.[54] In the Mediterranean region, study of feuds has been to a large extent confined to the Italian Peninsula and especially the *vendettas* of family clans that fought for control of the various *renaissance* city-states.[55] The arms permits that have been examined in this chapter have brought to light a fascinating case study featuring a violent dispute between two groups of individuals that is similar in character to those that took place in Italy and revolving around a struggle for power. In this case, however, the ultimate aim of this struggle was not control of a municipal government but rather of the highest office of communal governmental of a minority group.

---

[53] See Document 3.1 in the Appendix.

[54] There is indeed a vast literature on the subject of feuding. For Scotland, see Keith M. Brown, *Bloodfeud in Scotland, 1573–1625: Violence, Justice and Politics in an Early Modern Society* (Edinburgh, 1986); for England, see R. Fletcher, *Bloodfeud: Murder and Revenge in Anglo-Saxon England* (Oxford, 2004); for Germany, see Hillay Zmora, *State and Nobility in Early Modern Germany: The Knightly Feud in Franconia, 1440–1567* (Cambridge, 1997); for Iceland, see the works of Jesse Byock, *Feud in the Icelandic Saga* (Berkeley, 1982) and William Ian Miller, *Bloodtaking and Peacemaking: Feud, Law, and Society in Saga Iceland* (Chicago, 1990).

[55] For feuding in Renaissance Italy, see Trevor Dean, "Marriage and Mutilation: Vendetta in Late Medieval Italy," *Past and Present*, 157 (1997): 3–36; Edward Muir, *Mad Blood Stirring: Vendetta and Factions in Friuli during the Renaissance* (Baltimore, 1993); Osvaldo Raggio, *Faide et parentele: Lo stato genovese visto dalla Fontanabuona* (Turin, 1990).

APPENDIX[56]

Table 3.1 Timeline of Events in the Struggle for Power in Évora

c.1440	Murder of Aḥmad Caeiro by João Fernandes.
17 August 1443	Aḥmad, the son of Muḥammad Dedo, is granted a license to bear arms to defend himself against the relatives and friends of Aḥmad Caeiro.
25 April 1444	ʿUmār Caeiro is granted a license to bear arms to defend himself against the relatives and friends of Aḥmad Caeiro.
February 1450	The *alcalde* of the Muslim community of Évora complains to the Crown about the refusal of certain members of his community to pay the communal taxes.
3 May 1451	João Fernandes is allowed to serve out his period of exile in the more hospitable town of Arronches.
Late 1454/early 1455	The Crown receives reports that the Muslim community of Évora is without effective communal leadership.
8 February 1455	The Crown appoints ʿAlī Caeiro (the brother of Aḥmad Caeiro) to the office of *alcalde* of the Muslim community in Évora for three years.
20 June 1455	João Fernandes is pardoned for the remaining two years of exile.
15 January 1459	ʿAlī Caeiro is reappointed to the office of *alcalde* of the Muslims of Évora.
9 June 1459	Ḥuṣayn is granted a license to bear arms in self-defense against relatives and friends of Aḥmad Caeiro.
13 March 1462	Bakr Caeiro, Ibrāhīm Velho, ʿAbd Allāh Caeiro, ʿAlī Caeiro and Aḥmad Franco are granted licences to bear arms to defend themselves against the relatives and friends of João Fernandes.
28 May 1462	Sulaymān and his sons Ibrāhīm and Aḥmad, all of whom are free Muslims of Évora, are granted licenses to bear arms to defend themselves against a certain Ḥuṣayn.
12 December 1466	Aḥmad de Ceuta, "the boy," and ʿAbd Allāh of Ceuta are both granted permits to bear arms to defend themselves against the family and friends of João Fernandes.

---

[56] All Muslim names have been altered from their non-standardized medieval Portuguese transliterations to their modern transliterations: thus for instance *Foçem* is rendered as Ḥuṣayn (حسين), *Brafome* or *Brafeme* as Ibrāhīm (إبراهيم) and *Azmede* as Aḥmad (أحمد).

Document 3.1 A.N.T.T., *Chancelaria de D. Afonso V*, bk 36, fol. 122r

9 June 1459

Dom Afonso V, etc., to all the provincial governors, judges, justices, town governors and bailiffs of our realms to whom this [matter] may be of concern or [to whom] this charter may be shown, greetings. Know that Ḥusayn, a free Muslim residing in our town of Évora, had informed us that ʻAlī Caeiro, also a free Muslim of that town, as well as his sons, brothers, family and all his relatives are his greatest enemies and wish him great mortal harm as they believe a brother of his named Sulaymān to have been responsible for the death of Aḥmad Caeiro, brother of the aforesaid ʻAlī Caeiro. On account of the death [of Aḥmad Caeiro], his aforesaid brother [Sulaymān] was arrested, accused and freed. [Proof of] this acquittal has been shown to us by him [Ḥusayn]. His brother [Sulaymān], because of the aforesaid enmity and in fear of receiving some injury, received from us a licence to bear arms in self-defence. Moreover, because Ḥusayn is his brother and their enmity also extends to him, as it does to his aforesaid brother, his enemies have threatened him [Ḥusayn] and he fears that they will kill him or inflict some other harm upon him or wrong him in some way. [...][57] In no way does he dare to carry weapons for his own protection and, because of this, he begs us to grant him a licence and the authority to be able to carry as many weapons of any type as he may [wish to carry]. Having heard what he told us and examined his petition, and having seen the acquittal that the killer [his brother Sulaymān] was granted, and [considering] that he is the brother of the killer to whom the right to bear arms was granted. Furthermore, taking into account the causes of the enmity that exists against his brother and the said Ḥusayn, We, in agreement with the [reports] of our magistrates, hold it to be right and proper that the said Ḥusayn should have the right to carry however many weapons of any kind he wishes for the defence and safekeeping of his person notwithstanding any [previous] laws and municipal ordinances to the contrary that may have been established or promulgated either by ourselves or by the Kings that preceded us. In consideration of this, We order you to allow him to bear these weapons and not to confiscate or requisition them except in the event that he should be discovered carrying them at night outside of the permitted hours or using them illegally. Granted in Lisbon on 9 June. The King ordered this [licence to be made] via the Dr. Lopo Vaz de Serpa and by Gomez Lourenço. João de Vila Real drew up [this licence] in the year of Our Lord Jesus Christ of 1459.

---

[57] "And the brothers and family of the deceased and... ." This passage does not coincide with what follows it and appears to be a scribal error.

Document 3.2 A.N.T.T., *Chancelaria de D. Afonso V*, bk 1, fol. 1v

13 March 1462

Dom Afonso V, etc., to all the judges, justices, governors and bailiffs of our realms, and any other officials of our kingdoms to whom this [matter] may be of concern or [to whom] this charter may be shown, greetings. Know that Bakr Caeiro, a free Muslim living in our town of Évora, has informed us that he was accused of the death of a certain João Fernandes, an inhabitant of Arronches, who was killed in the said town. As a consequence of the aforesaid death, he [Bakr Caeiro] was prosecuted and received from us a safe-conduct [to present himself] before the magistrate of our court and he summoned the persons to whom the prosecution of the aforesaid death fell and they accused him in such a way that he and others accused of the death [of João Fernandes] were set free [from prison] by a royal judgment as we can clearly see from the acquittal that he received and presented to us. Notwithstanding the fact that he was not guilty of the aforementioned murder, and was absolved of any guilt, he claims to fear that the family and friends of the aforesaid João Fernandes wish to kill or injure or stab him since he is not able to bear weapons for his own safekeeping and protection out of fear and dread of our ordinance and prohibition against this. In order that he should not receive any injury without any reason, he has begged us to hear him and provide him with some rightful remedy and grant him the right to bear [weapons] in all our realms and dominion. We [thus] hold it to be right and grant [him] a licence so that he may be able to bear, for his protection and safekeeping, as many weapons of any type as he pleases throughout our kingdoms and dominion. As such, We order you not to confiscate nor requisition [any of these weapons] except in the event that he should be discovered carrying them at night outside of the permitted hours or using them illegally. Granted in Santarém on 13 March. The King ordered this [licence to be made] by Drs Lopo Vaz de Serpa and Lopo Gonçalves, both of whom are knights of his household, etc. Diogo Afonso drew up [this licence] in the year of Our Lord Jesus Christ of 1462.

Likewise another such [licence is granted] to Ibrāhīm Velho of the *comuna* of the free Muslims of our town of Évora.

Likewise another such [licence is granted to] 'Abd Allāh Caeiro, free Muslim resident of Évora.

Likewise another such [licence is granted to] 'Alī Caeiro, resident of the said town.

Likewise another such [licence is granted to] Aḥmad Franco, resident of Évora for the aforesaid case and death.

Document 3.3 A.N.T.T., *Chancelaria de D. Afonso V*, bk 1, fol. 25r

28 May 1462

Dom Afonso V, etc., to all the judges, justices, governors and bailiffs of our realms, and any other persons to whom this charter may be shown, greetings. Know that Sulaymān, together with his sons Ibrāhīm and ʿAḥmad, all of them free Muslim inhabitants of our city of Évora, have informed us that a certain Ḥuṣayn, a free Muslim inhabitant of the same town, together with all his *dijujdos*,[58] are their mortal enemies, holding them in great hatred and wishing them the greatest evil. All of this is because of the death of a certain ʿUmār who was the brother of Sulaymān and uncle of his sons Ibrāhīm and Aḥmad, whom Ḥuṣayn murdered and for which he is now in hiding. Although he is on the run, [Ḥuṣayn] has returned to these realms many times and they have been told that he is waiting for the opportunity to kill them, saying that he would deal with them just as he had dealt with the aforesaid [ʿUmār]. Since they frequently have to go by themselves to watch over their goods and properties, they [live in] fear [of] the murderer (*matador*) and his accomplices (*aderentes*) and wish to bear weapons to defend their persons but do not dare to do so in fear of our ordinances and laws against this. They have begged us to grant them a licence to bear weapons in all of our Lordship for their self-defence. Having heard what they said and listened to their claims as well as the account of our magistrate [in Évora], We hold it to be right and grant a licence to the supplicants so that they may [from now on] be able to bear as many weapons of any type as they wish in the whole of our lordship for their own protection notwithstanding any ordinances and laws to the contrary. We order you to allow them to bear these weapons and not to confiscate them nor detain them except in the event that any of them should be found [carrying the weapons about] at night outside of the permitted hours or using them inappropriately. Granted in Lisbon on 28 May. The King ordered this [licence to be made] via the Drs Lopo Vaz de Serpa and Lopo Gonçalves, etc. João de Vila Real drew up [this licence] in the year of Our Lord Jesus Christ of 1462.

---

[58] The meaning of this term is unclear but it probably refers to those people—friends and family—associated with Ḥuṣayn.

Chapter 4
Feudal War in Tenth-Century France

Dominique Barthélemy[1]

War in tenth-century France deserves a rethink in light of recent anthropological work on feud. Hostility between knights in the tenth century was less focused on avenging murders than on reclaiming castles and land. The goal of aggression was above all else land, and individuals took vengeance indirectly by pillaging the peasants of other lords. Moreover, true social stability coexisted with that form of controlled violence. The *Annals* of Flodoard were very conscious of that stability, but at the same time they reflect the biased manner in which excommunication was meted out for plundering and tyranny.

The *Histories* of Richer of Rheims communicate more explicitly about the discourses and ideas of avenging honor. But one can see also through Richer how the values of harmony and justice, equally present in the post-Carolingian world, permitted vassals to avoid taking vengeance for their lord when it proved inconvenient for them, and even to betray him under the pretext of justice.

Susanna Throop has proposed that we historians interested in the study of vengeance confront an interesting topic: the ideological construction and social dynamics of medieval vengeance. I believe we are all followers of the great Evans-Pritchard. His book on *The Nuer*, published in English in 1937, is the founding text of the anthropological study of internal warfare, or *feud*. His research allows us to consider the relative order of the post-Carolingian world in the footsteps of great historians like Karl Ferdinand Werner and Olivier Guillot, without denying its social stability or overestimating its centralized political structure, as they tended to do.[2] It is true that the tenth century was not a time of pure anarchy, but thanks to the feud, which is a social practice, there was some order inside that anarchy. Similarly, the excessive value placed on personal honor at that time should not be used as evidence for a lack of public order and justice. Vassalage and the fief were very much institutions allied with war. In the Frankish region between the Loire and the Rhine, and the Aquitaine of Gerald of Aurillac, castles existed and were

---

[1] Translated by S. Throop.
[2] Karl Ferdinand Werner, *Les origines (avant l'an mil)* (Paris, 1984), pp. 431–96, esp. pp. 432–6, where anarchy is judiciously refuted, but where at the same time all allusion to knightly brutality disappears. Olivier Guillot, "Formes, fondements et limites de l'organisation politique en France au Xè siècle," in *Il secolo di ferro: mito e realtà del secolo X (Settimane di studio del Centro italiano di studi sull'alto medioevo.38*, 1991), Tome I, pp. 57–116.

fought over as early as the tenth century, and acts of violence occurred that greatly resembled those in the year 1000.[3] Vassals were supposed to avenge their lord; if they had done so faithfully, war would have been everywhere and it should have been impossible to stop them, or excuse them.

According to Guizot—the phrase is well known—the "feudal regime" resembled "less a society than a war."[4] Was it not rather that the phenomenon of war resembled society? Sociology has helped us to pay more attention to the social arrangements between adversaries, and to the codes and purposes that governed violence. Moreover, although not all in that society, or in that war, should be considered "feudal," nevertheless clear feudal elements such as homage and the fief played a certain role that it would be wrong to deny. The crucial point is that these elements did not exist alone and they had their exact place in society. Susan Reynolds has justly demystified the "band of vassals" and the "private contractual relationship" between lords and vassals; in my view it is now necessary to restore to all these matters their vassalage, that is, in the Old French epics, the ethos and the behavior of adult noblemen in this society of vengeance.[5]

In order to understand a little something of war in northern France in the tenth century we have at our disposal in particular the two testimonies of the *Annals* of Flodoard and the *Histories* of Richer. Flodoard's *Annals* covered the period from 919 to 966. Richer's *Histories* began with the year 888, incorporated material from Flodoard for events between 919 and 966, and finally blossomed into an original account of affairs between 966 and the death of Hugh Capet in 996.[6]

Both these authors were clerics removed from events, yet nevertheless they were very different from each other in other ways. Flodoard, in his *Annals*, set down dry and neutral notes on the parchment; he seemed simply to take note of

---

[3] As Paul Hyams rightly notes: "Homage and Feudalism: A Judicious Separation," in Natalie Fryde, Pierre Monnet and Otto Gerhard Oexle (eds), *Die Gegenwart des Feudalismus. Présence du féodalisme et présent de la féodalité. The Presence of Feudalism* (Göttingen, 2002), pp. 13–49.

[4] François Guizot, *Essais sur l'histoire de France* (5th edn, Paris, 1836), p. 350. He adds this however: "mais l'énergie et la dignité de l'individu s'y maintiennent; la société peut en sortir."

[5] Susan Reynolds, *Fiefs and Vassals* (Oxford, 1994).

[6] Hugh Capet's death was a contemporary event that Richer himself observed from Rheims. *Les Annales de Flodoard*, ed. Philippe Lauer (Paris, 1905); abbreviated hereafter as *Annales*. On this author, see Michel Sot, *Un historien et son église au xe siècle: Flodoard de Reims* (Paris, 1993). The best edition of Richer is Richer von Saint-Remi, *Historiae*, ed. Harmut Hoffmann, *MGH Scriptores* 38 (Hanover, 2000); abbreviated hereafter as *Histoires*. On the text, see Michel Sot, *Richer de Reims a-t-il écrit une Histoire de France?*, in Yves-Marie Bercé and Philippe Contamine (eds), *Histoires de France, historiens de la France, Actes du Colloque International, Reims, 14 et 15 mai 1993* (Paris, 1994), pp. 47–58; Jason Glenn, "The Composition of Richer's Autograph Manuscript," *Revue d'Histoire des Textes*, 27 (1997): 151–89; Hartmut Hoffmann, "Die Historien Richers von Saint-Remi," *Deutsches Archiv für Erforschung des Mittelalters* 54 (1998): 445–532.

outstanding deeds arising from the competition between kings, counts, bishops and castellans. Vassalic campaigns to pillage peasants, besieged castles, acts of homage done for the sake of peace (sometimes temporary), the betrayal of those fallen in the castles—these events recurred each year, much more frequently than did formal battles. But there were few acts of personal vengeance for such offenses, except sometimes for a murder, as when Herluin of Montreuil avenged William Longsword.[7] From Flodoard alone it is difficult to know if honor was truly avenged in his society, and no doubt those who agree with Guy Halsall would derive evidence from this for his denial of feud.[8]

Richer of Rheims, on the other hand, as much in his interpolations from Flodoard as in his own work, often evoked vengeance and honor, and did so in clearly feudo-vassalic contexts. He was also closer than Flodoard to the ideals of vassalage, and much less interested in the supernatural than most of his historian contemporaries. But if we choose to utilize his legendary anecdotes and reconstructed discourse for a history of vengeance, some will object that we are examining fiction, not fact, as do those who criticize Miller and his study of Icelandic sagas.[9]

We run the risk then that we will simply encounter nonexistent vengeance in Flodoard and invented vengeance in Richer. All the same, it seems to me that one can find substantial evidence for vengeance in Flodoard, and that Richer did not invent anything simply to please himself.

Nonexistent vengeance?

Flodoard, it is generally agreed, recorded historical reality, and indeed his work first interests us because it is that of a person alive at the time he was describing—or rather, it represents the perspective that an individual could have had in his local and social environment. He recorded events, but in addition he had a certain manner of selecting them, qualifying them and connecting them in a causal chain. Moreover, although in his text there are few examples of acts of vengeance (i.e. of revenge or reprisal described as such), there was on the other hand something very feud-oriented in the way in which he selected events, year after year, and established connections between them. It seems that the king and the great lords

---

[7] *Annales*, p. 89 (943).

[8] Guy Halsall (ed.), *Violence and Society in the Early Medieval West* (Woodbridge, 1998)—esp. the *Introduction* (pp. 1–15) and the contribution of Matthew Bennett (pp. 126–40). Indeed one does not find archetypal "feud" in the chronicles of feudal France, but this does not prevent, in my view, the feudal logic so clearly discharged by the *chansons de geste* and the manuals of sociology from being worthwhile and relevant to the work.

[9] William Miller, *Bloodtaking and Peacemaking* (Chicago, 1990). See also Alessandro Barbero.

lived in conflict even in the tenth century, in the manner Patrick Geary has studied in the eleventh century.[10]

The main events Flodoard recorded were the relatively short seasonal campaigns, raids and castle sieges lasting less than two months, in which the knights played a great role and large-scale battles were rare (except at Soissons, in 922). Bloody vendettas and mortal hatreds were not common among the great men; the case of William Longsword was almost exceptional. Lords disputed goods, namely land and castles. They aimed their violence at these goods rather than at the men who possessed them, and they distributed part of these goods in return for their supporters' help.

The term "feudal war," although a convenient way to describe these things, in my view is a little broad for these events. What Flodoard twice called "enmities" between great men was in reality a rather limited form of violence.[11] There were many peace treaties, intercessions and mediations comparable to those studied by Hermann Kamp.[12] The act of homage was one way of making peace and initiating friendship through an integral gesture of allegiance, or of recognizing an established alliance when it was problematic in some way. It was often the sign that someone had changed sides.[13] Men frequently reneged on their alliances, but it seems to me that, far from creating disorder, these shifting allegiances instead tended to promote stability, to the extent that when one of the princes achieved an advantage, he would in turn disturb and provoke a strong coalition against him; the system resisted extreme change. It was "treason" that caused most cities and castles to fall—social maneuvers were more decisive than feats of arms.[14]

But the essential feature of this "feudal war" was undoubtedly the pillaging of the countryside, that is to say, the peasants. Indeed it could be suggested that this plundering and devastation, limited but nevertheless notable, was the latent purpose of "feudal war," as Gadi Algazi notes for Germany at the end of the Middle Ages.[15] Flodoard constantly noted depredation and pillaging, but in general he was not any more disturbed by these than by any other events. He did not so much possess the merit of seeing events clearly himself, as that of enabling his readers to do so.

---

[10] Patrick Geary, "Vivre en conflit dans une France sans État: typologie des mécanismes de règlement des conflits (1050–1200)," *Annales ESC*, 41 (1986): 27–42.

[11] *Annales*, p. 49 (931) and p. 136 (953).

[12] *Treugæ vel indutiæ belli* (pp. 105, 947); see, among others, p. 79, 85, 97, 123, 125, 132, 151. Hermann Kamp, *Vermittler in den Konflikten des hohen Mittelalters*, in *La Giustizia nell'alto Medioevo (secoli IX–XI)* (Spolète, 1997), pp. 675–710.

[13] *Annales*, p. 70 (938) and p. 118 (948).

[14] *Annales*, p. 46 (930), p. 70 (938), p. 72–3 (939), p. 82 (941), p. 91 (944), p. 122 (949) and p. 145 (958).

[15] Gadi Algazi, "Pruning Peasants: Private War and Maintaining the Lords' Peace in Late Medieval Germany," in Esther Cohen and Mayke de Jong (eds), *Medieval Transformations: Texts, Power and Gifts in Context* (Leiden, 2000), pp. 245–74.

For example, he routinely related the details of one day in 948 when the settlers of Cormicy, where he himself possessed a church, were killed.[16]

He also had his own way of selecting and relaying these events. Very often, he recorded an assault and its reprisal for a given year. This was particularly distinct for the events of 954 between Herbert III of Vermandois and Renaud of Roucy. After taking and retaking castles, they reached an agreement and reestablished equilibrium, and one senses that Flodoard communicated the official version of the events that had reset the social accounts at zero. Contrary to his usual practice, he not only recorded the reasons why hostilities had commenced in the first place, but also willingly emphasized their mutual character: "they plundered *each other*."[17] The formula Flodoard used was admirable, considering that each had in fact found fault not with the other himself, but with the other's peasants. Indeed, by taking the peasants as their targets they conveniently confirmed for each other that the lands were truly their own.

By failing to even mention violence done to peasants, this type of verbal formula euphemized indirect vengeance and constituted the creation of downright symbolic violence that was at the heart of the feudal war, even as early as the code of Charroux in 989 (second order).[18] Vassalage was the code and nature of this society of vengeance after the sociopolitical changes which took place between the years 880 and 900. It was also a formidable post-Carolingian inheritance that suggested that the vassals and lords defend the weak. Assuredly the knights of the tenth century defended right—but their own right, before all—and they protected the poor—but only those poor who depended on them, at the cost of heavy taxes and exposure to their adversaries.

Above all, noble men were courteous with each other. How wonderful indeed were their beautiful, peaceful deeds, the concern that people of good company showed for each other when they mutually pardoned each other the wrongs done to their peasants, that is to say, when they counted as nothing the suffering of a "lower order" of humanity! But then, their society did not recognize this reality. The discourse with which they regulated themselves (and their conflicts) and elaborated an official version of equilibrium was also the discourse with which they legitimized noble violence and failed to recognize peasant suffering. Moreover, this discourse also disclosed official reasons that a lord could use to justify not claiming all that he potentially could claim (in one sense), but rather to choose a path according to strategy and opportunity.

Well before 989 and the peace councils in Aquitaine, the Church had already realized that the plundering of the goods of the peasants was a great knightly

---

[16] *Annales*, p. 117 (948).

[17] *Annales*, p. 139 (954), followed on p. 140 by a negotiation *pro subreptis mutuo sibi castris*.

[18] Dominique Barthélemy, "Abolir la guerre féodale? La paix de Dieu dans le monde de la faide," in Pierre Bonnassie and Pierre Toubert (eds), *L'Europe de l'an mil* (Toulouse, 2003).

sin in post-Carolingian times. The Council of Trosly in 909 firmly condemned this harrying and devastation, ranking it among the other sins which could call down upon the Christian people the violent remonstrations of a vengeful God.[19] So too did the Council of Sainte-Macre in 935.[20] Despite the admonitions of the Aquitanian councils of 1000, Flodoard does not record the use of methods like sermons, anathema, tales of miraculous vengeance and focus on the diocesan community. But it is clear that excommunication was already being used by lords to destabilize an enemy, to promote the maneuverings of his vassals, who were supposed to be able to detach themselves from him without treachery (like those of Hugh the archbishop in 948) and to mount a royal campaign against him.[21] As one example, in 938 Louis IV could thus remove his sphere of influence from the pressure exerted by the lord of Montigny-Lengrain, knowing well that as soon as the latter was imprisoned and his life and limbs endangered, archbishop Artaud would intercede on his behalf.[22] Peace councils throughout the tenth and eleventh centuries faced the same problem: in principle, indirect vengeance was denounced, but in practice, personal vengeance was inadequate or impotent, and feudal war in fact had many good days ahead of it.

It becomes apparent that the social demand for vassals to be faithful to their lords during the process of regulating conflicts could be counterbalanced by reference to other norms and laws, like the law of the councils or implicit norms that public opinion would interpret for itself. These unwritten standards mutually impinged upon each other. It was necessary to love peace and display solidarity with the king, and at the same time, when these values contradicted the allegiance of vassals, then the time had come for vassals to protest or maneuver.

Although Flodoard did not document elaborate, well-delineated feuds described as vengeance like the great "bloodfeuds" of Merovingian times, nevertheless his world was completely feud-oriented. Perhaps even more fluidly feud-oriented, since conflicts over goods shifted with greater rapidity, and did so within a much greater social network, than did conflicts like that of Sichar and Chramnesind.

Invented vengeance?

Although Flodoard did not record details of the vassals' protests and maneuvers, Richer did do so in Book IV of his History, with the "treason" of the castellan of Melun, who in 991 abandoned Hugh Capet and allied himself to Odo I of Blois. Richer reconstructed a dialogue between Odo's messenger and the castellan, in

---

[19] In chapter 7: PL 132, col. 694–6; cited by Isolde Schröder, *Die Westfränkischen Synoden von 888 bis 987 und ihre Überlieferung* (MGH Hilfsmittel 3, 1980).

[20] *Annales*, p. 62 (935); equally evoked in Flodoard, *Historia Remensis Ecclesie* IV.25 (*Revue du Moyen Age Latin* 41, 1985, p. 530).

[21] *Annales*, p. 117 (948).

[22] Ibid., p. 69 (938).

which the latter gave his account. When he delivered the castle of Melun to Odo, he recalled a hereditary right and asserted the justice of his action, claiming that he did not wrong Hugh Capet since the king remained as overlord (even if the castellan carefully denied him the right to determine who was to be his vassal!). We see here two excellent arguments, each of which also adjoined a third: namely, that Odo would enrich the castellan.[23] I think that there was nothing in that passage that could not potentially have applied to one of the "treasons" so cursorily evoked by Flodoard. Even if Richer had given his own version of events, even if he had displayed his usual rhetoric, he does not in my view falsify the reality of events any more than when diverse chroniclers of the year 1100 reformed the words of Urban II at Clermont in 1095, each in his own manner.

Richer was less sensitive than Flodoard to the ecclesiastical arguments against plundering the countryside, but all the same he mentioned pillage at times.[24] He did not invoke Church law, but instead he gave the appearance of a quasi-Roman state, of a *res publica* with an equestrian order, harmonious ideals and treason law in which individuals feared the accusation of betraying the king. At the same time, Richer was very aware of the values of vengeance and honor; in his text these elements appeared clearly. These values together may seem very contradictory to us, but it seems to me that they only contradicted each other enough to create a living, dynamic society, where to live in conflict was also to live among contradictions, to manage them, to exploit them, to use them when a change of attitude was needed.

Thus Richer was familiar with vassalic ethos and close to his father, Raoul, who taught him the heroic legends of the times of Louis IV D'Outremer. These legends were a hundred years old, and Philippe Lauer has seen in this Raoul a "troubadour soldier," a bearer of epic traditions like Raoul d'Ivry, an inspirational figure who claimed the authority of Dudo of Saint-Quentin.[25] These traditions may well have existed: we possess a song, in Latin, about William Longsword that has the same hero, if not the attractive appearance, of Richer's text.[26] If only we knew if his father also peddled an ancient version of *Raoul de Cambrai*!

But Richer only tells us the histories of devoted vassals up until the death of a lord who was the king, which is a little too convenient, since it then was no longer a case of the contradiction between "the State" and "feudalism." The count of Normandy, William Longsword, had performed homage to Louis IV. The details of this ritual do not interest Richer very much, but he implies that it signaled the intention to return to the king all the power that such great men had previously taken for themselves.[27] To avenge the honor of his lord, he risked his

---

[23] *Histoires* IV.75 (pp. 283–4).
[24] Ibid., II.8 (p. 104) and III.74 (p. 210).
[25] Philippe Lauer, *Le règne de Louis IV d'Outremer* (Paris, 1900), pp. 267–76.
[26] Ibid., pp. 319–23.
[27] *Histoires* II. 28–34 (pp. 118–23).

own death, and there we see the real ideal that drove William, albeit an ideal a little bit transformed all the same by Richer's words.

This type of account, which presented a singularly idealized version of vassalage, seems to have had a true social function: it diverted attention and emotion away from the real suffering of the peasants to the risk of death (not insignificant, but hardly great) of the lords, from the actual deeds of war to the insults aimed at their honor. Moreover, in Richer's account we have a good example of power articulated at the same time by history and literature, since the history of William and the slightly more elite tale of Ingo in the time of the Normans were both true vassalic epics, close to the *chansons de geste* in spirit and themes, which included efforts to make peace as though claiming the other's defeat. The ancient versions of the *chansons de geste*, or even those of the twelfth century in their time, surely played an important ideological role: to promote belief in the courage and loyalty of knights and to claim that those knights were devoted before all else to direct acts of vengeance, at the same time as they themselves, through the implacable mechanism of indirect vengeance, always attacked the weak.

In any case, Richer does not hesitate to provide us with an abundance of rhetoric for the events of 978–80 in which the conversation of important individuals, glittering with salubrious expressions, said it all and contradicted it all at once.[28] It was as if the Franks had the same ancestry as the Greeks. Truly medievalists of yesteryear would have found in Richer an author who contradicted the paradigm of violent, vengeful anarchy. In 978, King Lothar commanded his "Gauls" to raid Aix-la-Chapelle as an act of retribution for a previous insult. When the Gauls had accomplished their vengeance, then the emperor Otto II could galvanize his own men in turn to attack Paris:

> Lothar sent you fleeing, it is necessary to erase this shame. And to do that you do not have the right to fear either war or death. Your nobility demands it, the moment has arrived, the means are present. Be ready to die rather than to serve, you who are in the army of the age and who have courage. Do not leave this outrage unopposed. Display great valiance, make those who mistook you for a base people fear you.

This passage was like one from the *chansons de geste*, in which the social stakes were expressed perfectly as *"Viva la muerte"*: it all came down to the ranking of interests.

After that speech there followed a German pillaging expedition that respected prestigious churches, and did not in fact meet the king Lothar and the duke Hugh Capet in battle. The day when the two armies faced each other was marked by a duel between a lone German, the instigator, and one Gaul, who "cleaned up the insult."[29] After the duel, king Lothar reflected on his interests and sent messengers

---

[28] Ibid., III.73 (p. 209), III.79–80 (p. 213), III.82–3 (pp. 214–15).
[29] Ibid., III.76 (p. 211).

to the emperor Otto with a collection of beautiful statements about public order and harmony, in the Carolingian manner. "And Otto responds—I know the evil that discord has done to the public order." It was time to meet, to give each other the kiss of peace, and to pledge their friendship. However, the reconciliation between Lothar and Otto in 980 was unknown to the duke Hugh Capet, who found himself suddenly, unexpectedly, isolated and threatened. What was he to do? He turned to his great vassals: "You are bound to me by homage and oath. There is no doubt, consequently, that you have sworn to me unbreachable loyalty, because of which I seek your counsel in all confidence. It is a matter of your life."[30]

The vassals of Hugh Capet advised him to wait for a good opportunity, not because their loyalty was limited or faltering, but because they took into account the repercussions of force. Before avenging himself on Lothar, Hugh would have to do his best to split him from Otto:

> If you rise against the two together, you will encounter all kinds of misery: you will be harassed by cavalry raids, by many ambushes, fires and plundering. And the worst thing would be the many rumors that would run through the treacherous people: it could be claimed that we were not making a legitimate defense against our enemies, but were quarrelling with the king like arrogant and forsworn rebels.[31]

The matter of "what would be said?" was a constant concern in the world of feudal war, since it was always necessary to mobilize one's supporters. Or more precisely, Hugh Capet's infraction of the fundamental norm of respect for superiors would constitute a good excuse for all those beneath him to part from him and from those who had thus counseled him. It would be possible to allege that "there would be then no offense or perjury in abandoning their lords and turning their heads against them with arrogance."[32]

In other words, these vassals were not duped by the heroic legends of Ingon and of William Longsword. Without refusing in principle to die for their lord, they threatened to betray him in times of great difficulty. They understood that it was necessary to specify when one would not die for one's lord, or even avenge him. But after all, did not Hugh Capet himself wish that such would be the case? Perhaps his vassals said precisely what he wished to hear. For in a vengeance-oriented society, people quickly became experts in the art of taking vengeance—or not—with great discrimination.[33]

---

[30] Ibid., III.82 (p. 214).

[31] Ibid., III.83 (p. 215).

[32] Ibid.

[33] Other versions of this study have been published in the *Bulletin-annuaire de la Société de l'Histoire de France*, 2003 (beneath the title "La féodalité et l'anthropologie"), and in my *Chevaliers et miracles en France autour de l'an mil* (Paris, 2004), ch. 1, "La chevalerie au Xè siècle."

Chapter 5
The Way Vengeance Comes: Rancorous Deeds and Words in the World of Orderic Vitalis[1]

Thomas Roche

The Norman monk and chronicler Orderic Vitalis needs no introduction.[2] His historical work, beginning as an interpolator to Guillaume of Jumièges's *Gesta Normannorum Ducum*[3] and then writing his own masterpiece, the *Historia Ecclesiastica*,[4] is well known to students of twelfth-century Western society. His rich narratives complement the scarcity of contemporary diplomatic sources, while his description of local aristocratic and monastic society provides insight on many legal points, including the issue of vengeance. As a matter of fact, most Norman feud-tales from around 1100 are only documented by Orderic.[5]

---

[1] This paper owes much to reflections exchanged with James Bickford Smith. I would also like to warmly thank the editors for their useful comments and their patience.

[2] Marjorie Chibnall, *The World of Orderic Vitalis* (Oxford, 1984). As this chronicler is the main source for Norman history from the 1070s to the 1140s, virtually every study on this era should be included in an Orderician bibliography. The latest survey is J. Bickford Smith, *Orderic Vitalis and Norman Society, c. 1035–1087* (Oxford University D. Phil Thesis, 2006).

[3] *The Gesta Normannorum Ducum of William of Jumièges, Orderic Vitalis and Robert of Torigni*, ed. Elisabeth M.C. Van Houts (2 vols, Oxford, 1992–5), hereafter *Gesta Normannorum*.

[4] *The Ecclesiastical History of Orderic Vitalis*, ed. and trans. Marjorie Chibnall (6 vols, Oxford, 1969–80), hereafter *Ecclesiastical History*.

[5] The only exception seems to be the story of Serlo of Hauteville, fleeing from a gloomy fate as criminal and seeking shelter in Brittany, as reported by Geoffrey Malaterra.

Most have already been commented on at length, for their own sake[6] or in relation to lineage-centered studies.[7]

The first aim of this chapter is to discuss the notion of "feud" as analyzed by recent historians in the light of the evidence brought by Orderic, and to show that this evidence cannot be treated as a whole. Then, I will focus on the root causes of various occasions of vengeance. Three levels will be considered: the discourse that Orderic promotes simply by the way he tells and explains events; the discourse that protagonists used, as reported—I should say reconstructed—by Orderic; and finally, the overarching discourse that Orderic creates surrounding these "discourses of rancor" by the way he uses them in his narrative.

Orderic's feuds

What do historians define as "vengeance" or as "feud", and how does this compare to the information Orderic brings us?

Historians and feuds

Historians at first regarded feuds as irrational blows of violence in medieval societies, just as colonialists denounced indigenous vendettas.[8] They disqualified pre-industrial "anarchy" because they referred to the model of the State—in Max

---

[6] Jean Yver, "L'interdiction de la guerre privée dans le très ancien droit normand," in *Travaux de la Semaine d'histoire du droit normand tenue à Guernesey du 26 au 30 mai 1927* (Caen, 1928), pp. 307–47; Matthew Bennett, "Violence in Eleventh-century Normandy: Feud, Warfare and Politics," in Guy Halsall (ed.), *Violence and Society in the Early Medieval West* (Woodbridge, 1998), pp. 126–40; Paul Hyams, *Rancor and Reconciliation in Medieval England* (Ithaca, 2003), pp. 116–36. On punishments, see Emily Tabuteau, "Punishments in Eleventh-century Normandy," in Warren Brown and Peter Gorecki (eds), *Conflict in Medieval Europe: Changing Perspectives on Society and Culture* (London, 2003), pp. 131–49. On William Pantoul accused of having murdered Mabel of Bellême and passing an ordeal, see Dominique Barthélemy, *L'an mil et la paix de Dieu* (Paris, 1999), pp. 559–61.

[7] On the Giroie and Bellême families, see Pierre Bauduin, "Une famille châtelaine sur les confins normanno-manceaux: les Géré (X^e–XIIIe siècles)," *Archéologie médiévale*, 22 (1992): 309–56; Jean-Marie Maillefer, "Une famille aristocratique aux confins de la Normandie: les Géré au XIe siècle," *Cahiers des Annales de Normandie*, 17 (1985): 175–206; Gérard Louise, *La seigneurie de Bellême (X^e–XIIe siècles): Dévolution des pouvoirs territoriaux et construction d'une seigneurie de frontière aux confins de la Normandie et du Maine, à la charnière de l'an mil* (2 vols, Flers, 1992–3).

[8] Alain Mahé, "Violence et médiation: Théorie de la segmentarité et pratiques juridiques en Kabylie," *Genèses*, 32 (1998): 51–65.

Weber's words, a community that "claims the monopoly of the legitimate use of physical force within a given territory."[9]

Comparison with traditional societies studied by twentieth-century anthropologists, such as Evans-Pritchard's Nuer, and the influence of functionalist theories, eventually brought about a revaluation of medieval vengeance.[10] It was now seen as an "institution," paradoxically helping society to keep its coherence, because it was no longer imagined as born out of unleashed passions but as settled by familial obligations, by a sense of honor, by "rules of the game" that prevented unbalanced outbursts of violence. Peacemakers in human societies could only belong to marginal groups: lineages of sorcerers, of holy men, or, for the Middle Ages, the Church. Accounts of medieval feud from the 1970s were usually founded upon this theoretical background, despite the fresh and developing discussions of contemporary anthropologists, which shifted attention to the mobilization process, to the use of legal arguments and procedure. If the topic of vengeance has created a huge literature, in anthropology as well as in history, this amount of work has yet not brought about an accepted definition.[11]

A first issue is the distinction between "feud" and "blood-feud." Even if these two words are sometimes used interchangeably, I will use them here to distinguish two ways of defining "vengeance."

For an historian with a state-centered mind and no anthropological awareness—mostly anyone writing before 1930 could fit—"vengeance" refers to violence with no restraint, usually in the context of intra- or inter-familial conflicts. It is the romantic view of the Mediterranean vendetta, as described by Prosper Mérimée in *Colomba*, or the fatalistic depiction of Albanian disputes, as narrated by Ismaïl Kadare.

Later on during the twentieth century, historians read anthropologists—Glucksmann's "Peace in the feud" had been seminal—and drew then a less negative vision of vengeance. To stress the otherness of medieval behavior, they had since rather used the Germanic "faida," in French "faide," in English "feud," to describe processes actually involving more than mere familial disputes—and becoming then "political." I will here keep the word feud for this neutral and sociological interpretation of vengeance (even if I think that feud is more in the historian's mind than in its sources), and distinguish it rigorously from "blood-feud," which I will use to refer to the negative view of vengeance as unrestrained and unavoidably bloody.

---

[9] H.H. Gerth and C. Wright Mill (eds), *Max Weber* (New York, 1970), p. 77.

[10] E.E. Evans-Pritchard, *The Nuer: A Description of the Modes of Livelihood and Political Institutions of a Nilotic People* (Oxford, 1940). The book was translated into French in 1968, with a foreword by Louis Dumont who stressed its structuralist aspects. Georges Balandier has pointed out, however, that Evans-Pritchard's work could also support his own views of a more dynamic political anthropology; see Balandier's foreword to the second edition of *Anthropologie politique* (Paris, 1995).

[11] Wiliam Ian Miller, *Bloodtaking and Peacemaking: Feud, Law and Society in Saga Iceland* (Chicago, 1990), p. 179.

However, to explain that the processes they examine are not unrestrained violence, recent historians still feel the need to oppose them to an ideal type of "unreasonable" vengeance. William Ian Miller, amongst others, distinguishes feud "from other types of violence like war, duels, or simple revenge killings."[12] Matthew Bennett rejects the notion of feud for eleventh-century Normandy, but what he is rejecting is the concept of the blood-feud. He concludes that "apparent feuds disintegrate upon closer scrutiny," but what he disqualifies seems rather to fit the blood-feud definition: "personal quarrels which could be resolved in a series of tit-for-tat revenge killings."[13] Moreover, what he pictures are not feuds, but "rather a self-regulating system operating in much the same way as the wars of princes, but on a smaller scale."[14] However, he is right to point to the difficulty of telling "what is feud" from "what is warfare."

So another issue arises: on what criteria could one extract from untangled legal and military processes a specific, self-coherent social phenomenon and name it "feud"? Actually, each historian puts the emphasis on one or another key element, often depending on the scope of their analysis: regulation of violence,[15] wish for redress of wrong,[16] obligation to suffer the possibility of being killed,[17] length and emotional strength,[18] to list a few. As some have stressed, feud is a multi-dimensional process, in words as in deeds, because of the variety of the acts it covers, and because of the multiplicity of the meanings it conveys.[19]

Yet there is another notion to contrast with feud: "public" war, a concept put forth by some past historians, who regarded feud as a symptom of the feudal anarchy. Medieval historians have with good reason played this view down, as notion of "public" and "State" cannot be applied to pre-industrial societies in the

---

[12] Ibid., p. 180.

[13] Bennett, "Violence," p. 136.

[14] Ibid., p. 127.

[15] Dominique Barthélemy, *La chevalerie, de la Germanie antique à la France du XIIe siècle* (Paris, 2007).

[16] Hyams, *Rancor*, p. 3.

[17] Miller, *Bloodtaking*, p. 181.

[18] John Hudson, "Faide, vengeance et violence en Angleterre (c. 900–1200)," in Dominique Barthélemy, François Bougard and Régine Le Jan (eds), *La vengeance, 400–1200* (Rome, 2006), pp. 341–82, especially p. 373.

[19] Miller, *Bloodtaking*, p. 180–81. Miller's views are adopted for eleventh- and twelfth-century France by Stephen White, "Un imaginaire faidal: La représentation de la guerre dans quelques chansons de geste," in Barthélemy, Bougard and Le Jan (eds), *La vengeance, 400–1200*, pp. 175–98, at pp. 178–81; see also his "Feuding and Peace-making in the Touraine around the Year 1100," *Traditio*, 42 (1986): 195–253. This is complemented by Chantal Senséby, "Récits de meurtre et de vengeance: De l'art de présenter les conflits et leur règlement aux XIe et XIIe siècles," in Dominique Barthélemy and Jean-Marie Martin (eds), *Liber largitorius: Études d'histoire médiévale offertes à Pierre Toubert par ses élèves* (Geneva, 2003), pp. 375–92.

sense modern writers understand them, and have instead promoted the notion of feud against the outdated view of "private war."[20] However, pushing this position too far could leave rather little room for the analysis of institutional change, which indeed occurred in the twelfth century with the renewal of monarchies.

I stop this short review of historiographical issues here, as I will discuss further below the modern analysis of feud by testing it against Orderic's text. Let's turn now to the notions our monk uses.

Orderic's words

Orderic Vitalis used various terms to depict what could be described as feuds. The word *talio*, rarely found, would seem to apply to particularly cruel deeds, which would fit in the blood-feud category as I defined it earlier. To coerce friendship between Ralph Harenc and Eustache of Breteuil, King Henry gave Ralph's son to Eustache as a hostage. That did not work: Eustache had the boy's eyes cut out and sent to his father. Ralph complained to the king and with his agreement mutilated Eustache's daughters, Henry's own granddaughters. Is this a striking example of how inescapable and mathematical could be the medieval unrestrained cruelty? We, as twenty-first-century citizens, reject with disgust those acts as blind violence. But notice that Orderic casts no blame at the king, or at Ralph. The categories he uses, the way he qualifies behaviors is "other." *Talio* is biblical—it evokes Ancient Hebrew Law as well as Old Gospel God's anger against his chosen yet unfaithful People. And that is what Orderic has in mind: that savage deed is indeed given as an example of where bad faith sometimes leads.[21]

The useful index and concordance Marjorie Chibnall has established in her edition provide us with facility to analyze Orderic's terminology. There are two traditional Latin words for vengeance: *ultio* and *vindicta*. *Ultio* and this family was clearly Orderic's preference, if we look at figures. The term *ultio* occurs 53 times, *vindicta* only 16; meanwhile, the whole *ultio* family (verb *ulciscor*, noun *ultor*, adjective *ultrix*) occurs twice as much as the *vindicta* family (verb *vindico*, noun and adjective *vindex*). However, as John Hudson has pointed out, these terms remain ambiguous, as they do not refer exclusively to "horizontal vengeance," but also to "vertical punishment":[22] justice or penalty, as war, cannot be easily distinguished from feud based solely on the terminology.

Another term widely used by Orderic is *guerra*, an appellation some historians identify with the notion of feud. It occurs 51 times in the *Historia Ecclesiastica*. The translation proposed by Marjorie Chibnall is "private war." However, the same term is used also to refer to other kinds of military conflict, for instance a

---

[20] Dominique Barthélemy, "La mutation féodale a-t-elle eu lieu?" *Annales HSS*, 47 (1992): 767–77, especially pp. 772–4. This article is included in his collection *La mutation de l'an mil a-t-elle eu lieu?* (Paris, 1997).
[21] *Ecclesiastical History* 6:210–12.
[22] Hudson, "Faide," pp. 348 and 381.

"public" war between King William and King Philip,[23] and a revolt against King Henry.[24] Indeed, the traditional term for "public" war, *bellum*, is sometimes used to qualify a conflict motivated by rancor, for example the war the King of Norway wages against his Irish father-in-law.[25] The clear distinction between *guerra* and *bellum* that does exist in a contemporary Angevin chronicle[26] is much blurred in Orderic's work.

Eventually, even less specific words can describe feuds in Orderic's text. Terms for "anger" are often used—and the emotional background of vengeance is discussed in greater detail below.

Telling feuds

A semantic approach to the definition of feuds needs to be compared with a chronological one. Recent historians have argued for an evolution of military— and social—practices of vengeance, from early medieval warriors executing their vanquished opponents to later medieval knights courteously ransoming their prisoners.[27] When it comes to Norman feuds, according to John Gillingham, blood-feuds date from before 1066, whereas *guerra* is a twelfth-century practice, connected to chivalry.

Orderic Vitalis offers a major piece of evidence in this respect. In his works, some instances of eleventh-century vengeance are reported briefly and, as they imply murder and retaliation, deserve the name blood-feud. Meanwhile, Orderic incorporates for the years c.1070–1140 several longer vengeance narratives, more accurate in their depiction of events (likely because he himself witnessed them) and less likely to include a death.

Is this twofold description of feud a sign of the growth of the chivalric ethos? Does the split in Orderic's approach to vengeance imply that Norman warriors c.1040 feuded to kill, whereas their grandsons c.1100 feuded to gain honor or wealth? The answer is surely not that easy. The distinction to stress is rather between two different kinds of feud-tales than between two kinds of feud.

---

[23] *Ecclesiastical History* 5:212.

[24] *Ecclesiastical History* 6:332.

[25] *Ecclesiastical History* 5:220.

[26] Bruno Lemesle, "Le comte d'Anjou face aux rébellions (1129–1151)," in Barthélemy, Bougard and Le Jan (eds), *La vengeance, 400–1200*, pp. 199–236, at p. 206.

[27] I summarize here in the shortest, and, I fear, most simplistic way ideas defended by John Gillingham, "1066 and the Introduction of Chivalry into England," in George Garnett and John Hudson (eds), *Law and Government in Medieval England and Normandy: Essays in Honour of Sir James Holt* (Cambridge, 1994), pp. 31–55 and Matthew Strickland, "Slaughter, Slavery and Ransom? The Impact of the Conquest on Conduct in Warfare," in Carola Hicks (ed.), *England in the Eleventh Century* (Stamford, 1992), pp. 41–60; see also his *War and Chivalry: The Conduct and Perception of War in England and Normandy, 1066–1217* (Cambridge, 1996).

Eleventh-century blood-feuds

Writing about eleventh-century Normandy, Orderic Vitalis gives us greater detail about feuds merely alluded to by William of Jumièges, such as the murders of Gilbert of Brionne or of Osbern the duke's steward. Details provided by Orderic can help reconstruct a feuding context to these deaths. For example, the assassination of Osbern by William of Montgomery (c.1040–42) was eventually avenged by his man Barnon of Glos, who entered the murderer's house at night and killed him and his companions.[28] The monk's narrative seems also to imply that the hanging of Walter of Sordenia by Bellême's men (in the 1030s) brought about the murder of their lord Robert, who was at that time kept in custody by Walter's sons.[29]

These tales are nonetheless laconic, the details scarce and the information scattered here and there in Orderic's writing. An extreme case in point is the death of Gilbert of Brionne (c.1040). In Orderic's interpolations to the *Gesta Normannorum Ducum*, Gilbert is said to have been killed along with Fulk Giroie and Walkelin of Pont-Échanfroi (Fulk's brother-in-law) by Odo the Fat and Robert Giroie, Fulk's own brother; the deeds were done by the will of Ralph of Gacé.[30] Ralph was the son of Archbishop Robert and a member of a ducal family. His feud with Gilbert probably had roots in the struggle for leadership when the actual duke, William the Bastard, was still a child: he replaced Gilbert as William's guardian. As Matthew Bennett has argued, this peculiar political background suggests that we question the use of the terms "vengeance" or "feud" in this case.[31]

Orderic does not offer any explanation for the presence of a member of the Giroie family on *both* sides. However, the monk does offer further information on the background of the relationship between the Giroie brothers and Gilbert.[32] Fulk's fidelity—fealty—to Gilbert is stressed twice in the *Historia Ecclesiastica*. Elsewhere, however, another part of the background is unveiled: Gilbert tried to take advantage of their father's death to take away from the young Giroies the village of Le Sap. Duke Robert brought peace between them, yet Gilbert did not give up his plans. According to Orderic, Gilbert was killed as he tried again to seize Le Sap. Only brief mentions of Gilbert's murder are found later in the *Historia*.[33]

Because Orderic had in mind either Giroie history or the anarchy of the 1030s, he fails to give a definitive account of this feud. Most of his eleventh-century

---

[28] *Gesta Normannorum* 2:94.

[29] *Gesta Normannorum* 2:56.

[30] *Gesta Normannorum* 2:94.

[31] Bennett, "Violence," p.132. But I have already stressed the weakness of Bennett's analysis: he contrasts once more the notion of a "private murder"—"part of a feud"—with the idea of "a clear political assassination." Feud is indeed part of medieval politics.

[32] *Ecclesiastical History* 2:24.

[33] *Ecclesiastical History* 2:120; 3:89; 4:208. William of Jumièges also mentions Gilbert's fate (*Gesta Normannorum* 2:92).

feud-tales are written on the same pattern: they are disconnected episodes set in the context of a broader narrative. The murder of William Repostel by Osmond Drengot (1020s–1030s) functions to introduce the Norman "conquest" of Southern Italy,[34] while the hostility between the Tosny and the Beaumont families (*c.*1040) merely preludes either an account of the Beaumont house[35] or the report of the monastic conversion of Robert of Grandmesnil.[36] In the same way, a battle between Gilbert of Brionne and Enguerrand of Ponthieu (*c.*1030) is mentioned only because it brought about the conversion of Herluin and the foundation of the abbey of Bec, and the beheading of a knight Gonthier (*c.*1020s) by Warin of Bellême, who was purportedly possessed by a demon, is reported because Orderic wishes to underscore the wickedness of this family.[37] Finally, the mutilation of William Giroie by William of Bellême, mentioned in the *Historia Ecclesiastica*,[38] is described with greater precision in the *Gesta*.[39] That Orderic may have heard the story from his brother monks, and that this event led to the (re)foundation of the abbey of Saint-Évroult explain why the chronicler devoted such space to this case. (Another exception to the trend is the tale of the Sors brothers, which I will discuss below.)

Ultimately, I fear, there is not much left in these earlier episodes for the historian interested in factual details of historical feuds. The way Orderic embroiders allusions to murders and feuds in his narrative implies one has to proceed cautiously when comparing these "facts" to those described for a later period.

Twelfth-century wars

Feuds *c.*1100–1140 reported in the *Historia Ecclesiastica* are no longer mere tangents but belong to the spine of Orderic's narrative as it approaches his own days and adheres to a less confused chronology. They come "naturally" under the monk's quill and they are told with greater precision, so the reader glimpses a subtler and more complex world than was described before. This has two consequences for our topic.

The first is the apparent scarcity of deaths during feuds between 1100 and 1400; these pages lack the bloody density of his eleventh-century tales. Indeed, as the range of violent deeds is more widely covered by Orderic's narrative, deaths seem rarer. The usual *guerra* instead targets peasants and goods. A feud between Rotrou of Perche and Robert of Bellême provides a clear example:

---

[34] *Gesta Normannorum* 2:154; *Ecclesiastical History* 2:56.
[35] *Gesta Normannorum* 2:96–8.
[36] *Ecclesiastical History* 2:41.
[37] *Gesta Normannorum* 2:50; *Ecclesiastical History* 6:396.
[38] *Ecclesiastical History* 2:14.
[39] *Gesta Normannorum* 2:108–10.

> They fought each other ferociously, looting and burning in each other's territories and adding calamity to calamity. They plundered poor and helpless people, constantly made them suffer losses or live in fear of losses, and brought distress to their dependants, knights and peasants alike, who endured many disasters.[40]

Violent deaths are reported in the broader course of events, for example accounts of sieges: we learn of Gilbert du Pin's death at Brionne, of Richard of Montfort's at Conches.[41] Richer of Laigle is similarly mortally wounded in a skirmish during the siege of Sainte-Suzanne. His men were eager to kill the youngster who shot the fatal arrow, yet in a last whisper the agonizing man pleaded for clemency.[42] Is mercy a new value? Orderic adds that Richer's companions left the boy unharmed, but *doubled their efforts* to win the siege. Rancor did not vanish—the boy's life was probably just not worth that of Richer.

The feeling that these later conflicts are less harsh and less bloody could be just a narrative illusion—or not. Orderic's assertion that only three knights died at Brémule battle is often quoted.[43] He points to the quality of chain-mail, to the appeal for ransoms, but also to the fact that "as Christian soldiers they did not thirst for the blood of their brother, but rejoiced in a just victory given by God"—note that the feud here is no longer theirs but God's. Yet we can still find disputes that might have deserved the "blood-feud" label. Roger, made viscount of Cotentin by King Stephen, was killed by Normans, causing his parents and friends to rally to Geoffrey Plantagenet's side as the battle against the Angevin army began.[44]

The second consequence of Orderic's more detailed accounts is the fascination they raise among historians. As my note on violent deaths has shown, it brings enough evidence to support one theory or another. Orderic finally seems an extraordinary anthropological informant, as each key element of an ideal feuding society can be exemplified by an extract from his work—and sometimes contradicted meanwhile from elsewhere.

Violence is regulated. There is a binary rhythm in feud: Roger of Tosny seized Vaudreuil castle; Galeran of Meulan struck back, taking the castle and destroying another at Acquigny; Roger then burnt three villages belonging to Galeran.[45] Yet this binary mentality does not prevent the same "player" from striking twice in a row, as the feud between William of Evreux and Ralph of Tosny shows: after some skirmishes, William unsuccessfully attacked Ralph's stronghold at Conches. Then his men plundered Ralph's lands to clear him of the shame of failure.[46] More than a strict alternation of hits, the process seems to aim to keep the balance of honor.

---

[40] *Ecclesiastical History* 6:396.
[41] *Ecclesiastical History* 4:210 and 214, respectively.
[42] *Ecclesiastical History* 4:48.
[43] *Ecclesiastical History* 6:240.
[44] *Ecclesiastical History* 6:512–14.
[45] *Ecclesiastical History* 6:458.
[46] *Ecclesiastical History* 4:214–16.

In such an honor society, players practice face-saving.[47] Men of the castle of Vignats clearly formulated the issue:

> The garrison in fact were hoping to be stormed in battle, for they were ready to surrender the castle in the face of a strong assault; they could not honorably (*dignabantur*), for fear of earning condemnation as faithless deserters.[48]

As a matter of fact, a Norman garrison had to endure King Henry's scornful reproaches that they had too easily given up the fight.[49]

Feud, as it is an inner war, has special rules.[50] Talking of feuds and rebellions caused by the rivalry between King Henry and his nephew William Clito, Orderic names them "more than civil war," and explains, as an anthropologist would do, self-restraint and balance-keeping in war:

> In the general confusion that always occurs in conflicts between kinsmen [King Henry] was unable to trust his own men. Men who ate with him favored the cause of his nephew and his other enemies ... Ties of blood bound together brothers and friends and kinsmen who were fighting on both sides, so that neither wished to harm the other.[51]

However, this wealth of information may become a trap for historians: extracting elements without paying heed to the aim of Orderic's discourse or his tendency towards understatement could be misleading.

Understanding vengeance

In the second part of this chapter, I will discuss a specific moment in feud—when it begins. I will focus now on how Orderic, or rather the feuders according to Orderic, express and explain their rancor, in order that I may stress the variety of interpretations that can be drawn.

Expressing feud

The way vengeance comes about is first shown by the way it is written up by Orderic. When he comes to discuss actual feuds, our monk talks about the flow of

---

[47] On the notion of face: Erving Goffman, *The Presentation of Self in Everyday Life* (New York, 1959).

[48] *Ecclesiastical History* 6:22.

[49] *Ecclesiastical History* 6:194.

[50] Raymond Verdier, "Le système vindicatoire," in Raymond Verdier (ed.), *La Vengeance* (2 vols, Paris, 1981), vol. 1, pp. 13–42.

[51] *Ecclesiastical History* 6:200.

passions and the tide of emotions. See, for example, how he explains the Tosny–Évreux feud that began c.1090, to some an exemplification of Robert Curthose's "anarchy":

> The Countess Helwise [of Évreux] was incensed (*irata*) against Isabel of Conches for some slighting remarks, and in her anger (*per iram*) used all her powers to urge Count William and his barons to take up arms. So the hearts of brave men were moved to anger (*in furore*) through the suspicions and quarrels of women.[52]

This short extract exemplifies the process of chain-reaction by which malevolent emotions fuel the feud. Vivid expressions of passion respond one to another: as Geoffrey Plantagenet, asking his father-in-law for castles, was rebuked by King Henry, he became *iratus*, which in return awoke Henry's *furor*.[53]

If Orderic usually recalls the emotional context of feuds, he does not provide us with their actual causes. Most often, he lets us know the state of hostility between two magnates only by telling us that "a feud has begun," and by reporting emotions and military deeds, giving no more clues. A usual premise was for a lord to plunder his neighborhood, in order to gather in his castle enough supplies to withstand a siege.[54] Explicit explanations are rare, and so are discourses from the opponents which could throw light on their inner motives. One instance of a formal ritual of defiance is mentioned—when Reginald of Bailleul came to King Henry's court to renounce his fealty.[55] However, Orderic only alludes to the words exchanged, but stresses once more the emotional side of the scene, especially the anger of King Henry.

This way of telling things is part of Orderic's world-view: human passions are boiling. Yet it could also be part of the world he describes, a world which puts emphasis on symbolic communication, on the defense of honor and face-saving. Emotions are a narrative device for Orderic as well as a social code. It is no wonder that historians of feud have been eager to renew the history of emotions. Feelings had long been an embarrassing matter for historians.[56] Marc Bloch notes with a sigh that "despairs, anger, impulsions, brutal changes in mind" challenge historians' rational minds.[57] However, he was also one of the first to try

---

[52] *Ecclesiastical History* 4:212.
[53] *Ecclesiastical History* 6:444.
[54] *Ecclesiastical History* 6:86 and 192.
[55] *Ecclesiastical History* 6:214.
[56] What follows is only a brief reflection on the history of emotions. A convenient survey is Hyams, *Rancor*, pp. 34–68; see also Barbara Rosenwein (ed.), *Anger's Past: The Social Uses of an Emotion in the Middle Ages* (Ithaca, 1998). For a sociologist's viewpoint, see Philippe Braud, *L'émotion en politique* (Paris, 1996).
[57] Marc Bloch, *La société féodale* (Paris, 1939), pp. 116–17.

to overcome a merely psychological approach by linking emotional instability to medieval insecurity.[58]

Another theory soon met success, Norbert Elias's civilizing process.[59] In a word, the Austrian sociologist used German literary sources from the later Middle Ages and French historiography of the High Middle Ages to demonstrate that emotional instability came from the lack of social and political control by institutions.[60] Indeed, modern state-building since the Renaissance implies the spread of strict rules of behavior that limit emotional displays. As historians of feud question the state-centered minds of their elders, they are bound to question—and disqualify—the "civilizing process."

In this context, how far can we rely on medieval "informants" such as Orderic? On the one hand, we might take what he tells as a given, treating his narrative as a pure reflection of his social context. On the other hand, we could consider his discourse as no more than an expression of his personal and monastic world-view.

In matters of feud, emotion and ritual, both attitudes have their supporters. The school of *anthropologie historique* centered on Jacques Le Goff has worked on the ecclesiological history of emotions, developing what we could call a speculative historical anthropology.[61] This contrasts with a pragmatic historical anthropology, which claims that expressions of emotions are part of a broader social code that

---

[58] Similarly, his colleague Lucien Febvre pointed to everyday-life contrasts between day and night, meager times and feast days ("Histoire et psychologie: Une vue d'ensemble" (1938) and "La sensibilité et l'histoire: Comment reconstituer la vie affective d'autrefois?" (1941), in *Combats pour l'histoire* (Paris, 1992), pp. 207–20 and 221–38). This kind of physiological explanation was later supported by Robert Fossier, who pointed to unbalanced food and abuse of alcohol or other psychotropic substances (*Enfance de l'Europe: Aspects économiques et sociaux* (Paris, 1982), p. 117). Furthermore, Febvre, maybe having in mind Nazi *grand-messes* at Nuremberg or their Communist equivalents on 1 May, insisted on the collective nature of emotions, as did contemporary sociologists such as Maurice Halbwachs ("L'expression des émotions et la société" (never published before), in *Classes sociales et morphologie* (Paris, 1972), pp. 164–73) or Marcel Mauss ("Les techniques du corps" (1936), in *Sociologie et anthropologie* (Paris, 1968), pp. 363–86).

[59] Norbert Elias, *Über den Prozeß der Zivilisation: Soziogenetische und psychogenetische Untersuchungen*, (2 vols, Basle, 1939), translated into English in 1969 and into French in 1974.

[60] For example, Achille Luchaire, i.e. historians who still saw medieval emotions as irrational, even pathological.

[61] Le Goff himself has devoted lectures to laughter in the Middle Ages ("Rire au Moyen Âge" (1989), in *Un autre Moyen Âge* (Paris, 1999), pp. 1343–56); one of his disciples, Piroska Nagy, has worked on the theology of tears (*Le Don des larmes au Moyen Âge: Un instrument «spirituel» en quête d'institution, V^e–XIIIe siècles* (Paris, 2000)). They hold on in a way to the "civilizing process," but instead of pointing to the role of state-building as Elias did, they stress control by the Church. Furthermore, they conclude that any history of emotions cannot but be a theological history; in Le Goff's words, to seek actual emotions would be "fishing" in the texts (Le Goff, "Rire," p. 1345).

rules medieval political communication.[62] Feelings mentioned in the evidence should not be read literally: the issue is not whether they were actually felt or whether they reflect the inner state of mind but rather to point at the range of meanings they could be given in interaction, whether consciously or not.

Stephen White and Gerd Althoff are surely right in describing social rules of emotional behavior, but only if regarded less as a formal code than as a miscellaneous panoply of gestures; and only if it is remembered that they are known solely through a narrative distorting glass.[63] Orderic, like any chronicler, plays on the multi-layered perceptions of emotions according to what he has to tell. Indeed, in a religious context tears refer to piety and closeness with God; in a feud-tale, they go with anger, to proclaim that a death or a wound is taken as an injury to avenge.[64] Speaking of one's resentment on the edge of feud, Orderic can depict it as mere anger, a sad anger, zealous indignation, an earthly embodiment of *ira Dei* against a trouble-maker, or condemn it as rage moved by devilish feelings of envy. But knights in the midst of battles, whether pious or sinner, are always described as "furious."

Vengeance as legitimation

Beyond the alternatives of "Orderic as a biased monk" and "Orderic as a fair informant," we have to question the points of convergence between the ideology of vengeance and the reality of feud. Can we point to the social efficiency of the discourse of vengeance? Is claiming vengeance useful? Can we find clues for a vengeance ideology in Orderic's world-view? And should we distinguish strictly between vengeance and rebellion?

First of all, in the same way that the emotions alluded to are part of social and literary codes and cannot be taken as concrete evidence for genuinely felt resentment, the justification given for a feud may not be the feud's cause. For instance, claims of inherited hatred hardly seem more than mere words. Have a look at Richard of Montfort's career: his brother Amaury was killed while helping Ascelin Goel to storm William of Breteuil's land. Orderic says then that Richard inherited his land as well as the will to avenge him.[65] Nevertheless, he displayed little indication of blood-thirstiness: indeed, he took a leading role in the peace

---

[62] Gerd Althoff, "'Ira regis': Prolegomena to an History of Royal Anger" and Stephen White, "The Politics of Anger," in Rosenwein (ed.), *Anger's Past*, pp. 59–74 and 127–52.

[63] Philippe Buc, "'Noch einmal 919': Of the Ritualized Demise of Kings and Political Rituals in General," in Gerd Althoff (ed.), *Rituale, Zeichen, Werte* (Münster, 2004), pp. 151–78.

[64] For example, William Giroie's friends and parents mourned him after his mutilation, but eagerly sought vengeance from William of Bellême (*Gesta Normannorum* 2:110). Bishop Ivo of Séez was sad and angry when putting fire to his church in order to get rid of the Sor brothers (*Gesta Normannorum* 2:112).

[65] *Ecclesiastical History* 4:200.

negotiations after William of Breteuil had been made prisoner in February 1091.[66] Richard was eventually killed at the siege of Conches, in November 1091 or 1092, when he sided with his former enemies William of Évreux and William of Breteuil against Ralph of Tosny. Orderic adds he was mourned on both sides, because he was a nephew to the Count of Évreux as well as a relative of Ralph's wife.[67]

Hatred between families is a specific social construct that can endure only if familial and political configuration does not evolve. As a consequence, it is possible to refuse rancor leading to feud. There is indeed no objective offense, but rather a process of the social assessment of particular acts, some regarded as meaningless, others becoming rated as insults. Gilbert of Laigle was killed c.1090 by knights serving Geoffrey of Mortagne. In order to prevent Gilbert's family, especially his nephew Gilbert, from viewing his death as an occasion for vengeance, Geoffrey labeled it "an accident" and hurried to give his friendship and his daughter to Gilbert junior. The wedding was even more welcome in that both men had a common enemy, Robert of Bellême. Orderic contrasts in his narrative the success of this peacemaking by wedding with the missed reconciliation of Ascelin Goël and William of Breteuil—the latter, captured, had to surrender the hand of his daughter as part of his ransom, but, ashamed, resumed the feud as soon as he could.[68]

Tales of unavenged deaths clearly demonstrate the importance of qualifying insults. Two sons of Giroie died from accidents. Arnold simply fell heavily onto a stone.[69] When Hugh, in contrast, was killed in a training exercise by his own squire, his brothers tried to avenge him.[70] The use of a weapon in the later case may explain why it is regarded as a murder, and not an accident. However, if they expressed the wish to avenge Hugh, the Giroie brothers did not display a strong will to hunt down the squire to kill him—one may wonder if the rancor was not, at least somewhat, faked, in order again to save face.

Similarly, introducing oneself as somebody's avenger implies more of a will to inherit than kill. At Robert Giroie's death, in strange circumstances[71] while in revolt against Duke William, his nephew Arnold resumed his fight at first, having in mind to keep the castle of Saint-Céneri for himself and not his young cousins.[72]

William Pantoul (c.1080) was accused of being an accomplice in Mabel of Bellême's murder by her parents, who sought his death.[73] It might seem at first

---

[66] *Ecclesiastical History* 4:202.
[67] *Ecclesiastical History* 4:216.
[68] *Ecclesiastical History* 4:200–202.
[69] *Ecclesiastical History* 2:28.
[70] *Ecclesiastical History* 2:30.
[71] Orderic says he was poisoned; however, poison stories in his works actually mirror miracle tales. Both seek causality of an extraordinary nature in order to make sense of a succession of unrelated events.
[72] *Ecclesiastical History* 2:80.
[73] *Ecclesiastical History* 3:160–62.

glance a perfect exemplification of blood-feud, yet William had actually taken no part in the assassination. The traditional interpretation is that the friend of an enemy is an enemy, and indeed William was the murderer's friend; William had reasons of his own to hate Mabel, as she had just seized one of the castles he held from her. What if the Bellêmes were simply disguising their resentment against an unreliable vassal behind words of vengeance? In any event their hatred was short-lived: once William had passed an ordeal, with the support of Saint-Évroult's monks, he remained a vassal of Roger of Montgomery—Mabel's husband, who confirmed his gifts to these monks[74]—and of Robert of Bellême, until he disinherited him in 1102.[75]

Monastic vengeance culture

Orderic habitually situates human passions, including feud, within a wider worldview:

> Just as the sea is never wholly still and safe, but is tossed continually as it ebbs and flows; and although it may seem calm sometimes to those who are safe on shore nevertheless by its continual movement and tossing fills sailor with fear: so this present age is continually troubled by change and fluctuates ceaselessly through all the changing moods of joy and sorrow. Amongst the perverse lovers of the world, who can never be wholly satisfied by the world, disputes frequently arise and grow to immense proportions. And when everyone strives to raise himself and become better than this equals, he forgets justice and defies the law of God; and as all snatch at the same things human blood is cruelly shed. The old history books are full of stories that prove this; and in our own day it is shown by the many rumors that pass through towns and villages, bringing to some momentary joy, to others weeping and mourning. I have briefly mentioned some events of this kind in my book, and now I can add accounts of others as I have learned them from my elders.[76]

This monk views his own times through Christian lenses: what happens around him renews what occurred in the Bible or in the age of the early Church.[77] In the world he writes of, he sees the hand of God justly punishing sinners, or the whisper of the Enemy of mankind inspiring dreadful deeds.

---

[74] *Ecclesiastical History* 3:138 and 154.

[75] *Ecclesiastical History* 6:24. Orderic does not explain this act. William joined then King Henry in his campaign against Robert. He might have acted this way by vengeance, however Orderic does not mention anything of this kind; the William Pantoul of 1102 may have been a son of the William of Pantoul *c.*1080.

[76] *Ecclesiastical History* 2:302–304.

[77] *Ecclesiastical History* 4:228: "I find many things in the pages of Scripture which, if they are subtly interpreted, seem to resemble the happenings of our own time."

The Sors affair is an exemplary depiction of Orderic's view of society, which is far from original. As he reports the career of Ivo of Bellême, bishop of Séez, Orderic mentions his harsh reaction against three men of the Sor family: because they had turned a cathedral tower into a stronghold and a "cavern of thieves" (*speluncam latronum*, a biblical phrase Orderic uses frequently), the prelate had to set fire to his own church to make them flee.[78] But the story continues. As the chronicler tells it, the three brothers die dramatically: the eldest was killed by a peasant he had tortured, as he was trying to flee from an unintended assault; the second was mortally wounded on his way back from plundering; the third was hit by a missile in a skirmish with another noble Norman.[79]

When writing this bloody tale, Orderic is no longer in the register for his eleventh-century feud-tales I have described above, one, that is, where he alludes to feuds in order to contextualize a character, a family or an epoch. He has switched to another narrative construction, the depiction of a miracle, wherein the chronological succession of events is interpreted as a causal chain that serves a moral purpose. The deaths of the three brothers are linked by Orderic (although they might not have occurred at the same time) and the text assumes implicitly that they are a consequence of the Séez incident. Moreover, Orderic places them in a wider moral context: to lay hands on church properties is to incur God's wrath. What he describes is not merely the trivial end of three petty knights, but three perfect exemplifications of righteous vengeance according to Christian and social values. Each died "instantly", that is, without *viaticum*, with no chance to gain salvation. Their honor died with them, as two were killed by peasants; the third is hit by a "missile" (*pilum*), a form of death probably not considered as honorable as a sword's blow.

This is not the sole example in Orderic's work. Under King Stephen's reign, the death of Richard *Silvanus* was pointed to as a divine punishment and his body was excluded from the cemetery.[80] Orderic uses a rare Greek word to refer to Richard, *biothanatus*, a term he uses when speaking of the violent deaths of impious characters.[81] In his view, a man's death can sum up his whole life, and indicate his

---

[78] *Gesta Normannorum* 2:112–14. Gérard Louise thinks they could be Bellême's relatives, but cannot prove it; Joseph Decaëns, "L'évêque Yves de Sées," in Pierre Bouet and François Neveux (eds), *Les évêques normands du XIe siècle* (Caen, 1995), pp. 117–37, describes them in a *mutationniste* way, as typical year-thousand *milites* benefiting from a feudal revolution, but is likely wrong in asserting their family is only known by this episode, as people surnamed "Sor" appear in the entourage of Roger of Montgomery (husband to the Bellême heiress)—see *Regesta regum Anglol-Normannorum*, vol. 2, ed. Henry A. Cronne and Charles Johnson (Oxford, 1956), vol. 2, nos 1307, 1466 and 1609. There might have been a link between Sor and the family of *Sordenia*, as Van Houts suggests (*Gesta Normannorum* 2:56, n. 4); they would have then switched from one fealty to another.

[79] *Gesta Normannorum* 2:114–16.

[80] *Ecclesiastical History* 6:492.

[81] *Ecclesiastical History* 5:292.

fate in the beyond. Speaking of the Bellêmes, Orderic says that their wickedness was "proved by their horrible ends ...; none of them has met an ordinary or normal death like other men."[82]

Yet on occasion God's vengeance is understated: Robert of Chaumont fell from his horse and died as he was coming back from looting lands belonging to the abbey of Saint-Ouen of Rouen.[83] Giroie son of Giroie died from a shot of madness after having plundered lands of the Church of Lisieux.[84]

Orderic contrasts virtuous characters, aware of heavenly everlasting goods, with an earthly society naturally shaped by mundane passions and twisted by the wheel of Fortune:

> Worldly honor, like a bubble, suddenly bursts and vanishes ... . Lovers of the world pursue corruptible things, are corrupted as they scale the steep heights of vice, and suddenly fall back to be besmirched in the depths ... leaving to those who still live and breathe nothing but cautionary tales.[85]

This rhetoric can eventually lead to the moral disqualification of the feuders. The feud between Roger of Tosny and Robert of Leicester during King Stephen's reign is compared to the Beast of the Book of Revelation.[86] In this case, both seem to incur Orderic's disapproval, but is our monk always so balanced?

His world-view implies that in relating feuds, the chronicler is not a fair informant—a fact that historians of Normandy should not play down; it also stresses the degree to which Orderic understands his world as a vengeance society, where even God feuds.[87]

Feuding with the king

Nevertheless, Orderic sometimes includes in his narrative short explicit explanations or long discourse in direct speech, which unveil how the opponents themselves are said to justify their bellicose attitude. We should keep in mind that these are Orderic's own literary constructions and not evidence for lay eloquence—a skill nevertheless usually pointed to by the monk when describing a noble character.[88] Yet, they cannot be wholly dismissed either. Even if the motives Orderic suggests

---

[82] *Ecclesiastical History* 4:152.

[83] *Ecclesiastical History* 2:154.

[84] *Ecclesiastical History* 2:30.

[85] *Ecclesiastical History* 6:476. See also 6:512: "In the ebb and flow of this world no power endures for long."

[86] *Ecclesiastical History* 6:458.

[87] See also *Ecclesiastical History* 6:8: "Transgressors who defy the Law deserve only/ Punishment from the wrath of heaven."

[88] Among many other examples, Count Helias of Maine is ready-tongued and persuasive (*Ecclesiastical History* 5:232).

in his emotional narrative most likely do not reflect actual words or thoughts of the protagonists, the norms they referred to are not mere monkish fancies. Orderic attributes to some thoughts they did not have; he bears testimony less to actual inner motives than to the way one could justify one's rancor.

Circa 1090, when Robert Curthose wanted to give back the stronghold of Brionne to Robert of Meulan and Roger of Beaumont, Robert's father, its castellan, Robert son of Baldwin, demurred. An heir to the aforesaid Gilbert of Brionne, he explained:

> If you wish to keep Brionne for yourself, as your father held it, I will restore it at once. Otherwise I will protect my inheritance, and will surrender it to no man as long as I live. It is common knowledge in this land that Richard the Elder, duke of Normandy, gave Brionne with the whole country to his son Godfrey, and that he at his death handed it on like fashion to his son Gilbert. Then after Count Gilbert had been brutally assassinated by evil men, and the guardians of his sons had fled with the boys to Baldwin of Flanders for fear of their enemies, your father kept a part of my grandfather's county in his own hand and alienated part to outsiders at his will. Long afterwards your father, having married to the daughter of Baldwin of Flanders, at his request restored Meules and Le Sap to my father Baldwin, and gave him his aunt's daughter in marriage. He also restored Bienfaite and Orbec to Baldwin's brother Richard. Finally by your favour, my lord, whom I wish to serve in all things, I now hold Brionne, my grandfather Gilbert's chief castle, and will continue to do so while God upholds my right.[89]

By recounting Robert's genealogy and reinterpreting his familial history, this speech intertwines references to hereditary right and to ducal favor—in a tone that turns bitter when alluding to William the Conqueror's unscrupulous gift of the land to "others." These two notions, heredity and fidelity, constitute the spine of discourses of rancor. Lords on the verge of fighting are eager to prove their rights, which are necessarily rooted in the past. References to hereditary rights are the most common, but cannot be distinguished from hereditary favor, and hatred too is said to be inherited. But past interferes with present and demands reinterpretation, since one is on the one hand tied to one's ancestors, and on the other entangled in the networks of lords and friends.

In these discourses rancor is mixed with defiance: it erupted because the duke (or the king) threatened hereditary rights. Hearing that King Stephen was coming, the sons of Robert of Beauchamp refused to deliver him their castle. Taking their point of view, Orderic takes care to explain that this attitude should not be labeled as rebellion, but as fear of losing the patrimony, since the king had just married a Beauchamp girl to his friend Waleran of Meulan's brother, Hugh le Poer.[90]

---

[89] *Ecclesiastical History* 4:208.
[90] *Ecclesiastical History* 6:510.

What is at stake in these discourses of rancor is the relationship with the duke or the king, as if there could be no real hatred without the inevitable involvement of a powerful man, according to Orderic. The main issue here is the capacity of duke or king to make inheritance settlements. When William of Roumare claimed his mother's lands and was rebuked by the king, he furiously began a *guerra* against him. Richer of Laigle asked King Henry for his father's inheritance, but after having been turned down several times, concluded a pact with his enemies, King Louis of France and Amaury of Montfort, who had himself rebelled in support of his claim to the county of Evreux. Richer's rebellion did not last long: after Henry had eventually accepted the bargain, the lord returned to his loyalty. However, his castle did not resist the French army long: obviously, the old pact was not forgotten.

In 1136, William of Pacy stormed lands he claimed by inheritance, as his father Eustace of Breteuil had held them, playing down the fact King Henry eventually seized them.[91] Discourses of rancor aim thus at disguising treason under the appearance of justice, as well as providing an attractive agenda in order to gather friends and allies—their support is far from being mechanical. The tale is devised so as to put all the wrongs on the opponent's side: a claim of denial of justice is the best kind of justification. Robert of Neubourg rebelled against Henry Beauclerc because the king dismissed the claims he had against Waleran of Meulan;[92] Amaury of Montfort pointed to the zeal and corruption of royal officers in his county;[93] Ascelin, son of André, joined the King's enemies because he could no longer stand the judges of the Archbishop of Rouen.[94]

Furthermore, Orderic himself sometimes points to the role of feud in the exercise of justice: William of Eu, who had rebelled against King William Rufus, was sentenced to mutilation. The punishment was inflicted by Hugh of Chester, who had his own reasons to resent William, who had, according to Orderic, first married then cheated Hugh's sister.[95] Similarly, Orderic explains that Robert of Bellême came to support Ascelin Goël's enemies from an "old hatred" against him; yet the chronicler lets us know by the way that Robert took part in the feud in the "public" army led by Duke Robert, *in expeditione generali*.[96]

What should a historian of feud think of so-called "rebellions"? As I recalled earlier, the theory of medieval feud was born out of criticisms of the old model of state-building. Feuds are no longer seen as a part of feudal anarchy, but as another kind of order; kings or dukes are themselves players in this game, but they learned from their courtiers and clerical propagandists to disguise their own vengeance under pretense of Roman law by accusing their enemies of "rebellion." Yet we

---

[91] *Ecclesiastical History* 6:456.
[92] *Ecclesiastical History* 6:200.
[93] *Ecclesiastical History* 6:330.
[94] *Ecclesiastical History* 6:216.
[95] *Ecclesiastical History* 4:284.
[96] *Ecclesiastical History* 4:288.

should be careful to not play down these discourses on rebellion too easily: even as pure embroidery, they do show the specific part princes played in the process of feuds.[97]

Furthermore, by stressing rules of conduct and "peace in the feud," feud analysis does not pay too much attention to political change. It is of course also a matter of time scale. Take for example the Beaumont-Meulan family and their enemies, the Tosnys. They fought each other in the middle of the eleventh century, according to Orderic's early feud-tales.[98] A generation later, they are adversaries again during Curthose's reign.[99] Another generation later, they sided with opposing rulers during the war between King Stephen and Count Geoffrey.[100] One might on the one hand stress the lasting structural feud between these two families. On the other hand, repeated reconciliations do not return the parties to their original positions, but rather imply, again and again, a shift in status; these parties have a history of their own.

Dukes and kings were traditional partners in the feud-game—one could gain their friendship and expect their help, as with any patron. Yet this friendship was so valuable that it became of itself a motive for feud. When Robert Curthose gave the castle of Exmes to Gilbert of Laigle, Robert of Bellême got angry, and began a feud against this neighbor.[101] Vengeance could also be sought against those who worked on removing ducal or royal friendship: c.1100, Ralph of Tosny and William of Évreux allied themselves against Robert of Meulan, whom they accused of setting William Rufus against them.[102] They had waited till King William's death, nursing their anger and resentment, from fear of his reaction.

Indeed, dukes and kings also had ideological and material means sufficient to play further. With the Church supporting them, they could disqualify their opponents on a moral level. Meanwhile, they could rally to their cause more lords than any other baron, mustering a powerful force when it came to castle sieges, for instance. A "friend" of this kind was valuable indeed. Furthermore, he was free to act within as well as outside "traditional" feuding culture, since he could manage other's feuds to balance local powers and enforce his own, and since he could impose, even against the tide, capital punishment or life imprisonment.[103] When King Henry ordered the blinding of Luke of La Barre, a petty knight caught in a rebel castle, voices protested; even the Count of Flanders began to plead for the king's mercy, because Luke had been captured in his lord's service. Henry refuted

---

[97] See, for the Plantagenet case in Anjou, Lemesle, "Le comte d'Anjou."
[98] *Gesta Normannorum* 2:96–8; *Ecclesiastical History* 2:41.
[99] *Ecclesiastical History* 5:300.
[100] *Ecclesiastical History* 6:458.
[101] *Ecclesiastical History* 4:200.
[102] *Ecclesiastical History* 5:300.
[103] Twelfth-century Normandy reminds of Ottonian Germany: Hermann Kamp, "La vengeance, le roi et les compétitions faidales dans l'empire ottonien," in Barthélemy, Bougard and Le Jan (eds), *La vengeance, 400–1200*, pp. 259–80.

the argument—since Luke had joined the rebels after he had already been forgiven once by the king—and expressed his rancor towards Luke's satirical songs.[104]

The game is somewhat risky: when push comes to shove, the king could not act except by hurting his own friends' pride. Vexing an heir or not sharing his favor widely enough could throw his barons into what *he* called "rebellion"; from their point of view, the king had hurt their honor, and as ex-friends they felt it legitimate to fight to call the king's attention to this insult. When Ralph of Tosny could not obtain Duke Robert's arbitration in his dispute against William of Evreux, he turned to another friend more willing to help, King William Rufus.[105] Rotrou of Mortagne, seeing that he could not rely on his friend King Stephen to rescue his nephew Richer, got angry and concluded a pact with Geoffrey Plantagenet.[106] In the computing of rancor, disappointment by princes rated high.

* * *

Orderic's tales show the extent of medieval vengeance ideology. They provide patterns for relations between lords and for the depiction of God's attitude or baronial relations with the king. The feuds he reports do actually fit into the model recent historians have proposed. Yet, conflicts were seldom restricted to equal partners for long: eventually the duke or the king was involved, even when he was not the grieved or the hated one.

Each act was interpreted as rancorous, malevolent or zealous. This interpretation is usually the privilege of God or the king: their vengeance belongs to a higher level. Furthermore, in Orderic's world, the criterion for telling negative from positive rancor is the relationship with his monastic community. Monks have feuds of their own, exemplified by the Bellême case. The core of this enmity lay in the character of Robert of Bellême, the persecutor, according to Orderic, of Serlo, abbot of Saint-Evroult then bishop of Sées.[107] The monks supported King Henry because they blamed their troubles more than they should have on the weakness of Robert Curthose. Defining Robert of Bellême as a wicked figure, indeed a devil—at first

---

[104] *Ecclesiastical History* 6:354.
[105] *Ecclesiastical History* 4:212–16.
[106] *Ecclesiastical History* 6:546.
[107] Kathleen Thomson, "Orderic Vitalis and Robert of Bellême," *Journal of Medieval History*, 20 (1994): 133–41. C. Warren Hollister, *King Henry I* (New Haven, 2001), p. 64, n. 155, dismisses her analysis, pretending that Orderic's evidence is confirmed by other Anglo-Norman chroniclers, and explaining Robert's pathological behavior by referring to "studies in abnormal psychology" (a leap a century backwards …). But Robert is King Henry's villain as well as Orderic's, and though Hollister stresses the connections these writers have with the court (pp. 1–21), he does not acknowledge the degree to which they spread parts of Henry's own propaganda. The same is also true of the bad press they give to Robert Curthose.

sight, a Norman priest took the *Mesnie Hellequin* to be Robert's army[108]—they naturally identified his adversaries as instruments of divine will. The pattern of divine vengeance mixed then with royal feud—a similarity that royal propaganda had more than likely supported.

Moreover, the ideology of fortune could be applied to princes too and emphasized the alternation between weak and bad dukes, and good ones. This does not prevent Orderic from reproaching William the Conqueror or King Henry, his "good" rulers: indeed, these reproaches are an element historians usually stress to prove Orderic's narrative is balanced and reliable, as well as fascinating. But it plays down Orderic's world-view, as well as political dynamics. To tell us that Robert of Bellême claimed lands beyond his ancestors' right is already to take sides; it strengthens Robert's opponents by disqualifying Robert's use of "legitimate yet rancorous heir" rhetoric, and all too easily traps historians.[109]

We should proceed with caution. Stressing change, we should not rely solely on Orderic's texts, since they too have a narrative dynamic of their own. Yet, any defiance towards theories of feud should not be based on nostalgic support of traditional event-shaped history that might be aiming to uncover confused medieval sources in order to determine some rational course of actions. We would do better if we tried to understand the actors in terms of their own values and social expectations. Rancor was certainly one of these.

---

[108] *Ecclesiastical History* 4:238.
[109] *Ecclesiastical History* 4:230.

Chapter 6
Verbal and Physical Violence in the *Historie of Aurelio and Isabell*

Marina S. Brownlee

Vengeance—indeed, genocide—is the graphic outcome invoked in the anonymously penned *Historie of Aurelio and Isabell*. This sixteenth-century translation and adaptation of Juan de Flores' fifteenth-century *Grisel y Mirabella* was republished in bilingual, trilingual and even quadrilingual versions, becoming, as Everett Olmstead observes, "one of the most widely read books of the 16th century, almost a class manual for the study of foreign languages."[1]

Not only a vivid installment in the long-standing Quarrel of the Sexes that occupied so many of the heated debates on the topic in fifteenth-century Europe, this text exerts a timeless, parabolic fascination deriving from the problem of language and its production of meaning, of referentiality—especially its susceptibility to contamination. For in the case of *Aurelio*, as in its model *Grisel*, the king's discourse is irreparably impaired, polluted by his incestuous desire for his daughter. And the consequences of such discursive perversion are devastating.

In earlier periods than our own, "discourse," as Michel Foucault acknowledges, "was not originally a product, a thing, a kind of goods; it was essentially an act—an act placed in the bipolar field of the sacred and the profane, the licit and the illicit, the religious and the blasphemous. Historically, it was a gesture fraught with risk before becoming goods caught up in a circuit of ownership."[2] Like its model text, *Aurelio* offers a stunning illustration of this Foucauldian insight, by

---

[1] Everett Ward Olmstead, "The Story of *Grisel and Mirabella*," in *Homenaje ofrecido a Menéndez Pidal: Miscelánea de estudios lingüísticos, literarios e históricos* (2 vols, Madrid, 1925), p. 369. It was translated into Italian by Aletiphilo. Further elaborating *Grisel*'s dissemination, Joyce Boro, in an unpublished study, indicates the following additional evidence: "Its first English translation, published in 1527–35, is preserved in a one-page fragment housed at Emmanuel College, Cambridge. *Grisel* was retranslated into English anonymously and printed as part of a quadrilingual, French, Spanish, Italian, and English edition in 1556, 1588 and 1608, entitled *The Historie of Aurelio and of Isabell*; and as part of a trilingual, French, Italian, and English edition in 1586. It was printed in 1606. It was also twice adapted into dramatic form: Swetnam's *The Woman Hater* was performed in 1619 and printed in 1620; and John Fletcher's *Women Pleased* was first printed in the collected works of Beaumont and Fletcher in 1647."

[2] Michel Foucault, "What is an Author?" in Josué Harari (ed.), *Textual Strategies: Perspectives in Post-Structural Criticism* (Ithaca, 1979), p. 148.

examining the relationship between natural law and judicial law as they pertain to the discursive authority of their world—defined by their guarantor, the king. It offers an exploration about language, about naming, about the legitimacy of discourse itself.

A feature which makes this text particularly appropriate to a volume devoted to the study of vengeance in the Middle Ages is not only the preponderance of vengeful words and deeds, their complexity and dire consequences, but the encyclopedic variety of vengeance which confronts the reader: divine vengeance, judicial, man-made (fallible) vengeance, clan/family-feud vengeance, socially-based vengeance, the private vengeance of competing suitors and, finally, gender-based vengeance. The analysis of *Aurelio* here focuses on the performative efficacy of discourse—the power of words to represent or distort human experience and on the potentially dire relationship of words to deeds, on their ability not only to cause the death of an individual, but to threaten the extinction of humanity itself. Isabell, a victimized princess and daughter, has a secret affair with Aurelio because her father (the King of Scotland) denies her the right to amorous fulfillment, even within the context of lawful matrimony. The father's subconscious but very real incestuous desire, a perversion of natural law, will result ultimately in the deaths not only of these two lovers, but of many other subjects as well. This causal relationship between the virtual yet cataclysmic incest and the linguistically polluted language of the otherwise virtuous monarch is established at the outset of the narrative proper:

> The king ... hadde none other children, and for the extreame merites and deserving of graces, that were in his daughter, the love without measure unto none of the foresayde demanders would he never geve her in marriage.[3]

Because the king's incestuous desire prevents him from giving his daughter in marriage, many knights vie for her hand, but lose their lives in the process. It is as a consequence of military not familial considerations (the deaths of valiant knights) that the king removes his daughter from public view by locking her away in a tower. This architectural detail underscores Isabell's imprisonment by her father's metaphorical, architectural phallus. It is ironically as a direct result of this imprisonment that she ultimately becomes involved with Aurelio. In spite of the King's profound commitment to justice, his impeccable behavior is undermined by his transgression of natural law, irreparably deforming his authority. Because of his unrecognized excessive attachment to his daughter, the king, in spite of his aspirations to being an impeccably just monarch, will initiate a chain reaction of vengeance that will lead not only to multiple deaths, but to a wholesale alienation of women at the untenable misogyny masquerading as justice that rules the kingdom. Provoked to the breaking point, they will not only commit torture and murder, but advocate the unconditional severing of any ties to men, including the care of their

---

[3] *Histoire de Aurelio, et Isabelle, [fille du]Roy d'Escose, nouuelement traduict en [quatre] langues, italien, espaignol, françois & anglois* (Antwerp, 1556), p. 7.

own male children. Taken to its logical conclusion, this unnatural behavior would lead to the very extinction of Scotland.

The text develops the sinister effects of the King's discourse by means of four striking debates: the first between Aurelio and the unnamed Other Knight, the second between Aurelio and Isabell, the third between Hortensia and Afranio, and the last between the Queen and the King. The first of these encounters is significant in that words fail to resolve the question of which knight is the more committed to Isabell. The unnamed knight, claiming that God is on his side, loses the duel. This defeat constitutes a notable departure from convention, whereby the judicial duel is meant to function as an index of divine justice, and those who invoke this form of adjudication tend to win since "right equals might."[4]

The reference here to a transcendent order—a misreading of it—is, moreover, the first in a series of allusions to a Christian axiology. Likewise the claim made later on, that Aurelio's death is a "miracle" because it demonstrates that he is guiltier than Isabell, represents a similar misappropriation of religious authority by society, whereas in fact Aurelio clearly commits suicide because of his altruistic passion. The attribution of an apocalyptic darkening of the sky as a reflection of the queen's attitude toward the death sentence for Isabell functions in a related (though opposite) manner.[5] Namely, whereas we would expect this meteorological phenomenon to be attributed to divine authority, it is explained instead as an instance of the "pathetic fallacy," whereby nature mirrors the human affect.[6] These are three in a number of examples of what might be termed negative religious evocation, designed to undermine not religion, but its human misinterpreters. This form of religious misinterpretation points to the global linguistic misappropriation exposed most visibly on the level of plot.

Isabell and Aurelio engage in great passion and are discovered in the same bed, at which point they are seized and incarcerated. The "Law of Scotland" stipulates that the initiator of the affair be burned at the stake, and the accomplice, exiled for life, and it is this crucial apportionment of guilt that the King seeks to determine.[7] True to his reputation for being just, the King proceeds in an orderly manner,

---

[4] As Howard Bloch explains, "the judicial duel belongs to the series of ordeals common to any primitive sense of justice in which legal process remains indistinguishable from divine law" (*Medieval French Literature and Law* (Berkeley, 1977), p. 18).

[5] *Historie de Aurelio*, p. 75.

[6] This term, coined by John Ruskin, but clearly in evidence for millennia (see his *Modern Painters, 1843–60*), refers to the personified attribution of human emotional response to nature, animals and even inanimate objects. ("Pathetic Fallacy," *Encyclopedia Britannica Online*, 11 July 2007, at http:proxy.library.upenn.edu:2913/eb/article-9058718).

[7] "In the [twelfth-century] lives of St. Kentigern we find very clearly explained a 'Law of Scotland,' according to which the king carries out, against his own daughter, the penalty of death for illicit love while unmarried" (Barbara Matulka (ed.), *The Novels of Juan de Flores and Their European Diffusion: A Study in Comparative Literature* (New York, 1931), p. 162).

appointing a panel of judges. Though they interrogate and even torture the lovers, they are unable to ascertain whether Aurelio or Isabell is more to blame, since they each swear to be the instigator of what the author refers to as the "filth and sin" that resulted in the illicit affair.[8] Here, as with the debate between Aurelio and the unnamed knight, words fail to determine the truth.

Because of this judicial impasse, the authorities decide that the issue of relative guilt can only be determined by means of yet another debate—this time between one man and one woman who will argue in general terms as to whether man or woman is more at fault in initiating seduction. The representatives chosen to debate this matter are Hortensia, a woman known for her "discretion" and "knowledge," and Afranio, who "knew the artes and malisses of the ladies."[9]

Debate is the form of verbal violence *par excellence*. Yet, although this type of dialogic confrontation was certainly widespread in the Middle Ages and beyond, the debate between Afranio and Hortensia is striking because it has nothing to do with the attitudes projected by Aurelio and Isabell.[10] On the contrary, their self-sacrificing bond of love could not be more alien from the thoughts, words—and, ultimately, deeds—of the cynical Hortensia and Afranio. Each contestant offers an arsenal of stock arguments to prove the greater guilt of the opposite sex. While she speaks of women as a "besieged castle" relentlessly assaulted by men, he observes that women are the daughters of Eve, hence the very cause of perpetual sin and chaos in the world.[11]

Both participants are calculatedly nonobjective. For this reason, they function as a cynical inversion of the King's unconscious lack of objectivity. At the same time, however, they are—in a fundamental sense—discursively analogous. Just as the King's discourse of regal impartiality is invalidated by its incestuous context, so is their totally biased, sexist invective. The epistemological fissure separating *signans* from *signatum* is exposed over and over. To further emphasize this perspective—that meaning is entirely contingent upon context, and that the distance separating word from deed can be very great—both contestants programmatically

---

[8] The Spanish original of Flores does not contain such harsh evaluative judgments. In general, the tone of *Aurelio* is morally charged in this way.

[9] *Historie de Aurelio*, p. 33.

[10] That this debate is not just extraneous and tangential is reflected in the title of another of the English adaptations of *Grisel: A Paire of Turtle Doves: or, the Tragicall end of Agamio, wherein (besides other matters pleasing to the reader) by way of dispute between a knight and a lady is described this never before debated question, to wit: Whether man to woman, or woman to man offer the greatest temptations and allurements unto unbridled lust, and consequently whether man or w[o]man in that unlawful act, be the greater offender.* (See Olmstead, "The Story of Grisel and Mirabella," pp. 371–2.) For a recent discussion and series of examples of debate literature from the Middle Ages, see Barbara K. Altmann and R. Barton Palmer (eds), *An Anthology of Medieval Love Debate Poetry* (Gainesville, 2006).

[11] *Historie de Aurelio*, pp. 60 and 70.

accuse one another (and the sex they represent) of linguistic counterfeit, of saying one thing while doing quite another. In this way they make explicit what has, until now, been presented only implicitly (i.e. the dangers of the word/deed dichotomy unwittingly embodied by the King).

Of paramount importance also is the explicit admission by each of the debaters that they believe the legal system to be just. Hortensia expresses confidence that she will win the dispute since the truth is clear. She tells the Queen that there is "no neade in that toward hir to use so many praires" because the facts speak for themselves.[12] Afranio, by contrast, not only accepts words of encouragement from the King's men, but even "infinite giftes and preceaux joules."[13] Though Hortensia invokes a litany of impressive reasons why men are more to blame for seduction (including even their corruption of nuns) and argues that women are sincerely looking for a licit relationship while men are merely "players," Afranio wins. On further reflection, Hortensia realizes that this outcome was preordained by the inescapable fact of gender-bias; the kingdom's most esteemed group of twelve judges are men, thus corruptible, able to be "blyndede of [Afranio's] affection" in an act of (willed or unwilled, nonetheless inescapable) gender solidarity.[14]

In this way, the *Historie* dissociates the debate from the causality of the King's incestuous inclinations—of which the Kingdom of Scotland at large is ignorant. As such, Afranio and Hortensia provide independent corroboration (and an extreme example) of the inescapably biased nature of any speech situation.

Afranio wins the debate as we are told simply that the judges declared Hortensia to be the more guilty, founding their decision on "many reasons" without disclosing any of them.[15] The fact that no concrete reasons are given suggests that the decision of the jury—like the very premise of the judicial debate—is questionable to say the least. This resolution, like the outcomes of the debates between Aurelio and the unnamed Other Knight, as well as the debate between the two lovers leaves us with the distinct impression that unbiased, objective discourse is virtually unattainable.

Once the sentence has been pronounced whereby Isabell is consigned to death by immolation, Hortensia invokes God "railing unto the hey magiste of God lyke as unto the sofferaigne and true iuge of mankynde."[16] The idea of having Isabell die because a jury believes that women are the instigators of illicit love is incongruous, and we feel Hortensia's horrific pain. Shortly after this desperate divine invocation, however, she stuns her audience with a call for the ultimate act of vengeance—genocide, the murder of all men. Given that men are our enemies, she reasons, we should cease to have contact with them:

---

[12] Ibid., p. 34.
[13] Ibid., p. 35.
[14] Ibid., p. 52.
[15] Ibid., p. 75.
[16] Ibid., p. 76.

> Alas what ill agreement was owers (Lorde God) what we putte ower honesties and renounce in the poore of owre ennemys ... Alas corssede wemen wherefor with so grete paines ans trauailles of bringing fourthe will you them that shame and deathe geuethe you for a recompence? For if you had beane all wyse, at the birthe of your sonnes, you sholde have geuên eynde vnto their daies, to the eynde that we hade not bidden subiect vnto ower ennemys but sholde have liffede ioifulley.[17]

Hortensia acknowledges that men "laugh at our tears."[18] Totally enraged, she condemns the accustomed lack of resolve in women, hoping to provoke vengeful behavior in her female auditors in an attempt to redress the accustomed male abuse:

> What blyndenesse, or lack of iudgemente, consente vnto that that we seake vengeance of this thinge of the whiche the men daieley pronounnethe vengrance? But what preuailethe againste them ower litell power sins that we life vnder their empire, the whiche lyke cruell tirantes forcethe hus, and of all ower honoure do stripe hus?[19]

Further, even if we see men die, we should do nothing to help them, "yet that we doo see them die disfavor for recompense" should be the rule.[20] The implications of such horrific vengeance against males are, of course, horrifying. For were women to follow this advice, the human race would literally perish. The fact that no one challenges Hortensia's grim, gender-based invocation, reflects the blind rage into which the assembled women have descended.

The final and briefest of the four debates occurs between the Queen and King. It is significant that here too words fail to convince, and the ensuing action does not result from rational discourse. The Queen pleads for Isabell's life, yet the King refuses to spare her, despite the Queen's valid assertion that:

> Wouldst thou not that it is a worke of grete and vertueux prince: to love better to pardonne him that hathe donne amisse, than to geve paine to him that hathe deseruede it?[21]

In total desperation, the Queen offers to sacrifice her own life so that Isabell may live. And, like the debate between Afranio and Hortensia, here too we find an incongruous proposal. While maternal devotion can account for some of the Queen's motivation, it is aberrant—in terms of judicial logic—that she should sacrifice

---

[17] Ibid., p. 77.
[18] Ibid.
[19] Ibid.
[20] Ibid.
[21] Ibid., p. 81.

herself for an illicit love committed by another woman. The King is profoundly moved by his wife's offer to spare their child by sacrificing herself instead, yet he is unwilling to accept the substitution because it would be grotesquely unjust. He affirms that:

> If in me life anney vertu of the same maey I praise and laude ... that the oneley iustice is me triumphe, me victory, and the most laudableste thinge that is in my realme.[22]

Nonetheless, the King belies this discourse of regal impartiality very boldly, contradicting both his words and actions—being himself so distraught as to offer his own life in place of his daughter's, as did his wife. At the same time, he indicates that if he lives, Isabell must perish. This decision by the King causes the Queen to break violently with him, saying,

> It pleases the my well that thy crualte maey so muche, that in one daie thou bideste alone, withoute wife and children.[23]

Her bleak aggression toward the King is quite unexpected because it departs from the norm of queenly decorum. Yet, of course, it is motivated by his own indecorous kingly comportment—his discursive counterfeit.

Isabel is forcibly taken from her mother's arms, and the lovers exchange their last words, full of anguished devotion. Aurelio says he must die, so as not to be one more example of the male faithlessness so graphically exposed by Hortensia's earlier debate. This evocation of Hortensia's exposé of male deception and infidelity is one more unanticipated turn in the text. For Aurelio is a paragon of fidelity and amorous self-sacrifice. Having uttered these words, he demonstrates their integrity through action—by leaping into the flames intended for Isabell, so that her life might be spared. She immediately lunges toward the fire, to join her beloved, but she is prevented from doing so, forcibly removed from the flames by the women around her—who seem incapable of understanding the power of love. For surely it would be a much crueler fate for Isabell to outlive Aurelio, just as he had perceived the impossibility of a meaningful existence without her.

The immortal bond of these two lovers serves as a paradigm that none of the people around them can comprehend—let alone imitate. Evidence of this fact is offered immediately thereafter, as the spectators claim to have witnessed a miracle. Heaven "hade miraculessley ordenede the death to him that was worthey against God gaue not the paine to him that deseruede it not."[24] Except for Isabell, no one understands Aurelio's motivation, yet they are eager to designate him as the sacrificial victim (the obviously guiltier party deserving immolation) so that she

---

[22] Ibid., p. 83.
[23] Ibid., p. 88.
[24] Ibid., p. 95.

may be spared. Similarly, the judges who had originally sentenced her to death are easily persuaded to revoke the sentence since Aurelio has died.

Just as Aurelio's words to Isabell were not understood by any of the spectators, they likewise assume that she will not kill herself—although she has explicitly indicated that she will do so.[25] Not only does she choose to end her own life, but the manner of her death is as violent as Aurelio's—she hurls herself into a den of lions where she is torn to shreds. The lion is not indigenous to Scotland, but there as elsewhere it is an emblem—indeed, the most often invoked emblem—of regal authority. For this reason, it is very appropriate that she is destroyed by her father's identity. It is, moreover, significant that these lions are anthropomorphically endowed with erotic sensibilities—described as "of hir delicate fleshe they fedde themselves," thereby echoing the King's incestuous subconscious.[26]

She kills herself because life without Aurelio has no meaning for her. And, although she has explained this fact *alta voce* to the assembled multitudes, they do not anticipate that she will, in fact, guarantee the truth of her words by her actions. It is equally revealing that rather than serving as an exemplary function of amorous and linguistic fidelity, the deaths of Isabell and Aurelio elicit a decidedly *un*exemplary reaction in the Kingdom of Scotland—resulting in even greater violence.

The escalation of violence is precipitated by Afranio's unanticipated infatuation with Hortensia following the death of Isabell. By means of a letter he declares his love to her, at the same time acknowledging that he is unworthy of her, and desirous of doing penance. The understandably incredulous lady shows the letter to the Queen, who sees Afranio's affective about face as an excellent opportunity for vengeance against her daughter's wrongful death. She thus instructs Hortensia to reply by feigning a reciprocal interest in him—a pretext designed to lure the unsuspecting misogynist to a grisly death.

For his part, Afranio's passionate declaration appears to be motivated by lust rather than love since he boasts to his friends that Hortensia will make an easy conquest. Upon arrival at her chamber, he learns otherwise, when he is seized by the incensed and bloodthirsty females, bound with rope, fastened to a pillar and gagged so that he can not utter any words. The verbal violence of the earlier debate that resulted in the deaths of the exemplary lovers is now replaced by physical violence, graphic vengeance by which he is tortured by a thousand different torments. As some women burn him with tongs, others flirt with cannibalism, tearing him to shreds with their nails and teeth.[27] This hint of cannibal behavior echoes the kingly lions consuming Isabell's flesh, and both cases of gustatorial violence are meant to be repulsive.

After he has been so brutalized that he seems on the point of death, the women stop tormenting him in order to partake of a sumptuous banquet. The banquet

---

[25] Ibid., p. 96.
[26] Ibid., p. 100.
[27] Ibid., p. 119.

takes place in close proximity to the mutilated Afranio so that he can witness their enjoyment, and so that his torturers can abuse him verbally before returning to their bloodthirsty physical vengeance. As the supper is concluded the women resume the torture of Afranio, described now explicitly in terms of food: "a verrey bitter sopper," of "divers tourments."[28]

Two religious images are recalled by the treatment of Afranio here, and they accord with the subverted religious motifs mentioned earlier. Martyrdom and the Last Supper are each being reenacted here in a perverted form.[29]

In addition, this supper clearly constitutes a subversion of romance celebration. Rather than ending the text with the normative banquet in honor of the couple (in commemoration of order restored), we find instead a graphically lurid destruction of that ideal as represented by the physical destruction of Afranio's body. Moreover, the manner of his death—the poet's gory dismemberment at the hands of outraged females—recalls the dismemberment of another infamous misogynist writer—that of Orpheus in Book 11 of Ovid's *Metamorphoses*. He likewise dies a victim of women (whom he has spurned since the time of Eurydice's death, favoring the love of young boys instead). It is from this affective switch that Orpheus is identified in the Middle Ages as the father of homosexuality. By this subtextual reminiscence the *Historie* underscores the fact that Afranio's view of women is anything but objective. His dismembered discourse contrasts sharply with Isabell's physical dismemberment as metaphor of spiritual union.

Afranio is a love-martyr *in malo*, the opposite of Isabell and Aurelio, which is why the women burn his ashes and carry them in pendants around their necks—rather than the traditional wearing of a locket containing a lover's portrait or lock of hair. His martyrdom thus reflects as badly on him as it does on the bloodthirsty women who effect it.

Given the violent dissolution of the three relationships portrayed in the text (those of Aurelio and Isabell, the King and Queen, and Afranio and Hortensia), it is tempting to read the text as an illustration of René Girard's axiom that desire inevitably breeds disaster rather than romance. According to the Girardian view, the fault lies with the lovers who succumb to their passion, thus causing a chain reaction of multiple deaths and savage brutality that threatens the very fabric of society. It is because desire threatens society that the couple must be ritualistically eliminated. Ritual, as Girard explains, is nothing more than the exercise of "good violence."[30] The importance of ritual sacrifice is paramount, its absence is cataclysmic:

---

[28] Ibid., p. 120.

[29] A.D. Deyermond notes this inversion in his book entitled *A Literary History of Spain* (London, 1971), p. 165. Rather than submitting to martyrdom willingly and for a noble cause, Afranio suffers reluctantly and for the ignoble cause of misogyny, which he claims to deny.

[30] René Girard, *Violence and the Sacred*, trans. Patrick Gregory (Baltimore, 1977), p. 37.

> Mimetic desire is simply a term more comprehensive than *violence* for religious pollution. As the catalyst for the sacrificial crisis, it would eventually destroy the entire community if the surrogate victim were not at hand to halt the process and the ritualized mimesis were not at hand to keep the conflictual mimesis from beginning afresh.[31]

Such ritual sacrifice serves as a form of catharsis, as an affirmation of the rules upon which a given community is predicated—that is the reason why societies create laws to punish transgressors. It is not that the crime will be undone by the act of punishing the guilty individual, it will serve instead as an example of behavior that society will not tolerate.

What we see graphically illustrated in the *Historie* is the opposite. After the twelve judges (clutching their bloodstained swords) pronounce the death sentence for Isabell, rather than reverting to the peaceful status quo of orderly behavior, Scottish society breaks down before our eyes. The only legitimate successor to the throne—Isabell—kills herself; the Queen not only becomes estranged from the King, she takes the law into her own hands with the help of many other equally disaffected females. Hortensia's call for genocide—initially perceived as the passing rage of a provoked female—by the end seems to be within the realm of the possible. For his part, the King is incapable of stopping the murderous females, much less of bringing them to justice.

Given that this is the case, that with the sacrifice of the lovers the violence does not end and society is not restored, it appears that it is not the lovers' desire that is at fault. If it were, their deaths would have ended the chain of destruction, as Girard's phenomenology of violence makes clear. One is tempted to conclude, therefore, that it is the law, or more precisely, the King as law-bearer, who is flawed, that, had he allowed his daughter to marry rather than preventing her from doing so out of his own incestuous desire, none of the tragedies would have occurred. In this connection, the fact that the incestuously inclined King is not eliminated indicates that we are not reading romance. (If we were, the virtuous heroine would have inherited the kingdom from an equally virtuous father. Alternatively, both lovers would have perished as a result of their sexually transgressive behavior.) But the *Historie* suggests something different.

Isabell dies as a result of her own linguistic integrity. Given the suggestion of incest that pervades the narrative, it is surprising—indeed shocking—that the father's incestuous urge does not achieve physical intimacy. The focus is not physical but verbal transgression. Unlike earlier medieval incest narratives, physical defilement is unnecessary.[32] In fact, its elimination here is very revealing. For, what is at issue is nothing less than a new attitude toward language. The text is

---

[31] Ibid., p. 148.

[32] For a recent consideration of the perennial literary interest of incest, irrespective of historical period, see Elizabeth Barnes (ed.), *Incest in the Literary Imagination* (Gainesville, 2002).

a negative, skeptical, nominalist recasting of the early medieval discursive principle whereby the continuity of language guarantees genealogical succession—as Isidore of Seville had posited, and as Howard Bloch explains.[33]

Juxtaposing the new attitude operative in the later Middle Ages with the earlier one, Bloch writes: "this [new] body of grammatical thought [the work of the speculative grammarians] is organized around synchronic categories; more committed to logical distinctions than to chronological sequence, continuity and origins; less oriented toward the 'verticality' of the single word—etymology or definition—than toward 'horizontal' problems of syntax and consignification."[34] Bloch thus describes a shift from a metonymic to a metaphoric attitude toward language, from a strict referentiality between *signans* and *signatum* to a problematization of referentiality. This change from consensus in the meaning produced by a given word to an awareness that meaning itself is contingent upon the perspective of the individual speaker or writer accords, moreover, with Roman Jakobson's observation regarding "the [diachronically] alternative predominance of one or the other of these two processes."[35]

Jakobson's observation of the cyclical nature of referentiality is especially pertinent in the case of the *Historie of Aurelio and Isabell*, a work of translation and adaptation that appears in the mid-sixteenth century. Although the quadrilingual text of 1556 is published in Antwerp, it reflects a striking discursive evolution taking place largely during the decade of the 1550s in Spain. We find in 1548 the appearance of the first epistolary novel in Europe (the *Processo de cartas de amores*) two hundred years before Richardson wrote *Pamela*, in 1552 the first Byzantine novel written in Spanish (*Clareo y Florisea*), in 1554 the first European picaresque novel (*Lazarillo de Tormes*), between 1550 and 1560 the first Moorish novel in Europe (*El Abencerraje y la Hermosa Jarifa*) and in 1559 the first Spanish pastoral novel. All of these texts—with the exception of the *Processo* and *Lazarillo*—immediately gave rise to continuations and adaptations. The reason why these two texts did not enjoy the popularity of the others at the time of their production is in large part due, I maintain, to their attitude toward referentiality. That is, they were problematizing the performative efficacy of words at a time when readers had a taste for romance rather than novel.

Definitions of the novel and novelistic discourse are admittedly diverse. Literary historians attempt to define a diachronic progression for this elusive type of fiction, while theorists posit ahistorical distinctive features (formal, semantic, sociological, etc.).[36] Nonetheless, amid this plurality of approaches and perspectives one feature

---

[33] "*Ex linguis gentes, non ex gentibus linguae exortae sunt*" (San Isidro, *Etmologías*, ed. José Ortiz Reto (2 vols, Madrid, 1983), vol. 1, 9.1.14).

[34] R. Howard Bloch, *Etymologies and Genealogies* (Chicago, 1983), p. 160.

[35] Roman Jakobson, "The Metaphoric and Metonymic Poles," in Roman Jakobson and Morris Halle (eds), *Fundamentals of Language* (Paris, 1971), p. 92.

[36] For a useful consideration of ways in which the novel has been theorized and represented, see Michael McKeon, *Theory of the Novel: A Historical Approach* (Baltimore, 2000).

remains constant—namely, the novel's status as Other, as oppositional discourse, as the paradigmatically non-canonical genre.

A protagonist's failure to conform to mythic paradigms (such as those celebrated by epic and romance) is one way of identifying the novel.[37] This distinction between myth and novel expresses itself not simply in actuantial terms, but in a consistent attitude toward language per se, as Bakhtin makes clear: "The novel and myth [are] two 'genres' that ... constitute the opposite poles of the intertextual continuum. Myth implies a transparency of language, a coincidence of words and things; the novel starts out with a plurality of languages, discourses, and voices, and the inevitable awareness of language as such; in this sense, the novel is a basically self-reflexive genre."[38] The impossibility of heroic self-fulfillment corresponds to the shift in focus from the successful physical adventures of the outerworld of romance to the fragile novelistic inner world of the individual human psyche.

In discursive terms, Bakhtin conceptualizes this shift by contrasting the monologism of epic and romance with the dialogism of the novel, where idealized literary discourse becomes undermined by its contact with the nonliterary, unheroic discourses of quotidian reality.[39] Romance, like epic, is "monologic" in nature, that is, it offers a univocal, transcendent model of referentiality that is exemplified by a single discursive system. The signifying potential of words is never questioned within such monologic genres. By contrast, novelistic discourse is "dialogic"—a confrontation of different discourses that inevitably has the effect of questioning the authority of each one. Clearly, these two genres represent two very different types of utterance—indeed, two opposing attitudes toward language and its performative capacity.

The dramatization of referentiality—and the chaos that ensues from its absence—explains why so much of the *Historie* is devoted to debates. The result is an illustration of the universality of linguistic transgression. Indeed, what we witness in this text is a new kind of incest—not physical but linguistic incest.

---

[37] As Northrup Frye explains, "Romance avoids the ambiguities of ordinary life, where everything is a mixture of good and bad, and where it is difficult to take sides or believe that people are consistent patterns of virtue or vice" (*The Secular Scripture: A Study of the Structure of Romance* (Cambridge, Mass., 1976), p. 50).

[38] Tzvetan Todorov, *Mikhail Bakhtin: The Dialogic Principle*, trans. Wlad Godzich (Minneapolis, 1984), p. 66.

[39] Bakhtin casts this tension in terms of the difference between "official" and "unofficial" discourse, in the Middle Ages for example, as follows: "It can be said, with some restrictions to be sure, that medieval man in a way led *two lives*: one *official*, monolithically serious and somber; beholden to strict hierarchical order; filled with fear, dogmatism, devotion, and piety; the other, of *carnival* and the *public place*, free; full of ambivalent laughter, sacrileges, profanations of all things sacred, disparagement and unseemly behavior, familiar contact with everybody and everything" (Todorov, *Mikhail Bakhtin*, p. 78).

Language is "deprived of its hallowed function as support of the law, in order to become the cause of a permanent trial of [every individual] speaking subject."[40] For Kristeva, poetic discourse is "incestuous" in that it routinely transgresses codified forms of signification and social hierarchies of decorum.[41] The *Historie* dramatizes the fact that not only poetic discourse—but *all discourse*—is inherently incestuous in the etymological sense of *in* (not) and *castus* (chaste). It is impure because of its adulteration or pollution of signification (either by conscious or subconscious motivation). Afranio functions as a paradigm of willed impurity, while the King offers an example of impurity that is unwilled.

A further and related displacement of our generic expectations is that the romance paradigm (on the model of Tristan) involves illicit love which shuns marriage. Here the situation is reversed—Isabell and Aurelio become furtively involved precisely because she is prevented by the King from marrying a vassal of his own choosing.[42] This reversal likewise signals the text's very *un*-romantic axiology.

The text ends with the words: "the grete malice of Affranio gave vnto the ladies victorey, and vnto him of his deseruinge rewarde."[43] And though Afranio's behavior was monstrous, so was that of his female torturers as well. As a result, the text is neither misandrist nor misogynist—or rather it is both. What is wistfully celebrated is the couple of idealistic lovers whose words guarantee their deeds—in other words the determinacy of signs. This successful private relationship bears no connection to the public and its laws. The admirable love and death of Isabell and Aurelio does not function exemplarily for the godless society of Scots; their amorously motivated words and actions do not convince others to emulate them. They are, as it were, two displaced romance characters lost in a novelistic world. What is denigrated is not the (putatively destructive) desire of Aurelio and Isabell, but the linguistic perversion of society itself—its lamentable ability to generate verbal ambiguity and distortion leading to catastrophic consequences. The text is

---

[40] Julia Kristeva, *Desire in Language*, trans. Thomas Gora, Alice Jardine and Leon S. Roudiez (New York, 1980), p. 137.

[41] Kristeva's interest here is for "the intrinsic connection between literature and breaking up social concord: Because it utters incest, poetic language is linked with 'evil': 'literature and evil' (I refer to a title by Georges Bataille) [and] should be understood, beyond the resonances of Christian ethics, as the social body's self-defense against the discourse of incest as destroyer and generator of any language and sociality. This applies all the more as 'great literature,' which has mobilized unconsciousness for centuries, has nothing to do with the hypostasis of incest (a petty game of fetishists at the end of an era, priesthood of a would-be enigma—the forbidden mother); on the contrary, this incestuous relation, exploding in language, embracing it from top to bottom in such a *singular* fashion ... defies *generalizations* [yet] still has this common feature in all outstanding cases: it presents itself as demystified" (ibid.).

[42] For a discussion of romance and the social threat it poses, especially in terms of the Tristan myth, see Denis de Rougement, *Love in the Western World*, trans. Montgomery Belgion (Princeton, 1983).

[43] *Historie de Aurelio*, p. 121.

much more than an illustration of the perennial conflict between law and desire, or misogyny and misandry. It is about the dangerous potential of language and about how subliminal factors can pervert justice and even go unrecognized since the king never admits his initial error in denying his daughter her right to matrimony. The adulterous affair, the carnage, the destruction of a peaceable kingdom and the threat of genocide all stem directly from the king's resistance to her marrying anyone, as the text makes clear. As such, *Aurelio* serves as a parable of language, its performative complexity and its horrific potential for vengeance.

Chapter 7
Was There Really Such a Thing as Feud in the High Middle Ages?[1]

Paul R. Hyams

Few of us, however hard we try, can avoid the urge to take vengeance for the wrongs that others do to us, to try and get our own back. We may restrain ourselves from action, but the urge is always there. The pull toward the taking of personal vengeance is at least as evident in the medieval West as at other times and in other places. It is, indeed, a staple theme of entertainment literature, quite as much in gentle late medieval romances as in the *chansons de geste* that seem to speak to us of earlier times and their mores. So widespread a cultural pattern necessarily moved clergy to the protection of their lay flocks, and so features in pastoral works as behavior to avoid or guard against. The fear was always that one violent act could beget another and lead participants into that much-cited "unending cycle" of tit-for-tat violence.[2] What gives this fear a certain plausibility is the way that we humans so commonly adduce a *casus belli*, some previous wrong done to ourselves or our associates and loved ones, in justification of any harm we may plan to commit against our fellows. We do this in many circumstances, from petty thefts represented as recalled loans all the way up to attempted genocide said to be in requital for the killing of God's son.

Any observer, even an alien spaceman with no knowledge of earthly tongues, would visually identify this behavior pattern in us humans. Indeed the urge to vengeance is often immediately apparent through body language. But every culture needs a form of words, a discourse, with which to explain, justify, plan

---

[1] This chapter revises arguments of my book *Rancor and Reconciliation in Medieval England* (Ithaca, 2003), esp. ch. 1, where fuller documentation may be found. My sense that the notion of feud required further thought was reinforced by my colleague Oren Falk, who read an earlier draft with a special intensity that compelled a number of developments and improvements, and I was further assisted by my co-editor, Dr. Throop, and Dr. Ionutz Epurescu-Pascovics while he was still my student. I am also grateful to both of the anonymous readers for their suggestions and especially to Guy Halsall for his courtesy which included forwarding some unpublished drafts. Important among recent work relevant to the topics covered here is John Hudson, "Faide, vengeance, et violence en Angleterre (ca 900–1200)," in Dominique Barthélemy, François Bougard and Régine Le Jan (eds), *La vengeance, 400–1200* (Rome, 2006), pp. 341–82. This time, alas, I was the one who did not find his study until mine was written.

[2] I suspect this actually happened much less often than was feared, and certainly less often than some lofty modern "observers" assert.

and persuade. This chapter aims to show one significant way in which the men and women of the High Middle Ages managed and waged their conflicts and vengeance within a set of behavior patterns—their repertoire, if you like—inherited from the past and widely recognized at the time.[3] Medieval men and women articulated these behaviors through a small group of locutions familiar to contemporaries, but which we historians can recover only with difficulty from written materials often quite distant from the acts themselves, the language independently important as the means by which this *imaginaire* was propagated, calibrated and renewed. We obtain thereby our glimpse of the modes by which medieval people made sense of the micropolitical choices they and their neighbors made. When they perceived themselves to have been wronged, they understood their situations and sought to decide their responses (if any) within a loose repertoire inherited from their forbears and internalized in advance as fair and just. Armed with a firm sense of obligations, duties and rights governing whether and how to seek redress in general, men and women might seek to replicate the *imaginaire* and meet their personal challenges by acting out this part of their inherited repertoire.

Since the particular behavior patterns to be considered here share common features with those that various Germanic languages apparently denoted by the precursors of our word "feud," I find it useful to refer to them as "feuds," despite some obvious dangers. Feud, like its unconnected dictionary neighbor "feudalism," is a much overused term, a notion in real peril of collapsing and losing all precision and utility.[4] I make no essentialist defense of my own usage of the term; I shall not argue that the word has a core meaning, some essential without which no feud can be real or true.[5] Nor is it defensible to reify feud as an "institution," as has sometimes been done in the past. Marriage can perhaps be viewed in institutional terms, so too the manumission of serfs. Both are organized within known and tighter repertoires mostly with set forms of words, legally enforced, and so have relatively predictable consequences.[6] Feud, in contrast, is only loosely predictable

---

[3] For reasons that will become apparent I avoid talk of "scripts," which seems to me to suggest much more of a set discourse and order of attack than I can see in the evidence. My initial shot at an alternative, "scenario," seemed at least more neutral. But now thanks to Sidney Tarrow, I can take from Charles Tilly, *Contentious Performances* (Cambridge, 2008), pp. 14–16 the term "repertoire," which it so happens that biologists also use in a comparable way to denote a set of behavioral acts performed in a particular context.

[4] I have myself objected to the continued use of "feudalism" and its cognates on very similar grounds, in my "The End of Feudalism?" *Journal of Interdisciplinary History*, 28 (1997): 655–62.

[5] Stephen Pinker, *How the Mind Works* (New York, 1997), pp. 323–7 offers a partial defense of essentialism as a move to facilitate our own daily life. I concede nevertheless that the approach remains inappropriate to scholarly study.

[6] Robert Bartlett, "'Mortal Enmities': The Legal Aspect of Hostility in the Middle Ages," *T. John Pierce Lecture* (Aberystwyth, 1998), however, demonstrates that *inimicitia mortalis* (for which see below) was recognized in some Continental law codes as a valid defense. This was not normally the case in England.

and not normally protected or enforced by laws. I therefore follow the well-established approach of those anthropologists who focus on process and practice, patterns set by nothing more formal than what has repeatedly been done in the past, and in the case of feud found workable as mechanisms for the control and limitation of the effects of violence.[7] Such a "processual" or "practice" approach assumes a degree of procedural and substantive flexibility—the actors, including bystanders, always have at their disposal more than one choice of how to respond.[8] This capital point is one to return to in due course.

But first an anecdote. John Cusin, a substantial Somerset landowner, was dining one afternoon in 1196 secure in his own home and surrounded by his household and family. Seven men burst in upon them, having somehow got past the gate keeper. Some of them seized John and dragged him by his feet into his bedroom. They then pulled torches from the fire, and waved them at his face close enough to singe his beard, pulled out his tongue, cut it off and laid it on his chest. Meanwhile their companions were ransacking the house. When they found John's valuables chest, they took out from it important title deeds, royal and other charters, and flourished them in the injured man's face. One they burned in his face. Only then was he pulled out of the house where one William Basher (sic!) beheaded him.

John's son, Simon, a clerk, witnessed as much of this as he could see from his relatively safe hiding place deep in the window recess. As soon as he could escape, he left the area and stayed away for three years. This was, as he later confessed, from fear of the family enemy, Thomas FitzJohn, son of a dominant local baron, William FitzJohn, and himself "almost lord of the whole *patria*." Telling the story later still at the presentation of his homicide appeal against his father's killers, Simon spared no pains to explain that everyone knew the FitzJohns to be responsible, though William himself was personally absent from the incursion. Significantly, the accusations never reached judgment or proof. High-level political influence apparently underpinned the peacemaking settlement laboriously brokered between the parties. No offenses having been proved, nobody was punished. The powers-that-be apparently considered inappropriate any punishment of the kind royal justices habitually meted out to other homicides—mutilation at best, and quite possibly hanging.[9]

---

[7] John L. Comaroff and Simon Roberts, *Rules and Processes: The Cultural Logic of Dispute in an African Context* (Chicago, 1981) is a classic expression of this approach. I have found Karen Sykes, *Arguing with Anthropology: An Introduction to Critical Theories of the Gift* (London, 2005), ch. 7 a useful sketch of the ways in which routine habits such as gift-giving and feud can be regarded as "knowledge practices" that come to be "weighted with meaning."

[8] There are, of course, real and important differences between these two approaches. But my limited concern in this chapter is simply to map a course which I can use, as a historian, to capture "feud" as represented by my sources.

[9] My *Rancor and Reconciliation*, pp. 274–6 outlines all the evidence I was able to locate.

Data concerning the previous relations between the Cusins and the FitzJohns is too scant for anyone to aver with confidence that their difference of opinion constituted a "feud," however one might choose to understand that. But most would agree that it was at least feud-like.[10] The FitzJohns had dispatched their men with instructions to destroy their enemies' most protected space. This would proclaim their supremacy to all; the nay-sayers had nowhere left to hide. Why they chose John Cusin and this moment is beyond our knowledge. But the tongue-cutting (linguectomy?) surely tells us that words, and the honor and esteem for which they contend, were central to the story. People had been saying things Thomas disliked, to the point that he felt compelled to act, in order to maintain his position over the inhabitants of his patch. This, he was announcing, is what happens to people who say bad things about *me*.

Here, then, as so often, is a snapshot which the historian needs to fit into an action movie he does not possess. There has to have been a pre-history to the scene the legal records preserve for us in such flickering brilliance. We must do what we can to supply enough of the surrounding context to make sense of our sources. But they too are designed to make specific points which the reader seven centuries later can easily misconstrue, especially if s/he thinks s/he knows the feud repertoire. The tellers of the tale evidently knew how to tell their story in more than one way; they tailored their narrative to their audience at the time. What we have on the royal plea rolls are versions designed to further the interests of the parties to a lawsuit before royal justices, but recorded by clerks concerned primarily to check that court rules were followed. Faulty pleas ensured that this one went to the gallows while that one escaped scot-free.

But there was also at least one quite different narrative created by, and aimed at, the neighborhood. This had to appeal to people who perhaps imagined their social relationships, and the politics of their neighborhood (their *patria*) in terms of alliance (*amicitia*) and enmity, love and hatred, and who took it for granted that men would and should affirm by force their view of their own reputation and position when it was challenged. We almost never possess this second narrative from the neighbors' perspective—there was in medieval northern Europe no tradition of recording it in writing.[11] And if we did, the true oral discourse in which

---

[10] The otherwise helpful subterfuge of labeling something "x-like" has the disadvantage of assuming the existence of a model (feud) of an institution or behavior pattern which it has failed to discover in action. It seems nevertheless worth extending its usage beyond the historians in search of lesbians who coined it (Hyams, *Rancor and Reconciliation*, p. 33).

[11] The revenge narratives of Renaissance Italy for all their rhetorical artifice perhaps come a little closer to the oral discourse into which we should really like to tap. See Edward Muir, *Mad Blood Stirring: Vendetta in Renaissance Italy* (Baltimore and London, 1998), pp. xxv–xxvi.

such matters were prepared, cooked, served and consumed would still remain way beyond our reach.[12]

But was *any* discourse of dispute in high medieval Europe also a discourse of feud? That may seem to depend on one's definition. I will in due course explain why definition is not, in my view, a useful way to tackle a social practice as amorphous as feud.[13] But I will first discuss briefly some apparently promising feud definitions and will review and revise a couple of my own *non-definitions*, before going on to examine a strong version of the case against labeling the phenomena under examination as feud. Finally, I will outline my ways of meeting the criticisms with an understanding of the way that medieval people just might have organized their acts of vengeance.[14] I adduce mainly English evidence. The anecdote with which I began is just one of a whole number of colorful feud-like narratives that can be found in England well into the age of the Common Law. We are of course very dependent on the chance that contemporaries had some interest in making a record, and that this interest did not distort the sequence of events beyond recognition. This rules out any statistical approach. The events we have may thus be exceptional, some even "entirely made in hindsight."[15] Others must decide to what extent the

---

[12] Stephen D. White has perhaps been the major proponent of this discourse view. I have benefited from various of his writings, now available in his *Feuding and Peace-making in Eleventh-century France* (Aldershot, 2005), but especially from "Un imaginaire faidal: La représentation de la guerre dans quelques chansons de geste," in Barthélemy, Bougard and Le Jan (eds), *La vengeance, 400–1200*, pp. 175–98. I am grateful to have been able to see this in draft form. For my taste, White makes the discourse too exclusively aristocratic; see here Dominique Barthélemy, *Chevaliers et miracles: La violence et le sacré dans la société féodale* (Paris, 2004), p. 14. Whatever may have been its origins and inspiration, it was widely shared, down to the village level, in thirteenth-century England (Hyams, *Rancor and Reconciliation*, ch. 8, esp. pp. 246–51). I should add that I feel no commitment to any strict Foucauldian sense of "discourse." A much broader alternative is offered, for example, by Emile Benveniste, *Problèmes de linguistique générale* (2 vols, Paris, 1966–74), vol. 1, p. 242: "toute énonciation supposant un locuteur et un auditeur, et chez le premier l'intention d'influencer l'autre en quelque manière."

[13] Cf. J.M. Wallace-Hadrill, "The Bloodfeud of the Franks," in his *The Long-Haired Kings* (New York, 1962), p. 123: "feuds remain undefined by those who have to resort to it."

[14] Guy Halsall seems to me to represent that strongest recent case. I am most grateful to him for letting me see the speaking draft from which he delivered his presentation to the Aarhus conference on "Feud, Vengeance, Politics, and History in Early Medieval Europe," and sad that he felt unable to develop it for publication. His earlier "Violence and Society in the Early Medieval West: An Introductory Survey," in Halsall (ed.), *Violence and Society in the Early Medieval West* (Woodbridge, 1998), pp. 1–45 had already moved me to an earlier and salutary process of rethinking.

[15] As Halsall has said of the great Durham conflict, on which I have expressed a view of my own (*Rancor and Reconciliation*, pp. 76–7 and 277–9). But all feud may be said to be "made" by observers. What one man calls feud may always be described by others as mere violence or a breach of the peace or, later, simply as crime.

argument is plausible for the different sources of Continental Europe. But England, given its reputation for precocious legal centralization and state apparatus, suffices as a worthwhile prima facie case.

* * *

Feud is certainly a term whose over-abundant usage appears to make it an excellent candidate for a moratorium. Anyone who has ever read texts in translation and later checked their readings against the original will have noticed how many quite different Latin and vernacular words and whole phrases end up rendered "feud." Peter Sawyer long ago alerted scholars to the notion's danger of imminent collapse.[16] It is a concept in need of pruning, to say the least, and two kinds of dead wood can go without regret. First, it is unnecessary to envision feud as in some way intrinsically in opposition to law and the state. Both direct action (in the sense of private enterprise acts to avenge perceived wrongs) and the enmities thus pursued can patently coexist comfortably alongside law and state apparatus. This was as true in the early Middle Ages as in more recent "traditional" societies. Thus the well-documented existence of a court system and governmental institutions, along with their records, in, say, Carolingian Francia and later in Anglo-Saxon England, is not in itself reason to deny that feud operated there too.

Equally, we need not limit the operation of anything we may call "feud" to clans and kinship. Because blood was thicker than water, medieval Europeans privileged among their "friends" those whom they regarded as blood kin. They consequently represented support groups, both their own and their enemies', as if they consisted primarily, even exclusively of kinsmen. Regino of Prüm's endlessly quoted remark on *"vindicta parentum, quod faidam dicimus"* should not lead us to read this convenient fiction as if it were fact. In time of peril men naturally hurried to choose allies from the ranks of powerful but unrelated lords, vassals and neighbors, and to refuse their support to habitually troublemaking cousins, or even formally to expel them from their own kindred.[17]

No definition will do then that separates feud from law or conceptualizes it merely as a function of kinship. But what might? Definition arguments among historians are among the most arid and unproductive of all their disagreements.[18] But one cannot analyze process without some delineation of what it is and where it starts and ends. In earlier work, I found it useful to offer two "working assumptions,"

---

[16] Peter Sawyer, "The Bloodfeud in Fact and Fiction," *Tradition og Historieskrivining*, Acta Jutlandica 63.2 (Aarhus, 1987), pp. 27–38.

[17] See William I. Miller, "Choosing the Avenger," *Law and History Review*, 1 (1983): 159–204, and my *Rancor and Reconciliation*, pp. 9–10.

[18] "Remember that we sometimes demand definitions for the sake not of the content, but of their form. Our requirement is an architectural one: the definition is a kind of ornamental coping that supports nothing." Ludwig Wittgenstein, *Philosophical Investigations*, ed. R. Rhees and G.E.M. Anscombe (New York, 1958), p. 217.

as I called them. Each springs from recorded observation of what people seem to have *done*, rather than what they might have *said* about their actions.

The simpler one presents confrontations between individuals as ones between political entities, which is what support groups really are, on a small scale. In effect, one treats personal relations as if it were international relations. This makes good prima facie sense. Feud support groups viewed without preconceptions emerge as small-scale political entities, recruited and deployed as such. So, when I see men strive to resolve their disputes by means of a peace treaty, as it were, rather than submitting them to a winner-takes-all tribunal capable of meting out punishment on the loser, I scent feud. Oversimplified possibly, but useful in that it includes within a single frame both the process of prosecuting perceived wrongs by violence or its threat, and the option of securing closure by peaceful means. This assumption goes far to collapse the debated distinction between feud and politics and demarcates a significant band within the spectrum of conflict resolution methods from the rest. It will not serve for all the questions that might be asked of violent conflicts, and can only serve as a "feud alert." Our notion of feud must do better than that.

My second non-definition started life as an extended definition exercise of the steps by which feud began and was prosecuted. In the absence of written rules, I necessarily derived my data very largely from descriptive sources. From this, I sought to set down as precisely as I could the ways in which medieval people pursued serial (or potentially serial) vengeance. Though factual in outward appearance, each one of the steps in the series is charged with justification, morality of various kinds, emotion and local politics. This was not, I was aware, what a definition ought to be like, but I could at the time find no better description.

I now see that what I was moving toward was the recording of a repertoire of practice. Like any such practice, this must have coalesced around some core underlying notions, in this case a particular concept of wrong. In the age before the legal revolution that saw the birth of the English Common Law and its Continental cousins, Europe had what has been called an undifferentiated notion of wrong very different from the legally defined ones that followed.

Anglo-Norman litigants and court-holders around 1100 still conceptualized party-and-party conflict and dispute resolution, whether on a horizontal or vertical dimension, through a notion of wrong that for the most part lacked the familiar modern legal distinction between crime and tort.[19] Until the importation of this distinction from the Roman law of the schools *c*.1166, they chose their procedures according to their goals, amongst which might be blood vengeance itself, and the power and resources at their disposal. There were thus until the generation following the adoption of the new conceptualization no observable "forms of action," and few special requirements for the form in which complaints had to

---

[19] The modern approach defines wrongs to be prosecuted and punished publicly on behalf of the state as crimes, while private or civil wrongs for whose redress individuals sued, usually in search of money damages, are torts (Hyams, *Rancor and Reconciliation*, pp. 220–24).

be made. Instead the same very general "undifferentiated" conception of wrong appears to underlie the whole discourse of dispute, including but by no means restricted to the way pleas were argued in duly constituted courts.[20]

This notion, doubtless vernacular and oral in origin, seems virtually ubiquitous in case narratives and a variety of other sources of the period. It was *not at all* restricted to issues of physical violence, though all kinds of dispute contain the potential for violence if unresolved with emotions left unchecked. Men pleaded conflict of all sorts, from property claims to personal grudges to external wars and Crusades, very largely in terms of licit redress (vengeance, if you prefer) for the wrongs that the other side had committed against them as individuals, and through them against the social groups of which they were members—the party of God or His son, or some local saint. None of this excludes what may be called Downwards Justice, where punishment, sometimes harshly afflictive, was imposed on those whose wrongs were deemed to have harmed a wider community.[21] Kings, bishops and powerful lay lords were quite happy to mutilate and hang killers, thieves and other offenders within this conceptual framework of wrong, without feeling the need to talk about "crime" in the later sense of the word.

The introduction into medieval Europe from the law of Rome of that foundational distinction split a previously undifferentiated notion of wrong into two discrete concepts. Wrongs that kings chose or were persuaded to prosecute came to be labeled crime, and their punishment was justified in terms of a public interest. But individuals might also proceed against many of the same wrongs on their own account by civil suits, called in England "trespass" from a French word for wrong.

Associated with this development was an emerging claim that something like a full monopoly of violence, or at least its regulation, ought to reside in some kind of public authority, which in England meant the king or his delegated agents. But the transition from old to newer understandings of wrong was much more drawn out and contested than many of us realized. Aggrieved individuals continued to have options beyond the new remedies provided by the king. For many decades after the new terminology of crime and tort had become second nature to the law professors and their many former students now practicing as lawyers or officials,

---

[20] I tried to explain my view in *Rancor and Reconciliation*, chs 6–7. Some previous scholars, seeking to understand the early common law, have talked in related terms but about an undifferentiated *action* or *procedure*. This is not my contention. It is the understanding of wrong that is undifferentiated (i.e. lacking the later distinction) and not any single action or procedure. I see little or nothing before Henry II's reign that deserves the name of action, itself a borrowing from Roman law. Admittedly, canonists and others did write about "crimen" and sometimes use this term in ways that reflect its meaning to Roman lawyers, but their work did not as yet, I argue, affect the general consciousness.

[21] I use this phrase when writing about early medieval Europe, to avoid anachronistic mention of "crime" or "criminal" before the introduction of the Roman law distinction between crime and tort, as in the following paragraph.

many lay people remained confident that they had the power, even the legitimate duty, licitly to avenge wrongs done them by extra-curial means including violent self-help. If English experience is at all typical, the "moment" of change lasted a long while. The king's principle was from the start that all convicted thieves, robbers and murderers should suffer penalties of life and member, in a fashion that relatively few other than the poor and friendless had in the past. But all animals were not equal, or so thought those of rank. The embarrassment and difficulty when the king and the justices knew the individuals involved, as they patently did the FitzJohns, is very evident in a significant body of cases from the early years of the thirteenth century. The law books specified corporal or capital punishment for criminals, but the politically influential continued to prefer for their own kind peace settlements that would last.[22]

Anyone who searches the abundant case records of the thirteenth-century royal courts for possible instances of vengeance and feud with a reasonably open mind will come up with a fair number of palpable hits. Other non-legal sources confirm the general picture. Obviously the procedures by which men and women prosecuted enmities and sought their vengeance in the thirteenth century through the good services of royal justices were very different from those of earlier times. The Angevin law reforms and the legal revolution that furnished much of their inspiration transformed the atmosphere of thought in multifarious ways. Although many of the detailed insights remain to be worked out, one can see a place for feud within the general picture along the following lines.[23]

Feud as practice[24]

1. Feud starts as an effort to avenge an act perceived as a wrong, generally violent injury and often a killing.
2. It represents this wrong as the act of an enemy and signals a lasting enmity between those who inflicted it and the "victim."
3. The wrong that provokes and justifies feud is understood to affect a larger group around the original victim that was in part known and even recruited in advance of trouble. That group's solidarity, threatened by its inability to protect its own, may now seem to need reassertion.
4. Given a similar sense of the vicarious liability of the injuring party's associates, these were sometimes targeted for vengeance in the principal's stead.

---

[22] Compare *The Treatise on the Laws and Customs of the Realm of England Commonly Called Glanvill*, ed. G.D.G. Hall (London and Edinburgh, 1965; repr. Oxford, 1993), Book 14 with the cases I discuss in *Rancor and Reconciliation*, pp. 191–6.

[23] The preceding paragraphs summarize a position I have argued in much more detail in *Rancor and Reconciliation*, chs 5–8.

[24] My earlier version of this model was in *Rancor and Reconciliation*, pp. 8–9.

5. The level of response is constrained by a notion of rough equivalence, requiring the keeping of a "score."
6. Emotions both fuel the response and help to determine its quantum and nature.
7. The response is open to public view and ritualized in ways that proclaim the acts to all as legitimate and honorable. This distinguishes it from the kind of secret killings and ambushes perpetrated by traitors and called by such names as murder and felony.
8. Action from the side of the "victim" nevertheless raises the high probability of a further tit-for-tat response from their enemies.
9. To dispel this and offer hopes of an end to the violence, something much more than the punishment of individual offenders is necessary, amounting to a veritable peace settlement between the wider groups involved.
10. This settlement, though widely recognized to be legitimate, is nevertheless understood in some broad sense to be distinct from any act of public authority.

Let me emphasize that this is not intended even as a crypto-definition. I did initially envision it as a kind of check list, though I was aware that the more elaborate and specific such a list gets, the more closely it approximates to a formal definition. With the help of Pierre Bourdieu, I now see more clearly why I found definitions of feud so unhelpful. Definitions, as he puts it, falsely objectify the subjective. In matters of life and death, men do not proceed mechanically by following definitions, painting by numbers, as it were. They act subjectively, as seems natural to them, doing what *feels* right. So I present the above as a description of what people appear actually to have done at critical times in the pursuit of their vengeance for wrongs. It presents a rough account of the practice of medieval English men and women in the taking of tit-for-tat vengeance. By formalizing to a degree what I think to have found in thirteenth-century England, I can offer a target for disagreement to specialists in other high medieval societies, whose vengeance paths and feud repertoires I believe to have been very likely described and argued in similar language, thus comparable yet culturally distinct.

Much more can be said about this non-prescriptive model of rather special vengeance behavior. A few comments of my own may help to advance the discussion and possibly also meet some of the objections that can doubtless be raised against it. I drew attention in points 3–4 above to the links between the principals (victim and offender) and the larger support groups whom they involved in their dispute, as have others in this volume. The eventual avenger was frequently quite distant from the original wrong that initiated the conflict. Feuds tend to ascend the social hierarchy. The victim and his closest kin often lacked the power and resources to act for themselves against any strong enemy. They therefore try to persuade a local lord or Big Man to take up their grievance as his own. Similarly, closure must be sought by agreement with the opposition's power leadership, which might again be quite distant from the individual actually responsible for the injury. The "Big Man" who had sent the men out from his house on their mission of vengeance, habitually kept himself absent when the blow was struck.[25] Lords must usually have been brought into the dispute if only to ensure that they would ratify any peace proposals.

The "publicity angle" to feud now strikes me as more important than I used to realize. Everyone needs to know what enmities are alive on their patch, and whether these, being pursued in honorable and open fashion, are to be considered licit. This point needs emphasis. The invaders need to persuade local society that they were "only" acting from the need to avenge a preceding wrong done to their side. Their claim was that their action was required by the norms, and so constituted neither simple predation nor, more dangerous yet, mere motiveless violence. In a word, if we assume that a notion of feud was familiar to them and their peers, their task was to bring their actions within its scope and thus legitimate them. The penalty for failure here was communal condemnation, which, even if it did not cause the whole body of the previously uncommitted to ride against them, would breed sympathy for the opposition's counter-measures.

One very attractive function of house assaults like that in which John Cusin perished was the visual demonstration that one had restored one's honor by the humiliation of one's foes. A very public invasion that annihilated the victim's most private and protected space made two important points. It established in the clearest possible manner the recovery of honor and social superiority. And it cleared the invaders of any suspicion of acting dishonorably themselves; they were neither secret murderers nor motiveless random killers.

The mention of publicity, of the need for honorable action to take on a "public" aspect, prompts one to ask to what degree feuding incorporated some version of the distinction between public and private spheres so familiar to the modern West in its various guises. Patently, feud decisions were never argued in the kinds of terms canvassed in the schools. Ideas of the "public interest" were hardly central to the standard discourse of dispute, organized around that undifferentiated notion of wrong already mentioned. By the twelfth century at the very latest, however, most people were aware that their kings, transformed by their coronations into a special, sacral kind of person, purportedly possessed a different authority to act against wrong than those over whom they ruled. Their advisers were coming to justify royal actions as acts of *publica potestas*. Their subjects (itself a fairly novel term at this time) certainly knew the difference between acts of force made licit by the giving of proper advance warning and the shameful, unadvertised violence of a *felun*. That is why avengers went to considerable ritual lengths to follow the "rules" and so proclaim their action legitimate. Ganelon's plea in the *Song of*

---

[25] Hyams, *Rancor and Reconciliation*, pp. 213–14 and 248–9 presents some evidence on the lord's role, including sending a raiding party off from his house, and on the occasional contract killing. F. Liebermann, *Die Gesetze der Angelsachsen* (3 vols, Halle, 1903–16), vol. 2, p. 180 gives some relevant references to earlier law, s.vv. *ræd* (3), and *rædbana*. Armstrong, in Chapter 2 above, cites a telling description of an act committed "per iniquitatis suae fautores, quorum ipse auctor et caput existit" (p. 68, n. 72).

Roland that he had acted in rightful prosecution of his private quarrel with Roland is only one of a whole number of fictional confirmations of this awareness.[26] Feuding was not, therefore, incompatible with a sense of the privileging of acts performed in the public interest over selfish and private ones. In order for us to strike the right balance here, we shall need to reread the sources more carefully than I have done so far.

What degree of the injury justified a violent response? How serious did a wrong have to be to justify the taking (or the threat) of vengeance against an enemy's life? Everyone agrees that the culpable killing without excuse of one's close relative or associate met the required standard. But a variety of lesser but still serious acts also sufficed to trip the wire. Fictional narratives that raise issues of rights as well as wrongs, and especially accounts of happenings that left one side with a sense of having been shamed in some way, suggest the kinds of offense serious enough to justify vengeance on life and limb. It would be relatively easy and very worthwhile to compile such a list, which would certainly comprehend serious assaults, especially rapes and arsons. A neglected source for comparison is the many regional lists of offenses deemed serious enough to be reserved for the attention of public justice in the shape of the Carolingian count and his successors. These so-called *vicaria* surely lie behind the lists of serious and so indictable offenses introduced into English legal practice from 1166 onwards as felonies.[27] They too show us from an unusual angle the kinds of offense most hated and feared by influential opinion over the period from the ninth to thirteenth centuries. The lists, differing in length and content from one Frankish county or region to the next, are good indicators of an early medieval ranking order of serious wrongs that passed formally unchanged into the High Middle Ages. This comparison of fictional with prescriptive sources suggests that private vengeance and royal justice drew upon a common cultural understanding of violence on a sliding scale.

* * *

In what I have written to this point, I have permitted myself to lapse frequently into feud language, thus apparently begging the very question I set out to answer. Let me now try to revisit the main question, armed with the kind of data briefly rehearsed above, and see if the notion of feud can be placed on some more scientific and defensible basis.

---

[26] *Chanson de Roland*, ed. G.J. Brault (University Park, Pa., 1984), ll. 3757–60 and 3827–30, also ll. 289–91 which contain the original and very public declaration of enmity.

[27] I set out what I knew of the development of *haute justice* in my "The Common Law and the French Connection," in R. Allen Brown (ed.), *Proceedings of the Battle Conference on Anglo-Norman Studies*, 4 (1982), pp. 84–5. The sense of "vicaria" as jurisdictional rights is to be distinguished from the territorial usage also familiar to Carolingian scholars. J. Boussard, *Le gouvernement d'Henri II Plantagenet* (Paris, 1956), pp. 313–19 documents Angevin usage.

I have endeavored to construct here from the various kinds of available evidence behavioral patterns followed in certain circumstances by some people in England between, say, the eleventh and thirteenth centuries, in order to avenge perceived wrongs done to the shame of themselves and their friends. The resulting loosely delineated notion of feud helps make sense of some of the more significant patterns of competitive behavior in medieval Europe. The nub of the argument is the utility of a single, crucial idea. Vengeance is always conceived in responsive, reactive terms; the avenger always claims that the other side had started the conflict, and committed the previous wrong. Similarly, so much direct action, violent and otherwise, is excused in retrospect (but also, one imagines, planned beforehand) as a response to some past wrong. In each case, the challenge for the principals on both sides of the dispute, and especially for their counseling friends, is how to minimize the overall cost of a satisfactory resolution of the issues in such a way as to restore with maximum speed the working equilibrium necessary for the world to get on with its life. Just how they might reach these decisions I leave to the final, speculative section of this chapter. But it should already be evident that the convenience of some notion of feud resembling the action model presented above, despite or maybe because of its definitional looseness, is that it gathers within a single repertoire a whole narrative of strike, counter-strike and effort at resolution. It offered contemporaries a kind of modular procedure, within which the decision to act or not was directed by answers to custom-set questions and allowed the actors to leave at any time they chose. The fact that it also enables us historians to situate within a posited continuous and dynamic narrative the few scrappy episodes or fragmentary narratives preserved by our sources hints at the conceptual advantages for participants.

Some objections to this approach

In our age of science, technology and high theory, this may not be enough to persuade. I therefore turn finally to consider a strong critique of conclusions like the ones I am advancing here. I test my position against arguments that Guy Halsall has rehearsed and developed in recent years from a close and intelligent reading of mostly early medieval evidence. Halsall finds it "odd" that most feud definitions are so "vague."[28] He identifies "true" feud as a long-term phenomenon, a form of exchange based on select past acts that legitimate current violent responses. Blood is taken for blood; compensation is acceptable only at a time when the other side cannot pay its blood debt.[29] This alone qualifies as "real" feud. The contemporary feud words on which I place considerable weight, he dismisses from relevance as

---

[28] Halsall, "Violence and Society," pp. 19–29, here at p. 19, also his "conference draft," pp. 2–3. Unless otherwise noted below, the quotations come from Halsall's unpublished conference draft.

[29] Halsall, "Violence and Society," pp. 20, 21.

referring to a "one-way relationship," seeking either to avenge or punish a past affront (invariably homicide) in such a way as to minimize the fear of retribution, or to exact compensation for it. These words were not used to denote "a lasting and reciprocal relationship of violence" and seldom a "lasting vendetta." What I here call "feud," picking up the term's Germanic precursors, he distinguishes as "customary vengeance," contending that Old English *fæhðe* and the rest, though they may also lurk behind such Latin locutions as *inimicitia*, actually mean "legal vengeance, usually as a right or threat."[30] He is especially keen to distinguish feud from politics including the "violent competition for resources between the powerful groups or families," a point he illustrates with an excellently nuanced account of the political context and character of the multi-generational conflict in eleventh-century Durham between the families of Earl Uhtred and Thurbrand.[31]

I accept many of Halsall's analytical points. Like Sawyer before him, he has richly earned our respect and gratitude for reminding us of the distorting conceptual baggage we carry into feud. So much of the literature is beset by assumptions, often incompletely argued out, though impossible to confirm from the sources. His call for clarity of thought is well made. The important distinction between single acts of vengeance and a continuing state of enmity had a contemporary importance, for example, that I at one stage tried to indicate with my own terminological coinage.[32] If the issue were no more than one-off acts of vengeance, the difference of opinion would be minimal. Iteration and reciprocity, within a chain of acts and reactions, forms the nub of the question here. There is no need to posit a romantic vision of cycles of unending violence. Yet I should not wish to talk of feuding relationships or discourse in the absence of a degree of reciprocity. I shall need to persuade readers that what I call feuds worked through continuing relationships between individuals, and (usually) also certain larger groups to which they belonged.

It is noteworthy that Halsall's analytical distinction between feud and customary vengeance, though useful in its sphere, is not to be found in contemporary sources. He notes the absence of any "clear term" for his feud, which does not, of course, necessarily diminish its ability to illuminate medieval ways of thought on conflict and violence. Much turns on the way one reads the primary sources, and more especially their silences. The attempt to reconstruct lost movies from the few "stills" that have come down to us will always require scholars to contest with each other the conceptual equipment with which we try to tackle the task. I might justify my own suggested premises by the need of the majority of the population

---

[30] Ibid., pp. 22–3, 25.

[31] This is the case I call "Earl Uhtred's Feud" in *Rancor and Reconciliation*, pp. 277–9. Whether one regards this as a series of linked conflicts or a single story depends partly on taste, quite largely also on the questions one wishes to pose. Robert C. Palmer presents a thirteenth-century mega-suit that might be said to present a comparable dilemma in *The Whilton Dispute, 1264–1380* (Princeton, 1984).

[32] Hyams, "Feud in Medieval England," *Journal of the Haskins Society*, 3 (1992 for 1991): 1–21, at pp. 6–7.

in the Middle Ages (as today) to get on with their lives in a very imperfect world without totally sacrificing their sense of decency and self-esteem. To register and account for the various manifestations of this need, the historian must, as Halsall agrees, focus on the relationships that are to endure. I differ from him only on how best to achieve this. I seek primarily to understand as best I can management of conflict in the medium to long term. In consequence I seek to bring together within a single framework the acts of violence and their motivations with the means by which adversaries and the wider society tried to contain these and limit the damage. In my view, this makes for a movie with not merely a more cheering, optimistic denouement, but also a richer message.

Much turns on the interpretation of the small group of terms by which contemporaries seem to have indicated vengeance behavior patterns. These include most obviously the slew of cognate words from the Germanic languages of the early Middle Ages that lie behind our modern English word "feud." Old French *faide*, Latin *faida* and their Germanic counterparts like Old English *faehðe* and Middle High German *vehde* were all used ostentatiously to describe dispute situations. Other terms that seem to occupy similar semantic space include Latin *inimicitia(e)* and vernacular equivalents, and another Germanic term that became thoroughly incorporated into Romance languages, *werra* (and the Old French *guere* derived from it).

It is risky to draw simple conclusions from so mixed a bag. A vocabulary shared throughout Western Christendom could indicate a common understanding of the situations to which it was applied across otherwise firm linguistic boundaries. One can surely claim that the vocabulary is common to a wide area, comprising most of Western Christendom. Pending a proper linguistic study, for which I am signally unqualified, I restrict myself to rehearsing a few points on matters directly relevant to the argument.

Enmity was a familiar notion in the Middle Ages. It came in various shapes and sizes. It received various restrictive labels; enmity could be mortal, public or (as variously expressed) ancient and long lasting.[33] *Inimicitia* thus denotes a superset of situations that takes in feud, as experienced and defined by modern observers, but also much else.[34] Roman law rules concerning one form, *inimicitia mortalis*, make it look very much a candidate to denote the kinds of events termed feud by modern scholars and perhaps also in vernacular conversation by participants at the time. But mortal foes and mortal enmities also appear all over the vernacular entertainment literatures.

---

[33] That hatreds are so often labeled ancient indicates a noteworthy community awareness of potentially life-threatening situations in their own midst (see Hyams, *Rancor and Reconciliation*, p. 247, n. 18).

[34] One good way to study its parameters would be to review glosses on the word's occurrence in the Bible, at locations like Gen. 3:15 and 26:21; Num. 35:23; Ezek. 26:15; Gal. 4:20; Sirach 6:17; I Macc. 7:26, 10:51; 11:12 and 13:6; II Macc. 3:3. I shall use as my own guide Pamela Barmash, *Homicide in the Biblical World* (Cambridge, 2005), ch. 2.

Enmity does not immediately entail action. Old French *guere*, in contrast, registers violence imminent or already begun. Stephen White's analysis of its usage in certain *chansons de geste* of the twelfth and early thirteenth centuries usefully begins by noting that every such act assumes wrongs to justify the action and stories by which each side justifies its own position.[35] The semantic field covered by *guere* is not quite as clear as a philologist might wish. It seems to cover conflicts not covered by Latin *bellum*, which essentially denotes the kinds of war started by a recognized authority like king or pope that can be justified along the lines of just war theories.[36] In the twelfth-century schools, and the courts they influenced, these were beginning to be conceptualized as public wars. In consequence, the modern Continental secondary literature describes as private war most situations where Anglophone scholars habitually talk of feud. It follows that any comprehensive account of feud in the High Middle Ages will have to take full account of their analyses too.

Two other Latin words must also come under scrutiny, *ultio* and *vindicta*.[37] Notably, both of them raise questions of interpretation, because they can each refer to either vengeance or punishment, and they sometimes seem to be innocent of any distinction between the two. *Vindicta* is especially interesting for its vernacular consequences. Its Old French cognates, verb and noun, appear from the very earliest texts, and its Italian form, *vendetta*, emerged as the description of choice for the kind of conflict patterns under examination here.[38] To assume that the different meanings that happen to accrue to any particular word imply some semantic or cultural association between them is an elementary linguistic error. Yet the way that both these words are capable of denoting such (to us) different responses to publicly identified wrongs remains striking. It does not seem much of a stretch to posit a semantic development by which the notion that a wrong to me and mine deserves vengeance is extended into a vindictive view that it should

---

[35] White, "Imaginaire faidal."

[36] F.H. Russell, *The Just War in the Middle Ages* (Cambridge, 1975), ch. 1. G.A. Raymond, "Military Necessity and the War Against Global Terrorism," offers a brief summary of the distinction between *bellum* and *guerra*, in H.M. Hensel (ed.), *The Law of Armed Conflict: Constraints on the Contemporary Use of Military Force* (Aldershot, 2005), pp. 11–12.

[37] See further now pp. 215–16 below.

[38] One main Romance derivative of *vindicta* is our word "vengeance." See *Dictionnaire de l'ancien français*, ed. J.A. Greimas (2nd edn, Paris, 2004), p. 613; *Altfranzösisches Wörterbuch*, ed. Adolf Tobler and Ernest Lommatsch (Berlin and Stuttgart, 1925–), Fasc. 88 [= vol. 11.1, 1989], cols 160–61, 177–8; and *Glossario degli Antichi Volgari Italiani*, ed. G. Colussi (20 vols. to date, Helsinki, 1982–2006), vol. 19, pp. 422–9. It was the *vindicta* root that spread into Romance languages, and not *ultio*—see W. Meyer-Lübke, *Romanische Etymologisches Wörterbuch* (2 vols, Heidelburg, 1911–20) and *Altfranzösisches Worterbuch*, ed. Tobler and Lommatsch.

receive afflictive punishment in the interests of all. Whether this development is plausible must be left to specialist linguists.

A definitive cross-cultural linguistic study of medieval vengeance words is both desirable and likely to be quite productive for historians. I should expect such an inquiry to conclude that men and women all over the medieval West did, indeed, share a broad understanding of the kinds of new and continuing hostilities that must be controlled for the safety of all, and around which local life must maneuver and organize itself, if reasonable order is to survive. It might also reveal that the distinction between vengeance and punishment was not much appreciated outside very learned circles until the advent of Roman law into the law schools gradually propelled it into a general acceptance. If these predictions are confirmed the second conclusion might prove as significant as the first.

In the meantime, we can still ask where all this leaves the case for using the notion of feud as an analytical tool in high medieval Europe after, say, 1100. I will once more work mainly from English evidence and partly by reference to Guy Halsall.

Halsall contends that the feud words from which our modern terms for feud are derived—*faide*, *vehde* and the like—denoted in the Middle Ages not what he calls feud but his "customary vengeance." He makes a number of constructive points about the actions these words actually covered, but the crux is that he believes that all of them denote "a one-way relationship" lacking reciprocity. The goal is vengeance without any danger of a come-back, something quite distinct in his view from the tit-for-tat patterns of genuine feud.

He is certainly right that many vengeance killings do not in fact trigger a response. One might point in illustration to the relation of Beowulf and Unferth in the Old English poem.[39] But the real question is this. Can one find in the Middle Ages at any stage a strategic procedure distinct from the reciprocity of "real" feud in which no response was expected or even perhaps, in some sense, permitted? This seems most improbable for more than one reason.

Remember first that there is no way to separate the two procedures from each other verbally. I cannot see that our feud words will fill the need. Like *inimicitia* and some of the other words discussed above, it seems possible to use them for both kinds of conflict, the ones stemming from strategic acts of vengeance that generate no counter-action and the other kind that occur within a tit-for-tat series. Indeed, as Halsall understands, words like *fæhðe* often take on a quite general meaning of conflict with no evident limitation to any particular kinds of situation. I shall suggest that this may in fact be their defining purpose. I strongly suspect that they are empty set terms, or something very close, which rely for their precise effect on the context and the way the protagonists understand their situation. But this is a non-specialist guess. We need a proper study of usage, carried out by a competent linguist conversant with the historian's extensive feud literature, including both Halsall's work and mine.

---

[39] *Beowulf and the Fight at Finsburh*, ed. F. Klaeber (3rd edn, Boston, 1950), ll. 587–9.

There certainly does appear to be an important difference between a cycle of violence and a one-off act of vengeance. One can imagine public opinion in a particularly egregious instance of wrong lining up squarely behind the one-off act, yet in mortal fear that the cycle with all its threats to the rest of the community will continue. But what are these cases where a one-off vengeance is approved by all where a further comeback would not be? I do not find this question easy to answer. The most likely such case is one where there has simply been no previous relationship between the parties. If a complete stranger attacks someone in the street, or rapes one's wife or daughter before one's eyes, many people today would permit his companion or her husband or father to kill with little compunction. We would probably not even call this vengeance taking; we would more likely talk of self-defense, which is how those who composed thirteenth-century legal records wrote these matters up.[40] If the wrongdoer was a kinless and lordless man, there would be no support group to target his killer anyway. If the wrong consisted of a killing in wartime, again a case without previous relationships to consider, we and they would describe any personal comeback in terms of something like Just War theory, not as feud.[41] All these cases appear exceptional. The norm for vengeance within established social relations, often said to be the standard case for murders today, looks to be an act where further comeback is possible, a possibility that peacemakers and others can never afford to ignore. In practice then acts of one-off vengeance without the likelihood of more must have been very rare indeed.

This may explain the lack of a contemporary model for them. Halsall recognizes the difficulty of positing a distinction that cannot be confirmed from contemporary terminology. He raises the possibility that even contemporaries might identify a one-off act of customary vengeance *after* a successful peace settlement had been made. This comes close to collapsing the two cases posited. The response to vengeance can never be automatic. Even in the clearest case of a feud model, the party last hit has options. He—such decisions generally fall on the men—may try and perhaps fail to take a life for a life; he may choose a cowardly way out; or—perhaps the normal case—he may seek a settlement. No law or documented custom of which I am aware absolutely rules out any of these or their variants. The closest case is to try and rule out all vengeance for the execution of wrongdoers, as is found in some early medieval laws.[42] Naturally, people will always take different views on the justice of executions and in a vengeance culture men will try and avenge even

---

[40] N.M. Hurnard, *The King's Pardon for Homicide Before A.D. 1307* (Oxford, 1969), ch. 3.

[41] But this case helps one understand why medieval chroniclers and fiction writers *do* in fact frequently use feud-like language to describe what we would certainly call warfare. A study of the semantic development of *guerra/guere* could be most instructive here.

[42] The Old English laws of Wihtred, 25; II Athelstan, 6.2–3; VI Athelstan, 1.5 (Liebermann, *Gesetze*, i. 14, 154, 174) banned the seeking of vengeance for a thief duly caught and killed in the act; a prudent executioner would ritually proclaim this invulnerability to all (Ine 16, 21, 35 (Liebermann, *Gesetze*, i. 96, 98, 104)).

the most just of killings, a tendency that is very hard to restrain. It thus makes little sense to me that a community which accepts the principle of licit blood vengeance could easily exclude all possibility of a likely violent response from a kindred (or equivalent) now one life behind on the scoreboard. In the eleventh century, one can see evidence for a sentiment that even accidental deaths or the execution of a hand-having thief caught in the act demanded some compensation, to avoid the danger that blood would be taken for blood.[43] No law that permits blood vengeance could outlaw a violent response to past vengeance. That some looser unwritten custom would permit such a rule is less plausible still.

The distinction between one-off and recurring efforts at vengeance, intellectually so attractive, begins to look like a distinction without a difference. But here Halsall's insight, that the classification of disputes tends to be made with hindsight, makes good sense. The truth surely is that nobody in a feuding culture can ever predict with certainty how the "victims" will respond to an act of vengeance. The newly aggrieved may at once seek further vengeance of their own. More likely, they will agree to "lump it," take their punishment, nurse their injuries and do nothing more; perhaps the neighborhood would have to beware of an ancient enmity thereafter. Or they might make it known that they would respond favorably now to peace overtures. There is really no way to be sure which or what combination of these to expect. Nor can one set a time limit on this uncertainty. The attention paid in the sources and secondary literature to the timing of revenge and to the duration of enmities implies just such an uncertainty. The last avenger in any series (even a series of one) can never be sure if he is home free. Often he will walk in fear.[44] The only way to remove this fear is to kill off all the opposition, to practice small-scale genocide and not necessarily that small in scale either. It has to be significant that just this intent is sometimes attributed to the villains of medieval romance. The killer of the father is made to try and wipe out the whole family so that he never need fear vengeance.[45] Though he naturally never to my knowledge succeeds, the theme is a neat illustration of the way that real life fears are sometimes played out in literary fiction. In real life, the best the fearful killer can do is to consult his friends, take their counsel and perhaps set in motion negotiations toward a peace offering and settlement.[46] Meanwhile, his enemies may well be taking their own counsel too. They must decide whether to swallow the insult or prolong the killing and the enmity. The very fact that we have to posit these possibly agonized faction debates supports the overall notion of a feud-like culture, for it will be in

---

[43] In addition to the last note, see *The Vita Wulfstani of William of Malmesbury*, ed. R.R. Darlington (London, 1928), bk. 2, pp. 15–6.

[44] A marvelous fictional depiction of this fear is to be found in Ismail Kadare, *Broken April* (New York, 1990). But Kadare is depicting a system in which further vengeance is known to be required. How realistic this is or was in his Albania I cannot say.

[45] I give a couple of examples in *Rancor and Reconciliation*, p. 64, n. 152.

[46] See "settlements, peace" in the index of Hyams, *Rancor and Reconciliation*.

the impassioned course of these debates that feud norms are rehearsed, modified and taught to the inexperienced, a point I shall develop in a moment.

For the moment it is enough to conclude that the process or possibility of serial vengeance, which I want to term feud, is a rather more contingent one than it is often portrayed. It is not just that later narrators make feud from what has already occurred. The actors themselves must improvise their responses in a world not without rules but certainly lacking anything of a set script or mechanical form to the waging of dispute and the treatment of wrong. This can serve as a cue to pose at last the question of how medieval actors may have exercised their agency in such situations.

* * *

I begin from the premises that the urge to avenge wrongs was well nigh universal, and irresistible to all save the very saintly, and that all vengeance carried the potential for further violence through a tit-for-tat response.[47] If these premises hold, intelligent people will take them into account when faced by what they perceive as wrongs. And their practice, the practice of the respected and successful taken as *good* practice, will influence those around them. This is what I was out to formalize through my multi-stage model of feud as practice above.

In principle, this kind of decision can be made by following binding and systematic rules of the kind that lawyers specify to effect, say, a valid will. This is patently not part of feud practice as it has been observed, and it would be surprising if it were, given the life and death stakes. Equally obvious, such matters cannot be entirely ungoverned in any society that hopes to avoid the descent into chaos. This is a point that holds for non-human societies too and from which originates the theories of the peace in the feud.[48] The most helpful way I have yet found to pin down the actual rule-driven but very non-mechanical processes by which people came to their decisions about vengeance is through the notion that Pierre Bourdieu has called the *habitus*.[49]

Habitus offers a route through which to deal with the agency of individuals living in groups. The goal is to get inside the decision-making of other humans and try to understand why some options *feel* more right to them than others. We seek to deduce from people's past practice the source of their individual decisions.

---

[47] It is not clear we should except the saintly. My friend Carol Kaske directed me to Psalms 138:21–2, and to Augustine's thoughts on this in his *Enarrationes in Psalmos* (MPL 37, col. 1801), with very selective quotations in the Glossa Ordinaria of the Vulgate Bible.

[48] Hyams, *Rancor and Reconciliation*, pp. 14–16, 87–92.

[49] Pierre Bourdieu, *The Logic of Practice*, trans. Richard Nice (Stanford, 1990), esp. ch. 3. I am well aware that this work, originally published in 1980, has provoked some often heated debate. I have no interest in exegesis of the details of Bourdieu's theory or others' objections. These would be out of place in a single chapter anyway. I use his work as a convenient metaphor through which to express my own position.

The idea is that individual men and women form from their experiences sets of dispositions about the world and their place in it alongside others. They use these dispositions to shape their responses to new experiences, which in turn constantly reshape the dispositions themselves. Early experiences carry particular weight and go far to fix an individual's direction on important matters for good.

This posits a system with so much feedback that it almost seems unnecessary to look for conscious decision-making at all. The *habitus* itself limits the number of possible choices, in part by excluding some as simply unthinkable. Individuals almost literally embody the *habitus*. That is, we internalize the more significant norms by which we live to the point where they become second nature and apparently spontaneous, or at least such that we can think of them as beyond argument, and speak of them as "reasonable" and common sense.[50] In this way we do in fact tend to make many decisions without calculation or conscious reference to norms at all.[51]

There is nevertheless considerable room in the schema for necessary strategic calculation. There has to be. Though some responses look automatic, especially with hindsight, there can be nothing pre-ordained about the really big decisions concerning matters like vengeance, life and death. The most the *habitus* can do in advance preparation is to set out general parameters. Each fresh situation demands decisions of its own. Even for the old chestnuts, the *habitus* will offer a range of possibilities from which the individual must choose, and in doing so slightly restructure his or her own *habitus* itself. Striving to reach a position that feels right, people individuate their own mix through a process of what the French call *bricolage*.[52] This looks to the individual. But whole groups share *habitus*, or rather its members' related but different versions of *habitus* overlap in a substantial way. This is because they are inherently likely to have passed through comparable sets of experience, processed these through similar dispositions, and gone on to further multiple feedback between individual experiences and dispositions and those of their neighbors.

I find that this schema offers me a framework within which to understand how the feud findings above just may have worked in real life. The men and women of the Middle Ages were arguably considerably more forthright in voicing their thoughts and feelings about hatred and violence than I was brought up to be in the mid-twentieth century. Direct action was common enough that violence was always recognized to be among the known options in reaction to serious wrongs. The limits within which this was thought licit were openly debated and, to that extent, agreed. There were, of course, no hard and fast rules, certainly no set script,

---

[50] Bourdieu nicely describes this as "like a train laying its own rails" (p. 57).

[51] Malcolm Gladwell, *Blink: The Power of Thinking Without Thinking* (New York, 2005) both illustrates a wide variety of this type of swift and unpremeditated decision and also marshals some quite persuasive evidence that this is the optimal way to make them.

[52] Bricolage is a central conceit of Claude Lévi-Strauss, *The Savage Mind* (Chicago, 1966).

but people knew their norms all the same.[53] Our best chance to seize these is to research them in the usual kind of way we seek to block in the rest of the secular culture of the time.[54] Past experiences of contemporaries in their dealings with friends and enemies combine with a general awareness of proper behavior as judged by one's peers to evoke on the appropriate occasion an avenging response over and against the *Patientia* which churchmen generally sought to promote, and pursue it through some or all of the known steps of an enmity.[55]

The young will have imbibed these norms more or less effectively as they grew up. They could hardly avoid hearing in the home the complaints of their elders concerning insults and wrongs of all sorts, they watched what eventually ensued, and listened to instructive tales of past satisfaction and resentment. In special cases, their elders (often women who could not easily perform the act themselves) pressed upon them concrete tokens of what was required, the bloody shirt or broken sword preserved precisely in order to goad them if necessary into avenging action. It is not necessary to believe that they all witnessed the spectacular episodes of the "classic" feud anecdote, which were probably rare enough. One can acquire the ethos and dynamic of vengeance quite well from much more mundane squabbles and the manner in which people waged and retold them. Children could rehearse and practice the principles perfectly well in schoolroom and schoolyard, or as childhood preparation for life through mock hunts or battles and in play of all sorts.[56] In such locations, they experienced in their own persons and on their own

---

[53] Scripts are written by an author different from the actors. They are generally supposed to stick to the allotted words. In a violent dispute, this is too much like painting by numbers. But real life is much freer. The closest medieval analogy might be the liturgical rituals for which we possess what appear to be properly drafted scripts. But my sense is that any able celebrant used them as prompts and improvised from them like someone playing jazz rather than an orchestral musician. But even this is too tight. There is no script-text. We just "know" roughly what we ought to be doing, for example that a wrong *ought* to receive an avenging counter-stroke. I note that my co-editor just talks sensibly about "established patterns of thought" (Throop, p. 199–200 below).

[54] I look especially to the late Georges Duby and the lines of inquiry he initiated in "The Diffusion of Cultural Patterns in Feudal Society", *Past and Present*, 39 (1968): 3–10. In *Rancor and Reconciliation*, ch. 2, I was semi-consciously seeking to reconstruct a relevant portion of the *habitus*.

[55] I give some account of *patientia*, and its more secular counterpart *debonereté*, in my "What did Henry III of England think in Bed and in French about Kingship and Anger?" in B. Rosenwein (ed.), *Anger's Past: The Social Uses of an Emotion in the Middle Ages* (Ithaca, 1998).

[56] I witnessed something very like this in a Palestinian village in the summer of 2007. An enmity smoldering between two half brothers burst out into violence. The wife of one was so angry she declared that she would bring in her brothers from their nearby homes, thus broadening the dispute. When the teenage full brother of the second brother heard this, he at once threatened to call his own brothers in from their work in the city. All of this was apparently spontaneous and without cogitation, something especially striking in the case of the teenager. Eventually, the

bodies the power of pecking orders, the shame and loss of face in social failure, the joy of victory in "getting their own back," the need to concede when the opposition was too strong or opinion too heavily against them, putting them "in the wrong."

Experiences naturally differed according to where one grew up and lived, at what level of society and so forth. But further research will show, I believe, that the general lines of a feud ethos were kept reasonably consistent within a wider shared culture in the same way that other behavior patterns and tastes were, by what people did and how they viewed and discussed this. That discourse of dispute mentioned earlier was the means through which people treated their conflicts and the issues these raised for them. It did much more than mere description. It constructed the events themselves. In an important sense, this is where feud was born.

This reaches beyond practice. The acts of vengeance and restraint, what men and women did, acquired meaning from the language with which people expressed them. A return to matters of language and vocabulary is therefore unavoidable, to justify the use of the "feud" words which still seem to me to meet our analytical needs. I strongly suspect that the actual oral usage of the Germanic feud words, Old English *fæhðe* and the rest, could it be recovered, would turn out to fit the case for feud as a known pattern of tit-for-tat vengeance much as in the practice model above. This is once again no simple matter of dictionary definitions. Our only evidence comes from written documents, which are far too distant from the oral locutions in which people conversed, debated and comforted each other. My untutored guess is that these feud words were quite elastic in their connotations. It is easy to document a non-specific, broad sense of dispute or conflict with many examples.[57] Only by linking a written text to observed events of tit-for-tat serial vengeance could one prove the more specific sense that I suspect. But texts highly suggestive of this do exist. Perhaps the strongest example comes from the Old English laws. Edmund's second code (*c*.943–6) is a clear indication of the way an accepted vengeance procedure of the type under consideration might be brought without too much protest under royal regulation.[58] Its first chapter labels as *fæhðe* a process that seems undeniably close to the feud practice outlined above; the regulatory purpose of the law seems to me to make best sense on this reading. Anyone who kills a man, it declares, is to bear the feud, unless within the prescribed period of a year his friends make a settlement providing for the payment of the proper wergeld. *Gif hwa heonanforð ænigne man ofslea, ðæt he wege sylf ða fæhþe.*[59] When a carefully drafted text like this one talks of people bearing a "feud"

---

actors found ways to restore relations, for the time being. I do not claim this unfortunate episode even as a pre-feud, but it certainly taught me something of how feuds might work.

[57] Illustrations s.v. *fæhðe* etc. in the Old English Dictionary Corpus are available at http://www.doe.utoronto.ca/.

[58] I have argued this in *Rancor and Reconciliation*, pp. 82–4.

[59] Liebermann, *Gesetze*, vol. 1, pp. 186–7 (I Edmund 1). The word *fæhðe* is in fact quite rare in the laws, and the closely associated text *Wer* does not use it at all (Liebermann, *Gesetze*, vol. 1, pp. 392–5).

with legally enforceable consequences for themselves and their supporters, the term has to mean something more precise than generalized dispute or conflict. The twelfth-century *Leges Henrici Primi* took this over as it stood, and likewise has the killer bearing the feud.[60] Twelfth-century translators and adapters apparently saw no incongruity in killers bearing the feud in this more specific sense.[61] This single example demonstrates that *fæhðe* (and its cognates) are capable of carrying the narrower sense required for the hypothesis as well as the more easily documented general one. Interpretation of all these texts is inevitably tainted with circularity, and the best that one can say is that other ones remain congruous with the feud-as-practice reading for which I am arguing.[62]

Much in oral converse turns on context. We learn to read between the lines and to learn from facial expression and body language when to deduce rules for action, approved and proscribed, from more general terms. I think it very possible that the feud words functioned in that manner. We possess a persuasive body of information from many different medieval communities and a variety of social milieux for an almost corporeal belief in the justice of seeking in person redress or vengeance for wrongs suffered in person. It is up to the linguists to determine whether it is plausible to see our feud words used for this purpose, or to find an alternative linguistic route to make their use accord with the perceived patterns of vengeance in the Middle Ages.

* * *

The very inclusive approach argued for here has the merit of encouraging the incorporation of vengeance and its accompanying violence into our assessment of the political culture of the societies under study. It has been said that all politics is local, a point perhaps more apt for our Middle Ages than in today's globalized world. I see feuds as a means by which men and women considered their local political options within a spectrum of possible choices aimed at a number of possible goals. Gadi Algazi has reminded us that feuds were "multi-layered

---

[60] *Leges Henrici Primi*, ed. L.J. Downer (Oxford, 1972), 88. 12–12d. See in particular 88. 12a which says "ipse sibi portet homicidii faidiam," using a French form that 88. 13 shows to come from the *Lex Salica*. For the post-Conquest development of the term "feud," see E.J. Dobson, "The Word Feud," *Review of English Studies*, 7 (1956): 52–4 and the *Middle English Dictionary* (http://ets.umdl.umich.edu/m/med/) s.v. "féd(e)".

[61] *Leges Henrici Primi*, 88. 12a. The contemporary Quadripartitus translation of II Edmund 1 is "inimicitie factionem," and *fæhðe* is also translated by "factio" elsewhere (Liebermann, *Gesetze*, vol. 1, pp. 122–3 (Ine 74. 2), 187, 189 (II Edmund 7)).

[62] Some of the Old Testament renderings are very suggestive, though they tend to refer to intra-kin or divine vengeance. Take, for example, the accounts of Cain and Abel and the confrontation of Abraham and Lot in "Genesis A" (http://www.georgetown.edu/labyrinth/library/oe/texts/a1.1.html), ll. 1023–35, 2037–73.

practices with multiple uses and unexpected hidden edges."[63] No single approach will capture everything that is important about them.

White has recently categorized the literature on these directions under three heads. First, feud can be identified with the emotions that animated it, primarily but not exclusively honor and shame. It may then be analyzed in terms of its "my turn/your turn" rhythm and the exchange metaphors used to imagine it. A second approach stresses the legal dimension. The avengers contend that their direct action is made licit by the wrongs that have preceded it. Their adversaries may debate and seek to refute this position. Thus talk plays a highly significant role in the proceedings. And third, there is the political dimension. Approaching disputes from this direction emphasizes the instrumentality of the actors' goals, the quest for wealth, power and status. As White shows, one can easily find passages in *chansons de geste*—and, one may add, many other kinds of text too—to describe *gueres* and feuds in each of these ways.[64] I believe we can generalize White's postulate of a shared, highly flexible discourse of *guere* in eleventh- and twelfth-century France *mutatis mutandis* to a broader swathe of the High Middle Ages and other areas of Western Europe. To decide the degree to which this might be acceptable, it is essential to cast one's net wider than any "strict constructionist" definition of feud would permit, in order to include the multivalence that appears to be a major feature, even a selling point, of the vengeance processes under scrutiny here.

It would be excellent if this chapter provoked more detailed studies of practice in different localities and at different dates, and so advanced our understanding of the diverse but mutually intelligible modes in which many people in the High Middle Ages struggled to implement their right to answer wrong, by seizing on their own initiative the fullest satisfaction they could reasonably obtain. Whether particular instances of the taking of vengeance are to be considered as feud in the sense I have suggested remains a question of iterative fact, and one which will not easily be decided at that.[65] That is as may be. I continue to find it helpful to talk of feud, and to seek out instances of feud and feud-like behavior from the period for analysis.

---

[63] G. Algazi, "Pruning Peasants: Private War and Maintaining the Lord's Peace in Late Medieval Germany," in E. Cohen and M. de Jong (eds), *Medieval Transformations: Texts, Power, and Context* (Leyden, 2001), p. 259, as cited by White, "Imaginaire faidal," p. 179, n. 10.

[64] White, "Imaginaire faidal," pp. 182–5.

[65] John Hudson examines evidence concerning noble disputes in twelfth-century England and is not convinced that he can find a form distinctive enough to be called feud ("Faide, vengeance et violence en Angleterre (ca 900–1200)," pp. 368–73).

Chapter 8
Zeal, Anger and Vengeance: The Emotional Rhetoric of Crusading[1]

Susanna A. Throop

In a world still beset by religious violence, the medieval crusading movement continues to fascinate the West—the Hollywood release *Kingdom of Heaven* and the extensive popular literature on the Knights Templar now available in your local bookstore are but two examples of this appetite for information, accurate or otherwise, about the movement. The topic has proved fertile ground for scholars as well, with multiple academics researching all aspects of crusading, from weaponry and tactics to gender and religious politics. Others have looked at questions fundamentally tied to the social sciences: Why did people participate in these expeditions? And how did people at the time describe and explain their actions?

One such ideological question to receive renewed attention is how the concept of vengeance was used to motivate and justify the crusading movement in twelfth-century Europe.[2] Until recently historians have not focused on this line of thought, and above all, have assumed the idea of vengeance to be self-explanatory. Historians like the great Carl Erdmann considered the idea of crusading as vengeance "an obvious improvisation suggestive of how immature the idea of crusade still was," despite significant primary source evidence to the contrary, and even more recent historians such as Jonathan Riley-Smith and Jean Flori have promoted the general assumption that perceptions of the crusade as vengeance only flourished among the laity at the very beginning of the First Crusade, a vivid example of the laity's limited comprehension of theological subtlety and their general emotional

---

[1] I am grateful above all to the Gates Cambridge Trust, whose generous financial assistance made this research possible. Many scholars have helped me clarify my thoughts on this topic, including Jonathan Riley-Smith, my co-editor, Miri Rubin, Carl Watkins, Norman Housley, both anonymous reviewers, and the medievalists at the University of Edinburgh, the University of St. Andrews and the International Medieval Congress at Leeds, who listened to papers of mine on the matter and contributed many helpful suggestions and insights.

[2] My "Vengeance and the Crusades," *Crusades*, 5 (2006): 21–38, and Philippe Buc's contemporaneous piece, "La vengeance de Dieu: De l'exégèse patristique à la Réforme ecclésiastique et la Première Croisade," in Dominique Barthélemy, François Bougard and Régine Le Jan (eds), *La vengeance, 400–1200* (Rome, 2006), pp. 451–86. I am grateful to Dr. Buc for graciously sending me a draft of his article before formal publication. See also my forthcoming monograph *Crusading as an Act of Vengeance, 1095–1216* (Ashgate).

over-enthusiasm. In fact, recent work has shown that the idea of crusading as vengeance appeared in the texts with greater frequency as the twelfth century progressed. Moreover, various aspects of the idea of crusading as vengeance were propagated extensively in religious literature by key figures like Bernard of Clairvaux and Pope Innocent III, suggesting that it would be inaccurate to conclude the ideology's popularity was limited to the laity or the lowlier clerics.

It is significant, however, that earlier scholars assumed that the notion of crusading as vengeance was due to over-emotional reactions—the concept of "vengeance" in our own times is steeped with emotional overtones, resonating with the "passions" that we assume drive people to seek vengeance. To a large degree, the emotional aspect of vengeance would seem to imply an inherent irrationality as well. These are, I would argue, reflections of our own culture and do not necessarily tell us anything new about medieval perceptions of vengeance. As William Reddy has noted, extensive research in the social and natural sciences has led to the theory that emotional change within any given culture is the product of humanity's emotional capacities and a specific historical context.[3] No scholar who accepts in this way that emotion is subject to the influence of culture and history could simply assume that the emotional component of medieval vengeance is self-explanatory and universal. Since *vindicta* and *ultio*, the two primary medieval Latin terms I have investigated, did not signify precisely the same concept in the twelfth century as the modern English term *vengeance* does today, the emotions associated with *vindicta* and *ultio* may have been in some way understood differently than the emotions the modern individual ascribes to vengeance. The question needs to be asked, what emotions did twelfth-century contemporaries relate to vengeance, and how did those emotions further connect to the idea of crusading as vengeance in particular?[4]

The evidence for the importance of *zelus*

When reading the primary source evidence for crusading in twelfth- and early thirteenth-century Latin texts, it quickly becomes apparent that one word was time and again used to describe, expand or otherwise modify the idea of crusading vengeance: *zelus*. Not merely the proximity of the words in the texts is suggestive—the frequency with which the terms appear is related. As the twelfth century progressed, the idea of crusading as vengeance appeared more frequently in the texts and, at the same time, the term *zelus* appeared more frequently alongside those references to vengeance.

---

[3] William Reddy, *The Navigation of Feeling: A Framework for the History of Emotions* (Cambridge, 2001), p. 45.

[4] For a broader answer to the first part of the question, see Barbara Rosenwein's "Les émotions de la vengeance," in Barthélemy, Bougard and Le Jan (eds), *La vengeance, 400–1200*, pp. 237–56.

I believe it is well worth outlining the evidence in detail on the following pages, so that the reader can gain a sense of scope of the passages in question. For convenience I have translated *zelus* and its derivatives as "zeal," but the deeper, more exact meaning of *zelus* will be discussed at much greater length later in the chapter.

Early twelfth-century sources

In crusading texts from the early twelfth century, *zelus* was associated with crusading by only two writers that we know of. Orderic Vitalis wrote of Raymond of St. Gilles that on the way to Jerusalem from Antioch "in no way giving way to laziness or indolence, rather he was continuously hostile to the gentiles owing to zeal."[5] Describing the violent persecution of the Jews by First Crusaders on their way to the East, Ekkehard of Aura wrote that "they had enough to do, either to eliminate the execrable Jewish people they discovered, or even to compel them into the lap of the church, serving with the zeal of Christianity even in this thing."[6] Later in the same work he noted that those who persecuted the Jews "[had] the zeal of God, but not according to the knowledge of God." In other words, the crusaders were motivated by the right sentiment, but nevertheless acted against God's plan.[7] Their fault lay in their action, not in the emotion that moved them.

Mid-twelfth-century sources

Crusading texts in the mid-twelfth century revealed more frequent connections between zeal, crusading and vengeance. King Louis VII of France supposedly went on crusade because "zeal for the faith burned in the king."[8] Bernard of Clairvaux wrote similarly to those preparing for the Second Crusade.[9] After the Second Crusade, Peter the Venerable asked King Roger II of Sicily to attack the Greeks for their alleged role in the expedition's failure: "therefore rise up, good prince … rise up to aid the people of God, just as the Maccabees were zealous for the law of

---

[5] Orderic Vitalis, *Historia Aecclesiastica*, ed. Marjorie Chibnall (6 vols, Oxford, 1975), vol. 5, p. 134. All translations are my own, except where otherwise noted. Roche has also noted the general association of "zeal" and vengeance/feud in Orderic's history, which suggests to my mind that the relationship between the two ideas existed in a broader cultural milieu, not only in the context of crusading (Roche, above pp. 127 and 135).

[6] Ekkehard of Aura, *Hierosolymita*, Recueil des Historiens des Croisades, Historiens Occidentaux 5 (Paris, 1895), p. 20.

[7] Ekkehard of Aura, *Hierosolymita*, p. 21. See more on this passage below, starting at p. 184.

[8] Odo of Deuil, *De Profectione Ludovici VII in Orientem*, ed. Virginia G. Berry (New York, 1965), p. 6.

[9] "the zeal of God burns in you." Bernard of Clairvaux, *Epistolae*, ed. J. Leclerq and H.M. Rochais, S. Bernardi Opera Omnia 8 (Rome, 1977), vol. 8, p. 314.

God; avenge such shames, such injuries, so many deaths, such great and impious shedding of blood of the army of God."[10] Peter, bishop of Oporto, was depicted exhorting the Second Crusaders before the siege of Lisbon with the vocabulary of vengeance, justice and zeal: "good men with good minds, implement legitimate deeds of vengeance here and now. *Cruelty for God is not cruelty but piety*. With the zeal of justice, not the bile of anger, wage just war."[11]

Late twelfth-century sources

In late twelfth-century crusading texts, references to zeal and vengeance with regard to crusading substantially increased in number. At Damascus the army of King Baldwin II of Jerusalem was described as "having zeal for the faith, immediately they all strove to avenge their injuries."[12] Baldwin III was described in similar terms at the siege of Edessa.[13] William of Tyre also depicted Pope Urban II speaking at Clermont: "therefore, let us be armed with the zeal of God, let us as one gird on our powerful sword, let us go forth and be powerful sons ... anyone who has zeal for the law of God, he will help us."[14]

People in western Europe purportedly responded with enthusiasm to calls for the Third Crusade:

> zeal incited [the men] to greater fervor to embrace the journey without delay ... [the pope] ran forward to the cross held by the priests with speedy zeal and pious passion, so that now it is not a question of who will be signed with the cross, but rather who will not take on such pious work.[15]

Kings Philip II of France and Henry II of England took the cross "incensed with zeal for God."[16] When King Richard I's men captured a Muslim vessel in June 1191, the Muslims killed a few Christians in the fighting. In response, according

---

[10] Peter the Venerable, *The Letters of Peter the Venerable*, ed. G. Constable (2 vols, Cambridge, Mass., 1967), vol. 1, p. 395.

[11] *De expugnatione Lyxbonensi*, ed. C.W. David (New York, 1936), p. 80.

[12] William of Tyre, *Chronicon*, ed. R.B.C. Huygens, Corpus Christianorum, Continuatio Mediaevalis 63 (Turnholt, 1986), p. 609.

[13] "zeal seized arms to take vengeance on the iniquitous." William of Tyre, *Chronicon*, p. 719.

[14] William of Tyre, *Chronicon*, p. 134. William also described the First Crusaders before Jerusalem was taken: "there was in that group not one man who was old or sick or from a small estate whom zeal did not move and whom the fervor of devotion did not incite to the battle." William of Tyre, *Chronicon*, p. 970.

[15] *Itinerarium Peregrinorum et Gesta Regis Ricardi*, ed. W. Stubbs, Rerum Brittanicarum Medii Aevi Scriptores 38.1 (London, 1864), p. 139.

[16] Rigord, *Gesta Philippi Augusti*, ed. H.F. Delaborde, Oeuvres de Rigord et de Guillaume le Breton 1 (Paris, 1882), p. 84.

to the *Itinerarium peregrinorum*, the crusaders "pregnant with fervent anger and zeal for vengeance ... raged courageously at the bitter insult."[17] In 1199 Pope Innocent III wrote to the Armenians "may the house of the Lord employ your zeal so that [you may] take vengeance for the injury done to the Crucified One and to his Temple and his inheritance."[18]

Zeal was invoked to describe actions against Jews and heretics as well as Muslims. When preachers spoke convincingly against heretics in southern France, purportedly the crowd were "moved with vehement admiration and inflamed with zeal for the Christian faith."[19] Kings Henry II of England and Louis VII of France had supposedly taken action against the heretics "filled with zeal for the Christian faith ... they decided that they would eliminate the aforesaid heretics from their borders."[20] Rigord reported that King Philip II of France felt likewise about the Jews in France: "inflamed with zeal for God he commanded that ... the Jews should be captured ... despoiled ... and sent forth, just as the Jews themselves despoiled the Egyptians."[21]

Some of Philip's actions against Christian enemies were also attributed to zeal for the Christian faith.[22] When he moved against Hugh of Burgundy in 1185, Philip, "inflamed with zeal for the Christian faith ... told [Hugh] that ... he must restore things stolen to the aforesaid churches and must not do such things again, and, if he did not want to restore that money to the churches, [Philip] would take serious vengeance upon him."[23]

Some writers in the late twelfth century connected zeal with crusading through self-sacrifice rather than aggression. In 1181 Pope Alexander III described the crusaders in 1096 as "zealous for the law of God, they were able to tolerate the slaughter of the faithful with patient mind."[24] In 1187, Pope Gregory VIII wrote in his crusading bull *Audita tremendi* that the Christians should "pay attention to how the Maccabees were zealous for divine law, experiencing great dangers to free their brothers, and they learned to relinquish not only their belongings, but even their persons for their brothers."[25] Zeal was associated with self-sacrifice

---

[17] *Itinerarium Peregrinorum*, p. 208.

[18] Innocent III, *Die Register Innocenz' III*, ed. O. Hageneder and A. Haidacher (Graz, 1964–2001), vol. 2, p. 468. (*Etsi modernis temporibus*).

[19] *Gesta Regis Henrici Secundi*, ed. W. Stubbs, Rerum Brittanicarum Medii Aevi Scriptores 49.1 (London, 1867), p. 201.

[20] Roger of Howden, *Chronica*, ed. W. Stubbs, Rerum Brittanicarum Medii Aevi Scriptores 51.2 (London, 1868–71), p. 150.

[21] Rigord, *Gesta Philippi Augusti*, p. 16.

[22] Rigord, *Gesta Philippi Augusti*, p. 16 and 37.

[23] Rigord, *Gesta Philippi Augusti*, p. 51.

[24] Alexander III, *Epistolae*, ed. J.-P. Migne, Patrologia Latina 200 (Paris, 1855), col. 1294. (*Cor nostrum*).

[25] Gregory VIII, *Epistolae*, ed. J.-P. Migne, Patrologia Latina 202 (Paris, 1866), col. 1542. (*Audita tremendi*).

on the field of battle as well. When Reynald of Châtillon died, the *Itinerarium peregrinorum* lauded his martyrdom: "O zeal of faith! O fervor of the soul!"[26] Similarly, when a woman died of exhaustion after carrying stones at Jerusalem, the *Itinerarium peregrinorum* noted that "without a break the tireless woman went back and forth, exhorting others more diligently, driven by zeal to find the end of her life along with the end of her labors ... O admirable faith of the weak sex! O inimitable zeal of the woman!"[27]

Early thirteenth-century sources

Early thirteenth-century crusading texts also revealed textual connections between zeal, vengeance and crusading. According to Arnold of Lübeck (writing sometime before his death in 1212), in 1187 Pope Clement III "incit[ed] all to zeal against the impious and to vengeance for the holy blood."[28] Arnold of Lübeck also noted that Emperor Frederick I was moved "to the vengeance of the zeal of God and the vengeance of the holy land."[29] This was confirmed by Robert of Auxerre, who wrote that "Frederick Augustus was happy when he heard the news ... a discrete man and one zealous for justice."[30] The Third Crusade was undertaken "by many, inflamed with zeal ... with fervent zeal."[31] Each man who took the cross, "zealous to take vengeance for the house of God went forth to avenge the just blood."[32] Ralph of Coggeshall also described the Third Crusaders as "inflamed with zeal for God."[33] According to a German chronicler, even the Byzantines in 1189 reportedly "marvelled that ... [the Third Crusaders] did this with one agreement or promise, by which they swore, to take vengeance for a zealous God and the holy land and the effusion of just blood of the servants of God."[34]

Peter of Les Vaux-de-Cernay described crusaders in southern France in 1209 as "on fire with zeal for the orthodox faith."[35] Robert of Auxerre noted that those who fought the Cathars were "armed with zeal for the faith against the deserters

---

[26] *Itinerarium Peregrinorum*, p. 16.

[27] *Itinerarium Peregrinorum*, pp. 101–2.

[28] Arnold of Lübeck, *Chronica*, Monumenta Germaniae Historica, Series Scriptores 23 (Hanover, 1869), p. 169.

[29] Arnold of Lübeck, *Chronica*, p. 172.

[30] Robert of Auxerre, *Chronicon*, Monumenta Germaniae Historica, Series Scriptores 26 (Hanover, 1882), p. 252.

[31] Arnold of Lübeck, *Chronica*, p. 203.

[32] Arnold of Lübeck, *Chronica*, p. 170.

[33] Ralph of Coggeshall, *Chronicon Anglicanum*, ed. J. Stevenson, Rerum Brittanicarum Medii Aevi Scriptores 66 (London, 1875), p. 24.

[34] Arnold of Lübeck, *Chronica*, pp. 172–3.

[35] Peter of Les Vaux-de-Cernay, *Hystoria Albigensis*, ed. P. Guébin and E. Lyon (2 vols, Paris, 1926), vol. 1, p. 74.

of the faith."[36] According to Robert, in 1210, "the pilgrimage [to Languedoc] was celebrated ... because of the zeal for the faith inflamed in the minds of the faithful against those who corrupt the faith."[37]

James of Vitry made it clear that he admired zealous Christians, or, at least, that he chose to depict individuals worthy of praise as zealous. Robert of Courçon, a papal legate, was "a man literate and devout, affable, generous and benign, having zeal for God and ardently desiring the liberation of the holy land."[38] Reiner, the prior of Saint Michael, "inflamed with zeal of the faith he did not fear to go to the enemies' army [and preach]."[39]

Pope Innocent III continued to use the word *zelus* often in the thirteenth century. In 1206 he wrote to Peter II of Aragon that good men, who "are zealous about divine law," should take as their own what formerly belonged to heretics in southern France: "while you endeavor to exterminate them with zeal for the orthodox faith, you may retain [their goods] freely for your own use."[40] In 1208 he wrote "the Lord of vengeance descends to earth with those who are on fire with zeal for the orthodox faith, to avenge the just blood ... may pious zeal inflame you to so avenge the injury of your God."[41] He also wrote to King Philip II of France and, later, the Frankish nobility, using practically identical words.[42] In that year Innocent also wrote to all clerics that "on fire with zeal for the orthodox faith, you have decided to fight heretical depravity."[43] Those crusaders who fought the Cathars were "on fire with zeal for the orthodox faith to avenge just blood," and "the zeal of the Lord had armed [them] in a holy army against the subverters of the faith."[44] And as Innocent began preparations for the Fifth Crusade, he wrote that he hoped that "those inflamed with zeal for the Christian faith ... [would] avenge the injury of the Crucified One."[45]

As in the late twelfth-century crusading texts, there was one example of zeal inspiring self-sacrifice in the early thirteenth-century sources. In one of James of

---

[36] Robert of Auxerre, *Chronicon*, p. 272.

[37] Robert of Auxerre, *Chronicon*, p. 275.

[38] James of Vitry, *Lettres de Jacques de Vitry*, ed. R.B.C. Huygens (Leiden, 1960), p. 100.

[39] James of Vitry, *Lettres*, pp. 132–3.

[40] Innocent III, *Epistolae*, ed. J.-P. Migne, Patrologia Latina 215 (Paris, 1890), cols 915–16. (*Cum secundum evangelicam*).

[41] Peter of Les Vaux-de-Cernay, *Hystoria Albigensis*, vol. 1, pp. 60 and 63 (see also p. 74).

[42] Innocent III, *Epistolae*, ed. Migne, vol. 215, cols 1358 and 1359. (*Si tua regalis* and *Rem crudelem audivimus*).

[43] Innocent III, *Epistolae*, ed. Migne, vol. 215, col. 1469. (*Cum orthodoxae fidei*).

[44] Innocent III, *Epistolae*, ed. Migne, Patrologia Latina 216 (Paris, 1891), col. 152 (*Nuntios et apices*); vol. 215, col. 1356 (*Ne nos ejus*); and vol. 216, col. 151 (*Habuisse bajulos Dominici*).

[45] Innocent III, *Epistolae*, ed. Migne, vol. 216, col. 822. (*Pium et sanctum*).

Vitry's *exempla*, a pilgrim was captured by the Muslims in the holy land. He faced death because the Muslims believed him to be a Templar and they (so the story went) killed all Templars. At first the pilgrim truthfully denied he was a Templar, but finally, "inflamed with zeal for the faith he said, with his neck stretched forth, 'in the name of the Lord I am a Templar.'" He was killed immediately and "went to the Lord, happily crowned in martyrdom."[46]

Clearly the term *zelus* was increasingly used in crusading texts in the twelfth and early thirteenth centuries, often alongside the vocabulary of vengeance. But what did the medieval Latin word actually mean? What concepts underpinned its usage? What can it tell us about medieval emotions—and medieval vengeance?

Christian love and righteous anger

On closer examination, the context of the evidence itself, in particular the evidence related to specific passages from the Bible, provides crucial information about the meaning of the term. The biblical verse Ekkehard of Aura cited when referring to those who had killed Jews on their way to the East in 1096 was Romans 10:2–3. In this passage Paul expressed his doubt that the Jews could or would come to know Christ: *testimonium enim perhibeo illis quod aemulationem Dei habent sed non secundum scientiam ignorantes enim Dei iustitiam et suam quarentes statuere iustitiae Dei non sunt subiecti.*[47]

Romans 10:2–3 was frequently cited to signify right intention but incorrect action. For example, Bernard of Clairvaux wrote to a young monk that he should desist from his desire to live an eremitical life: "acquiesce to the counsel of your seniors, since although by chance you may have the zeal of God, [it is] nevertheless not according to the knowledge [of God]."[48] The idea that zeal was good, and blameless, even if the action it motivated was not, was also evident in a letter from Bernard of Clairvaux to another professed religious: "for you may have the zeal of God in this matter, and thus your intention should be excused; but I do not see that in any way your will has been enacted according to the knowledge [of God]."[49] Zeal for God and intention were set apart from knowledge of God and action.

Similarly, in one of James of Vitry's *exempla*, a group of Dominicans heard the confession of a community of nuns. Shocked by the sins some of the nuns had committed, the Dominicans concluded that all were "evil" and publicly proclaimed this, causing great scandal. James disapproved of the public disclosure, and

---

[46] James of Vitry, *The Exempla*, ed. T.F. Crane (London, 1890), p. 39.
[47] Romans 10:2–3. I discuss the significant relationship between *zelus* and *aemulatio* at length below.
[48] Bernard of Clairvaux, *Epistolae*, vol. 8, p. 508.
[49] Bernard of Clairvaux, *Epistolae*, vol. 7, p. 294.

commented "I have known some of those preachers who are called truly religious and are seen to have zeal, but not according to the knowledge [of God]."[50]

In addition, there was already a historical precedent for using the verse to evaluate the guilt or innocence of those who committed violence for religious reasons. Departing from the Augustinian tradition, Bede had used the verse to question the Jews' ignorance of their crime in killing Christ in reference to Christ's request on the cross that God forgive his murderers.[51] Bede held that those possessing zeal but doing the wrong thing should be forgiven, since they acted out of ignorance and right intention. Some of the Jews, on the other hand, acted with wrong intention, and should not be forgiven. It should be noted that Bede's judgment that some of the Jews had wrongly intended to kill Christ did not resurface in textual sources until the twelfth-century *Glossa Ordinaria*.[52]

It seems reasonable to conclude that, at least within a religious context, zeal was used to signal the partial mitigation of guilt—it was the right sentiment, even when it motivated a wrong action. This is very different from our modern notion of zeal as simply a "passion," a strong emotion that derives its moral value from context. In the medieval sources I have examined, there appears to be no such thing as "bad" zeal—zeal was always "good," even when the actions it inspired were not, and thus the possession of zeal partially mitigated responsibility for those "bad" actions.[53]

Some texts even suggested that because zeal was the right sentiment, the possession of zeal would in general lead to success. For example, Joachim of Fiore wrote of the Second Crusade that

> [all were] zealous for the injury of their King and desiring to take vengeance on the unfaithful people ... There were many such zealous ones and they were moved, not only in spirit but in body. Wherefore then did they fail? I think that [it was because] in being zealous they did not maintain the proper order (*rectum ordinem*).[54]

Joachim was clearly very surprised that the zeal of the Christians had not guaranteed their victory, and concluded that although they rightly possessed zeal, their actions were not governed by the proper discipline. Many things could compromise the actions of the zealous—lack of discipline, as with Joachim above, or ignorance of

---

[50] James of Vitry, *The Exempla*, p. 36.

[51] Jeremy Cohen, "The Jews as Killers of Christ in the Latin Tradition, from Augustine to the Friars," *Traditio*, 39 (1983): 1–27, at p. 11. Cohen cites Bede, *Lucae Evangelium Expositio*.

[52] Cohen, "The Jews as Killers of Christ," p. 11.

[53] Of course, I cannot claim to have exhaustively looked at every medieval text in existence. Only time (and more research) will tell if this argument will hold up.

[54] Joachim of Fiore, *Expositio in Apocalypsim* 6.1 (cited by Benjamin Kedar, *Crusade and Mission: European Approaches Toward the Muslims* (Princeton, 1984), p. 222).

"God's will," as with Bernard and Ekkehard—but it was not because the zeal itself was problematic.

Looking beyond the biblical passages, zeal was intimately connected to the concepts and terminology of justice and love.[55] In 1133 Peter the Venerable wrote to Pope Innocent II about the sentence handed down on the murderer of Thomas, prior of St. Victor:

> since therefore the king's sword was withheld in this [matter], we seek, and all who are zealous for the law of God pray you with us, that the episcopal, that is, the spiritual sword [in this case excommunication], which is the word of God, according to the Apostle, should not be hidden ... so that the impious may be punished with deserved vengeance and others may be deterred.[56]

Those who were "zealous for the law of God" prayed that the "impious may be punished with deserved vengeance." Arnold of Lübeck was fond of the appellation "a man zealous for justice," and used it to praise Bertold archbishop of Bremen, Pope Urban II and Henry of Glinden.[57] Bernard of Clairvaux urged Pope Eugenius III to be more zealous and actively avenge injuries to the papacy and God: "your zeal, your clemency, and the discretion [which serves] to moderate between these virtues should be known; as often as you pardon injuries, you should avenge them, having prudently observed the means, the place, and the time for each."[58] Bernard also urged Eugenius to love justice, according to Proverbs 1:1: "it is of little account to possess justice, unless you love it. They who possess it, possess it; those who love [it], are zealous. One who loves justice seeks justice and prosecutes it."[59]

The moral argument connecting vengeance and justice was not that *all* acts of vengeance were just, but that vengeance could be, and sometimes necessarily was, just. Thomas of Chobham summarized the complicated position taken by the Church on vengeance, noting that "it is permitted for the laity to seek to regain their belongings from criminals through judgment and to demand the death penalty if they are evildoers and murderers, as long as they do this with a zeal for justice and not a vengeful desire [*libido*]."[60] Here Thomas did not distinguish between actions per se, but rather between the emotional motivations behind those

---

[55] Sometimes *caritas*, but also *amor* and others.
[56] Peter the Venerable, *The Letters of Peter the Venerable*, vol. 1, p. 25.
[57] Arnold of Lübeck, *Chronica*, pp. 131, 158 and 231.
[58] Bernard of Clairvaux, *De Consideratione ad Eugenium Papam*, ed. J. Leclerq and H.M. Rochais, S. Bernardi Opera Omnia 3 (Rome, 1963), p. 428. The translation of *donandis* is debatable. The more usual sense of the word would lead to the following translation: "as often as you give injuries, you should avenge them." But the verb can also mean to forgive, pardon or remit, and I chose—conservatively, I think, given the rest of the passage—to use this sense when translating.
[59] Bernard of Clairvaux, *De Consideratione*, p. 437.
[60] Thomas of Chobham, *Summa Confessorum*, ed. F. Broomfield (Paris, 1968), p. 436.

acts, approving of a "zeal for justice" and condemning "vengeful desire." But a few pages on, Thomas qualified this statement, implying that in some cases even "vengeful desire" was appropriate: "for it is one thing to avenge one's own injury, and another to avenge a common injury."[61] For Thomas of Chobham vengeance by the laity could be licit or illicit—the moral value of retributive action was complicated and hinged upon internal motivations and whether the injury was considered to be personal or communal.

The connection between justice, vengeance, love and zeal dates back at least as far as Anselm of Lucca, who wrote that "just as Moses the lawgiver by divine inspiration allowed to the people of God an eye for an eye, a tooth for a tooth, and so forth to repress the ungodliness of the peoples, so we will and applaud that princes should exercise vengeance against the enemies of the truth according to zeal, to a purpose of divine love and to the duty of godliness."[62] Zeal was a sentiment that drove the actor to pursue just vengeance on wrongdoers—because it was compatible with the "purpose of divine love."

The relationship between zeal and love was emphasized by other writers as well. The Anonymous of Halberstadt noted that when Arnulf was made bishop of Halberstadt he was "aroused by the zeal of love and devotion."[63] Suger of St. Denis also made it clear that one who has "zeal according to the knowledge [of God]" would act "out of love for the Church."[64] Moreover, at least sometimes zeal was an emotion tied to the desire to force non-conforming members of society to convert to orthodox Christianity. Bernard of Clairvaux wrote of the use of force to convert heretics that

> we approve the zeal, but we do not recommend the deed, since faith should be suggested not enforced. Although it is beyond doubt better that they be coerced by the sword, namely [the sword] of those who do not carry the sword without cause, than that they be allowed to drag others into their error. For that man is *the minister of God, he takes vengeance in anger on he who does wrong.*[65]

---

[61] Thomas of Chobham, *Summa Confessorum*, p. 440.

[62] Anselm of Lucca, *De Caritate* (cited and translated by Herbert Cowdrey, "Christianity and the Morality of Warfare during the First Century of Crusading," in Marcus Bull and Norman Housley (eds), *The Experience of Crusading* (2 vols, Cambridge, 2003), vol. 1, pp. 175–92, at p. 179).

[63] Anonymous of Halberstadt, *Gesta*, Monumenta Germaniae Historica, Series Scriptores 23 (Hanover, 1874), p. 92.

[64] Suger of St. Denis, *Epistolae*, Recueil des Historiens des Gaules et de la France 15 (Paris, 1878), p. 529.

[65] Bernard of Clairvaux, *Sermones super Cantica Canticorum*, ed. J. Leclerq and H.M. Rochais, S. Bernardi Opera Omnia 2 (Rome, 1958), pp. 186–7. Reference to Romans 13:4.

In this sense zeal was again completely compatible with the notion of Christian love as correction that motivated crusaders. And, again, as with Ekkehard, there was partial approval for the zeal of those who converted others by force. The action was wrong, but the driving emotion was right.

It would seem from the evidence that because those who were zealous acted out of a love for God and justice, their zeal could limit their culpability, even when their actual deeds were inappropriate. But what was the specific sentiment of zeal that was understood in this way?

Charles Du Cange gave an in-depth analysis of the vocabulary associated with *zelus* and the great variety of meanings the terms could signify, and the primary sources I have looked at bear out his conclusions. I have already shown that "zeal" was linked with love, and Du Cange also linked *zelus* with passionate love. *Zelus* could signify passion or love (*studium* and *amor*), and similarly, the verb *zelare* could mean to favor (*favere*), to be passionate (*studere*), to desire (*expetere*) and to very much wish (*peroptare*).[66]

Appropriately then, *zelare* was to burn or be fervent (*fervere*). Indeed, images of fire surrounded *zelus* in the primary source passages. Crusaders were *zelo accensi*, *zelo succensi*, *zelo inflammati* and *zelo incensi*. Zeal was often burning, *zelo fervente*, and it was eager, *alacri zelo*. As Bernard of Clairvaux urged Pope Eugenius III, "if you are a disciple of Christ, ignite your zeal."[67] The connection between fiery images, *zelus* and love for God may have been related to the way in which the Holy Spirit manifested as Pentecostal flame upon the heads of the disciples in the Acts of the Apostles.[68]

Also appropriately for such committed love, *zelare* could mean to protect unthinkingly (*impense protegere*).[69] A *zelator* was both desirous (*cupidus*) and a guardian (*fautor*).[70] The loving, protective aspect of zeal goes some way towards explaining the connection between zeal and vengeance, since I have already discussed how Christian love was used by some to encourage vengeance for God and other Christians.

But there was another aspect of *zelus*. The verb *zelare* could mean to love jealously, and the adjective *zelosus* meant one "burning..full with love, to us *Jaloux*," while *zelotes* signified a rival (*aemulator*).[71] A *zelator* was a rival and

---

[66] Charles Du Cange, *Glossarium Mediae et Infimae Latinitatis* (6 vols, Paris, 1840–50), vol. 6, p. 933.

[67] Bernard of Clairvaux, *De Consideratione*, p. 409.

[68] Acts 2:1–4. I am very grateful to Gary Dickson for bringing this point to my attention.

[69] Du Cange, *Glossarium*, vol. 6, p. 932.

[70] Du Cange, *Glossarium*, vol. 6, p. 932.

[71] Du Cange, *Glossarium*, vol. 6, p. 932 and vol. 6, p. 933 (Du Cange here called attention to Exodus 20:5, a verse with significance for this chapter and discussed below accordingly. The term *aemulatio* will also be further analyzed below).

enemy (*aemulator, inimicus*).⁷² William of Tyre noted that when Hugh II of Jaffa was suspected of dallying with his cousin's wife, King Fulk I of Jerusalem "inflamed with the zeal of a spouse was said to conceive inexorable hatred against him."⁷³ Pope Innocent III elsewhere discussed the example of the spouse faced with a rival: "who can endure a rival with equanimity? Suspicion alone fiercely afflicts the zealous, for it is written, *they will be two in one flesh*, but a zealous man cannot suffer two men in one flesh."⁷⁴ It would seem that jealousy and rivalry were also emotional components of zeal.

As well as signifying passion and longing, *zelare* could mean to mock (*irridere*), and *zelus* sometimes meant anger (*iracundia*) and hatred (*odium*).⁷⁵ Niermeyer also defined *zelus* as "hatred, envy, [and] jealousy."⁷⁶ Of course, the images of flames and burning emotion associated with zeal in the sources are as potentially appropriate for depicting anger and hatred as love and devotion.

The textual evidence given above has in part elucidated what the term *zelus* meant. As a general term, it was an emotional composite of the modern concepts of love, passion, jealousy, protectiveness and angry hostility. In a Christian context, because it was directly associated with the desire to pursue God's purpose, on the one hand it was a virtuous loving passion and on the other one apparently centered on hatred, anger and jealousy. When this sentiment led a Christian to incorrect action, it nevertheless served to mitigate the offence.⁷⁷

Emotion and action

As the twelfth century progressed, and the popularity of the idea of crusading as vengeance increased, the term *zelus* appeared more frequently in crusading texts. The actions zeal inspired crusaders to take were both acts of violent persecution (often labeled acts of vengeance) and acts of self-sacrifice. Why was *zelus* especially associated with crusading, both as vengeance and as self-sacrifice?

The concept of zeal as Christian love desirous of doing God's purpose was linked to crusading in now-obvious ways, as Jonathan Riley-Smith's previous work

---

⁷² Du Cange, *Glossarium*, vol. 6, p. 932.

⁷³ William of Tyre, *Chronicon*, p. 652.

⁷⁴ Innocent III, *De Miseria Condicionis Humane*, ed. R.E. Lewis (London, 1980), p. 123. Reference to Genesis 2:24.

⁷⁵ Du Cange, *Glossarium*, vol. 6, p. 932 and vol. 6, p. 933.

⁷⁶ Jan F. Niermeyer, *Mediae Latinitatis Lexicon Minus* (Leiden, 1997), p. 1138.

⁷⁷ The correlation of *zelus* with anger, jealousy, hatred and hostility may seem to contradict my assertion that there was no "bad" zeal (above, p. 185). Were not anger, jealousy, hatred and hostility always perceived as "bad" feelings in the Middle Ages? The short answer is apparently not always—their moral weight appears to have depended on whether those feelings were morally justified. For more on this, please see my discussion of *ira per zelum* below, pp. 190–91.

on the matter has shown, and also to the ideology of crusading as vengeance.[78] But the concept of zeal as a sentiment involving hatred, anger and jealousy has been less analyzed in relation to crusading ideology.

The very existence of a connection between zeal and anger/hatred hints at why zeal was associated with the terminology of vengeance. Paul Hyams has noted the ways in which the terminology of anger and vengeance were associated and used together to justify acts of violence. For example, in 1281 Archbishop Pecham stated at the Council of Lambeth that *ira* was "a passion for vengeance."[79] Fortunately, it is possible to take analysis beyond this hint. Anger is one emotion that other medieval historians have examined, and these studies, together with medieval Christian perceptions of anger, are extremely helpful in defining the aspect of zeal as anger/hatred and its relationship with crusading.

In the ninth century Hincmar of Rheims differentiated between virtuous anger, directed inwards against the sinful self, and vicious anger, directed outwards at others. According to Hincmar, only anger against the sinful self was acceptable in a Christian.[80] But by the time Thomas of Chobham wrote his *Summa Confessorum* in the late eleventh or early twelfth century, anger against the self was no longer the only acceptable anger: Thomas of Chobham also condoned anger against "wrongdoers." He called this anger against the wrongdoer *ira per zelum*.[81]

For Thomas, *ira per vitium*, anger stemming from vice, was shown when "someone moves to kill or injure another, and if reason does not immediately proceed to refrain that motion to injure."[82] It was least sinful when the anger led only to hatred, moderately sinful when anger "burst forth in general disorder" and most sinful when "from anger proceeds assault and homicide."[83]

Ira per zelum was a different matter:

> Anger through zeal is when we are angry against vice and against the vicious, and we can hope that this anger increases, because it is a virtue. Nevertheless we ought to resist it as much as we can lest it become fastened [to us], that is lest the outward agitation increase ... However that which is called anger through zeal is a virtue, especially when someone moves through hatred of the vicious, and is impassioned to eliminate them ... The Lord was moved by such anger when he threw out the sinners and merchants from the temple.[84]

---

[78] Jonathan Riley-Smith, "Crusading as an Act of Love," *History*, 65 (1980): 177–92.

[79] Paul Hyams, *Rancor and Reconciliation in Medieval England* (Ithaca, 2003), p. 50.

[80] Hincmar of Rheims, *De Cavendis Vitiis et Virtutibus Exercendis* (cited by Richard Barton, "'Zealous Anger' and the Renegotiation of Aristocratic Relationships in Eleventh- and Twelfth-Century France," in Barbara H. Rosenwein (ed.), *Anger's Past: The Social Uses of an Emotion in the Middle Ages* (Ithaca, 1998), pp. 153–70, at p. 157).

[81] Barton, "Zealous Anger," p. 157.

[82] Thomas of Chobham, *Summa Confessorum*, pp. 414–15.

[83] Thomas of Chobham, *Summa Confessorum*, pp. 415 and 420.

[84] Thomas of Chobham, *Summa Confessorum*, p. 414. Reference to Matthew 21:12–13.

Anger through zeal (as opposed to vicious anger) was characterized by how rational (i.e. morally justifiable) the sentiment of anger was in the circumstances. Of course, anger against sin was always eminently justifiable.[85] So in part zeal was a component of the emotion of righteous, or justified, anger against the wrongdoer. This association with righteous anger corresponds to the way in which zeal was portrayed as a virtue that mitigated guilt.[86] Zealous righteous anger also complements the idea of zeal as love, since from Augustine onwards Christians were urged to undertake chastisement and punishment of sin in a spirit of love.

If *ira* signified the emotional arousal of anger, and *ira per zelum* signified "righteous anger" as apart from other forms of anger, then it would seem that *zelus* could be defined in part as the desire to eliminate what was wrong, just as when Christ threw people out of the temple in Jerusalem. This was confirmed by Pope Innocent III, who described the three natural powers of man: "the potential for reason, so that he may discern between good and evil, the potential for anger, that he may reject evil, and the potential for desire, that he may long for good."[87] Zeal was in some ways both the anger that led one to reject evil and the love that led one to desire good, both according to the purposes of God.

The role of zeal as loving anger that rejected what was evil and promoted what was good (according to divine will) is confirmed by an examination of the Hebrew tradition of zealotry. This tradition stemmed from the exemplary Old Testament story of Phineas who took violent action to stop the Israelites from mixing with other races and thus ended a plague and restored God's favor.[88] Jewish zeal involved both non-physical and violent coercion, and was, at least for some modern scholars, concentrated "on the internal affairs of the Jewish community ... obsessed with sin and sinners."[89] For Paul, writing in Galatians, Judaism was the

---

[85] Daniel Smail, "Hatred as a Social Institution in Late-Medieval Society," *Speculum*, 76 (2001), pp. 90–126, at p. 115.

[86] Edward Muir and Natalie Zemon-Davis have noted that anger was sometimes used to mitigate guilt in courts of law in the later Middle Ages, though not (apparently) in ecclesiastical courts (Smail, "Hatred as a Social Institution," p. 101). Perhaps *ira per zelum* was one form of anger that could have been used in ecclesiastical courts in that way, since many clearly felt it mitigated guilt because it indicated right intention.

[87] Innocent III, *De Miseria*, p. 99.

[88] Numbers 25:11. To see how Phineas still serves today as a symbol of the justifiable use of violent force to enact divine will, one need look no further than the so-called "Phineas Priesthood," purportedly a paramilitary faction of the modern "Christian Identity" movement. See Timothy K. Beal, "The White Supremacist Bible and the Phineas Priesthood," in Jonneke Bekkenkamp and Yvonne Sherwood (eds), *Sanctified Aggression: Legacies of Biblical and Post-Biblical Vocabularies of Violence* (New York, 2004), pp. 120–31.

[89] David Rhoads, *Israel in Revolution, 6–74 C.E.* (cited by Robert Hamerton-Kelly, *Sacred Violence: Paul's Hermeneutic of the Cross* (Minneapolis, 1992), p. 73, n. 24). Richard Horsley, *Jesus and the Spiral of Violence* (cited by Hamerton-Kelly, *Sacred Violence*, p. 73, n. 24).

old way of "zeal for the Law," whereby religious faith equaled action.[90] To possess zeal was to act on God's behalf in the Jewish tradition, and intriguingly this tradition (and not Paul's New Testament reinterpretation) seems to have continued to be true of the term *zelus* in the twelfth century.

The working definition of zeal as a desire to eliminate actively what was wrong and promote what was good on God's behalf is perfectly compatible with the demonstrated connections between zeal, anger and Christian love. It may seem incongruous to connect anger and Christian love, but the link was not only evident in contextual evidence, but also in direct statements by those who promoted crusading. For Bernard of Clairvaux, the love of God fed the hatred of those who did not love God:

> it is certain that if [a man] should not return immediately to the love of God, it is necessary that he know, that not only is he now nothing, but nothing at all, or rather, he will be nothing for eternity. Therefore that man [should be] set aside; not only now should he not be loved, moreover he should be held in hatred, according to this: "*will I not hate those who hate you, Lord, and will I not languish over your enemies?*"[91]

Fervent love for God and the godly necessitated fervent hatred for the ungodly, and *zelus* seems to have reflected the need to act that was required by both love and hatred. The zealous individual loved God and fellow believers, was angry at those who did not, and took action.

One such action was vengeance, for at least two possible reasons. Stephen White has already connected anger and vengeance in medieval social relationships. In his outline of how anger functioned as a political tool in medieval France, White outlined a basic pattern of emotional transformations, a "script" for the quasi-ritual enactment of lordly anger. If a lord was injured, he would feel shame. That shame would lead to zealous anger, and the anger to acts of vengeance. Richard Barton demonstrated that this anger was specifically known as "zealous anger." In a sense, a display of anger could also serve to indicate to others that a prior action was indeed an injury in cases where there was uncertainty about the action.[92] Eventually, vengeance led to reconciliation and resumed peace.[93] Daniel Smail has further shown that if vengeance was not taken, the anger did not fade but rather was deemed hatred, a long-standing and publicly recognized hostile relationship between those involved.[94]

---

[90] Hamerton-Kelly, *Sacred Violence*, p. 74.

[91] Bernard of Clairvaux, *Sermones super Cantica Canticorum*, p. 82. Reference to Psalms 138:21.

[92] Stephen White, "The Politics of Anger in Medieval France," in Rosenwein (ed.), *Anger's Past*, pp. 127–52, at p. 140. Barton, "'Zealous Anger,'" p. 157.

[93] White, "The Politics of Anger," pp. 142–4.

[94] Smail, "Hatred as a Social Institution," pp. 90–92.

The reason why White called the pattern he identified a "script," and why Smail followed his lead, is because these patterns seem to have been almost universally recognized, understood and manipulated within western medieval discourse. To make reference to part of the pattern was to bring to mind the rest of it; hence, to display lordly anger was to firmly state that an injury had been committed and that due vengeance would follow. Like any metaphor, "script" is imperfect, in that it may seem to suggest a strictly controlled series of events without room for individual decision-making.[95]

The "scripts" of White and Smail correspond almost perfectly to the evidence found in crusading texts in the twelfth and early thirteenth centuries. Christ, or the Church, or Christianity, was "injured" in some way, either by the taking of territory or the killing of Christians. Upon hearing of this shameful injury, Christians were moved by anger to avenge the injury. Both Latin and vernacular texts marked the importance of shame and anger as emotions that motivated crusaders. A vernacular example is found in one of the interpolations of the *Chanson d'Antioche*, where Peter the Hermit recounted his experiences in the Holy Land:

> I am Peter the Hermit who made this voyage
> to avenge God for this grievous shame
> that they have done against him...
> I went to Rome, full of grief and rage,
> the pope heard my grief and my pain;
> he sends letters to you and your barons.[96]

However, the correspondence between the ideology of crusading as vengeance and the "script" is at first glance imperfect because it would seem that in the context of crusading Christian anger and desire for vengeance did not fade once vengeance had been taken. The understanding that Jerusalem had already been destroyed as vengeance for the crucifixion in 70 C.E. did not stop some in the twelfth century calling for further vengeance for the crucifixion, and the success of the First Crusade did not stop the movement of Christians to the East to fight Muslims from the early twelfth century onward. But the extraordinary twelfth-century failures of the Christians in the East, especially the fall of Edessa and loss of Jerusalem, in a sense created new injuries to be avenged, and of course the Latin Christians in the East were under military pressure from their Muslim neighbors, pressure easily interpreted as injury.

---

[95] Of course, for most actors a script is merely the starting point for improvisation and, indeed, complete rewriting. That said, after consideration of my co-editor's convincing arguments against "script" (Hyams, p. 172 above), I have decided to use the simple term "pattern" for my own discussion of such things—at least for the time being.

[96] *La Chanson d'Antioche*, ed. J. Nelson, The Old French Crusade Cycle 4 (Tuscaloosa, 2003), p. 352.

Nevertheless, one would imagine that when a specific injury had been avenged, at the least the angry desire for vengeance would be attributed to a different injury. Instead, the same themes in the rhetoric of crusading as vengeance for the same injuries only escalated, if anything, as time went on. So the correlation between the "script" outlined by White and Smail and crusading depends greatly on what was deemed to have been the primary injury deserving vengeance, whether it was thought that vengeance had successfully been achieved and (perhaps) whether a particular injury was judged likely to motivate sufficient numbers of Christians. In any event, Smail's conclusion that unfulfilled vengeance led to hatred, a formalized antagonistic relationship, would seem compatible with Christian attitudes towards Islam as the crusading movement continued.

The virtuous *ira per zelum* also led humans to take vengeance because to medieval minds, divine anger at sin led God himself to take divine vengeance. God's vengeance was to come in this life and the next; in the words of Pope Innocent III, "if a just man is barely saved, how can the impious man and the sinner be spared?"[97] For "God is eternally angry at the reprobate, because it is just that since the impious delayed in [the time available to him], God should take vengeance in his [eternity]."[98] Or, as Bernard of Clairvaux wrote in 1138, when confronted with sin "God sees and grieves, he is wretched and he girds on his sword to take vengeance on the malefactors, but also to praise the good."[99] In essence, according to medieval interpretations, zeal as righteous anger rooted in love for what was good and the desire to eliminate what was evil was a pattern established by God himself.

God enacted this emotional pattern in part through crusading. Baldric of Bourgueil made that clear when he wrote at the beginning of his account of the First Crusade "*[God] changes kings and times*: he corrects the pious, that he might advance them; he punishes the impious, that he might set them straight."[100] That God was following a traditional sequence of divine zeal and vengeance through crusading was also communicated by one of Innocent III's letters. In 1206 he wrote "[God] *said I the Lord am zealous, avenging the sins of the father, even to the third and fourth generations, on those who hate me*, that is, on those who imitate their fathers' hatred against me."[101] In this passage Innocent quoted Exodus 20:5–6, but with significant changes. The text of Exodus 20:5–6 in the Latin Vulgate reads: *ego sum Dominus Deus tuus fortis zelotes visitans iniquitatem patrum in filiis in tertiam et quartam generationem eorum qui oderunt me et faciens misericordiam in milia his qui diligunt me et custodiunt pracepta mea*. Innocent accurately remembered that the Old Testament text described God as *zelotes*. However, he rephrased

---

[97] Innocent III, *De Miseria*, p. 227. Reference to 1 Peter 4:18.

[98] Innocent III, *De Miseria*, p. 217.

[99] Bernard of Clairvaux, *Epistolae*, vol. 7, p. 381.

[100] Baldric of Bourgueil, *Historia Jerosolimitana*, Recueil des Historiens des Croisades, Historiens Occidentaux 4 (Paris, 1879), p. 9.

[101] Innocent III, *Epistolae*, ed. Migne, vol. 215, col. 805. (*Nisi cum pridem*).

visitans iniquitatem as *vindicans peccata*, explicitly linking the punishment of sin with divine vengeance.

To a certain degree, then, Exodus 20:5–6 was a pattern of thought establishing divine zeal leading to divine vengeance, and purportedly spoken in God's own words. James of Vitry confirmed that pattern in a letter written in 1221 from Egypt, relating that Damietta was in Christian hands but that

> many of our men, unmindful and ungrateful of such blessings, *provoked the Lord to anger* with various crimes ... for which the Lord, angry, permitted them to perish in the sea and on the land in manifest vengeance, with some held captive by the Saracens, some drowned in the sea, and others [killed] by their own.[102]

This vision of a zealous God who sought angry retribution on the wrongdoer and lovingly praised the good was directly related to the idea of crusading as vengeance, not only because the Muslims had committed the singular crimes of killing Christians and taking land in the East, but also because the targets of crusader violence were all repeatedly described as those who maliciously turned away from God by rejecting Christianity again and again, *qui oderunt [Deum] in tertiam et quartam generationem*, so to speak. The Jews were certainly often described willfully perpetuating the sins of their fathers. As Arnold of Lübeck wrote, "those [Jews] were satisfying the standards of their fathers, calling down on themselves and their own as they said: *his blood be on us and on our sons*."[103] The heretics in Toulouse supposedly passed their unfaithfulness from generation to generation: "from father to sons with successive poison the superstition of infidelity was spread."[104] The Muslims surely also were "those who imitate their fathers' hatred": to Christian eyes, Muslims were "the enemies of the cross of Christ, who ought to be his sons."[105] More specifically, Muslims were "the offspring of adultery," the sons of Ishmael—truly their sins were in the family, so to speak.[106]

If one of the main reasons why vengeance was sought through the crusades was the "injury" of willful disbelief, it is no surprise that Pope Innocent III applied Exodus 20:5–6 to the crusades, directly suggesting that *zelus* was the angry desire for vengeance on the malicious unfaithful who had injured God. God, as a zealous God, grew angry at sin and took vengeance, and the crusaders in effect enacted this divine characteristic by also taking vengeance on Muslims, heretics and

---

[102] James of Vitry, *Lettres*, pp. 134–5. Reference to Deuteronomy 4:25 and 9:18.

[103] Arnold of Lübeck, *Chronica*, p. 190.

[104] Peter of Les Vaux-de-Cernay, *Hystoria Albigensis*, vol. 1, pp. 7–8 (see also p. 2).

[105] Peter the Venerable, *Summa Totius Haeresis Saracenorum*, ed. J. Kritzeck, *Peter the Venerable and Islam* (Princeton, 1964), p. 206. Peter of Blois, *Conquestio de Dilatione Vie Ierosolimitane*, ed. R.B.C. Huygens, Corpus Christianorum, Continuatio Mediaevalis 194 (Turnholt, 2002), p. 84.

[106] Albert of Aachen, *Liber Christianae Expeditionis*, Recueil des Historiens des Croisades, Historiens Occidentaux 4 (Paris, 1879), p. 469.

sometimes Jews. Or rather, more precisely, the pope, who authorized the crusades, enacted that divine characteristic as God's representative. As Bernard of Clairvaux advised Pope Eugenius III, "let him fear the spirit of your anger, who does not fear men or the sword. Let him fear your words, who is contemptuous of admonitions. He at whom you are angry will think that God is angry, not a man."[107]

There was another factor in the increasing depiction of zeal as a crusading virtue, particularly in the context of Romans 10:2, the verse that was used to indicate correct intention but incorrect action. Ekkehard of Aura, Bernard of Clairvaux and Bede all used the term *zelus* to indicate that correct intention. But the word in the Latin Vulgate is not actually *zelus*, but *aemulatio*: *enim perhibeo illis quod aemulationem Dei habent sed non secundum scientiam.* The authors just mentioned substituted *zelus* for *aemulatio*, but Guibert of Nogent did not. He wrote of the First Crusaders that "they seemed to have the *aemulatio* of God, but not according to his knowledge, nevertheless God who bends many deeds begun in vain to a pious end ... brought success out of their good intention."[108] For some at least, it would seem that *zelus* and *aemulatio* were interchangeable terms, and were used in the same way to signify good intention.

This is rather surprising: *aemulatio* is not a term one would normally expect to be used in a positive way within a Christian context. The classical term signified "rivalry, emulation, competition," and the verb *aemulor* "to rival, vie with, emulate, envy, be jealous of."[109] Du Cange rather unhelpfully noted that *aemulamen* often meant *aemulatio*, and also simply an example (*exemplum*), without signaling what kind of example he meant (positive or negative).[110] He (or his editor) further stated that the verb *aemulare* meant "to excite jealousy, *donner de la jalousie*, or rather to act like a spouse."[111] Niermeyer, meanwhile, defined *aemulatio* as "ardent zeal, indignation, hostility," and the verb *aemulari* as "to be zealous, to be angry."[112]

The context of Romans 10:2 confirms that the term connoted some sort of mimicry, a desire to imitate: *for I allow that they* [the Jews] *have the* aemulatio *of God but not according to knowledge of Him*. The verse also upholds the negative connotations of jealousy and rivalry, since the term was applied to the Jews' unsuccessful and ultimately wrong religious beliefs and practices; they were trying to be godly, but because they ignored true knowledge of God through Christ, Paul felt they would always fail to see the truth.

Aemulatio therefore did not mean precisely the same as *imitatio*, though certainly the two terms are closely related. Giles Constable has argued that the term

---

[107] Bernard of Clairvaux, *De Consideratione*, p. 466. It is debatable to what degree the crusading armies also perceived themselves as God's agents directly.

[108] Guibert of Nogent, *Dei Gesta per Francos*, ed. R.B.C. Huygens, Corpus Christianorum, Continuatio Mediaevalis 127A (Turnholt, 1996), p. 120.

[109] Charles Lewis, *An Elementary Latin Dictionary* (Oxford, 1977), p. 34.

[110] Du Cange, *Glossarium*, vol. 1, p. 117.

[111] Du Cange, *Glossarium*, vol. 1, p. 117.

[112] Niermeyer, *Lexicon Minus*, p. 374.

imitare implies conforming to and identifying with an ideal.[113] *Aemulatio* seems to have contained a sense of aroused emotion and hostile, obstinate perseverance, not merely passive conformity. In a sense it may be closer to the notions of *imitatio* as passionate longing highlighted by Christina Heckman.[114] What is striking then, at first glance, is that this term and its frequent substitute, *zelus*, both associated in part with a negative connotation of hostility and rivalry, were used to depict a Christian crusading virtue that was linked with a virtuous love for God.[115]

A clue may lie in the fact noted above that in the sources crusading zeal led to two actions, the first vengeance and the second self-sacrifice. Crusading texts in the later twelfth and early thirteenth century more than once portrayed individuals giving up their lives selflessly because they were moved by zeal. I propose two potential reasons for this association: zealous self-sacrifice through crusading as an act of love, and zealous self-sacrifice through crusading as *aemulatio Dei*.

Part of the classic understanding of crusading as an act of love hinged upon the willingness of the crusaders to sacrifice themselves for their Christian brothers in the East.[116] With the term *zelus* so closely tied to the notion of love, particularly Christian love, it is not surprising therefore that some texts described those who possessed zeal willing to sacrifice their lives through crusading. This basic explanation accounts for most of the passages expressing zeal as self-sacrifice noted in this chapter.

However, it does not account for the striking *exempla* of James of Vitry in which a Christian who was not a Templar was captured by Muslims. He faced death only if he was a Templar, but "inflamed with zeal for the faith" he falsely claimed to be a Templar, thus choosing to die for an untrue statement.[117] He was not a crusader, killed in battle; he was a Christian pilgrim, captured alone, choosing to lie and die, rather than speak the truth and be spared, because he was "inflamed with zeal."[118] What was this "zeal" that so drove him to dishonesty and self-sacrifice?

---

[113] Giles Constable, *Three Studies in Medieval Religious and Social Thought* (Cambridge, 1995), p. 146.

[114] Christina Heckman, "*Imitatio* in Early Medieval Spirituality: *The Dream of the Rood*, Anselm, and Militant Christianity," *Essays in Medieval Studies*, 22 (2005): 141–53.

[115] This usage, along with the apparent medieval continuation of a Jewish sense of true faith as zealous action on behalf of God, deserves further independent research. It should be noted that Christina Heckman's work at least partially supports the complex relationship between *aemulatio*, *imitatio*, *zelus* and vengeance that I outline here. For example, she, too, marks the potential danger of strongly affective religious belief, namely that it "could lead to despair or violence just as easily as it could aspire to sublime identification with the divine" (Heckman, "*Imitatio* in Early Medieval Spirituality", p. 150).

[116] Riley-Smith, "Crusading as an Act of Love," p. 182.

[117] James of Vitry, *The Exempla*, p. 39.

[118] It is interesting that the description of this pilgrim rather resembles the description of Christ found in *The Dream of the Rood*—see Heckman, "*Imitatio* in Early Medieval Spirituality," p. 143.

I proposed above that crusaders saw zeal as a characteristic of God the Father, a divine attribute the pope imitated and they enacted through love for God and their fellow Christians. Christians, especially Christian leaders, were to act as God's ministers, possessing zeal and taking vengeance, as evidenced by the popular biblical verse applied to crusading, *minister enim Dei est, vindex in iram ei qui malum agit*.[119] Crusaders were also encouraged to be like the second person of God; the *imitatio Christi* was another, albeit limited, strain of crusading rhetoric.[120] In the early Church, martyrs were the most perfect imitators of Christ, and the imitation of Christ was seen as a "process of divinization or deification."[121] Crusaders who imitated Christ bore their sufferings in silence and relinquished their lives when necessary, thereby coming closer to the divine.

In comparison with *imitatio*, the *aemulatio Christi*, zeal as emulation, based on what we know of the term *aemulatio*, surely involved attempting to accord to an ideal, but in an envious, perhaps competitive way. The Jews aimed at the emulation of God but failed; this was negative imitation in the way that Satan had tried to be like God and fallen from divine grace.[122]

Nevertheless, some in the Church attempted to harness *aemulatio* for good ends. Bernard of Clairvaux wrote to Pope Eugenius III that he must act as a good example for the people around him and below him in the Church hierarchy. The rebellious people of Rome were "impious in God, rash in holy things, always seditious, rivals (*aemuli*) with their neighbors, inhuman to outsiders."[123] Eugenius should counter that by encouraging them to attempt to rival each other in virtue, as Bernard himself did with the pope: "I rival you with good rivalry [*aemulatione bona*]"[124] This corresponds with what Miller has already noted, using very similar vocabulary, about the contrast between envy as admiration ("understood as emulation") and negative envy.[125] The almost competitive desire to emulate another could be directed towards virtuous behavior, suggesting that just as crusaders were described imitating Christ through martyrdom in battle, some, like James of Vitry's knight, were described emulating Christ through zeal: not passively accepting unavoidable death in battle through humility and submission to God's will, but actively seeking it out of defiant, almost angry love for God

---

[119] Romans 13:4.

[120] William Purkis, "Elite and Popular Perceptions of *Imitatio Christi* in Twelfth-Century Crusade Spirituality," in K. Cooper and J. Gregory (eds), *Elite and Popular Religion*, Studies in Church History 42 (Woodbridge, 2006), pp. 54–64.

[121] Constable, *Three Studies*, pp. 149 and 150.

[122] It should be noted that whereas to the best of my knowledge *zelus* was "never bad", *aemulatio* was clearly at times an undesirable characteristic—and yet *zelus* was apparently used as a synonym for *aemulatio* by medieval writers. This deserves further investigation.

[123] Bernard of Clairvaux, *De Consideratione*, p. 452.

[124] Bernard of Clairvaux, *De Consideratione*, p. 453.

[125] William Miller, *Humiliation* (Ithaca, 1993), p. 129.

and, perhaps, a competitive desire for virtue. Crusading texts therefore presented both the imitation and emulation of the second person of the Trinity as goals to be aimed at, culminating in the action of self-sacrifice, although imitation and emulation seem to have differed distinctly with regard to the emotional state of mind leading to that self-sacrifice.[126]

One of the main components of the medieval concept of zeal was to take action on God's behalf based on an angry desire to eliminate evil and on love for the good. Given this, it is not surprising that individuals described as possessing zeal might try to take action in two ways compatible with two related, but distinct, emotional states. Predominantly those who were zealous were depicted seeking to enact the vengeance of God through righteous anger, but at times the desire to emulate God led some to express zeal through self-sacrifice.

Conclusions

I have demonstrated that zeal was linked to the ideology of crusading through a number of emotional patterns. There was the "script" proposed by White, Barton and Smail, in which injury led to lordly anger, which in turn led to vengeance.[127] If the desire for vengeance was unfulfilled, anger grew to hatred, another emotion that was used as a narrative strategy to justify actions and mitigate guilt in medieval society.[128] Moreover, there was a long-standing biblical pattern of God's anger at sin and love for the good leading him to seek divine vengeance upon wrongdoers.

It must be noted that the emotional patterns that I and others have described are broad and simplistic. Human psychology is never as simple, nor as clearly delineated, as these models may suggest—as Kedar has rightly noted, individual preconceptions "dictated the extent to which the data [of rhetoric] were absorbed."[129] In fact, the patterns were effective *because* they were simple and broad and flexible. They were templates that could be loosely applied to a variety of circumstances with great effect, they contained various options and choices for action, and thus they were compatible with whatever other factors influenced individuals within their own minds as they considered and wrote about crusading.

The fact that the ideology of crusading as vengeance grew during the period in question and became more and more associated with the emotional terminology of zeal may have been due to the fact that there were already these established

---

[126] It is possible, of course, that this difference is so distinct only to the over-scrupulous (and hind-sighted) eyes of modern historians. The necessary caveat, then, is that my careful dissection of meaning is meant to enhance our own understanding of a distant time, rather than to describe a literal play-by-play of conscious thought in the Middle Ages.

[127] White, "The Politics of Anger," pp. 142–4. Barton, "'Zealous Anger,'" p. 157.

[128] Smail, "Hatred as a Social Institution," pp. 95, 101 and 109.

[129] Kedar, *Crusade and Mission*, p. 87.

patterns of thought tying together love of God, anger at sin, a passion for justice and the vocabulary of vengeance. It is crucial that there was more than one such pattern, since the rhetoric was aimed at specific audiences. Multiple patterns ensured more people—in more "emotional communities"—were likely to find a reason in their own minds to link zeal, crusading and vengeance.[130] And even minimal, partial reference may have evoked the entire, commonly understood patterns in individual minds. Thus these pre-existing patterns of thought linking emotion, religion and violence were powerful motivating tools at the disposal of those who encouraged the crusading movement and sought a united Christendom, internally reformed and externally expanding.[131]

There may have been a further dimension to the way in which these patterns worked. In his work on reports of religious visions collected in the much later Spanish Inquisition, William Christian has come to some startling conclusions about the way emotion was interpreted in the later Middle Ages. Apparently the emotional reaction of the subject of the vision was an important criterion in deciding whether it was a vision from God or from the Devil. The reasoning for this went back to Thomas Aquinas, who in turn relied on the *Life* of St. Anthony by Athanasius: "if fear is followed by joy, we know that the help of God has come to us ... If, on the contrary, the fear remains, then the enemy is present."[132] After extensive research Christian concluded that "certain emotions seem to have been moral indicators, or signifiers ... a form of obscure communication from God. Like dreams, they were messages to be deciphered."[133] I know of no work done to test or verify this conclusion outside the Spanish Inquisition, but if it were true that in the medieval period as a whole the right emotion could serve as an indicator of moral rectitude, then patterns would have been recognized and triggered not only intellectually, but also emotionally: *feeling* the emotion of zeal may have confirmed for the individual that her actions were godly, apart from any intellectual understanding of the situation. Thus the ideology of crusading as vengeance may have functioned both intellectually and emotionally.

John Cowdrey has noted that at the time of the First Crusade martyrdom was not a crucial component of crusading ideology, but rather a "catalyst," a concept that enabled the crusaders to understand "how they could at one and the same time"

---

[130] Kedar, *Crusade and Mission*, p. 101. Barbara Rosenwein, *Emotional Communities in the Early Middle Ages* (Ithaca and London, 2006).

[131] Those who sought both internal reform and conversion of the Muslims were usually described as zealous. For example, St. Dominic (*Acta canonizationis S. Dominici*, cited by Kedar, *Crusade and Mission*, p. 121), Ramon of Penyaforte (cited by Kedar, *Crusade and Mission*, p. 138) and St. Francis (James of Vitry, *Lettres*, pp. 132–3).

[132] William Christian, *Apparitions in Late Medieval and Renaissance Spain* (Princeton, 1981), p. 193.

[133] Christian, *Apparitions in Late Medieval and Renaissance Spain*, p. 201.

kill and be martyred.[134] I suggest that the emotional rhetoric of zeal functioned in a similar way as a catalytic discourse that suited both anger and love, imitation and emulation, vengeance and self-sacrifice, and that because it was such a flexible tool, the emotional rhetoric of zeal was utilized more and more through the twelfth century and into the thirteenth to promote and explain the actions that resulted from crusading ideology.

---

[134] H.E.J. Cowdrey, "Martyrdom and the First Crusade," *The Crusades and Latin Monasticism, 11th– 12th Centuries* (Aldershot, 1999), p. 53.

Afterword
Neither Unnatural nor Wholly Negative: The Future of Medieval Vengeance

Paul R. Hyams

This volume contains a variety of able and engaging studies on and around the subject of vengeance. It was not intended to present its readers with a unified view and I see no reason to force the contents into an awkward and closed synthesis. Instead I consider in this Afterword some of the many ideas for the next stage of research on medieval vengeance provoked by my privileged opportunity to read and meditate on the book.[1] My specific responses to the arguments in these studies did, however, return often to what struck me as a key question which analysts of behavior patterns like vengeance might usefully pose. This asks how "natural" is vengeance. The many different meanings that we invest in words like "natural" and its cognates mostly share an intention to assess behavior through rhetoric. One way we seek to decide whether violence, for example, is permissible in particular circumstances is by analyzing and presenting it as natural. Vengeance is by definition retaliatory. Thus the notion that meeting force with force is licit when other violent acts are not is implied in all our studies of vengeance in this book. It is, indeed, axiomatic; medieval legal writers constantly deploy the tag *vim vi repellere*. I am drawn to characterize this as a natural use of force, and not deterred by the fact that medieval writers do not themselves, so far as I am aware, invoke Nature in this way.[2]

In what follows, I shall first make some remarks about the roles of reason and emotion in the taking of vengeance. I shall then turn to the most noted type of vengeance, so often known as feud, and will ask briefly what this patterned version can teach us about the broader subject. Finally, I reengage with the question of naturalness via a consideration of vengeance as threat and a comparison of human with non-human responses to injury and wrong. I hope that my discussion will help to advance the study of vengeance, a primary goal of this book. More specifically, I shall try to demonstrate the manner in which the volume as a whole advances understanding of the rhetoric and logic of getting even with perceived enemies,

---

[1] The substantial contribution of Dr. Throop to this Afterword virtually qualifies her to be named co-author. The errors are, however, my responsibility as always.

[2] The tag comes from the Roman law corpus, Dig. 9.2.45.4, where it is presented as a justification for self-defense, A. Berger, *Encyclopedic Dictionary of Roman Law* (Philadelphia, 1953), p. 765. I do not myself know of any studies of the naturalness argument in the Middle Ages.

the ways medieval men and women articulated and conceptualized vengeance and tried to achieve it.[3] In all this, I shall pay special attention to the Bible, that springboard to moral reflection in medieval Christendom, in the hope of provoking more serious if retrograde study of biblical proof texts as one fruitful entry point to contemporary attitudes toward vengeance.[4]

* * *

Newton's Third Law of Motion is often simplified as follows: "every action has an equal and opposite reaction." This Law of Reciprocal Actions is about as natural a phenomenon as one can find. If it is true, as has been argued here, that people who see themselves as having been wronged feel an almost insuperable urge to return the favor, if possible with added interest, this speaks strongly for the naturalness of vengeance. Newton may prompt us to ask whether it may not even be in some sense hard-wired into us as an instinctive reaction, a possibility to which I shall later return.

Obviously human reactions to the actions of others raise very different questions from the kind that trouble specialists in thermodynamics.[5] Physicists, operating as they claim to do at the very pinnacle of human reason, seldom acknowledge the need to consider emotional questions. In contrast, many historians now question the old opposition of Reason and Emotion and have begun to study the part emotions have played in past actions alongside, for instance, more calculated decision-making.[6] Vengeance, though often involving much calculation, was also deeply infused with passion, in ways that defy easy analytical separation. To strike the right balance between reason and emotion, or rather to measure the tensions that unite the two, is a scholarly challenge that will guide us into a deeper but messier view of political decision-making in general. Barbara Rosenwein, the most prominent current guide for medievalists, declines to see vengeance as any kind of simple universal and so allows for differing attitudes to it within what she calls

---

[3] I shall refer frequently here to William Ian Miller's recent splendid study, *Eye for an Eye* (Cambridge, 2006), and I look forward to scrutinizing its data and many arguments in more leisurely fashion than has been appropriate here.

[4] I owe my keen, non-specialist interest in the study of the Bible to a revered teacher and pioneer in the field, Beryl Smalley, and her great book, *The Study of the Bible in the Middle Ages*. I take my few illustrations from the Ordinary Gloss that accompanied most schools Bible MSS in the two centuries from the mid-twelfth, using the facsimile 1480/1 text of *Biblia Latina Cum Glossa Ordinaria*, with introduction by K. Froehlich and Margaret T. Gibson (4 vols, Turnhout, 1992). This is obviously only a preliminary foray into the mass of Bible commentaries.

[5] One to be discussed below is whether the human reaction to wrong must necessarily prove either "equal" or "opposite." See below starting at p. 211.

[6] In practice, most of us still emphasize in particular studies one approach over the other, analyzing either calculation (sometimes as "rational choice") or the passions involved.

"emotional communities."[7] (Others might call these competing or cooperating discourses.) She regards these emotional communities as located within particular societies and capable of evolving and changing according to circumstances.[8] From exemplary close readings of texts, she infers that "les émotions ne sont connues que lorsqu'elles sont exprimées."[9]

Of course writing is not the only means to express emotion or, for that matter, reason. We must also watch for actions and other non-verbal utterances, the gestures that are mostly lost to us, and even such material objects as tombstones, inscriptions and emotionally charged bloody shirts for goading mothers to find and flourish at the right moment.[10] Medievalists are unlikely to find more than the very occasional written reference to such things, which points to the complexity and almost limitless range of the search for evidence of vengeance.

Take as illustration the legal records from which I am myself accustomed to begin. These mostly document motives like vengeance only by chance or mistake. Western legal systems have since the twelfth-century emergence of professional (or, better, relatively full time) lawyers quite consciously obscured emotions as largely irrelevant to their purpose. In their determination to identify and focus on "legal" issues, they launder vengeance and its related emotional motivations out of the official record. The important exceptions occur when motive is in some sense written into the procedures and definitions, as in the matter of the Portuguese petitions for exemption from the bans on bearing arms in François Soyer's chapter above, which nicely demonstrates that the student of vengeance (and similar emotions) can make use of a wide range of evidence.[11]

* * *

[7] She tackles our specific topic in "Les émotions de la vengeance," in Dominique Barthélemy, François Bougard and Régine Le Jan (eds), *La vengeance 400–1200* (Rome, 2006), pp. 237–56, but scouts the whole subject in her *Emotional Communities in the Early Middle Ages* (Ithaca and London, 2006). "Les émotions de la vengeance," pp. 240–42 gives references to the literature, including her own contributions.

[8] To the four examples she offers in "Les émotions de la vengeance," one might add by her own testimony counter-communities from the direction of the Church.

[9] "Les émotions de la vengeance," p. 241.

[10] Miller, *Eye for an Eye*, ch. 7 carries both recent thoughts on goading and references to earlier studies. I wish some of the goading objects had survived, in the way that our archives retain some of the objects deposited to memorialize livery of seizin to land, as noted by M.T. Clanchy, *From Memory to Written Record* (2nd edn, London, 1993), pp. 257–60. On gestures, English-speaking readers can follow the leads given by such as Gerd Althoff, *Family, Friends and Followers* (Cambridge and New York, 2004); Philippe Buc, *The Dangers of Ritual* (Princeton, 2001); Geoffrey Koziol, *Begging Pardon and Favor* (Ithaca, 1992).

[11] Soyer, above Chapter 3. Among other instances are the English inquisitions *De Odio et Athia*, on which see my *Rancor and Reconciliation in Medieval England* (Ithaca, 2003), pp. 246–51, and Natalie Z. Davis, *Fiction in the Archives: Pardon Tales and their Tellers in Sixteenth-Century France* (Stanford, 1987).

Feud is the mode of vengeance-seeking that most often catches the imaginations of scholars and ordinary folk alike. It is odd how little has been done to examine how its spectacular processes illuminate the broader subject, or even to decide what space they occupy within it. As an initial approximation, one might say that feud is one of the main ways in which cultures formalize the working of vengeance, embody it within some patterned format, presumably in order to minimize the risks of dissolution into uncontrolled violence and chaos. Earlier study of feud was bedeviled by some false assumptions stemming from a sense of its alien nature. Feud was a deliciously scary feature of "savage" customs from "primitive" worlds as different as could be from our own "higher" cultures. This central error of approach impeded the critical realization of how often very feud-like patterns operated alongside, and often within, formal laws and states. Yet the feud concept itself predates in an important sense the notion of the state, a point illustrated by Jackson Armstrong's demonstration that feuds can transcend their boundaries.[12] The premise for successful feuding, then, might just be the existence of a noble caste that privileges personal links above national loyalties and which, some would say, has lasted even into the early twentieth century.[13]

Understanding the dynamics of the process raises myriad further questions. How, for example, do participants know what to do? What kinds of constraints operate on the principal avengers and on those ubiquitous third parties, whose role goes far beyond collateral damage waiting to happen? It used to be thought that one could answer such questions in terms of feud as an institution that worked through more or less binding rules. But institutional arguments have failed to explain the dynamics of the avenging process. Recent studies, including several in the present book, approach the problem in part through the use of two kinds of image. I argue in my own chapter that the "script" image does not suit our analytical purposes.[14] Let us instead consider the powerful notion of the rules of feud, often seen as operating within or for a game, as in Gerd Althoff's *Spielregeln*.[15]

Viewed from a rules-of-the-game perspective, feud apparently requires the spontaneous acceptance by everyone around, players and spectators alike, that the violence and threats involved do in fact constitute a vengeance game, whose rules everyone knows, or ought to know. Some very familiar legal maxims lend a

---

[12] Armstrong, above Chapter 2.

[13] I have in mind here the survival of a transnational noble caste, as depicted in Renoir's great movie *Règle du jeu* (1939). Less controversially we need to consider the effect of recent re-evaluations of the ethos of chivalry by scholars like John Gillingham and others. This is not to confine the urge to vengeance to the nobility, as I note below at p. 212.

[14] See above pp. 181–2.

[15] Gerd Althoff, *Spielregeln der Politik im Mittelalter: Kommunikation in Frieden und Fehde* (Darmstadt, 1997). I note that "Spiel" can mean "play" as well as "game." Since "free" play is thought by many to require neither rules nor a rule-giver, this could modify the argument in the text below.

certain plausibility to this claim.[16] But most, though not all, games with rules have, like laws, law-givers who at least claim the authority to enforce and implement them.[17] In contrast, the feuding societies of the Middle Ages knew no equivalents to an MCC (the Marylebone Cricket Club whose rules took over the game of cricket) or the Football Association, which launched Association Football on an unsuspecting world.[18]

Patently, this issue is of some general interest, with implications far beyond feud and vengeance.[19] It is therefore worthwhile to test the *Spielregeln* approach.[20] One might ask first how one began and ended a feud. Feud actors were expected to make explicit their contention that they were not wrongdoers but pursuing a "legitimate" vengeance. Prudent players therefore publicized their intentions in ways designed to be easily understood within their neighborhood. One method used the well-known ritual of defiance (wrongly linked to "feudalism") to publicize the initiation of a feud which might be ended with an act of homage to

---

[16] I have in mind "ignorance of the law is no excuse" and "to a willing person, no injury is done," medieval coinages which both appear in modern law dictionaries. Canon lawyers incorporated *ignorantia iuris non facti excusat* among the *regulae iuris* in the thirteenth-century Sext, VI, 5.13. The principle of *volenti non fit iniuria* was obviously known early; Gratian's *Decretum*, C. 22.4.23 cites a passage from Ambrose, *De Officiis*. See VI, 5.13.27 for *scienti et consentienti non fit iniuria neque dolus*.

[17] This is not a universal feature. Our word "rule" has a very wide usage range and can cover some quite vague regularities. Children, especially, often play without set rules, and—at least in my memories—frequently squabble about whether some act is fair. But most who theorize about games in the context of law and rule-giving appear to have something fairly formal in mind. In the midst of this theorizing, it is tantalizing to note that the official empowered to settle disputes in ancient Rome was known as a *vindex* (G.E. Mendenhall, *The Tenth Generation: The Origins of the Biblical Tradition* (Baltimore, 1973), pp. 75–6).

[18] *The Rules of Association Football 1863* (Oxford, 2006), with introduction by Melvyn Bragg, is well worth reading in this context.

[19] The possibility that a number of principles like those in the two maxims cited just above reached Western laws as summaries of feud and vengeance process is surely worth further investigation. It is one more reason for cultural historians to take legal maxims seriously. See more generally Peter Stein, *Regulae Iuris: From Juristic Rules to Legal Maxims* (Edinburgh, 1966), and perhaps the appendix to my own "Due Process Versus the Maintenance of Order in European Law: The Contribution of the *Ius Commune*," in Peter Coss (ed.), *The Moral World of the Law* (London, 2000), ch. 5.

[20] One question I shall leave aside here concerns the kind of player who fares best in the game. William Miller has much to say among his various writings on feud and similar matters. One should start with his foundational work on the possibly aberrant Icelandic feud in *Bloodtaking and Peacemaking: Feud, Law, and Society in Saga Iceland* (Chicago, 1990) and go on to more recent and generalizing work such as his *Eye for an Eye* (2006). It is a pity that Stephen Jaeger did not consider this matter in his *The Origins of Courtliness* (Philadelphia, 1985).

publicize and seal a peace settlement.[21] In this way a man could proclaim to the world his sense of wrong and the rupture of bonds that might otherwise prevent him from taking vengeance for it. This was initially a threat.[22] His newly declared enemies were being warned that to deter him from taking blood, they must take steps to requite him by other means or at least enter into negotiations.

Any reasonably frequent repetition of such public acts accepted as demarcating enmity would educate the young of the area in the rules of vengeance in general. How such acts initially established themselves it is probably impossible to determine. The medieval sources speak less of ritual *acts* than of some *state* of enmity, perhaps deemed old or ancient, known to be in force.[23] This must usually have been the most that locals could tell an inquirer. An original *casus belli* soon passed out of mind once an enmity was properly launched.[24] Who needed it? The details of an enmity's origins were important only to the principals and their very close friends and advisers, and then mostly in the early stages of proceedings. Their neighbors, if wise, concentrated more on where the urge toward vengeance lay, the current "score," and where to watch for the next strike. It is thus possible that formal declarations of feud were as rare in the High Middle Ages, say, as settlements with multiple homages. If so, this would of itself weaken the notion of formal *Spielregeln*.

But if such rules did govern the play, scholars need to consider what happened on their breach. What happened, for instance, if one side played out of turn and killed twice in succession? Most feud models make much of the requirement for proportionate response.[25] In this volume, Thomas Roche notes that such cases did occur in the Middle Ages.[26] We need to seek out and evaluate other examples. The need to condemn such unfair play probably explains why some of these incidents are recorded, and also perhaps explains why secret killings were singled out for special condemnation under the name of murder.[27]

---

[21] In "Homage and Feudalism: A Judicious Separation," in Natalie Fryde, Pierre Monnet and Otto Gergard Oexle (eds), *Die Gegenwart des Feudalismus* (Göttingen, 2003), pp. 13–49, I even suggested that this might lie at the origin of one or both acts.

[22] On which more below.

[23] I note some specific examples from my own work in *Rancor and Reconciliation*, pp. 193–4 and 247.

[24] It helps to hang the memory on a dramatic event. These can be manufactured if wished. An elderly Oxford don once told me his father's experience of a good walloping on Mafeking night, in the summer of 1900, performed, he was told, in order that he would never forget the impact (sic!) of the news. Miller, *Eye for an Eye*, p. 90 quotes Nietzsche to the effect that "pain is the most powerful aid to mnemonics."

[25] Cf. T.H. Clutton-Brock and G.A. Parker, "Punishment in Animal Societies," *Nature*, 373 (1995): 209–16 at p. 215 on quantum of response among non-humans.

[26] Roche, above p. 123.

[27] J.M. Kaye, "The Early History of Murder and Manslaughter, Part I," *Law Quarterly Review*, 83 (1967): 365–95, T.A. Green, *Verdict According to Conscience* (Chicago, 1985),

Consider further the rule of proportionate response to wrong. Potential avengers must often have been tempted to exceed the mean and pursue absolute vengeance, in order to preclude the risk of future retribution from the other side. This is the micropolitical equivalent of genocide, to kill the whole of the enemy's family and thus leave nobody qualified to seek vengeance. People do seem to have feared extirpation; there are certainly literary instances where the villains try (but fail) to achieve it.[28] Whether it actually occurred and whether it could be considered vengeance, legitimate or otherwise, may be debatable. One might guess that such overkill—French contemporaries might say *desmesure* or *outrage*—remained vengeance but was perhaps not to be excused as feud. If even a sizeable proportion of real (or even literary) revenge acts aimed at the goal of ruling out all future response in this manner, I should feel it necessary to reassess the feud hypothesis I made in my own chapter above.[29] But that said, it seems beyond question that the proverbial idea of the punishment fitting the crime was already current.[30]

The basic principle that justice is about leveling things (the *talion*) may indeed be universal among humans, who have encapsulated it in a variety of images, "an eye for an eye," the scales of justice and so on.[31] As I have argued earlier in this volume, the implied claim has a very broad scope; it is always possible to

---

pp. 53–9 and index s.v., and B.R. O'Brien, "From Morðor to Murdrum: The Preconquest Origin and Norman Revival of the Murder Fine," *Speculum*, 71 (1996): 321–57, esp. pp. 30 and 37, review technical English evidence that throws light on the problem. But murder, in the sense of homicide aggravated by, *inter alia*, its secrecy, is a European phenomenon which demands comparative study at some stage.

[28] Cf. *Middle English Verse Romances*, ed. D.B. Sands (New York, 1966) for "Havelok the Dane," ll. 325–7, 509–12. A proverb in the *Poetic Edda* (*Sigrdrífmal*, 35) translated at http://www.northvegr.org/lore/poetic2/027_02.php: "I counsel you tenth; trust not ever the words of a wolf's kin,/If you have killed his kin/Or felled his father:/Wolf's bane is in his blood/Though he be glad of your gold" illustrates the basic sentiment and shows the familiarity of the idea within saga culture.

[29] I have in mind especially proposition no. 5 on p. 160 above.

[30] Cf. Matthew 5:29–30 and the glosses on first 5:29, "erue enim" ("Ad litteram nullum membrum erui proicitur") and especially 5:30 "abscide eam et proice": "Si quis hoc predicat de membris, affectu pietatis non debet audiri. Sed ut improbitas morum et pravitas actionum inde resecetur, ut quicquid in oculo mentis de via iusticie et morum probitate nos subuertit et quicquid contra operationem virtutum extra pulsat, procul pellatur." Cf. Stewart Rapalje and Robert L. Lawrence, *Dictionary of American and English Law* (2 vols, Jersey City, 1883), vol. I, p. 327 for the maxim "culpae poena par esto. Poena ad mensuram delicti statuenda est," with which one may fairly compare Dig. 48.10.31 and Dig. 48.19.11pr. I am very grateful for assistance on this tricky maxim from Charles Donahue Jr.

[31] This is the leitmotif of Miller, *Eye for an Eye*, which has fascinating details on "evening up", pp. 17–19. Laura Nader expressed her sense of the required reciprocity of vengeance in the title she gave, "To Restore the Balance," to her influential chapter in Nader (ed.), *Law in Culture and Society* (Chicago, 1969), pp. 69–91.

meet any act of vengeance with a similar counter-act.[32] There is, of course, no requirement to do so, which is one reason why vengeance so seldom produces feud. Much in feud practice does, however, appear to derive from a concern for proportionality and balance. An avenger who goes beyond the tipping point risks losing the privilege that comes from having his act validated by inclusion within the feud process.[33] Yet even the balance image is not universally simple. Some victims were simply too inferior to their enemies in power and social standing to harbor serious thoughts of getting even by force. If they were not to "lump it," to swallow their injuries without compensation, they had to try and persuade someone of equivalent standing to their enemy to make their injury his and avenge them alongside himself. The victim and his party always sought more than the mere restitution of actual loss, which is what Latin *dam(p)num* seems so often to mean. This is nicely shown by the formulaic claims in the action of trespass.[34]

The notion of satisfaction seems well suited to cover this more complex notion of balance. The primary dictionary meaning of Latin *satisfactio* in the Middle Ages is penitential; it denotes what a penitent was required to do to level his or her account with God. But the word is also common in secular law.[35] Satisfaction is more obviously proactive than monastic *patientia*, different in kind from the emotions behind the *clementia* expected of kings and the courtesy or *debonereté* of their nobles.[36] But general dictionaries are inadequate for our purposes. A full lexicographical study would illuminate the workings of medieval vengeance, and ought to include the major vernaculars, most especially Old French.[37] Still, Latin scholarly writings alone confirm that restitution had to go beyond ancient man-prices to include something for damage to feelings and status. Saint Anselm's

---

[32] See above pp. 168–9.

[33] The particular factors that determine whether acts lie within the feud process have much in common with the criminal defenses permitted in medieval and later law. A re-examination of these in this vengeance perspective would be enlightening about the boundaries of licit vengeance.

[34] J.S. Beckerman, "Adding Insult to *Iniuria*: Affronts to Honor and the Origins of Trespass," in Morris S. Arnold et al (eds), *On the Laws and Customs of England: Essays in Honor of Samuel E. Thorne* (Chapel Hill, 1981), pp. 159–81 strongly suggests that formulas that initially showed the weight disputants placed on honor and shame progressively weakened into mere forms of words. This swift disappearance of honor from the legal equations surely deserves closer attention than it has received.

[35] *Mediae Latinitatis Lexicon Minus*, ed. J.F. Niermeyer (Leiden, 1997), s.v., esp. senses 1 and 2. Miller, *Eye for an Eye*, ch. 10, esp. pp. 140 ff., explains the etymological implications of satisfaction.

[36] I made some preliminary explorations into this area in "What Did Henry III of England Think in Bed (and in French) About Kingship and Anger?" in Barbara H. Rosenwein (ed.), *Anger's Past: The Social Uses of an Emotion in the Middle Ages* (Ithaca, NY, 1998).

[37] A.J. Greimas, *Dictionnaire de l'ancien français* (2nd edn, Paris, 2004), s.v. *Satefier*, *satisfaire* is suggestive.

exposition of sin as a dishonoring of God offers a convenient illustration. He argues that the repentant needed to offer Him something more than simple contrition, "secundum exhonorationis factam molestiam" or, more bluntly, "pro honore ablato."[38] Injured mortals would surely expect similar assuaging.

Patently, equal balance was no matter of simple arithmetic, of the kind that an older tradition read into early medieval secular compensation payments and the "tariffs" of the penitentials. I am led to think more in terms of unwanted gifts than commercial transactions.[39] Their *positive* reciprocity constitutes an obvious analogy to the *negative* reciprocity of vengeance. But the whole ethos of gifts weighs against calculation to be overt; this would appear cheese-paring and dishonorable, and would diminish the felt value of the gift. Would-be peacemakers, wary of comparison with Judas and his 30 pieces of silver, endeavored to include in their settlement proposals such indications of sincerity as declarations of contrition and gestures of abasement like peace homage or pilgrimage. In such ways, people hot for vengeance might see their enemies paying for the pleasure they would otherwise seek in a revenge killing by themselves suffering pain.[40] The notion might, as Dr. Throop has argued above, raise the whole question of self-sacrifice, extending even to voluntary martyrdom.[41] But overall we need to view the balance

---

[38] *Cur Deus Homo*, I.11; *Meditatio Redemptionis Humanae* in F.S. Schmitt (ed.), *Sancti Anselmi Opera Omnia* (6 vols, Seccovii, 1938–), ii.68; iii.87, cited by Christina M. Heckman, "*Imitatio* in Early Medieval Spirituality: *The Dream of the Rood*, Anselm, and Militant Christology," *Essays in Medieval Studies*, 22 (2005): 141–53, at pp. 146–7.

[39] A good place to start on the burgeoning literature is Gadi Algazi, Valentin Groebner and Bernhard Jussen (eds), *Negotiating the Gift: Pre-modern Figurations of Exchange* (Göttingen, 2003), and especially the contributions of Algazi.

[40] Joanna Bourke, *An Intimate History of Killing* (New York, 1999) highlights the excitement of killing, also Miller, *Eye for an Eye*, pp. 143–5. As Sigmund Freud is quoted as remarking in his *Civilization and Its Discontents* (e.g. Jed Rubenfeld, *The Interpretation of Murder* (New York, 2006), pp. 61, 365), "Satisfying a savage instinct is incomparably more pleasurable than satisfying a civilized one." This simplifies the accepted text, to be found in *The Standard Edition of the Complete Psychological Works of Sigmund* Freud, ed. J. Strachey et al. (London, 1953–74), vol. 21, p. 79. The way believers were invited to identify with the cruelty of Christ's killers is sadly relevant here (Heckman, "*Imitatio* in Early Medieval Society," pp. 149–50). But even more to the point are the customs which authorize the relicts of a victim to personally perform the execution of judgment against the killer, P.C.M. Hoppenbrouwers, "Vengeance is Ours?' The Involvement of Kin in the Settlement of 'Cases of Vengeance' in Later Medieval Holland," in Isabel Davis, Miriam Müller and Sarah Rees-Jones (eds), *Love, Marriage, and Family Ties in the Later Middle Ages* (Turnhout, 2003), pp. 214–75, at p. 272; *Rancor and Reconciliation*, p. 250. The alacrity with which parents attend the capital punishment of their children's killers in the U.S. today hints at the relish with which executions were perhaps performed in the Middle Ages. This illuminates people's disappointment when God did not carry out threats made on His behalf, see below p. 213.

[41] Throop, above Chapter 8, esp. pp. 197, 209.

image as something much less than a binding model or rule and more like "a kind of constitutive metaphor."[42]

I shall, indeed, wish to move cautiously myself in future with the whole rules approach, which makes it all too easy to distort and trivialize an activity that is literally a matter of life and death. We should ask ourselves how great a weight of moral ideology or religious dogma could persuade *us* to regard any rules as binding in such circumstances.[43] We have in our own culture very recently seen the Laws of War and the Geneva Conventions come, to put it mildly, under severe pressure. Perhaps in "olden times" honor, shame and the preservation of face were once powerful enough to bring most nobles into line behind a feud rule book. It is hard to see such forces extending to ordinary men and women of the lower classes, who also experienced anger and sought vengeance. But an inquiry along class lines might help us to understand later medieval moves to confine any privileging of vengeance to the nobility.[44] Inferiors were virtually compelled to talk their lord into taking over the feud if they were to have any chance of avenging their wrongs. Success must have been rare and probably costly too. An examination of the social origins of the minority actually convicted of crimes of violence would suggest that the poor man's vengeance was most likely to be punished as crime.[45] Therefore feud must be, I repeat, an odd game, if it is one at all.

* * *

One reason why scholars may have so embraced the image of a game and its rules might be our tendency to focus on the more colorful anecdotes, especially those which involve killings. Football is about more than scoring goals, and the same applies to vengeance. It has often been noted that for strategic purposes—the hope of changing an enemy's behavior, say, and reaching a settlement—the *threat* of killing is as good as the act itself. In many ways it is in fact better, since it minimizes the danger of counterstrokes. Johnson illustrates the mechanics of this in the present volume, when she observes that "the same Irish saints who curse

---

[42] Miller, *Bloodtaking and Peacemaking*, ch. 6; the quoted phrase comes from p. 184.

[43] One might investigate commentary on the biblical episode of the Binding of Isaac in this light. The differences of interpretation between Christian and Jewish exegetes seem quite revealing, see http://en.wikipedia.org/wiki/Binding_of_Isaac.

[44] This might be one fruitful way to approach the classic ideas of Otto Brunner, *Land and Lordship: Structures of Governance in Medieval Austria*, trans. Howard Kaminsky and James van Horn Melton (Philadelphia, 1992) and the debate they provoked among historians.

[45] I think this could be done in England, for instance, better than the hints I managed in *Rancor and Reconciliation*, ch. 5. Certainly, the impulse to take violent revenge for what was perceived as wrong emerges just as strongly from the poor as the rich, when the sources permit it to be visible, as in *Rancor and Reconciliation*, pp. 246–51.

also cure."[46] Their very raison d'être is to change their subjects' behavior and they reach beyond simple deterrence to endeavor to construct the conditions of positive relations essential for a lasting settlement.[47] Irish saintly power operates in two distinct modes, we are told. The holy men sometimes make direct statements in prophetic form of what is to transpire. But quite often, apparently, they are simply present and obvious while nasty things happen around them to those who deserve them. Each of these forms carries general lessons for students of vengeance.

You do not have to be a saint to make use of the maledictory prophecy format.[48] It is reasonable to call it a format, since Johnson argues for a phenomenon that is as much a matter of rhetorical form as any reality.[49] This works very conveniently for saints who can achieve their ends without their evident vindictiveness attracting moral blame, as when a saint harms an undeserving bystander in order to punish a different sinner. In contrast, they may even repeat the biblical injunctions to leave vengeance to God. The format shares one important feature with the feuding process—the requirement that would-be avengers publicize their intentions works to pressure adversaries into the peacemaking process and offering peace terms. The sagas contain enough prophetic curses to suggest a wider pattern, and confirm Johnson's view that the phenomenon is largely a matter of reporting style.[50] Some of her Irish saints are yet more cunning, or disingenuous, and somehow manage to take credit for defeating the evil without actual prophecy.[51] Punitive miracles simply happen in their neighborhood, without any apparent act, speech or gesture of invocation on their part. This, though again presumably a literary device, may reflect a sense of the workings of individual conscience under the pressure of public opinion, a further incentive to send out peace feelers.

In such ways, the reported behavior of exceptional holy men seems to reveal patterns followed also by more ordinary individuals in time of distress. If this impression is correct, we should likewise pay attention to another way in which all threats, tacit or broadcast, are supposed to be exceptional. Johnson cites an eighth-century prohibition against pronouncing curses unless the wrongdoer "does not fear God's face." They are to be launched "not in the spirit of desire but [merely]

---

[46] Johnson, above Chapter 1, p. 37.
[47] On this see Armstrong, above Chapter 2, pp. 71–2.
[48] Johnson, above Chapter 1, pp. 16–19.
[49] Johnson, above Chapter 1, p. 7, n. 10: "textual devices, not ... reports of true occurrences." Johnson's position has the disadvantage perhaps of apparently removing the hope of illuminating actuality.
[50] *Grettir's Saga*, trans. Denton Fox and Hermann Pálsson (Toronto, 1974), ch. 34; *Gisli Sursson's Saga*, ed. V. Olason, trans. M.S. Regal (London, 1997), ch. 24. I am assured that one could add greatly to these examples. I shall look out for the pattern in Old French literature too, where a different rhetoric will make it harder to spot.
[51] Johnson, above Chapter 1, pp. 19–21 terms this Passive Retaliatory Judgment.

of forewarning."[52] All direct action ought to be a last resort, reserved for those who will not see the error of their ways. The proper goal for a Christian is correction rather than the execution of a justice that should be left to God. Of course the snag is the possibility that the sinner actually will repent, and leave the cursing saint looking as foolish as the biblical Jonah felt outside Nineveh, a sentiment that might easily be studied further through the commentaries.[53] Threats sometimes work better than their makers intend.

* * *

Modern investigations into medieval vengeance ought to strike a positive note. Much of the scholarship still views the phenomenon in largely negative terms. Many would prefer to dismiss the whole topic as one belonging to some less developed, even "primitive" stage of human development that we ought to transcend. Vengeance and feud were once assigned essentially to savage cultures, including those of "Dark Age" Europe. Most readers of the present volume, however, will be prepared to take a different view. More recently, a number of philosophers have gathered to lend their support to a revaluation of vengeance, and W.I. Miller's recent book *Eye for an Eye* presents persuasive reasons (a number of which I have referred to above) why historians should move in a similar direction.[54]

In conclusion, I therefore wish to draw together very different kinds of material to support two of Miller's propositions. Miller wants us not to think too badly of revenge. There is no avoiding the urge to vengeance anyway. It is inextricably engrained into human nature, and responsible for much that is positive in our lives. His overall argument on this is premised on the belief that a "sharp distinction between retributive justice and revenge cannot be maintained." Now he may be correct about this at some philosophical level, but historians cannot ignore how deeply such a distinction has been incorporated within our everyday language. It is therefore important to investigate the way this distinction arose in the West, not least because the critical period appears to have been the High Middle Ages.

---

[52] Ibid., p. 16. The last phrase is my paraphrase of "non optantis animo, sed prophetantis."

[53] Cf. Ionas, iv.1, gl. "Et afflictus est" which suggests that Jonah's sadness reflected his imminent loss of prophetic status, and ibid., iv.4, gl. "putas ne": "[Deus] interrogat ipsum iratum ut vel causas ire respondeat, vel si ille tacuerit verum Dei iudicium ex eius silentio conpletur." Also Ionas, iv. 9, gl. "Putas ne bene." And cf. above n. 40 for the pleasure of righteous killing, which an unperformed threat did not give.

[54] I first picked up on this in *Rancor and Reconciliation*, pp. 38–9 with the help of R.C. Solomon, *A Passion for Justice* (Cambridge, Mass., 1990), but I am now advised to read P. French, *The Virtues Of Vengeance* (Lawrence, Kan., 2001) and J.G. Murphy, *Getting Even—Forgiveness and its Limits* (New York, 2003).

First, we see a distinction between—in effect—vengeance and punishment. This is much less evident in the early Middle Ages than it is later. It is well known that two of the main Latin words used to denote these matters, *ultio* and *vindicta* and their associates, sometimes indicate vengeance, sometimes punishment. The lexicographer will find some cases of each word that denote a vengeance idea, some that seem to speak of punishment and quite a number that can easily be read to mean either or even both. To this enigma, one attractive solution assumes that outside a narrow circle of very well-educated Latinists, the majority of writers were more or less innocent of the distinction we now make in the West between barbaric vengeance and properly just punishment.[55] And if that was true of the *literati* who wrote in Latin, the likelihood is that the line between vengeance and punishment was in the popular consciousness dim to the point of non-existence.

This difficulty is very characteristic of the "long" twelfth century, when an unprecedented volume of collective thought in writing was sharpening analytical practice in a direction that became an individuating characteristic of Western thought into our own age. In this "Twelfth-Century Renaissance", there originated a slew of the learned (mostly legal) distinctions that have long demarcated Western culture from its neighbors.[56] The process of generating and assimilating these distinctions was a complicated one. Yet scholars familiar with the categories of our own day often exaggerate the ease with which that modern thought world was constructed. Occasionally they imagine a distinction which did not yet exist.[57] The period before a new distinction emerges is not its pre-history—it is an entirely different era. People cannot ignore or flout a *future* distinction, because it simply does not exist for them. This may well be the case with the conceptual opposition of vengeance and punishment. If so, the ambiguity of *ultio* and *vindicta* and their like would be genuinely insoluble. Some kind of conjoined "vengeance-punishment" may have been organic to early medieval majority culture, as it perhaps remains even today among some minority groups. How to test a hypothesis of this nature is a question for another occasion. The challenge is a troubling one.

I take the easier course by illustrating the chronological progression through texts from the decades around 1100 that seem almost to portray the distinction

---

[55] Dr. Throop has explained to me that the existence of this distinction among the Romans is problematic enough to need its own careful inquiry. Medievalists might help here by seeking the sources for its inception in our own time period.

[56] Haskins' classic ascription of the major advances to his twelfth century is finally coming under direct challenge, C. Stephen Jaeger, "Pessimism in the Twelfth-Century 'Renaissance'," *Speculum*, 78 (2003): 1151–83 and Jaeger, "John of Salisbury: A Philosopher of the Long Eleventh Century," in John Van Engen and Thomas Noble (eds), *The Twelfth Century* (South Bend, IN, forthcoming).

[57] I noted a couple of important examples of such legal distinctions in *Rancor and Reconciliation*, ch. 7, esp. pp. 218–24. That between crime and tort took a full century to solidify in England from the third quarter of the twelfth century.

in the process of emerging.⁵⁸ Turn first to the *Cur Deus Homo* of Anselm of Canterbury written in the 1090s with help from a monk summoned for the purpose from Bec.⁵⁹ Boso, an old collaborator of Anselm's, had asked if God ought not to forgive His enemies as He told humans they should theirs. Anselm replied sharply that *vindicta* was God's business, but then went on to imply that God often left His anger to be executed by human justice if exercised "recte."⁶⁰ This seems a neat combination of divine vengeance and human justice.⁶¹ Then there is Romans 13;4, a key biblical proof passage that reads (in the traditional translation):

> For he is God's minister to thee, for good. But if thou do that which is evil, fear: for he beareth not the sword in vain. For he is God's minister: an avenger to execute wrath (*vindex in iram*) upon him that doth evil.

The twelfth-century Ordinary Gloss seems to want to have this both ways. Its author explains *vindex in iram* as "propter iram Dei vindicandam, vel vindex in iram Dei ostendendam, quia hec *punitio* indicat persistentes in malo gravius *puniendos*."⁶² Out of anger comes unequivocal punishment. Even if this gloss is grappling with divine rather than human anger, it is noteworthy that enmity and anger leads in the glossator's mid-twelfth-century view to punishment from above. Something of the same flavor emanates from St. Bernard's admonition in the aftermath of the Second Crusade that Pope Eugenius should temper clemency to sinners with zeal in their punishment.⁶³ His language, "qualis ... in donandis iuiuriis, qualis si in ulciscendis" reads more like an injunction to *avenge* Christendom on sinners than an invocation of papal justice. Yet there are again elements of both, for by this

---

⁵⁸ What I said above, Chapter 7, p. 166, already needs modification in the light of what I have learnt from discussion with my co-editor. She is not, however, responsible for this formulation.

⁵⁹ I follow R.W. Southern, *Saint Anselm: Portrait in a Landscape* (Cambridge, 1990), ch. 9, but owe the thought to Heckman, "*Imitatio* in Early Medieval Spirituality," pp. 148–9.

⁶⁰ *Cur Deus Homo*, I.12, ed. F.S. Schmitt, *Opera Omnia* (3 vols, Edinburgh, 1947), ii, p. 70.

⁶¹ Heckman also cites *The OE Version of the Heptateuch, Ælfric's Treatise on the Old and New Testament and his Preface to Genesis*, ed. S.J. Crawford (London, 1922), pp. 71–2. Cf. also for England, Wulfstan's legislation in II Atr 2.1; II Cn 40.2 and their precursors, F. Liebermann, *Die Gesetze der Angelsachsen* (3 vols, Halle: Max Niemeyer, 1903–16), i.222, 340–41.

⁶² Gl. "vindex in iram." I do not attempt here to trace the sources of these glosses, or their precise date.

⁶³ Throop, above Chapter 8, p. 186 cites this. Commentators take the word "donandis" to mean the same as "perdonendis."

time churchmen were coming to see that all such acts should be performed "zelo justicie" and without rancor.[64]

We need to study these and doubtless many other similarly ambiguous undifferentiated texts, to ascertain both the nature of the ambiguity and the precise time frame within which it was resolved. But even when we understand the medieval conceptual transition better, scholars will still wish for certain purposes to use the analytical distinction of our own day. We would not wish to avoid some assessment of the balance between punishments imposed by an authority posing as an impersonal dispenser of justice and private individuals in search of the satisfaction of personal vengeance. The differential consequences are too important culturally to be ignored. Medieval states and proto-states sought to enforce their will on wrongdoers without having to face any tit-for-tat comeback from their family and friends.[65] Their rulers' self-representation as acting in the name of *publica potestas* (public authority) was bound to exert an influence on the understanding of vengeance words and the texts that contained them. This line of inquiry will surely uncover in due course interesting discoveries in the Carolingian and later commentaries on those Old Testament texts that describe an often angry God in very personal terms, a God who can be offended, shamed and dishonored in much the same way as a human man or woman, and who, rather like them, seems to experience joy at the expunction of wrong and its culprits.[66]

My final question takes me beyond humankind altogether. Do non-human animals practice and/or recognize vengeance? Even in our hyper-culturalist age, I find that a number of ideas from studies of animal behavior seem useful to the historian.[67] A small but growing literature suggests that non-human animals can recognize vengeance and that some at least incorporate it into their normal activities.[68] When biologists press the claims of biological over cultural determinants of human behavior, many of us are quick to see a self-serving element in their work, which we fondly believe to be absent from our own. Setting that aside, one of the prime challenges of our day for history and the social sciences is surely to assimilate the best of the biological approaches through so-called evolutionary

---

[64] Dr. Throop gives some examples out of many for this commonplace phrase in Chapter 8 above.

[65] Hence, for example, those Old English laws that forbade vengeance taken for legitimate executions of thieves (John Hudson, "Faide, vengeance et violence en Angleterre (ca 900–1200)," in Barthélemy, Bougard and Le Jan (eds), *La vengeance 400–1200*, pp. 341–82, at pp. 353–4.

[66] I have, at Dr. Throop's urging, myself used Timothy Gorringe, *God's Just Vengeance: Crime, Violence, and the Rhetoric of Salvation* (Cambridge, 1996) as a guide here.

[67] F. de Waal, *Peacemaking Among Primates* (Cambridge, Mass., 1989), pp. 261–3 is especially to be recommended in the present context, and cf. his *Good Natured* (Cambridge, Mass., 1996), pp. 154–62.

[68] Clutton-Brock and Parker, "Punishment in Animal Societies," cited above, is a good survey of fairly recent studies.

psychology with the best of the textual and other insights of postmodernism and other brands of culturalism, while gently abandoning the associated lunacies.[69] Medieval historians certainly appear to have something substantial to gain from the attempt.

Students of non-human animal behavior look for instances of negative reciprocity, that is, actions that respond to unwanted acts the animals have received from others of their kind. This can cover all the acts which students of human behavior carefully divide into vengeance and punishment in human parlance. And biologists, like historians and other students of human behavior, juxtapose this negative reciprocity with the positive acts whose importance, perhaps even centrality, historians have learned to study under the head of gift exchange. A first lesson from this literature is to ponder how biologists can collapse the distinction between vengeance itself and punishment, which is so patently important to many human cultures, not least that which was developing during the European Middle Ages. One sees how greatly any such distinction rests on a communication system equipped to display within itself the richness of thought and feeling underlying human cultures. Although we have learned to surrender belief in a human monopoly of "culture" in some important senses, few non-human communication systems come anything close to the capacity of human language to convey and transmit these subtle distinctions and nuances.

Animal analogs may assist us first to single out the dynamics common to all or many species, including some with minimal ratiocinatory capacity, and then will prod us to determine what is—and is not—distinctively human. The ability and need to distinguish between "horizontal" acts of vengeance and the more vertical or "downwards" imposition of punishment, as in the semantic progress of such words as "ultio" and "vindicta" just discussed, seems to be one of the most distinctive of these characteristics. This important finding should reassure us as to the essentially cultural character of the distinction and thus the value and importance of the text-based efforts to penetrate its inner workings.

In other instances, animal observations add context to ones concerning past humans. Many animals, for example, muster support from kin and other allies when competing for dominance. They craft friendships in terms of shared interest, stemming especially from previous consciously reciprocal acts, in other words from something very close to gift exchange. Instantaneous negative reciprocity, on the other hand, might be purely instinctual. Any lapse of time would, however, rule it out for any animal unable to identify an individual enemy or offender as the one that had inflicted the previous harm. Memory and the ability to retrieve or revive it are thus confirmed as a necessary premise for vengeance. There is plentiful anecdotal evidence that some animals, dogs and horses, but also ravens and other corvids, can identify humans who have maltreated them in the past—and

---

[69] P.J. Richerson and R. Boyd, *Not by Genes Alone* (Chicago and London, 2005) shows this process under way.

in the ravens' case, their cars too![70] Animal kin recognition is obviously securely documented from observational as well as experimental studies. We can be confident that our primate cousins (chimpanzees etc.) strike lasting alliances in order to dominate their peers and spread their genes more widely than they could manage otherwise. The mechanics bear resemblances to those noted by students of medieval and other micropolitics.[71]

The other suggestive link between human and non-human behavior patterns is in the means used by and on adversaries to promote reconciliation. These generally include actual physical contact and visible gestures, stretching at times to "makeup" sex. The differences are again as telling as the resemblances. Animals, perhaps because they are closer to the evolutionary process and less buffered by culture, focus more directly on changing their enemies' behavior in ways that favor their own evolutionary success via dominance and sexual opportunities, and so on. Humans apparently settle a lower proportion of their conflicts than non-humans, and are, to say the least, unusual in regard to the ease with which they kill their own species. Very few animals if any perform capital punishment on offenders and then do not even proceed to eat the corpses.

This pitifully thin sample of comparisons could usefully encourage us to pay fuller note to the contentions of biologists and their colleagues. It reinforces the sense, for instance, that the study of medieval vengeance has focused too closely on the spectacular cases that led to violence and bloodshed. We should, perhaps, integrate this sub-field more closely into the broader study of conflict in general. More importantly, these data bolster the arguments for seeing vengeance as a natural part of medieval (and modern) life. There is no danger that such an approach will generate a biological determinism, so long as we continue to immerse ourselves primarily in our written sources, and recall the much larger amount that has been lost.[72] Despite the great advances made during my working lifetime that have destroyed claims of a human monopoly of culture, I see little likelihood that new discoveries are likely to dethrone human culture based around the language instinct as the richest game in town, representing much the most complex buffer between any species and the machinations of its selfish genes. In the meantime, the understanding of medieval vengeance has at least as much to gain from further study as that of animal punishment.[73]

---

[70] Bernd Heinrich, *Ravens in Winter* (New York, 1989).

[71] De Waal (above n. 67), should suffice to make the interim case. Evidence suggestive of early medieval polygyny might also be considered here, as, for example, in Margaret Clunies Ross, "Concubinage in Anglo-Saxon England," *Past & Present*, 108 (1985).

[72] Recent trends in biology help here. My layman's impression is that students of genetics emphasize first the complexity of the interplay between genes and behavior, but also that they make much of the way environment (read: culture?) affects and can in early development change nerve connections and thus the way that biological factors present and function.

[73] Clutton-Brock and Parker, "Punishment in Animal Societies," p. 215: "firm experimental evidence ... is now badly needed."

Vengeance emerges from scrutiny as natural in several senses. The urge to avenge wrongs and insults may be hardwired. But the forms within which men and women conceive of vengeance and seek to control it to their own ends are mostly contrived and cultural. They try to implement these in ways that *seem* as natural as they can be. When they refer to feud support groups, for instance, as if these consisted of blood kinsmen alone, they were knowingly stretching a point, using the kinship metaphor to make what were often highly instrumental political acts seem more natural. The whole complex apparatus of feud required conscious human intervention at every point, in a way that was not necessarily true of one-off vengeance. It may have originated in conscious calculation long ago, but could only have reached its present form through generations of imitation and adaptation to events.[74]

Thus they were able to pay lip service at least to the principle of leaving vengeance to the Lord, secure in the knowledge that this licensed their own powers-that-be to implement that vengeance on the Lord's behalf, and so gave rulers the opportunity (then as, alas, still now) to pursue their own vendettas while passing the responsibility on to the Lord. The results are not always bad. Peace in the feud may be neither automatic and easy nor ever comfortable and complete. Yet until the advent of political entities with the power to claim in plausible terms a monopoly of the use of force, the tit-for-tat of vengeance and its response may have offered the best chance in an imperfect world of peacemaking and the staving off of chaos. The prime responsibility of nation states, we believe (or did until 9/11 appeared to change the rules once more) is to keep order, do good justice and ensure the security of those who live within their frontiers.

Our residual problem today may be that the very instincts and emotional drives that served defensible ends in the early Middle Ages as the least bad solution to the challenge of managing violence, and the vices that promote it, have easily survived into the age of nation states and beyond. This is our legacy to our children and grandchildren. It is also an invitation to medieval historians to integrate the specialist study of vengeance into the general political and social history of their period, and see if this does not reveal what worked well and less well for our medieval predecessors and how their circumstances shifted the priorities. The more we know, the more we recognize our remaining ignorance. Here we surely have, as Marc Bloch might have said, "une enquête à poursuivre," and one that the contributors to the current volume can fairly claim to have usefully set in progress.

---

[74] The discussion in Richerson and Boyd, *Not by Genes Alone*, ch. 4 of the interaction of imitation and social learning, though rather different in direction, is full of analyses useful to the student of Bourdieu's *habitus* (which it does not, however, mention) and for our own interest in vengeance.

Index

Aaron 22
Abbey of Bec 122
Abbey of Saint-Évroult 122, 129
Abbey of Saint-Ouen of Rouen 131
Abel 22
Abiram 33
Abravanel 92
Abret, Abraham 89
Acquigny 123
Acquittal (*sentença de luyramento*) 99 (*see also* Pardon)
Acts of Andrew and Matthias 33
Acts of Thomas 23, 33
Adomnán 8, 14, 17, 18, 22, 25, 34
Áed Dubh 19
Áed Róin, King 29
Aemulatio see Emulation
Afonso V, King of Portugal 85, 92
Afranio 139–42, 144, 145, 149
Aggression 181
Aḥmad, son of Muḥammad Dedo 94
Aithech fortha 32
Aix-la-Chapelle 112
Alcalde or *al-qāḍī* (judge) 96, 97
Alcobaça, Cistercian monastery of 90
Alenquer 89
Alentejo region 93
Alexander III, Pope 181
Algazi, Gadi 52n, 108, 174, 175n, 211n
Allegiance 2, 108
Alliance 108, 154, 156
Alquiveny, Aḥmad 92
Althoff, Gerd 127, 205n, 206
Ambition 81
Ambush 69
Anarchy 121
Anathema 110
Angevin chronicle 120
Annals of Flodoard 105, 106
Anonymous of Halberstadt 187

Anselm of Canterbury 216
Anselm of Lucca 187
Anthropology 1, 3, 105, 126
  Anthropologie historique 126
Antioch 179
Antwerp 147
Apocryphon 21
Apostasy 18, 19
Apostles 22, 33, 36, 37
Aquinas, Thomas 200
Aquitaine 105, 109
Arbitration 81
Archbishop Artaud 110
Archbishop Pecham 190
Archbishop Robert 121
Archbishop of Rouen 133
Archibald, earl of Moray 70
Armenians 181
Armstrong, Jackson 2, 54n, 72n, 79n, 81n, 82n, 161n, 206, 213n
Arnold of Lübeck 182, 186, 195
Arnulf, bishop of Halberstadt 187
Arrogance 23 (*see also* Pride)
Arronches 94, 95
Ascelin, son of Andre 133
Assythment 75, 78
Athanasius 200
Audita tremendi 181
Augustine 191
Augustinians 185
Aurelio 138–41, 143–5, 149
Avenge *see* Vengeance
Axiology 149

Bacéne 27
Bachall 32
Bagasse 91
Bakhtin, Mikhail 148
Baldness 31
Baldric of Bourgeuil 194

Baldwin II, king of Jerusalem 180
Barnon of Glos 121
de Barros, Maria Filomena Lopes 96
Barthélemy, Dominique ix, 3, 109n, 116n, 118n, 119n, 120n, 134n, 151n, 155n, 177n, 178n, 205n, 217n
Barton, Richard 192, 199
Basher, William 153
Beauclerc, Henry 133
Beaumont family 134
Bede 185, 196
Bellême 121, 129, 131, 135
Bellême family
    Ivo of 130
    Mabel of 128, 129
    Robert of 122, 128, 129, 133–6
    Warin of 122
Bennett, Matthew 107n, 116n, 118, 121
Bernard of Clairvaux 178, 179, 184, 186–8, 192, 194, 196, 198, 216
Bertold, archbishop of Bremen 186
Berwickshire 59
Berwick-upon-Tweed 55, 65
Bethada 5, 7–9, 24–6, 34, 35
Betrayal/treachery 17, 30, 105, 107, 110, 111, 113
    Treason 108, 110, 133
    Treason law 111
Bible
    Acts 37, 188
    and Cursing 16
    Deuteronomy 5n, 73n, 195n
    Exodus 188n, 194–5
    Galatians 191
    Genesis 37, 189n, 74
    Matthew 190n, 209n
    New Testament 13, 16, 17, 23, 33, 35–7, 192
    Old Testament 13, 16, 17, 22–4, 33, 35–7, 191, 217
    Pentateuch 36
    Revelation 131
    Romans 184, 198
    and Vengeance 22, 39–50, 119, 129, 198–9, 204, 213
Biothanatus 130
Bishop of Séez 130, 135
Bishop of St. Andrews 55, 76

James Kennedy, bishop of St. Andrews 58, 61, 66, 70
St. Andrews Cathedral 76
Blasphemy 28, 32, 137
Blessing 37
Blindness 26, 27, 28, 33
Bloch, Howard 139n, 147
Bloch, Marc 71n, 125, 220
Blood (bodily fluid) 40, 49, 122–3, 130, 163, 169, 172, 180, 182–3, 195, 205, 208, 209
Blood (symbol) 124, 156, 220 (*see also* "Blood-feud" under Feud)
Blood-thirstiness 127
Book of Lismore 9
Book of Wisdom 23
Boso 216
Bourdieu, Pierre 67n, 160, 170, 171n, 220n
Brémule 123
Brigandage 26
Brionne 123, 132
Broichan 18, 19
Brownlee, Marina 3
Bucar family
    Aḥmad 92
    'Alī 92
Byzantines 182

Caeiro 96
Caeiro family
    'Abd Allāh 95
    Aḥmad 93–8
    'Alī 94–7
    Bakr 95
    'Umār 94, 96
Cáin Adomnáin 20, 25
Cain 22
de Cambrai, Raoul 111
du Cange, Charles 188, 196
Cannibalism 144
Carolingian 113, 217
Castellan of Melun 110
Castile 88, 90, 94
Castle of Melun 111
Castle of Saint-Céneri 128
Castro, Américo 86
Castus (chaste) 149
Cathars 182, 183

Catharsis 146
Cego, 'Alī Chanque 87
Ceuta 96
de Ceuta family
    'Abd Allāh 95
    Aḥmad 95
Chansons de geste 112, 151, 166, 175
Chanson d'Antioche 193
Charity 23
Charroux 109
Chevalerie 106
Chibnall, Marjorie 115n, 119, 179n
Chirnside 76
    William of 69, 70, 72, 76, 77
Chivalric epics 112
Chivalry 111, 120
Chramnesind 110
Christian, William 200
Church 129, 134
Church of Lisieux 131
de Clare, Richard 32
Clement III, Pope 182
Clermont 111, 180, 210
Clito, William 124
Cockburnspath 60
Cogitosus 8, 20, 23
Coirpre mac Néill 17
Coldingham
    Bailiary of 55, 58, 64, 67, 74–6
    Barony of 61
    Prior of 61, 65
    Priory of 53–5, 59, 62, 65, 66, 68, 71
Collectio Canonum Hibernensis 16
Collyngwood 77
Colmán mac Luacháin 29
Compensation payments 211
Competition 196
Compromise 72, 75, 78, 80, 81
Comunas 86, 91
Conches 123, 128
Conciliation 79
Conduct 134
Conflict 1, 2, 21, 27, 51, 52n, 53–4, 55–6, 58, 60, 64, 66, 68, 71–5, 79–82, 85, 87n, 97–8, 108–11, 116n, 117, 119, 120, 123–4, 135, 146, 140, 152, 157–8, 160, 163–7, 173–4, 219
    (*see also* Dispute)

Conflict management/resolution 51, 53, 63, 72–3, 75, 77–80, 98, 141, 157, 163
Constable, Giles 180n, 196, 197n, 198n
Contention 23
Convivencia 86
Corictic 11, 30
Cormicy 109
Council of Lambeth 190
Council of Sainte-Macre 110
Council of Trosly 110
Courage 112
Cowdrey, H.E.J. 187n, 200, 201n
Crichton, Chancellor 58
Crime 15n, 29–31, 51–3, 85n, 89, 94, 115n, 146, 155n, 157–9, 185, 186, 195, 209, 210n, 212, 215n, 217n
    and Tort 157–9, 215n
Crusades 177–9, 181–3, 188, 193, 197, 198, 200
    Crusading texts 189, 193
    First Crusade 177, 178, 193, 194, 200
    Second Crusade 179, 180, 185
    Third Crusade 180, 182, 216
    Fifth Crusade 183
Cur Deus Homo 216
Cursing/malediction 5–7, 9, 14–16, 19, 23, 25, 27, 29, 30, 35, 37
Cusin, John 153, 154, 161
Cusin, Simon 153
Cusins 154

Damascus 180
Dampnum 210
De Duodecim Abusivis Saeculi 19, 20, 23, 36
Deafness 28
Debonereté 210
Defiance 125, 136
Definition(s) 6, 7, 9, 25, 52n, 94, 116, 117, 118, 119, 120, 147, 155, 156–8, 160, 163, 167, 173, 175, 189, 191, 192, 196, 205
Derclaid 17
Desire (*libido*) 145–6, 149, 150, 186, 188
    Vengeful desire 187
Devil 200
Devotion 189
Diarmait mac Cerbhaill 34

Dib línaib 25
Díbergaig (brigands) 18, 23
Díguin 15
Discourse 137–49 *passim*, 151–2, 155, 158, 161, 164, 173, 175, 193, 201, 205
Dishonor 7, 67, 81, 217 (*see also* Humiliation)
Disobedience 23
Displicuit 15, 19, 20, 31
Dispute 2, 8, 52–5, 58, 61–2, 64–6, 71–3, 75, 77–82, 90, 96, 98–9, 108, 117, 123, 129, 135, 140n, 141, 153n, 155, 157–8, 160–61, 163, 164n, 165, 169–70, 172n, 173–5, 207n (*see also* Conflict)
Distinction between
    Crime and Tort 157–8
    Feud and Bloodfeud 117
    Feud and Customary Vengeance 164, 168
    Feud and Politics 157
    Guerra and *Bellum* 120, 166
    Myth and Novel 148
    Public and Private 161
    Retributive Justice and Revenge 214
    Vengeance and Punishment 167, 215
    Vengeance, single and iterated acts of 164, 169
Dominicans 184
Douglas (Black), Earls of 54, 56–8, 63, 65, 66, 70, 74, 81
    Archibald, 4th Earl of Douglas 58
    Archibald, 5th Earl of Douglas 57, 64
    William Earl of Douglas 68, 70
    William, 8th Earl of Douglas 63, 64, 74
Douglas (Red), Earls of Angus 56, 57, 58, 60, 61, 63, 66, 75, 81
    James, 3rd Earl of Angus 57, 62, 64, 73
    William, 2nd Earl of Angus 56, 59
    William, 8th Earl of Angus 58
Drax, William 60, 61, 64
Drengot, Osmond 122
Dudo of Saint-Quentin 111
Duel, judicial 139
Dunbar castle 56, 63, 68, 70, 75
Dunbar, Earls of March 56, 69, 70, 75, 81
    Archibald, son of Earl of March 63, 69, 70
    George, 10th Earl of March 56, 58, 69
    Patrick 56, 69
Dunglass, Collegiate church of 76
Durham 55, 59, 60, 62, 82, 164
    Prior of 55, 59, 64, 74, 77

Edessa 180, 193
Edinburgh 57, 68
Egypt 181, 195
Ekkehard of Aura 179, 184, 186, 188, 196
Elias, Norbert 126
El Abencerraje y la Hermosa Jarifa 147
Elijah 13, 22, 33, 35–7
Elisha 22, 35, 37
Elvas 90, 91
Emasculation 30
Emotion 124–7, 131–3, 157–8, 175, 177–201 *passim*, 203–5, 210
    Anger 2, 5, 6, 18, 73, 81, 120, 125, 127, 134, 189–94, 199, 200, 201, 212
    Divine 216
    Human 216
    Ira per zelum 190–91, 194
    Iratus 125
    Righteous 191, 194
    Vicious 190
    Virtuous 190
    Zealous 192
Envy 189
Fear 2, 134, 153, 169
Grief 2, 81
Jealousy (*jaloux*) 188–90, 196
Joy 217
Love 2, 140, 154, 186–9, 191, 197–9, 201
    Christian love 188, 189, 192
    Illicit love 143, 149
    Love of God 188, 192, 200
    Passionate love 188
Passion (*studium*) 178, 185, 188, 189, 200, 204
Rancor 116, 123, 124, 128, 132, 133, 135, 136, 217
Resentment 134
Shame 2, 67, 81, 162, 163, 173, 175, 192, 193, 217

Taboo 2
Zeal 127, 133, 135, 178–201, 216
  Zelo justicie 217
Emotional communities 200, 205
Emulation 37, 149 (*see also* Imitation)
  Aemulatio 184, 188–9, 196–9
  Aemulatio Christi 198
Énda 13, 24
Enemy 159, 160, 162, 188–9
  Common enemy 128–9
  Family enemy 153
  of God 10n, 42–3, 46, 49, 192, 195, 216
  of Mankind (i.e. Satan) 129, 200
Enguerrand of Ponthieu 122
Enmity 53, 108, 154, 165, 166, 169, 172, 208 (*see also* Hatred and Malice)
  Capital (*Inimicicias capitales*) 53
  Mortal (*Inimicitia mortalis*) 53n, 103, 108, 152n, 165
  Relations d'inimitie 106
Epic 148
Erdmann, Carl 177
Esáin (driving away) 15
Essentialism 152
Étach (refusal) 15
Eugenius III, Pope 186, 188, 196, 198, 216
Eurydice 145
Eustache of Breteuil 119, 133
Evans-Pritchard, E.E. 105, 117
Évora 93, 94, 96, 97, 98
Evreux 125, 133
Excommunication 105, 110
Executions 25, 34, 42, 49, 72, 87, 168–9, 211n, 217n
Exempla 33, 184, 196, 197
Exmes 134
Eye for an Eye 214

Face-saving 125, 173, 212
Faide chevaleresque 109
Failbe, King 27, 32
Fáistinid 16
Faith 119
Faithfulness 78, 81
Fasting 12–15, 23, 24, 29, 30
Favor (*favere*) 188
Fealty 121, 125

Feargaigther 30
Fernandes, João 93–6, 98, 100, 102
Fervent (*fervere*) 188
Feud 2, 51–3, 72, 81, 94, 97–9, 105, 107, 110, 116–31, 133–6, 152–7, 159, 163, 165–70, 172–5, 206–10, 212, 220
  Blood-feud 52n, 71n, 72n, 75n, 78n, 80n, 86, 93, 98, 99n, 110, 117–21, 123, 129, 155n, 156n
  Definition of 116, 117–20, 155, 160, 163, 165, 173, 175
  Feud-game 134
  Feud-like 81, 82, 154, 155, 168, 169, 175, 206
  Feud-oriented 107
  Feud repertoires 160
  Feud-tales 115, 122, 127, 130, 134
  Knightly feud 3, 110
  Law and 80, 82, 131n, 133, 152n, 153, 156, 165, 168, 169, 179–80, 180, 181, 186, 187, 206, 210n, 217
  Score 160
Feudalism 106, 152
Fíachu mac Néill 17
Fidelity 132, 143, 144
Fief 105, 106
FitzJohns 154, 159
  Thomas FitzJohn 153, 154
Flodoard 107–11
de Flores, Juan 137
Flori, Jean 177
Forgiveness 13, 16, 26, 31, 135, 185, 186, 214n, 216
  Failure to forgive merits vengeance 32
Foucault, Michel 137
Franco, Aḥmad 95
Franco family 96
Frederick I, Emperor 182
Freud, Sigmund 3, 211n
Friend, Friendship 77, 78, 81, 108, 156
Fulk I, King of Jerusalem 189

Gaels 36
Game image 117, 133, 134, 135, 149, 206–7, 212, 219
Ganelon 161
Gauls 112

Geary, Patrick 53n, 71n, 72, 75n, 79n, 108
Generosity 23
Geneva Conventions 212
Genocide 137, 141, 146, 150–51, 169, 209
Geoffrey of Mortagne 128
Gerald of Aurillac 105
Gerald of Wales 5, 7
Germany 108
Gesta Normannorum Ducum 115, 121, 122
Ghālib 93
Gifts 211
Gift-exchange 75, 79, 218
Gilbert du Pin 123
Gilbert of Brionne 121, 122, 132
Gilbert of Laigle 128, 134
Gillingham, John 120, 206n
Girard, René 145, 146
Giroie family
    Arnold Giroie 128
    Fulk Giroie 121
    Giroie son of Giroie 131
    Hugh Giroie 128
    Robert Giroie 121, 128
    William Giroie 122
Glossa Ordinaria 170n, 185, 204n, 209n, 216
Glucksmann, Max 117
Goading 172, 205
God 119, 129, 141, 200
    of Vengeance 10, 32n, 39, 46, 110, 131, 135, 158, 186, 194–5, 216
    Old Gospel God 119
Goel, Ascelin 127, 128, 133
Gonçalves, Martim 93
Gontheir 122
Grace 14, 37, 198
Gregory VIII, Pope 35, 181
Grisel y Mirabella 137
Guedelha, ʿAlī 95
Guibert of Nogent 196
Guillaume of Jumièges 115, 121
Guillot, Olivier 105
Guilt 185, 191, 199
Guizot 106

Habitus 170, 171, 220n
Hailes castle 56, 63, 69, 70, 71
Halsall, Guy ix, 52n, 107, 116n, 151n, 155n, 163–9

Harenc, Ralph 119
Harmony 105
Hatred 128, 154, 171, 189, 190, 192, 194, 199 (*see also* Enmity and Malice)
Hay, Edmund 77
Heaven 20, 143
Hebrew 191
Heckman, Christina 197, 211n, 216n
Helwise, Countess 125
Henry of Glinden 186
Henry I, King of England 119, 120, 124, 125, 133–6
Henry II, King of England 180, 181
Hepburn family 53, 62, 63, 69–72, 74–6, 79, 81
    Sir Adam, of Hailes 56, 57, 61–4, 66, 68–70, 73, 77–9
    Agnes 79
    Archibald 79
    Patrick 63, 68–70, 75–9
    William 78
Herbert II 109
Heredity, rights of 132, 133
Herluin of Montreuil 107, 122
Hincmar of Rheims 190
Historia Ecclesiastica 115, 119, 121, 122
Historie de Aurelio and Isabell 137, 138, 141, 145, 146, 147, 148, 149, 150
Histories of Richer of Rheims 105, 106, 110
Holy Spirit 188
Homage 106, 107, 108, 111, 113, 207
Homicide 190
Honor 2, 7, 11, 14–15, 27, 29–30, 32, 42, 53, 67–8, 77–8, 81–2, 98, 105, 107, 111–12, 117, 120, 123–5, 130–31, 135, 160, 161, 175, 210–12, 217
Honor-price (*enech*) 11, 14, 15, 27, 29
Hortensia 139–46
Hospitality 14, 17, 24, 25
Hostility 125, 197
House assault 153, 161
Hudson, John vii, 118n, 119, 120n, 151n, 175n, 217n
Hugh Capet, King of France 106, 110–13
Hugh le Poer (brother of Waleran) 132
Hugh of Burgundy 181
Hugh of Jaffa 189
Hugh of Chester 133

Hugh the archbishop 110
Human reason 204
Hume family 53, 60–64, 66, 70, 71, 73–5, 78, 79, 81
    Alexander (of that Ilk) 58–79
    Alexander (of that Ilk (younger)) 58–62, 79
    David, of Wedderburn 58–68, 71, 73–8
    Ellen 79
    George 77, 78
    Patrick 66, 67
    Thomas 78
Humiliation 29, 30, 161 (*see also* Dishonor)
Humility 16, 23, 198
Ḥuṣayn 94, 95
Hyams, Paul 3, 52n, 68n, 71n, 72n, 79n, 98, 106n, 116n, 118n, 125n, 154n, 155n, 157n, 161n, 164n, 165n, 169n, 170n, 190, 193n, 205n

Icelandic sagas 107
Imitatio see Imitation
Imitation 143, 194–9, 211n, 216n, 220 (*see also* Emulation)
    Imitatio 196, 197, 199
    Imitatio Christi 35, 36, 198
Incest 2, 137, 138, 141, 144, 146, 148, 149
Infancy Gospel of Thomas 22, 33
Ingo 112, 113
Injury 2, 11, 15, 27, 30, 53, 77, 82, 95, 101–2, 127, 153, 159–60, 169, 180–81, 183, 185–7, 190, 192–5, 199, 203, 207n, 210–11
Innocence 185
Innocent II, Pope 186
Innocent III, Pope 178, 181, 183, 189, 191, 194, 195
Insults 7, 128
Integrity 143, 146
Intercessions 108
Isabell 138–46, 149
Ishmael 195
Isidore of Seville 147
Itinerarium peregrinorum 181, 182
d'Ivry, Raoul 111

Jackobson, Roman 147
James I, King of Scotland 56, 59, 76, 82

James II, King of Scotland 57, 58, 59, 62, 82
James of Vitry 183, 184, 195, 197, 198
James the Gross 57, 58, 62, 64–8, 74
Jerusalem 179, 180, 189, 191, 193
Jesus/Christ 13, 20–22, 35, 37, 185, 193, 196
Jews 85, 86, 88, 89, 92, 93, 179, 181, 184, 185, 191, 195, 196, 198
Joachim of Fiore 185
Johnson, Máire 2, 18n, 212–13
João I, King of Portugal 85, 88
João II, King of Portugal 85, 92
Judaism *see* Jews
Judiarias 86
    Judiaria Grande 87
Justice 2, 52, 105, 138, 146, 158, 174, 180, 186–8, 200, 214, 216, 217, 220
    Downwards 158
    Retributive 214

Kamp, Hermann 108, 134n
Kin, Kinship 2, 70, 71, 77, 78, 81, 96, 98, 156
King (unnamed) 139, 142, 143, 145, 146, 149
Kiss of peace 113
Knights Templar 177, 184, 197
Kristeva, Julia 149

Land, importance of 68–70, 108, 109
Languedoc 183
Láparo, Qāsim 87
Lasair 25, 36
Last Supper 145
Latrones 18
Latrunculi 18
Lauer, Philippe 106n, 111
Law 150, 156, 158, 159, 162, 192
    Ancient Hebrew 119
    Anglo-Saxon 168n, 173, 217n
    English Common 155, 157, 174
    of God 22
    of Innocents 18
    Judicial 138
    Mosaic 35, 36
    Natural 138
    Roman 165, 167

Secular 210
of War 212
Lazarillo de Tormes 147
Lebor Gabála Érenn 36
Le Goff, Jacques 71n, 79n, 126
Leges Henrici Primi 174
Les 13
Letter of Jesus on Sunday Observance 17, 31
Levites 22
Life of St. Anthony 200
Linguectomy 154
Lisbon 85, 87–9, 91–3, 180
Literati 215
Little, Lester 5, 6n, 7n, 16n
Livingstons 58
Local conflict 54, 64
Lochru 10, 11, 21
Loegaire 17
Loire 105
Longing 189
Longsword, William 107, 108, 111–13
Lords and lordship 64, 72–4, 81, 106
Lord of Montigny-Lengrain 110
Lothar, King of France 112, 113
Louis IV, King of France 110, 111
Louis VI, King of France 133
Louis VII, King of France 179, 181
Loyalty 78, 81, 112, 113
Luke of La Barre 134, 135

Maccabees 179, 181
Madness 30
Maedóc 13, 28
Maldacht 9
Malice 68–9, 149, 195 (*see also* Enmity and Hatred)
Manuel, King of Portugal 86
Marriage 58, 63, 67n, 78–9, 128, 132, 138, 149, 152, 211n
Martyr 198
Martyrdom 145, 200, 211
Marvão 93, 94
Master Abraham 89
Master José 88
Matador 99
Mediations 108
Merchant 31
Mercy 13–15, 19, 23, 134

Merovingians 110
Mesnie Hellequin 136
Metamorphoses 145
Meulan family 134
Galeran of 123
Robert of 132, 134
Waleran of 132, 133
Miller, William Ian 68n, 71n, 99n, 107, 117n, 118, 156n, 198, 204n, 205–14 *passim*
Military service 89
Miracle, Miracle story 6, 22, 31, 32, 37, 130, 139, 143, 150
Miracula 7
Mock (*irridere*) 189
Montfort family
Amaury of Montfort 127, 133
Richard of Montfort 123, 127, 128
Mór feirge 25
Morocco 88, 89
Mortal hatreds 108
Moses 13, 16, 22–4, 33, 35–7
Mourarias 86, 87
Mouros forros 86
Muirchú 8, 21
Murder 17, 25, 47, 87, 93–6, 98–100, 102–3, 105, 107, 120–22, 128–9, 138, 141, 159–61, 168, 185–6, 208
Muslims 85, 86, 89, 91–4, 96, 180, 181, 193, 195, 197
Muteness 28, 32
Mutilation 133, 153, 154
Myth 148

Navarro 92
Negative or maledictory prophecy 9, 16, 17, 19, 23, 25, 35, 37
Negotiation 80
Negro 92
Niermeyer 189, 196
Nietzsche, Frederick 1, 208n
Nirenberg, David 87
Nisbet, James 69, 70
Nisbet, Robert 69, 72, 76, 77
Normans 112
Northumberland 65
Norway, King of 120
The Nuer 105, 117

Oath 113
Odo the Fat 121
Odo I of Blois 110, 111
Ogle, John 77
Oll, John, Prior of Coldingham 61–6, 68, 70
Olmstead, Everett 137
O'Leary, Aideen 21
Orpheus 145
Osbern the duke's steward 121
Other Knight 139, 141
Otto II, Emperor 112, 113
Outlaws 18
Ovid 145

Pagan 17, 23
Pantoul, William 128, 129
Paralyzed 29
Pardon/s 31, 87, 89, 93–6, 100, 109, 142, 168n, 186, 205n (*see also* Acquittal)
Paris 112
Passive retaliatory judgement 9, 19, 20, 21, 23, 26, 28, 29, 30, 34
Pasturing 21
Patience 172
Paul the apostle 22, 184, 191, 196
Paupers 23
Peace 192, 220 (*see also* Reconciliation)
　Pacification 72, 78, 80, 81
　Peace homage 211
　Peace of God 109, 110
　Peace offering 169
　Peace settlement 153, 169, 208
　Peace treaties 108, 157
　Peacemaking 53, 72–81, 98, 128, 153
　　Lords' role in 72–4
Peasants 130
Penance 13, 19, 20, 23–6, 28, 30–32, 34, 35, 144
Pedro, Prince 85, 88, 92, 93
Penitentials 18
Pentecostal flame 188
Peter, Bishop of Oporto 180
Peter II, King of Aragon 183
Peter of Les Vaux-de-Cernay 182
Peter the Hermit 193
Peter the Venerable 179, 186
Philip II, King of France 120, 180, 181, 183

Phineas 191
Piety 127
Pillaging 18, 108, 109, 111, 112
Pilgrimage 211
Pilum 130
Piperdean 57, 69
Plantagenet, Geoffrey 123, 125, 134, 135
Power struggle 96–8
Prayer 9–12, 14, 19, 21, 24
Pride 18, 135 (*see also* Arrogance)
Private contractual relationship 106
Processo de cartas de amores 147
Processual approach 153
Profane 137
Prophecy 16, 22, 23, 34, 36, 37
Protagonist 148
Proverbs and maxims 206–7, 209
Provocateurs 23
Psalter 35
Publica potestas 217
Public order 105
Publicity 66–7, 76, 79, 138, 160–61, 162n, 184, 192, 207–8, 213
Punishment 5, 20, 23, 25, 26, 28, 32, 116n, 160, 208n
　Capital punishment 95, 134, 159, 211, 219
　Divine punishment 39–40, 129–30, 131n, 186, 191, 194, 195, 216
　Legal/of crime 52, 133, 146, 153, 157, 158, 209
　in Relation to vengeance and feud 119, 157, 164, 166–7, 169, 186, 195, 212, 215–18

Quarrel of the Sexes 137
Queen 139, 141–6
　Queen mother (of Scotland) 58, 63

Rabi-menor 97
Raids 80
Ralph of Coggeshall 182
Ralph of Gace 121
Ralph of Tosny 123, 128, 134, 135
Ransoms 123, 128
Raymond of St. Gilles 179
Reais brancos 87
Rebellion 132–5

Reciprocity 6, 70, 164, 167, 204, 209, 211, 218
Recompense *see* Retribution
Reconciliation 113, 192 (*see also* Peace)
Reddy, William 178
Regal authority 144
Reginald of Bailleul 125
Reiner 183
Religious faith 192
Renaud of Roucy 109
Repertoire 152, 154, 160, 163
Repostel, William 122
Reprisals 98
Res publica 111
Restitution 12, 20
Retaliation *see* Revenge
Retribution 7, 11, 12, 20, 23–6, 29, 35, 37, 75, 80–82, 112, 142, 164, 187, 195, 209, 214
Revenge 2, 9, 21, 66, 70, 214
  Revenge acts 209
  Revenge killings 98, 118, 209
  Revenge narratives 154
Reynald of Châtillon 182
Reynolds, Susan vii, 106
Rhine 105
Richard I, King of England 180
Richardson 147
Richer of Laigle 123, 133, 135
Richer of Rheims 107, 111, 112
Rigord 181
Riley-Smith, Jonathan ix, 177, 189, 190n, 197n
Rivalry 188, 196, 197
Robert, Duke of Normandy 121, 132–5
Robert of Auxerre 182, 183
Robert of Beauchamp 132
Robert of Chaumont 131
Robert of Courçon 183
Robert of Grandmesnil 122
Robert of Leicester 131
Robert of Neubourg 133
Robert son of Baldwin 132
Roche, Thomas 3, 179n, 208
Roger II, King of Sicily 179
Roger of Beaumont 132
Roger of Montgomery 129
Roger of Tosny 131

Roger, Viscount of Cotentin 123
Roland 162
Romance 148, 149, 151
Rosenwein, Barbara 5n, 6n, 7n, 67n, 125n, 127n, 172n, 178n, 190n, 192n, 200n, 204, 210n
Rotrou of Mortagne 135
Rotrou of Perche 122
Roxburgh 54
Royal justiciar 65

Sacred 137
Sacrifice
  Ritual sacrifice 145, 146
  Self-sacrifice 143, 181, 183, 189, 197, 199, 201, 211
Sailm escaine (cursing psalms) 10
Saint Áed mac Bricc 31
Saint Andrew 33
Saint Anselm 210
Saint Baithéne 28
Saint Berach 29
Saint Brigit 5, 8, 9, 10, 12–15, 19, 20, 23–5, 27, 28, 34–6
Saint Camna 28
Saint Ciarán of Saigir 28
Saint Coemgen 31, 36
Saint Colmán Élo 18, 28
Saint Columba 5, 8–10, 14, 15, 17–19, 22–4, 30, 34
Saint Comgall 30
Saint Cuthbert 55
Saint Eógan 24
Saint Faenche 24
Saint Féchín 28, 32
Saint Fínán Cam 32
Saint Finnchua 30, 36
Saint Finnian 29
Saint Fintan 30
Saint John 22
Saint Michael, Prior of 183
Saint Mochoemóg 27, 36
Saint Mocholmóg 29
Saint Mochta 31
Saint Patrick 5, 8–15, 17, 21–4, 29, 30, 31, 34–6
Saint Peter 21, 22, 36
Saint Ruadán 34

Index

Sanctity 21, 23
Santarém 88, 89
Satisfaction 210
Savage 206
Script 152, 160–62, 192–4, 199, 206
Seduction 140, 141
Séez incident 130
Self-defense 85, 91, 93–5, 101, 103, 149n, 168, 203n
Senán 32
Sensory deprivation 26
Serlo, abbot of Saint-Evroult 135
Sharpe, Richard 9
Sichar 110
Siege of Sainte-Suzanne 123
Signans 140, 147
Signatum 140, 147
Silvanus, Richard 130
Silves 92
Sin 129, 140, 195
Smail, Daniel Lord 51n, 53n, 68n, 191n, 192–4, 199
Snádud 15, 24
Soissons 108
Solomon, Robert 3, 214n
Song of Roland 161, 162
Sors affair 130
Sors brothers 122
Soyer, François 2, 86n, 89n, 205
Spanish Inquisition 200
Spielregeln 206, 207, 208
Stability 105, 108
States 51
Status 67, 81
Stephen, King of England 123, 130–32, 134, 135
Stewart dynasty 82
Stirling 58, 70
Suger of St. Denis 187
Sulaymān, brother of Ḥusayn 94
Sulaymān (unknown) 95
   Aḥmad, son of Sulaymān 95
   Ibrāhīm, son of Sulaymān 95
   'Umār, brother of Sulaymān 95
Summa Confessorum 190

Talio 119 (*see also* Tit for Tat)
Tariffs 211

Tax collector 32
Taxes 97
Teviotdale 67
   Archdeacon of 66
Thermodynamics 204
Thieves 20
Thomas of Chobham 186, 187, 190
Thomas, prior of St. Victor 186
Throop, Susanna 105, 151n, 172n, 203n, 211, 215n, 216n, 217n
Tírechán 8, 13
Tit for Tat 117, 120, 151 (*see also Talio*)
Torture 87, 130, 138, 140, 144–5, 149, 153
Tosny 122, 125, 134
Transitus Mariae 33
Treason *see* Betrayal/treachery
Troubadour 111
Tuathal, King 29, 30
Turtugud 15

Uí Eircc 17
Ultio 9, 119, 166, 178, 215, 218
Urban II, Pope 111, 180, 186

Vanity 31
Vasquez, João 95
Vassal 105, 106, 110, 111–13, 129, 156
Vaudreuil castle 123
Vecinos 86
Velho, Ibrāhīm 95
Vendetta 9, 108, 117, 164, 166, 220
Vengeance 1–6, 9, 10, 12, 14, 15, 19, 22–6, 28, 29, 30, 32–5, 37, 51, 69, 70, 73, 75, 79, 81, 98, 105–7, 109, 111–13, 116–18, 120, 124, 127–9, 133–8, 141, 142, 144, 150–52, 155, 157–63, 165, 167, 168, 170–75, 177–82, 186, 187, 189, 190, 193–5, 197–201, 203–20
   Acts of vengeance 192
   Blood vengeance 157, 169
   Clan/family-feud vengeance 138
   Customary vengeance 164, 167, 168
   Divine vengeance 138, 194
   and Gender 23–6, 35
   Gender-based vengeance 138
   Indirect vengeance 110
   Judicial or legal vengeance 138, 164

Manmade (fallible) vengeance 138
Miraculous vengeance 110
Personal vengeance 110
Private vengeance 138
Saintly vengeance 2, 7, 18
Serial vengeance 173
Socially-based vengeance 138
Vengeance paths 160
Verdier, Raymond 1n, 124n
Vermandois 109
Viaticum 130
Vicaria 162
Vigil 13, 23, 24, 29,
Vignats 124
Vindicta 9, 119, 166, 178, 215, 216, 218
Vindex in iram 198, 216
Violence 1, 2, 53, 63, 65, 66–70, 73, 80, 81, 87, 97–9, 106, 108, 109, 123, 144, 146, 158, 164, 165, 168, 171, 190, 203
   Assault 190
   Depredation *see* Pillaging
   Illicit 137, 187
   Licit 137, 141, 161, 171, 175, 187, 203
   Public monopoly of 158
   Vim vi repellere 203
Virtue 199
Vitalis, Orderic 115, 116, 119–36, 179
Vitae 5, 8–10, 12–15, 17–31, 33–6
Vulgate 194, 196

Walkelin of Pont-Échanfroi 121
Walter of Sordenia 121
War 106, 168
   Bellum 120, 166
   Casus belli 208
   Distinction between feud and 105–6, 116n, 118, 119, 124, 166
   "Feudal war" 108, 110
   Private (*guerra*) 52n, 53, 97, 108, 119, 120, 122, 133, 166, 175n

Just 166, 168, 180
Public 118, 120, 166
Right to bear arms and 85, 89
Scottish Wars of Independence 54
Vengeance and 118, 158
Weapons
   Arms-permit 94
   Ownership 85, 91
   Right to bear 85, 86, 88–96, 98, 99
Weber, Max 117
Wergeld 173
Werner, Karl Ferdinand 105
Wessington, John 59, 60, 61, 62, 64–7, 71, 73–5, 77, 81
William of Breteuil 127, 128
William of Eu 133
William of Évreux 123, 128, 134, 135
William of Montgomery 121
William of Pacy 133
William of Roumare 133
William of Tyre 180, 189
William Rufus, King of England 133–5
William the Bastard 121, 136
William the Conqueror, King of England 120, 121, 128, 136
Wish (*peroptare*) 188
White, Stephen 67n, 68n, 71n, 75n, 81n, 118n, 127, 155n, 166, 175, 192–4, 199
Women
   and Vengeance 5, 15, 20, 28, 30, 34, 125, 141, 144, 172
   and Zeal 182
   Hatred of 138, 150
Wrong, notion of 109, 111, 118, 133, 157–75 *passim*, 185, 187, 191, 203–30 *passim*
   Undifferentiated notion of 157–8, 161

York 54